YOUR PUREBRED PUPPY

A Buyer's Guide

SECOND
EDITION

MICHELE WELTON

AN OWL BOOK
Henry Holt and Company
New York

Henry Holt and Company, LLC
Publishers since 1866
115 West 18th Street
New York, New York 10011

Henry Holt® is a registered trademark
of Henry Holt and Company, LLC.

The original edition was published in 1990 by Michele Lowell.
Distributed in Canada by H. B. Fenn and Company Ltd.

Library of Congress Cataloging-in-Publication Data
Welton, Michele.
Your purebred puppy: a buyer's guide / Michele Welton—2nd ed.
p.   cm.
"An owl book."
ISBN 0-8050-6445-1 (pbk)
1. Dog breeds.   2. Dogs—Buying.   I. Title.

SF426.W45   2000   00-026269
636.7—dc21

Henry Holt books are available for special promotions
and premiums. For details contact: Director, Special Markets.

First published in hardcover in 1990 by
Henry Holt and Company

First Owl Books Edition 1991
Second Owl Books Edition 2000

Printed in the United States of America

3   5   7   9   10   8   6   4   2

To Ralph,

Sharing the bridge across forever . . .

life is good.

CONTENTS

ACKNOWLEDGMENTS

I am grateful to the many club members and breeders who contributed breed information and "proofed" the profiles for accuracy. Special thanks to:

Don Abney, Anna Adams, Julie Adams, Barbara Adcock, Ken Adcox, Harilyn Adler, Debi Allen, Dottie Allen, Sherilyn Allen, Jan Allinder, Bill Amesar, Kurt Anderson, Virginia Antia, Maria Arechaederra, Aaron Armendariz, Dave Arnold, Kim Augustine, Brenda Bagwell, Bonnie Bailey, Lisa Baird, Marge Bakken, Carole Baldwin, Dyane Baldwin, Erica Bandes, Tina Barber, Nan Barcan, Robin Barfoot, Gloria Barrick, Jim Bass, Jackie Baugh, Leslie Bauman, Nancy Baun, Frank Bays, Beth Beatty, David Bergeson, Roberta Berman, Pam Bethurum, Trudy Bettinger, Barbara Beuter, Knox and Letrina Biles, Mary and Stephen Bilson, Elizabeth Binney, Grace Blair, Joanne Blair, Sue Boice, Donna Bollard, Ellen Bonacarti, Barb Bornstein, Gretchen Botner, Sue Bower, Lee Boyd, Diane Boyle, Mary Bradley, Margo Brady, Ellen Brandenburg, Daphne Branzell, Vicki Bratton, Margie Brinkley, Barbara Brooks, Edith Brown, Lucia Brown, Lyn Brownell, Marilyn Bubb, Connie Buckland, April Burchfield, Celaine Burns, Margaret Burz, Shelley Cafferty, Suzie Caldwell, Linda Campbell, Donna Canfield, Thomas Carneal, Debbie Carsillo, Jackie Carswell, Irene Cartabio, Margo Carter, Nicholas Carter, Sue Carter, Peg Carty, Deb Casey, Paula Cash, Kathy Caslin, Irene Castillo, Joanne Chanyi, Christi Chism, Jan Christoferson Barringer, Virginia Ciofletti, Mary Ciszek, Karen Clanin, Agnes Clare, Dave Clayton, Lisa Clowdus, Gaye Cocoman, Margory Cohen, Diane Collings, Sandra Combs, Betsy Conway, Margery Cook, Catherine Cooper, Gail Cooper, Dawn Cope, Ginger Corley, Vicky Creamer, Anne Crockett, Libby Crookham, Stacey Csisek, Mary Lou Cuddy, Gayle Cummings, Barbara Curtis, Barbara Curtiss, Gerry

Dalakian, Donna Dale, Peggy DaValt, Ruth Davis, Donna Davison, Dominique de Caprona, Linda Deckard, Jona Decker, Genevieve Deltieure, Kim Demchak, Charlene Denys, Laura Diebold, Terry Dineen, Donna Dodson, Leona Domino, Nancy Drabek, Bill Dreker, Terry and Ann Duffin, Kathy Dullinger, Eva Dunkel, Dan Durigan, Kay Durr, Jenny Durrance, Beverly Dye, Edy Dykstra-Blum, Stace Eakle, Robert and Debra Earl, Scott Ekblad, Kim Elanges, Lori Elvera, Audie Emery, JoAnn Emrick, Jacquelyn Engle, Carol Ericsson, Michael Ertaskiran, Dorothy Everett, Sue Ewart, Claire Fairchild, Martha Feltenstein, Merrilee Finch, Barbara Fitzpatrick, Jane Flanagan, Jennifer Floyd, Janet Foltz, Leslie Forrest, Kim Foster, Fay Fowler-Gross, Lis Frankland, Janice Frasche, Marge Gagliardi, Linda Gagnon, Jean Gamble, Chrystyne Gettman, Steve and Ceci Giacoma, Joan Gibson-Reid, Jason Givens, Eibhlin Glennon, Paul Gluck, Dorothy Goodale, Cindy Goodman, Amy Gordon, Faith Gordon, Marsha Gray, Madeleine Greenwood, Jan Gribble, Ann Grundy, Cynthia Grupp, Deborah Gschwender, Sherry Guldager, Jean Hale, Mary Ann Hall, Jeannie Halmo-Cone, Valerie Hamilton Preston, Kristy Hanes, Terry Hansen, Lisa Hardy, Karolyn Harris, Diane Hartney, Melissa Harvey, Christine Hawley, Brenda Heinsohn, Richard Hellman, Connie Hendricks, Marie Henke, Cheryl Hennings, Beverly Henry, Deb Henson, Lucy Heyman, Ann Hickman, Susan Hiller, Debbie Hirst, Ed and Kristie Hodas, Janelle Holmes, Keith Holroyd, Ginny Holtz, Patty Hoover, Retha Hopkins, Laurin Howard, Linda Hruby, Carol Hughes, Melinda Hughes, June Hulit, Melinda Hutchings, Alison Ibbitson, Sandi Ilmanen, Nancy Inlow, Mary Iverson, Sue Jackson, June Jarvis, Kathy Jodoin, Eric Johnson, Terry Johnson, Anne Jones, Brenda Jones, Dianna Jones, Robin Jones, Kimberly Jordan, Victor Kaftal, Kathy Kail, Martha Kalina, Debbie Kay, Gail Kaye, Ruth Keller, Carolyn Kembrodt, Kerry Kern-Woods, Alfred King Sr., Jennifer King, Melody Kist, Julia Kleutsch, Debbie Kloehn, Jessica Kloss, Paula Knight, Ray Knudson, Peggy Kopf, Nancy Korman, Linda Kornhi, Lynne Kuczynski Veazie, Joy LaCaille, Paula Lacker, Liz Ladd, John Landis, Laura Lanham, Tammy Lanktree, Tammarie Larson, Carolyn Lathrop, Gwen Ledford, Ruth Libner, Dori Likevich, Alice Linn, Doug Ljungren, Barbara Lounsbury, Linda Love Banghart, Leslie Lucas, Tracey Luty, Julie Lux, Ara Lynn, Janet Maas, Mike MacBeth, Dana Mackonis, Ellie MacNair, Mary MacQuiddy, Mikael Magnerholt, Shellie Magraw, Carol Makowski, Joyce Maley, Kathy Marshall, Nancy Martin, Marjorie Martorella, Marilyn Matthes, Jessica Maurer and Penthea Burns, Lori McClelland, Beth McCutchen, Linda McKay, Patty Metzger, Paul Milbury, Sandy Miles, Erin Miller, Kyle Miller, Merry Jeanne Millner, Pam Mills, Sharon Mitchell, Lori Moody, Stella Moore, Ermine Moreau-Sipiere, Lori Morgan, Carol Morris, Marge Morris, Anna Morton, Patty Munnikhuysen, Pat Murphy, Teri Murphy, Dorothy Mustard, Coleman Nemerov, Dee Nichols, Lori Nickeson, Helene Nietsch, Phyllis Noonan, Lovey Olbrich, John O'Malley, Jan Oswald, Carole Fry Owen, Bobbie Oxley, Barbara Pagurek, Larry Painter, Elizabeth Pannill, Robyn Paugh, Carol Paulsen, Sharon Pederson, Janine Peters, Bruce Petersen, Renae Peterson, Jeanie Philip, Helen Phillips, Edwin Plummer, Ann Potter, Bonnie Prato, Rita Prindle, Julie Quirk, Stephanie Rameika, James Rea, Helen Redlus, Colleen Reiss, Alice Rendall, Diane Revak, Deann Richardson, Kelly Riggs, Kathy Ringering, Judy Robb, Lyn Robb-Pritchard, Eleanor Robins, Kley and Lorie

Robinson, Kay Rodgers, Christine Roesler, David Ronsheim, Carole Ross, Dolores Russell, Nancy Russell, Vanessa Rydholm, Sharon Saberton, Sharon Sakson, Trudi Sample, Diane Sandberg, Lisa Sanders, Linda Scanlon, Christi Scarpino, Edell Schaefer, Patti Schaefer, Sandra Schickedanz, Karlene Schoonover, Michele Schuler, Barbara Schwartz, Dean Scott, John Scott, Katherine Settle, Don Seymour, Kristina Sherling, Catherine Shields, Paige Shriver, Doris Slaboda, Chuck Slemaker, Suzanne Sliney, Ann Smart, Donna Smiley-Auburn, Elena Smith, Jan Smith, Shen Smith, Sue Smith, Michelle Smith Barbour, Gail Smyka, Stephanie Snowden, Joan Staby, Carolyn Stewart, Winifred Stout, Ellen Straub, Fran Strayer, Sandra Stuart, Jodi Suda, Donna Sullivan, Lou Swafford, Katherine Szafran, Nancy Talbott, Donna Tanner, Betty Taylor, Ann Thibault, Gina Thomas, Debbie Tissot, Patte Titus, Caroline Tobin, Viv Toepfer, Linda Trader, Mary Jo Trimble, Kathleen Tumey, Karen Ursel, S. M. Uzoff, Janet Van Wormer, Janet Varner, Wynne Vaught, Dia Vickery-Landon, Jan Vincent, Pamela Voit, Mary Wakeman, Marsha Wallace, Sherry Wallis, Dorothy Warren, Laura Weber, Linda Weisser, Patricia Weissleader, Lynn Whinery, Mary Wieland, Beverly Willeford, Sue Williams, Susie Williams, Dorothy Wilson, Judi Wilson, Lorene Wilson, Karen Wisnieski, Peggy Wolfe, Becki Jo Wolkenheim, Marra Wollpert, Jack Wright, Theresa Wright, Linda Wroth, Heidi Yager, Rich Yates, Steven and Cody Young, Valerie Young, Linda Zaworski, Karen Zumwalt, Patricia Zupan.

Thank you to my agent, Jane Gelfman, whose energy, professionalism, and persistence helped get this revised edition under way. From one dog person to another, thank you, Nancy Clements, for your willingness to work with me on both professional and personal issues.

And all my love to Mom and Dad, Nana and Ray, who gave me the support I needed to get back on the writing track.

YOUR
PUREBRED
PUPPY

STEP ONE

◆ ◆ ◆

Deciding to Get a Purebred Dog

◆ 1 ◆

Should You Get a Dog?

So you think you want a dog.

Let's consider your decision some more. Let's talk about what it will mean to you, to your family, and to your present lifestyle. Let's be very sure you're making the right decision, because there's more to owning a dog than you might have thought.

There's money. The purchase price will run from $50 (for a puppy from an animal shelter) to $300 to $600 (for a puppy from a responsible breeder). If you're interested in a dog for showing or breeding, you'll probably have to pay even more. If you're interested in a breed that has difficulty whelping puppies, such as a Bulldog, you'll probably have to pay more to cover the breeder's cost of Caesarean sections. (Though the ethical question "Should dogs that consistently require C-sections be bred at all?" is one you may decide to take into consideration when choosing a breed.)

If you're interested in a breed not recognized by the American Kennel Club (AKC), you may have to pay more. To establish a foreign breed in this country, breeders must spend money to import good representatives, so they usually charge more for puppies until the breed becomes more common.

But for a nice puppy of most breeds profiled in this book—for a puppy not destined to be a show dog, stud dog, or brood bitch, but simply a cherished member of your family—you shouldn't have to pay more than $600.

Unfortunately, the breeders of certain breeds have decided that their pups should be priced in the $800 to $1,500 range. Though their breed is no more valuable or "special" than any other breed, these breeders create the illusion that it is by promoting one or two characteristics as unique and then inflating prices to suggest exclusivity and stimulate demand. If you pay astronomical prices, you are rewarding these breeders not for producing better dogs, but for their marketing prowess in convincing you that they have.

An inflated price tag does not automatically equal a superior dog. Much more important than how much a dog costs is how carefully he was bred (including genetic health checks done on parents and grandparents), how skillfully he was socialized to get along with the world, and how compatible his physical traits, behavior, and personality are with your own needs, wants, and lifestyle.

No breed is perfect. All breeds have good points and bad points. Each breed is right for some people and wrong for others. The goal of this book is to find the dog that is right for *you*. And he doesn't have to cost a thousand dollars.

How about the opposite, then—a low price tag? Can you find a nice puppy at the animal shelter for fifty dollars? Of course. Many people have found their beloved dog this way. However, a low price does mean you're taking a risk in the most important areas of genetic health and temperament, since it's a virtual certainty that no genetic testing was done on the puppy's parents; indeed, the pup's background may be entirely unknown. So spending less money doesn't buy you less love. But usually it does buy you less security.

In addition, you have to be careful that in looking for a "bargain" you're not encouraging the wrong people. For example, breeders who mate dogs without testing for genetic health problems usually charge lower prices, but in the process they are adding defective genes to the gene pool and pushing the breed along the road to ruin. If you buy a puppy from them, you're rewarding them for their irresponsibility. One of the most important contributions you can make to the world of purebred dogs is to support only responsible breeders. That usually means $300 to $600 for a good puppy.

The money outlay doesn't end when you hand over your check and scoop up your puppy.

You'll have to choose a veterinarian to provide ongoing medical care. It may surprise you to learn that there are *two* philosophies of veterinary medicine in the United States: the AVMA (American Veterinary Medical Association) and the AHVMA (American Holistic Veterinary Medical Association). They hold opposing views on critical health issues such as feeding practices, frequency of vaccinations, and reliance on antibiotics and other drugs and chemicals to prevent and treat common health problems.

Although a few vets belong to both organizations, 99 percent of the vets in your local telephone book will belong only to the AVMA, which currently holds the reins of power in the United States. This medical philosophy is also referred to as *western* or *allopathic*. If a body part is not working well, it is removed surgically or attacked with chemicals and drugs.

AHVMA medicine, also referred to as *natural* or *holistic*, is gaining ground for its gentleness and sensibleness. The major tenet of natural medicine is that a living creature can resist and overcome many health problems if he is given the building blocks to strengthen his own immune system. A holistic vet promotes wellness from within, advising fresh foods, supplements, and raw meaty bones for building the body and keeping teeth clean and strong, as well as limited vaccinations and a chemical-free household so the immune system is not constantly stressed. Additional tools include medicinal herbs, vitamins and minerals, enzymes and antioxidants, chiropractic manipulation, acupuncture, and homeopathy.

I recommend using an AHVMA vet for everyday health care, reserving the aggressiveness of

AVMA medicine for emergencies or major surgery such as hip reconstruction. Holistic vets have graduated from the same universities and teaching hospitals as AVMA vets. They have the same access to antibiotics and other drugs, and they use them when necessary. However, they seek the most minimal remedy that will do the job, and that is often a natural product. The majority of allopathic vets, on the other hand, know very little about natural health care, so when they recommend treatment, you are receiving only some of the available options—in my opinion, the harshest ones.

You can locate a holistic vet in your area by calling 410-569-0795 or visiting the AHVMA Web site at www.altvetmed.com.

Once you get your puppy home from the breeder, you'll have to start filling him with food. I recommend fresh foods: meats, vegetables, and a little cereal or grain. You'll find easy-to-prepare, vet-approved recipes in natural health care books such as *Dr. Pitcairn's Complete Guide to Natural Health for Dogs and Cats*, by Dr. Richard Pitcairn, DVM. An alternative to fresh foods is an all-natural (no chemical preservatives), meat-based (meat is the first ingredient *and* the second or third ingredient) commercial diet such as Innova or Flint River Ranch. You'll find these at natural pet supply stores and holistic veterinarians and over the Internet. I do not use or recommend common commercial diets such as Science Diet, Iams, Eukanuba, Gaines, or Purina.

Other "doggy essentials" that should find their way into your shopping cart include a buckle collar with identification tag, a leather or nylon/cotton leash, a brush and comb, and nail clippers. Add a tiny container of Kwik-Stop styptic pow-

der for your first nail clipping venture, as you're likely to cut the nails a bit too short. Hard rubber toys and Nylabones are useful for chewing, but I don't use or recommend rawhide, pig's ears, or cow's hooves because of the risks of choking and intestinal blockage. Dishes should be stainless steel, ceramic, or glass; plastic can cause facial warts and allergies. And don't forget the aforementioned book by Dr. Pitcairn, which should be your everyday health book.

A crate or pen, $30 to $150 depending on size, is recommended as a housebreaking aid and den. Trimming shears and clippers, if needed for your breed, run about $100, or you can pay a grooming shop $20 to $50 every few months. If you take frequent business trips or if your family enjoys long vacations, boarding or pet-sitting costs may be a factor at $10 to $30 per day. And the most important $50 you'll spend in your dog's life is enrollment in a public obedience class after you've taught him the basic obedience exercises in the ideal learning environment of your own home.

So *money* is indeed involved in owning a dog.

Time and patience are involved, as well: time and patience for feeding your dog, for housebreaking him, for grooming him, for cleaning his yard, for walking him, for taking him to the vet, for playing with him, for training him, for talking to him, for loving him.

Don't try to deceive yourself about the amount of time and patience you need to live with a dog. It's hard to stand outside in the rain or snow every two hours trying to housebreak a puppy. It's harder still when he simply gazes around at all the sights, then wets on the floor as soon as you come back inside. It's hard to resist strangling him when he chews your shoes into sandals, but it's also hard to be firm when there he sits, sprawled awkwardly on one hip, cocking his head quizzically at you, panting and smiling.

It's hard to spend hours training him to sit and stay. It's harder still when you give him a sit command in front of your friends and he gazes back at you with wide-eyed innocence. It's hard to clean the house for guests and then chase after the dog as he gleefully tracks in mud, overturns his food bowl, splashes in the water bowl, throws up on the carpet, sweeps his tail across the coffee table, and sheds loose hairs all over the sofa. It's hard to bandage a bleeding paw or pull off a tick or use a rectal thermometer or race frantically to the vet in the middle of the night. And sometimes it's even hard to remember to rub his ears every night because he's waited all day for you to come home.

Time and patience. Be honest—do you lose your temper when the blockheads all around you don't seem to understand the perfectly clear things you're telling them? It's not a sin to have little time and less patience, but it *is* a hint that you should look for a different type of pet—perhaps a goldfish.

If you believe that you have the time and patience, how about the *consideration*: consideration not only for the health and safety of your dog, but for the rights of other people? A considerate person trains his dog to be well-mannered. A considerate person doesn't let his dog bark incessantly, threaten the mailman, stalk the neighbor's cat, bowl over visitors, or snatch ice cream cones from little children.

A considerate person doesn't let his dog run free, as in "I'm going to let my dog run loose— he'll be happier." Is happiness being crushed by a car? Caught in an animal trap? Chewed up in a dogfight? Blinded by stones pegged by bullies? Shot by the game warden for running deer or livestock? Poisoned by irate neighbors for digging up their lawn? Perhaps your happy dog will cause an accident. Have you ever swerved sharply to avoid a dog dashing across the street? If by good fortune there wasn't a car coming in the opposite direction, there may be next time.

If you are so unconcerned about the lives of innocent people that you would allow your dog to risk causing injury or death, you should not have a dog. If you will not recognize the rights of your neighbors to be able to enjoy their own homes in peace and tranquility, you should not have a dog. And if you will not protect the life of your dog by confining him safely, you should not have a dog.

And finally, the most important factors involved in owning a dog: *communication* and *love*. You and your dog are two different species. Since you, presumably, are the more intelligent, you must communicate with him and love him in ways that he will understand. When you interact with your dog and speak to him, you must ask yourself what his canine eyes are seeing, what his canine ears are hearing, what his canine mind is understanding. Your interpretation of your words and actions may not be the same as his interpretation, and his interpretation is what counts. You must communicate so that *he* understands.

First and foremost, recognize your dog for what he is: a wonderful and unique creature with talents and abilities all his own. It is not only incorrect but wasteful and demeaning to consider him a furry person. His thought processes are very different from yours; he is much less complex and thus he seldom needs to read self-help books. He has basic instincts and basic ways of responding to actions.

He has definite limits to his physical and mental capacities that you need to understand—first, so that you do not ask too much of him, and second, so that you do not ask too little.

Let's take a practical, close-up look at your dog. What does the world look like to him? Looking through his eyes is like looking through the eyes of a nearsighted person without glasses. The world looks fuzzy and vague. If you crouch down to his eye level, you'll get an idea of his perspective on the world. Things look towering, don't you think?

Can he see details? Although his vision is fuzzy, he may wag his tail when you smile and drop his tail when you frown, because most dogs are very observant at picking out details in your expression. You may think he is slinking away from your shredded slipper because he feels guilty, but usually he's reacting to your outraged expression and threatening body posture. He knows from past experience, not from any sense of guilt, that this particular facial expression and body posture don't bode well for him.

His peripheral, sudden-movement vision is far better than yours. Even when he's looking in another direction, he'll suddenly spy the wriggle of a mouse in deep grass. His night vision is better than yours because he can dilate his pupils more, and widening his pupils lets in whatever little light can be found. Can he see color or just shades of gray? The debate rages, but interestingly, many dogs seem to prefer rubber balls that are red, and many dogs are suspicious of black clothing.

What does the world smell like to him? Just as your world is full of sights, his world is full of smells. He relies upon his nose as you rely upon your eyes. He can pick out, from a dozen articles, the single one touched by his owner—and thus bearing his owner's scent—just as easily as you can pick out a green ball from a pile of blue ones.

He actually creates mental pictures based on smells. When the family car pulls into a campground where he has been before, he will get excited. He can't read the campground sign, but he recognizes the tree and wildlife scents, and from past experience he associates these with a fun-filled weekend: Oh, boy! But when you lead him toward the veterinarian's front door, he will balk. He can't read the veterinary sign, but he recognizes the medicinal scents, and from past experience he associates these with examining tables and probing fingers: Oh, no! (He also recognizes and reacts to your happy "campground" attitude and your nervous "veterinary" attitude.)

What does the world sound like to him? He hears much better than you do—softer sounds over greater distances at higher frequencies. Some dogs burrow under the blankets long before you hear the faint roll of thunder. Some dogs appear to hear (or otherwise sense) imminent avalanches and earthquakes.

Use a low, pleasant voice when you talk to your dog. Just as with children, who must of necessity stop their crying in order to hear what you're saying when you speak in a quiet voice, dogs tend to pay closer attention. Does he understand your words? Not unless you link them to the appropriate object or action. Puppies learn language just as babies do: by your saying "toy" over and over while holding up a toy. Until you connect a word with the correct object or action, words are only meaningless sounds. When you listen to a conversation in a foreign language, the words are not connected to anything concrete and you have no idea what they might mean. But if a Frenchman repeats "*pomme*" while showing you an apple, you get it. You may not know how to spell it, but you understand that the sound "*pomme*" refers to the red fruit with the stem and green leaves. In the same way, when you're first teaching your dog what words means, you need to use short, simple words (sounds) and consistently connect them to the appropriate object or action.

You must also recognize his most important instinct: the pack instinct. It is instrumental in making your dog a full-fledged member of your family. Dogs are sociable animals who like to live with other sociable animals in a group or pack. Within the pack there is a hierarchy. At the top is the most dominant animal, the pack leader, who establishes and enforces rules, carries out discipline, and makes decisions. Next in line is the number-two animal, then the number-three animal, right down to the most submissive one of all. Pack animals are not unhappy with this hierarchy. On the contrary. Knowing exactly where they stand with one another and exactly what the rules are makes for a strong feeling of security and fellowship. The survival of the pack depends upon every member being able to handle his respective position.

The pack instinct is the main reason dogs wedge themselves into our families, rather than prowl along the fringes, like most cats. Cats are solitary animals who like to do their own thing. Dogs are pack animals who like to belong. That one instinct makes a tremendous difference in the way each pet—dog or cat—should be raised. It also creates a greater responsibility than if you'd decided to get a cat.

How so? When a dog joins your family, even if your family is only yourself, a pack is formed. Oh yes, in his mind it certainly is, and his instincts compel him to seek out its structure. Who is the leader? Who is the follower? If you don't establish yourself as the leader, he may seize the position himself, for most dogs are not comfortable in a leaderless world. When a dog assumes the dominant role, this is an unpleasant state of affairs that can actu-

ally jeopardize the dog's safety, because there will be many times when you'll have to do things with him that he may not enjoy, such as examining his teeth. You must be the leader so that he will allow you to do anything with him. He must accept your judgment as to what is best for him.

I can hear somebody out there wailing, "My dog would never let me touch his teeth!" Stop that. What are you going to say when he chokes because he wouldn't "let" you pull a bone out of his throat? And how are you going to train him?

"Oh, but he loves me!" you protest. "Dogs want to please the people they love." Don't all obedience instructors wish! Dogs want to please the people they respect: leaders. Dogs will coexist with, ignore, or challenge followers. They will love you either way, for dogs don't equate love with respect. They love blindly; they respect only those who have earned it. So teaching them to respect you will in no way diminish their love for you, and teaching them to respect you is mandatory if you are to take proper care of them.

Do you wish you'd decided to get a cat?

A complication: In a multi-owner household, even if one person establishes himself as the leader, the dog may test another person. He may respect the person he recognizes as being above himself on the ladder, but not the person he places below himself. Obedience instructors often hear: "Duke listens to me but not to my wife." Or vice versa. Dogs often seem to pester guests who don't like them because they pick up on the guest's uncertainty and test to see if they can dominate. Sometimes it's done playfully, sometimes seriously. Remember, in a dog's mind, life is filled with leaders and followers, and he likes to find out who's who.

A second complication: children. Dogs usually consider children below themselves in pack position. A child should never try to boss a dog who considers that child a subordinate, because the dog may defend against what he sees as a threat to his pack position. A child should *gradually* be moved up the ladder above the dog by feeding the dog, holding the leash, and enforcing simple commands. Young children should never wrestle with a dog or play tug-of-war or chase. These games only reinforce the dog's speed and strength compared to the child's.

A third complication: In a multi-dog household, if an unruly dog dominates an obedient dog, the obedient dog may follow the unruly one into bad behavior. It's important that both dogs see you as a strong authority figure so that they don't ignore you to follow each other.

How does one establish oneself as a pack leader? Fortunately, with most dogs it's very easy. Most dogs are happy to be followers if you are willing to be the leader. You demonstrate your leadership with a series of daily actions that, taken together, equal authority and direction:

- Teach him obedience exercises such as sit, lie down, stay, and come.
- Frequently initiate eye contact with him.
- Don't play aggressive games such as wrestling or tug-of-war. Stick with cooperative games such as fetch, hide-and-seek (you hide, he seeks), and find-the-hidden-toy.
- When you tell your dog to do something, speak in a low, declarative voice. Don't use a pleading or wheedling tone.
- Use simple words and equate them directly to specific objects or actions: "Go for a walk?" "Want your supper?" "Find your ball." "Good sit."
- Be utterly consistent with your words and rules. If "down" means lie down, it

can't also mean stop jumping or get off the sofa. If your dog can't climb on the bed on Monday, he can't climb on it on Tuesday either. Consistency is the most important aspect of training a dog.

- Praise him when he does something you like, even if that something is merely lying quietly at your feet or chewing on his bone.
- Stop him immediately when he does something you don't like. Don't let things pass because you're too busy doing something else. Misbehavior must be immediately pointed out to your dog and corrected with a firm "No."
- Don't pet your dog every time he nudges and shoves and demands attention. Tell him to sit, and pet him only after he obeys. Consider it the equivalent of saying please.
- Require that he stand still or sit still for grooming. Tolerate no fussing when you clip his toenails or clean his teeth.
- Require that he take food gently from your hand—no snatching.
- Require that he behave in public. Smiling and making excuses while he lunges at other animals, jumps up on people, or hauls you around on the leash only diminishes you in his eyes and makes your breed look uncontrollable to the general public.

I can hear you breathing a sigh of relief at how nonpunitive these actions are. You were probably afraid, with all that pack-leader talk, that you'd have to abuse your dog to convince him who was boss. Not at all. Psychological superiority is far more important than physical superiority. Convince the twenty-pound puppy with a firm voice and confident attitude that you are in charge, that you will make all the decisions, that you have everything under control, and the hundred-pound adult won't question you.

You also demonstrate leadership by immediately putting a stop to any sign of canine dominance. This is more apt to occur in some breeds than in others. Not all dogs want to dominate. Be gentle with dogs who already roll onto their backs or look apologetic at any sign of displeasure from you. They have accepted your leadership, and any further display of strength on your part would be unfair according to their social code.

What does a dominance test look like? It sounds ominous, but your dog is not going to pounce on you in the middle of the night. Just as your own buildup of leadership is a series of little actions, your dog's buildup of leadership is, too. He may protest giving up a toy. He may shove his head into your lap, insisting that you pet him. He may mumble his displeasure if you walk past his dish while he's eating or touch him while he's sleeping. He may mouth your hand when you try to clip his nails. He may bark at you when you give a command. He may shriek at guests, ignoring your attempts to shush him. Urinating on your belongings is an unmistakable dominance challenge!

How should you respond? Just as a child learns that when he puts his hand close to the fire he experiences a sharp discomfort that suggests "It would not be to your advantage to do that again," so your dog should learn that when he attempts to dominate you, he experiences a sharp discomfort that does not merely suggest, but *commands* "It would not be to your advantage to do that again."

Pack leaders discipline calmly. They don't nag, shout, wave rolled-up newspapers, or let the discipline drag on. They do it in a few seconds and are done with it and they bear no grudges. In a sharp, guttural voice, say, "No. Stop." And since words are meaningless sounds until you connect them with something, add a squirt of water from a spray bottle or the thwack of a fly swatter against the wall or table. With a young dog, an effective disciplinary method is to grasp the loose skin on either side of his neck near his face, lift his front end off the ground, maintain eye contact until he looks away, then release him.

Discipline cannot leave the slightest doubt in the dog's mind that you will not accept this behavior. A dog will weigh his enjoyment of a behavior against the discomfort of its correction, and he will decide which takes precedence. If you are to understand your dog, communicate with him, and love him, you need to recognize that he learns almost everything from cause and effect, from event and result, from your reactions to his actions.

We've talked about money, time and patience, consideration, communication, and love. Those are the responsibilities of dog ownership. Those are the things that you as an owner must give to your dog. And what do you get in return?

The rewards can't be measured tangibly, but that's the case with most rewards of great value. A dog offers you pride in his appearance and behavior. A dog offers you the opportunity for accomplishment: that of having raised and trained him well. A dog offers you fun and play and old-fashioned belly laughs: great for your spirits and your blood pressure. An old saying goes, "With a dog, not only can you make a fool of yourself without him laughing at you, but he will make a fool of himself, too."

A dog is a furry shoulder to cry on when you're feeling depressed or lonely or sick. If you're homebound or grieving from personal loss or stress, a dog gives you something to live for: He depends on you for his own life. Elderly people benefit enormously from keeping a dog.

Finally, a dog offers you companionship and devotion and a unique, unconditional love that is neither greater nor lesser, but simply different, from its human counterpart. An epitaph on a beloved pet's gravestone reads, "The reason I loved him is plain to see—with all my faults, he found beauty in me."

Senator Graham Vest said it best when he spoke his famous "Tribute to the Dog" over a century ago:

Gentlemen of the Jury: The one absolutely unselfish friend that man can have in this selfish world, the one that never proves ungrateful or treacherous, is his dog. A man's dog stands by him in prosperity and in poverty, in health and sickness. He will sleep on the cold ground, where the wintry winds blow and the snow drives fiercely, if only he may be near his master's side. He will kiss the hand that has no food to offer, he will lick the wounds that come in encounters with the roughness of the world. He guards the sleep of his pauper master as if he were a prince. When all other friends desert, he remains. When riches take wings and reputation falls to pieces, he is constant in his love as the sun in its journey through the heavens.

Is this trade-off between what you give and what you get worth it? That is what you must decide before you buy a dog. Those who decide no are undoubtedly missing out on a lot, but there are many legitimate reasons not to get a dog.

You may not be able to afford one, although so long as food and health needs are unfailingly taken care of, other costs can be kept down with a little thought. Don't deny yourself the love and companionship of a dog simply because of limited funds.

You may work long hours or participate in so many activities that little time would be left for the dog.

You may travel and cannot bring a dog along or board him.

You may like an immaculate environment.

You may consider a dog to be a possession that can be locked in the garage or tied outside when you're not showing him off.

In all these cases, you should not get a dog. Both of you will be unhappy.

And don't let a friend lay on you that classic pressure: "Don't you want to teach your children responsibility?" If you yourself are not committed to caring properly for a dog, what you will be teaching your children is irresponsibility. If feeding and exercising and training are neglected, if the dog is bred indiscriminately and new, unwanted lives carelessly brought into the world, if he is dropped off at the pound when he becomes inconvenient, you will be teaching your children that the life of an animal is not worth much, that it can be used and tossed aside at whim. Many children progress from a callous and uncaring attitude toward the life of an animal to a callous and uncaring attitude toward all life.

So, yes, you have a perfect right to decide no.

Those who decide yes should be willing and able to take on the pleasures *and* the responsibilities, and willing and able to make a commitment.

That's exactly what this is: a commitment to be fully responsible for the life of another living creature. If you have a child, you may already understand that this type of commitment requires that you love, provide, teach, share, enjoy, discipline, worry, laugh, cry, and eventually let go.

But there is a difference—a big one. With a child, your relationship changes as he grows; as he gradually becomes more independent, you gradually let go. Your dog, on the other hand, regards you as his whole world throughout his short life, and the letting go is often sudden and always final. Someday you may find yourself standing in the veterinarian's office for the last time, having reached the final and most difficult stage of the commitment you made when you brought home that little puppy.

So you think you want a dog. Do you know for sure now?

If you've weighed the advantages and disadvantages, the pluses and minuses, the rewards and responsibilities, and come out on the yes side, we have to find you a dog: the right dog for you.

◆ 2 ◆

Should You Get a Purebred or a Mixed Breed?

Purebred or mixed: Which is the better dog? Each side has staunch proponents, but in the end, every dog is a combination of heredity, environment, and plain old roll of the dice. If two dogs stand side by side, one purebred and one mixed, either may be the more beautiful, the more intelligent, the better family pet. When one purebred is compared to one mixed breed, either may come out ahead. It is only as a group that purebreds have a big advantage over mixed breeds. The advantage is that of predictability.

People began selective breeding based on working ability. The best herding dogs were bred to one another, and some of their puppies were found to have strong herding instincts. The best hunting dogs were bred to one another, and some of their puppies were found to have strong hunting instincts. Only later were dogs selected for specific physical features (prick ears in one herding breed, hanging ears in another) and specific temperaments (friendliness in one hunting breed,

aloofness in another). Selective breeding, in its simplest terms, means breeding *like* to *like* to get more little likes.

But in more accurate terms, selective breeding means breeding *like genes* to *like genes*.

Uh-oh, not that old high school science of genetics!

Just five quick points:

1. Traits such as herding and hunting instincts, prick ears and hanging ears, friendliness and aloofness, are determined by genes, which pass from parent to offspring during conception. So when dogs with a certain trait were bred, it was expected that the gene carrying that trait would be passed along to the puppies. Sounds logical, doesn't it?

2. It didn't always work. Sometimes two dogs with the desired trait—say, prick ears—couldn't seem to pass prick ears

along to their offspring. How could that be? The two dogs, Mom and Dad, had the prick ears, right? That meant they had to have the "prick ears gene," right? And that gene had to pass along to their offspring, right?

3. Not necessarily. Let's look at Dad first. Since Dad had his own mother and father, he had to have received two genes for ears when he was born: one from Mother and one from Father. Since he'd turned out with prick ears himself, one of those genes had obviously been for prick ears, but the other one might have been for hanging ears. So he could have passed either "prick" or "hanging" to his own offspring. The same with Mom. Remember dominant and recessive genes from high school biology? Two brown-eyed parents can have a blue-eyed child if both parents have a recessive (hidden) gene for blue eyes and these recessive genes come together in the child.

4. So the traits that a puppy displayed depend on the gene *combinations* they inherited, and those often included hidden genes that didn't show on the outside. In our example of breeding for prick ears, a lot of trial breeding had to take place so that all the dogs with hidden genes for hanging ears could be identified and removed from the breeding pool.

5. Now that only "prick ear genes" were available to be passed to each puppy, whole litters began sharing not only a set of the same traits, but a set of the same genes. With no more undesirable (hanging ear) genes in the picture,

the desirable (prick ear) genes were considered "fixed" and could be passed on to the next generation, and the next and the next, so the breed could continue to look as its developers wanted.

For example, Daisy is a Golden Retriever. Golden Retrievers have fixed genes for large size, a golden coat, and hanging ears. When Daisy is bred to Toby, another Golden, their puppies will inherit their fixed genes and turn out large, with a golden coat and hanging ears. Unless some strange mutation crops up, you cannot get a fifteen-pound Golden, a spotted Golden, or a prick-eared Golden out of two Golden Retriever parents, because those genes are not present in any parent in this breed.

This is the science behind all purebreds: fixed, predictable genes. And this is the advantage of a purebred puppy: Because he is born with a fixed set of genes, we know what he will look like and act like as an adult.

Act like? Yes, temperament and behavior are hereditary to some extent. Every dog starts with an innate genetic temperament that stems from general breed temperament (most Goldens are friendly) and individual parental temperament (Daisy is *very* friendly, while Toby is moderately so). When you're looking at a purebred litter and can confirm that the temperament of both parents—and grandparents, too, if you can see them, and other relatives—falls into the correct parameters for that breed, you can feel pretty secure that this litter is very likely going to fit in, as well.

Temperament and behavior are influenced (sometimes slightly, sometimes heavily) by environment. This includes how and where the puppy was raised during his first few months, how thoroughly he was socialized, whether his experiences and interactions with the world have been positive or negative, and so on. The environment *you* provide after you get him home is also important. But it all starts with the innate genetic temperament that can be predicted because of the purebred's fixed genes.

A mixed-breed puppy, on the other hand, inherits random, unfixed genes from his parents. Whether these genes contain traits that are going to appeal to you cannot be determined until the puppy is grown. And since these genes are unfixed and often wildly contrasting, they cannot be passed on predictably to his own offspring. Thus, a mixed breed should never be bred, for no matter how beautiful or intelligent he is, he doesn't have the fixed genes to consistently reproduce his appearance or intelligence.

Are there any advantages to a mixed breed over a purebred? Yes. Because his genes are mixed, the mixed breed often has a more middle-of-the-road temperament, while many purebred temperaments are *very* friendly, *very* independent, *very* energetic, and so on. Mixed breeds make wonderful pets—no doubt about it. I have owned them all my life and love them dearly. The trick is in trying to choose (guess, really), from the myriad gene combinations out there, the mixed breed who is going to turn out to fit your family. Even more problematic is realizing that even if the dog you choose happens to fit in well, his parents have not been tested for anything. That may not have been a concern in your grandparents' days, but today genetic health problems are rampant in the canine world. It is in these areas—predictable genes and screening for genetic health problems—that purebreds, who also make wonderful pets, come into their own.

Now, how many purebreds are there? There are more than three hundred breeds in the world, but many of these are not present in the United States

or are represented by only a few specimens. Importing a foreign breed is possible, but complex and expensive, so most people will want to choose a breed that is already reasonably well represented in this country. In this book, you'll find profiles for two hundred breeds and varieties. (A variety is the term used for different sizes or coats allowed within a breed, for example, Toy Poodle or Miniature Poodle, Smooth Dachshund or Long-haired Dachshund.)

Of these 200, 146 are registered with the American Kennel Club, the largest purebred registry in the United States. Many of the others are recorded with the AKC's Foundation Stock Service (AKC-FSS), which is sort of a waiting area for breeds that don't yet have enough representatives to warrant the time and expense of offering classes for them at dog shows. As time goes on and the AKC decides that a breed has enough representatives recorded, it will move the breed into the AKC Miscellaneous Class, where dogs can be shown but not yet attain championships. If there is enough show activity in the Miscellaneous Class, the breed will be granted full recognition.

Some of these "rare" breeds are already fully recognized by other registries. The United Kennel Club (UKC) is the second-largest registry in the United States, while States Kennel Club (SKC) is third largest. So, to the list of AKC and AKC-FSS breeds you'll be choosing from, we've added some UKC and SKC breeds—the ones most likely to suit a good number of prospective owners.

We've also added some breeds registered by the Federacion Cynologique Internationale (FCI), a Belgium-based registry used by most European, Asian, African, and South American countries. The FCI is old and well respected and is *not* to be confused with a new, minor registry who call themselves the "FIC." In the same way, the Canadian Kennel Club (CKC) is a reputable registry not to be confused with the Continental Kennel Club, so make sure the breeder means Canadian Kennel Club when he claims that his dogs are CKC-registered.

Finally, we've included some nice breeds that for various reasons have not yet been recognized by any major organization. But they *are* purebred. As you now know, purebred means that a type of dog has been so consistently bred to other members of the same type that the genes have been fixed and will be passed predictably from parent to offspring.

Note that the "poo breeds" (such as the "cock-apoo") are not purebred. Such a dog is a mix of cocker spaniel and poodle, comes in a hodge-podge of nonstabilized types, and does not have the fixed genes for consistently reproducing itself. It would also be instructive to ask if the parents used in these crossbreedings have been genetically tested for the wealth of health problems present in Cockers and Poodles. Individually, of course, mixed cocker-poodles can make wonderful pets, but you should consider what type of breeder and breeding program you're supporting when you pay several hundred dollars for a poo puppy rather than adopting one from the animal shelter.

If you've decided that you do indeed want a purebred, our next step is to find out what kind of physical appearance, temperament, and behavior you're looking for in a dog. Then we can find the purebreds who are most likely to have the genes and characteristics that will best match you.

STEP TWO

◆　◆　◆

Choosing the Right Breed

❖ 3 ❖

Evaluating Your Personality and Lifestyle

A major cause of problems between an owner and his dog is that the dog doesn't suit the owner and/or the owner doesn't suit the dog. Incompatibility includes a permissive person choosing a strong-willed Chow, a person who hates to groom choosing a shaggy Old English Sheepdog, a sociable family choosing a suspicious Komondor, or a family with toddlers choosing a fragile Chihuahua.

Some people choose a breed because they like its muscular appearance or flowing coat or angelic face, or because there's a litter handy right up the street, or because their uncle had one who could practically talk. In a week or a month or a year, these people may discover, to their dismay, that they've started a ten- to fifteen-year commitment with an incompatible breed. Owner and dog will end up in a discouraging battle as the owner struggles to change the dog's natural characteristics to ones that he would prefer.

It's so much better to figure out what you want first. And if your research reveals that the breed you were thinking of getting is unsuited to your personality and lifestyle, pat yourself on the back. It's an awful feeling to dislike a dog who doesn't suit you, and it stabs at your conscience when you have to search for a more suitable home for him. And think of how the dog would feel about being shuffled around simply because he is acting as his genes compel him to act.

"He digs in my flower beds!" wails the gardening enthusiast. Of course he does—he's a Fox Terrier, bred to dig vermin out of their underground dens. It's in his genes.

"He barks and barks!" wails the writer who can't concentrate on her work. Of course he does—he's a Finnish Spitz, bred to bark continuously while hunting. It's in his genes.

"He's so aloof with my friends!" wails the society woman. Of course he is—he's a Neapolitan Mastiff, a wary guarding breed. It's in his genes.

Remember that most breeds were developed for a reason, and the reason usually had to do with working ability. The instincts and characteristics that best suited that working ability are still going to come through today because of the purebred's fixed, predictable genes.

You might curse those fixed genes as you're replanting your flower bed or plugging cotton in your ears or apologizing to your miffed friends, but these three owners could just as easily have made those fixed genes work for them instead of against them. The gardener could have chosen a dignified Pekingese. The writer could have chosen a quiet Greyhound. The society woman could have chosen a friendly Bichon Frise. They just didn't know.

But you do. You can start your owner-dog relationship off on the right foot by evaluating yourself and your lifestyle, deciding which canine characteristics would best suit you, then choosing a breed that tends to have those characteristics. Some behaviors and personalities are influenced by early environment and can be modified (even changed) by proper handling and training, but it will be less frustrating all around if you start by choosing a breed that is at least reasonably compatible with your wants and needs.

THE QUESTIONNAIRE

The following questionnaire asks about your needs, wants, personality, and lifestyle. Your answer to each question will reveal a specific trait that you're looking for in a dog. Start by taking out a sheet of paper and listing the following categories:

1. Experience Required:
2. With Children:
3. Size:
4. Coat:
5. Exercise Required:
6. Trimming/Clipping Required:
7. Amount of Shedding:
8. Activity Indoors:
9. Ease of Training:
10. Sociability with Strangers:

As you answer each question, you'll be instructed to write a word or phrase beside the matching category on your sheet of paper. When you've answered all ten questions, you'll have a list of ten traits you're looking for in a dog.

1. Experience Required
Answer T(rue) or F(alse)

_____ I have been successful in training a dog to be well-mannered and obedient.

_____ I understand the concept of pack leadership and I'll make a good leader.

_____ I like to make decisions.

_____ I don't "reason" with young children; *I* establish the rules for expected behavior.

_____ I often feel I have better judgment than most people.

_____ I enjoy teaching others how to do something.

_____ I hold definite opinions on many subjects.

_____ I stand up for myself when I think I'm right.

If you answered True to at least six of these statements, you should be equipped to handle a breed who will try to test your leadership. Write the following two phrases beside Category 1: *Best for experienced owners* and *Fine for novice owners.* Otherwise, write *Fine for novice owners.*

2. With Children

Do you have children or oft-visiting relatives under age eight? Are there neighborhood children under age eight who would regularly come into close contact with your dog? Are you planning to have a baby within your dog's lifetime? If you answered yes to any of these questions, write *Good with children* and *Good with children if raised with children* beside Category 2.

If you answered no to all of these, write *Good with children* and *Good with children if raised with children* and *Good with older, considerate children.*

Unfortunately, many people will ignore these recommendations. They will go right ahead and choose a toy breed, or a very sensitive breed, or a very feisty breed. It seems that many parents are convinced that their youngsters are different, that they would never pester or hurt a dog, and that therefore any breed will do just fine.

Granted, this can be the case. But too often it isn't something deliberate that a child does that results in injury—to dog or child or both—but something accidental. For example, most kids (many adults, too) have no idea how quickly and easily a toy breed can be injured or killed. That a child meant well is little solace to a five-pound dog who has been stepped on, sat on, rolled on, squeezed, or dropped. You can supervise them twenty-four hours a day, but the day your child plays Speed Racer with his tricycle will be the day your toy dog will be in the wrong place at the wrong time.

Genetic temperament also plays a role here. Some breeds simply don't like the loud voices, yo-yo emotions, herky-jerky movements, and unpredictability that go along with wee human beings. Sensitive breeds are too easily intimidated or startled, while feisty breeds may decide not to put up with nonsense from little life-forms whom they view as below themselves in importance. Some breeds are so territorial that they may view playful wrestling as an attack upon your child. Some breeds are so rambunctious that toddlers can be sent sprawling from an exuberant leap or the enthusiastic whipping of a heavy tail.

So if you have small children, play it safe for both dog and child. Stick with breeds that thrive on the bumping and tumbles and Indian war whoops that result from living with kids.

Caution: All children, young or old, must be taught to be gentle with all dogs. Buying a tolerant, easygoing breed does not give any child license to be rough or abusive. Even breeds considered good with children *can bite* if they are hurt, teased, or frightened; if they are not raised and trained properly; or if they are not chosen carefully from a responsible breeder who screened their ancestors for stable temperament.

3. Size

Many people have preconceived ideas about various sizes of dogs. They may feel that all little dogs are cuddly, or the reverse—that all little dogs are snappy. They may feel that all big dogs are tough and protective, or the reverse—that all big dogs are tolerant and easygoing. Not true. Almost every type of temperament is available in almost every size dog. However, some practical generalities about size can be considered.

Little dogs, about the size of a Toy Poodle, and *small* dogs, about the size of a Cocker Spaniel, can live comfortably in tight quarters. Some breeds in these size categories can get most of their exercise running around indoors, while others need a lot more outdoor exercise than you might think. Little and small breeds are easy to restrain on a leash and can be picked up when necessary. They are often allowed by landlords. They are easy to clean up after and convenient to travel with. They usually enjoy a long lifespan of twelve to sixteen years. Note that there are not many little and small breeds recommended for small children.

Medium dogs, about the size of an English Springer Spaniel, generally need a brisk walk every day and a chance to run in a safe, enclosed area as often as possible. They are not that difficult to clean up after and are fairly convenient to travel with. Lifespan is in the ten- to fourteen-year range. There are comparatively few breeds in this size range, which is a shame, because many people prefer medium-sized dogs.

Large dogs, about the size of a Golden Retriever, need lots of daily exercise. Without training, dogs of any size can be unruly on a leash, but those who are large can be unmanageable. Poor socialization in a large dog, particularly in a guarding breed, can be dangerous. These dogs are sometimes objected to by neighbors and typically not allowed by landlords. They produce a sizable amount of waste, and unless well trained, they can be awkward to travel with. Lifespan ranges from eight to fourteen years. Their sturdiness and athleticism mean that a high percentage of these breeds are playful and understanding with children.

Giant dogs, about the size of a Saint Bernard or Great Dane, have the same pros and cons as large breeds, though they require *less* hard exercise because of their sheer bulk and slower metabolism. They make impressive companions when socialized and trained well, but as you might imagine, dogs of this size take up a lot of real estate in your home, yard, car—and on your furniture, if you are so inclined. They are expensive to feed, board, medicate, and buy supplies for. Puppyhood and adolescence can last three or four years in these

breeds. They are mature adults for perhaps another three years, age rapidly, and pass on at between seven and ten years.

Which sizes would be acceptable to you? Write your choices (as many as you like) beside Category 3.

4. Coat

Dog coats vary in length and texture:

Smooth coats (Doberman, Chihuahua) need only an occasional quick brushing to remove surface dirt and dead hairs. Brush more often when the dog is shedding. If you live in a cold climate and hope to spend a lot of time outdoors with your dog, this type of coat may not be your wisest choice. At the very least, a heavy sweater will be required, for both you and your dog!

Short coats (Labrador Retriever, Pembroke Welsh Corgi) need about five minutes of brushing once a week to remove surface dirt and dead hairs. Brush every day during shedding seasons.

Thick, medium-length coats (Siberian Husky, Pomeranian) need ten to fifteen minutes of brushing twice a week to remove dead hairs. Brush every day during shedding seasons, using a shedding blade or "rake" to pull out the chunks of dead undercoat.

Feathered, medium-length coats (Golden Retriever, Cocker Spaniel) need ten to twenty minutes of brushing and combing two or three times a week to prevent tangles and remove dead hairs. Pay special attention to the silky feathering on their ears, chest, stomach, and legs. Keep their bottom (anal area) trimmed for cleanliness. Brush every day during shedding seasons.

Long coats (Afghan Hound, Lhasa Apso) need ten to twenty minutes of brushing and combing every day or every other day to prevent tangles and remove dead hairs. Brush every day when the dog is shedding. Keep their bottom trimmed for cleanliness. Some breeders will shriek in outrage when they read this, but these breeds are often more comfortable and easier to keep clean and neat if you trim or clip the coat shorter.

Wiry coats, usually with bushy eyebrows and a beard (Schnauzers, many terriers) need ten to twenty minutes of brushing and combing once or twice a week, especially the longer "furnishings" on their chest, stomach, and legs. Beards should be combed daily, as food, water, and saliva can soak in and form mats. Keep their bottom trimmed for cleanliness. Wiry coats have the advantage of shedding lightly, but they must be clipped regularly.

Curly (Poodle, Bichon Frise) coats need ten to twenty minutes of brushing and combing two or three times a week to prevent matting. Most curly coats tend to shed lightly, but they must be clipped regularly.

Which coats would be acceptable to you? Write your choices beside Category 4.

5. Exercise Required

If you don't plan on taking your dog for regular walks, write *Low* beside Category 5. If you will take your dog for regular walks and occasional runs (in a safe, enclosed area), write *Low* and *Medium*. If you're willing to commit to a regular schedule of jogging or hiking or biking, write *Low* and *Medium* and *High*, but be sure you will follow through if you do choose a *High* breed. They'll bounce off the walls if you don't.

If you're a dyed-in-the-wool outdoorsman, you should skip the *Low* breeds entirely and opt only for *Medium* and *High* breeds that will match your activity level. And if you're looking for a jogging or biking companion in a hot or humid climate, make a note that short-nosed breeds (Bulldogs, Bullmas-

tiffs, Pugs), black dogs, and long-coated or thick-coated dogs may suffer heatstroke from too much exertion in warm weather.

6. Trimming/Clipping Required

Which one of these statements fits you best?

a. I only want a breed with a no-fuss coat (no trimming at all), such as a Beagle or Labrador Retriever.

b. I wouldn't mind a breed that needed minor trimming/clipping every four to six months, such as a wire-coated terrier.

c. I wouldn't mind a breed that needed extensive clipping every six to ten weeks, such as a Poodle, Schnauzer, or Cocker Spaniel. I could learn to use clippers or I'd pay a professional groomer.

If you chose a, write *Low* beside Category 6. If you chose b, write *Low* and *Medium*. If you chose c, write *Low* and *Medium* and *High*.

7. Amount of Shedding

Every animal with hair sheds at one time or another, because hair dies and must be replaced. Out with the old hair, in with the new. So the shedding question becomes, How much does he shed?

Many breeders and breed clubs promote their breed as shedding "less than other shorthaired breeds (longhaired breeds, black and white breeds, potbellied breeds with long noses, etc.). They're not trying to deceive you, but frankly, breeders are "into" dogs more than the average person. They don't notice and/or mind clumps of hair snaking under their refrigerator, and when they rise from the sofa, they absently brush their pants off. Shedding is not a problem if you don't mind the extra vacuuming and slight untidiness. And to cut down on shedding, brush more often, since dog hair that ends up in your comb and wastebasket doesn't end up on your floor.

If you hate the idea of hair on your clothes and furniture, or if anyone in your family is allergic to dogs, you need a breed that sheds very lightly, so write *Low* beside Category 7. However, in the case of allergies, you should understand the sensitivity that causes the allergy. Some people are sensitive to canine fur, some to dander, some to saliva. Yes, saliva. A low-shedding, low-dander breed like the Poodle or Bichon Frise will do you little good if your puppy loves to give kisses and you're allergic to saliva. Doctors can prescribe shots and/or pills to reduce allergic reactions, and there are products that may reduce dander, but sensitivity usually grows with exposure. No dog should suffer the trauma of being uprooted to a new home or stuck outdoors because you didn't do enough homework before bringing him home. Visit several breeders of the breed you're interested in and monitor your reactions.

Nonallergic people have more options. If vacuuming a few times a week during shedding seasons (typically a few weeks in the spring and fall) is okay and you wouldn't die of embarrassment if a visiting friend left with a few hairs stuck to her pants, write *Low* and *Medium*. Do note that with central heating, many dogs today don't go through the traditional spring and fall sheds, but shed lightly year-round and somewhat more heavily when "blowing their coat" twice a year, which may or may not occur in the spring and fall.

If you wouldn't mind vacuuming every day, sweeping dust bunnies from under the cabinets, and pulling out fistfuls of dead undercoat during the major shedding seasons, write *Low* and *Medium* and *High*; in other words, you would

accept any amount of shedding. Just be sure you really feel this way; preferably you have had some experience with heavy-shedding breeds. Sometimes people think they wouldn't mind, then discover that the reality of hair in the butter dish is worse than they had imagined.

8. Activity Indoors

Answer T(rue) or F(alse).

_____ I don't like to sit idly for very long; I prefer to be moving or doing something to keep myself busy.

_____ I use a lot of gestures when I talk.

_____ I am a fairly fast talker.

_____ I am a fairly fast walker.

_____ I am a fairly fast eater.

_____ I get quite tense, displeased, or upset when I'm stuck in traffic.

_____ I'm annoyed by active, inquisitive children who won't "settle" somewhere.

If you answered True to at least five of these statements, an active dog would probably drive you crazy. Write *Low* beside Category 8.

If you answered True to three or four of these statements, write *Low* and *Medium*.

If you answered True to none, one, or two of these statements, you could probably live with any degree of activity. Make your decision based on the following: If you'd prefer a dog who is lively and inquisitive indoors, who shadows you from room to room, who frequently tries to engage you in interactive play, who checks out doors and windows to see if anything interesting is going on that he should know about, write *High* and *Medium*. If you'd prefer more of a couch potato in the house, write *Low* and *Medium*. If it honestly doesn't matter to you, write *Low* and *Medium* and *High*; in other words, any degree of activity is fine.

9. Ease of Training

Which one of these statements fits you best?

a. I'm unwilling or unable to do any obedience training with a dog.

b. I'm willing to train a dog who is very attentive and responsive, but I'd become annoyed or discouraged with a slow learner or a somewhat stubborn dog.

c. I'm willing to train almost any kind of dog except one who is very self-willed or independent.

d. I'm confident that I can learn to train any dog. I'll find a skilled instructor or an excellent book or video, and I won't get impatient or discouraged even if he is very difficult to train.

If you chose a, check back to Category 3 (Size) and be sure it says *Little*, because only little dogs can get by without any obedience training . . . though training does benefit them, and they enjoy the bonding experience. For Category 9, write *High* and *Medium*, because if you're not planning to do any training, you'll need a little breed who is naturally responsive and mannerly. (There aren't many.)

If you chose b, write *High*. If you chose c, write *High* and *Medium*. If you chose d, write *High* and *Medium* and *Low*.

Breeders tend to get huffy when their breed is labeled *Low*. Immediately they'll rattle off the names of all the individuals who have achieved high scores and advanced titles in obedience competition. It's true: every breed can be trained successfully to the highest level of obedience, and in experienced hands, virtually every breed can be attentive and responsive.

However, with a novice at the other end of the leash, some breeds have proven to be much easier than others to work with. They are more inclined to forgive mistakes made by inexperienced owners. They accept that the object of the training session is to learn certain words and actions, and once learned, they're happy to perform them just to please you. These are the breeds we label as *High*.

Other breeds sense immediately that they're dealing with a beginner. Often these dogs learn quickly, but their attitude is "What's in it for me?" They feign deafness ("Huh? Did you say something?") or wide-eyed innocence ("Honest, I just don't understand what you want me to do"). They put their own spins on an exercise ("Let's see what she does if I roll over on my back with my feet sticking up in the air"). They're easily bored by repetition ("I already *did* that once") and they'll manipulate you with whines, whimpers, and nudges ("I'm tired and my paw hurts . . . let's do something else").

Keeping the attention of such breeds is a challenge, one that is best met by owners who know something about canine behavior and training. Thus, this category has less to do with intelligence than with a breed's likelihood of capitulating easily to the training attempts of the average owner.

10. Sociability with Strangers

If you'd like your dog to be friendly, to trust strangers, to bark when someone comes to the door but then welcome them inside, write *High* beside Category 10. If you'd rather he be more discriminating, more reserved, if you'd prefer that he observe people from a distance and then approach them in his own time when he is satisfied that they're "good guys," write *Low*. *Medium* breeds may be somewhere in the middle, or they may be those in which members range from *Low* to *High*, depending upon the breeder's goals, the temperament of the parents, and the degree of socialization the puppy receives from both the breeder and owner. If any reaction to strangers is fine with you, write *High* and *Medium* and *Low*.

Ten questions answered! You now have a list of ten traits to look for in a dog. But before we start combing through all two hundred breeds and varieties to find the ones that match your list, let's make sure you can consider all two hundred. There are two special circumstances that would require you to eliminate the majority of breeds before you start comparing.

Special Circumstance 1: Are you planning to use your dog to hunt birds or small game, to herd or guard livestock, to compete in the German protection sport of Schutzhund, or in some other specialized activity? If yes, only certain breeds are capable of performing such demanding work. People who are already involved in these activities are your best advisers to those breeds, so you should put your search on hold until you've had a chance to talk to them.

Call a veterinarian, animal shelter, or boarding kennel. Ask for the name and number of your local breed or obedience club, whose officers or other members might know individuals involved in your chosen activity. Also call breeders of *any* breed capable of performing the activity, even if it is not a breed that interests you. Ask if they participate in the activity or know anyone who does. Follow all leads and try not to hang up the phone without asking, "Do you know anybody else who might know . . ."

Once you've researched the activity and know which breeds perform best, you can continue your search to find out which of those would be the best match for you.

Special Circumstance 2: Do you want your dog to be a watchdog? First, let's define the way I'm using the term. A watchdog barks when he sees or hears someone or something near his property. Because every breed can and usually will bark or offer some kind of alerting behavior, every breed is a potential watchdog. Some breeds are more consistently watchful than others, but when an individual dog happens not to be alert to strangers, that is usually the individual, not the breed.

The majority of burglars will shy away from homes in which any dog is barking. Thus, even the barking of a little dog or a friendly dog whose bark is one of welcome rather than warning is all the "watching" that most families need. If you're looking for a dog whose appearance and behavior would give burglars even greater incentive to stay away, choose a medium or large or giant dog who looks imposing and who is aloof with strangers.

Now, if you're looking for a dog who is inclined to do more than bark, please consider the following: Some breeds are naturally protective, but they must be taught how to protect, i.e., where and when to bite. Professional training is expensive, and the result is the equivalent of a loaded gun. Guns often do more damage to the innocent than to the guilty, and a dog has no safety catch and cannot be unloaded. (Proponents of guard dogs argue that a dog, unlike a bullet, can be recalled, but they will also agree that few dogs are that well trained.) And training carries no guarantee of protection because a professional criminal has many ways of dealing with a trained dog: Mace or a bullet, for example.

Perhaps you want a naturally protective breed but don't want to go to the trouble and expense of professional training. Perhaps you believe that an untrained Doberman will protect you "naturally."

You may be in for a shock. Let's say the burglar isn't even a professional with a gun. Let's say he simply ignores your barking Doberman and breaks into your house, where he's promptly bitten. Don't you agree that a man who was already bold enough to enter a home in which a big Doberman is barking is going to fight back?

You bet he is. And since an untrained dog usually bites at the leg, the burglar, with both hands free, will knock your beloved dog's brains out with the nearest chair or stab him with a pocketknife. A few really tough dogs might continue to make a fight of it, but most inexperienced dogs who suddenly find themselves in a real fight with a human being will back down. Now the tables have turned as the angry burglar chases your bewildered dog with murderous intent.

Many a protective dog has lost his life trying to defend his owner's TV set, while the dog who is "so friendly he'd escort the burglar to the silverware" escapes unharmed. Thus it can be a disadvantage to own a protective breed, for no TV set is worth serious injury or death to a dog who is a member of your family.

But what if it's not your home and property that is endangered, but yourself—by, say, a mugger on the street? Wouldn't you want your dog to pro-tect you then? Actually, he may not have to, because most muggers, like most burglars, will shy away from anyone with a dog. Dogs can bark, and barking draws unwanted attention. But if you believe firmly in self-defense and you want your protective dog to be similarly equipped, consider joining a Schutzhund club. Schutzhund is a rigorous German sport that combines tracking, obedience, and protection. The training is exciting, and the result is a dog-owner team that works together in a close relationship.

Final recommendation: If all you want is a dog who barks or otherwise alerts you that people are approaching, you can make your choice from among all the breeds. But if you must have a breed with some size, muscle, and a reputation for defending his home and family, read the profiles carefully to see what is said about protective instincts and territoriality. Unless it is specifically mentioned, a breed should be considered to be only average or below in these areas.

Once you've gone ahead and brought home your protective breed, don't ever allow him to threaten anyone. Let him serve as an imposing presence that will discourage most criminals, but reassure yourself that he will never die because he actually bit a criminal who then called his bluff.

◆ 4 ◆

Using the Breed Profiles

Okay, it's time to find the breeds that match your list of ten traits.

Start by turning to the breed profiles that begin on page 39. The first profile is that of the Affenpinscher. You'll notice that the profile is divided into three sections. The top section corresponds to the first four categories on your list: Experience Required, With Children, Size, and Coat. The middle section is a chart that corresponds to the final six categories on your list. Right now we'll use just these top and middle sections to find the breeds that best match you.

The first category is Experience Required. Suppose you have written *Fine for novice owners*. The Affenpinscher matches you in this category, so use your pencil to put a check mark on the Affen's profile, just to the left of *Fine for Novice Owners*. One category matched.

Next is With Children. Suppose you've listed *Good with children* as your choice. The Affenpinscher doesn't match you here, so you can't put a check mark on this category. Go through the remaining categories, putting a check mark beside each in which the Affen matches you. When you've compared all ten of your desired traits with all ten Affenpinscher traits, count the check marks, put the total beside the Affen's name at the top of the page, and move on to the next profile: the Afghan Hound.

You'll notice that some breeds have multiple ratings within a category. For example, a breed may be listed as both *High* and *Medium* in Ease of Training, meaning that the breed as a whole falls between these ratings, or that about half its members are easy to train, while the other half are a bit more stubborn or independent. Even if you've listed only *High* as your choice, you should still consider that the breed matches you in this category.

Yes, combing through all the breeds will take some time, but do it carefully, perhaps over a few quiet evenings. You don't want to eliminate a suitable breed because you weren't paying attention to comparing, check-marking, and totaling.

After you've found the total for each profile, turn your list over and write down the breeds with the highest scores. Since the highest score any breed can get is 10, you'll list all these "perfect" breeds first. Depending on how strict your desired characteristics were, you may have no perfect breeds, or you may have a dozen.

Next, revisit any breed who scored 9 and find the nonmatching category. If upon reflection you feel you could live with a dog who doesn't match you in that category, add the breed to your list. For example, if a nine-point breed is small in size rather than the medium you wanted, perhaps you'll decide that his small size is forgivable. On the other hand, if he's giant instead of medium, perhaps you'll decide that even though he matches you in all the other categories, you simply don't want a giant dog. Only you know which traits are critical to you and which ones allow room for compromise.

Once you've picked out your ten- and nine-point breeds, you may even want to add eight-point breeds if your list is still very short. When you've compromised as much or as little as you feel comfortable with, take a look at your list. You're going to own one of these breeds!

No? You wouldn't think of owning a Tasmanian Klutzhound? Why not? Did you have a bad experience with one? Many people approach buying a dog with preconceived notions about certain breeds. Perhaps an X breed growled at you in 1955. Perhaps a Y breed represented an evil demon in a B movie. Perhaps a friend told you that a Z breed is the dumbest breed in the world and he should know because his aunt had one and it used to sit all day staring at the bathroom sink, waiting for the water to drip.

If you're too quick to form an opinion based on a single experience with an X, Y, or Z breed, you're ignoring the hundreds of experiences that were used to create the profiles. If a breed has delighted hundreds of owners, it will delight you, too, as long as it's compatible with you and as long as the individual you choose has been well-bred and well raised. Try not to prejudge an entire breed because of a single experience. Try to be open-minded.

But it's true, you do have to narrow your list of suitable breeds. We'll use the bottom section of the profiles to do just that. Turn to the profile of your first suitable breed and look at the rest of the page below the chart.

TEMPERAMENT

This paragraph describes the breed's overall personality, behavior, ideal owner or environment, attitude toward other pets, training hints, and tendencies toward undesirable behaviors such as excessive barking or chewing when left alone.

Of course, every dog has his own individual personality, his own quirks and idiosyncrasies that make him unique. And every dog of every breed exhibits, at one time or another, great intelligence, silliness, resourcefulness, playfulness, laziness, a sense of humor, affection, devotion, independence, jealousy, sweetness, and stubbornness.

But overall, most individuals within a breed are more likely to act "this way" than "that way." More Bassets will be placid than energetic, and more Jack Russell Terriers will be energetic than placid. More Cavaliers will be sweet-natured than feisty, and more Miniature Pinschers will be feisty than sweet-natured. Proper raising and training can modify behavior and control misbehavior, but to minimize unnecessary power struggles, look for a temperament that sounds very close to what you want.

HISTORY

This paragraph briefly touches on the breed's origin and past uses, and names the primary registry for the breed in the United States. In most cases, this will be the AKC (American Kennel Club), in which case the popularity of the breed will be given: *24th of 146* means that out of 146 breeds recognized by the AKC in 1998, the breed ranked 24th in number of individuals registered that year.

Popularity has its advantages and disadvantages. Popular breeds are easier to find, and there are plenty of representatives from which to choose the best individuals. On the flip side, popular breeds have typically been exploited by irresponsible breeders, so you must be extra careful. Less popular breeds have not been damaged by mass breeding, but you will have to search harder for a puppy and you may end up on a waiting list.

Other registries with a good reputation include the UKC (United Kennel Club), FCI (Federacion Cynologique Internationale), SKC (States Kennel Club), CKC (Canadian Kennel Club), and AKC-FSS (the AKC's Foundation Stock Service).

PHYSICAL FEATURES

This section includes the typical height and weight range found in the breed, grooming required, and colors. It also states whether the breed's ears and tail are natural or surgically altered.

Grooming

Grooming requirements range from the occasional quick brushing of a smooth coat, to untangling the silky feathering of a spaniel-type coat, to deep brushing with a shedding blade to remove the dead undercoat of a spitz-type coat.

Most wiry coats must be "stripped" (dead hairs plucked out by hand or with the aid of a stripping knife) or clipped with electric clippers. Wiry coats are supposed to be hard in texture, and clippers tend to soften the coat, making it more likely to mat, so breeders will advise against it. However, most professional groomers don't offer stripping, which is tedious to do and sometimes uncomfortable for the dog. Clipping is far more convenient, comfortable, and common.

Long coats may be trimmed or clipped to various lengths for ease of maintenance and/or to produce a cute, perpetual puppy look. Some breeders will look aghast if you mention clipping their long-coated breed, so it's best to keep it to yourself if that's what you're planning to do.

Colors

Brindle? Blue merle? Sable? Not to worry: All color terms used in the profiles are described in the glossary at the end of the book.

Type of Ears

Natural ears may hang down alongside the head, as in a Beagle or Labrador Retriever. Or they may start out hanging in a young puppy, then prick up on their own at two to six months of age, as in a German Shepherd. Or they may fold forward, with the base of the ear pricked and the pointy top of the ear drooped forward, as in a Collie or Airedale. Or they may fold backward, flattening along the skull, as in a Greyhound. All of these ear carriages are natural.

Cropped ears are man-made. Cropped ears start out hanging and would continue doing so except that a veterinarian intervenes at six to twelve weeks of age. He anesthetizes the puppy, cuts the rounded hanging ears into a triangular shape, and bandages them into an upright position over the skull.

Proponents of cropping argue that this causes no pain, while opponents assert that it causes agony. Much depends on the skill of the veterinarian, the effectiveness of the anesthetic, and the individual sensitivity of the puppy. But there seems little doubt that having one's ears shaved and injected with a numbing anesthetic cannot be a pleasant experience. Awakening from anesthesia in a state of confusion is an equally stressful event, not to mention that one's ears are now stitched along the edges and stretched upward with bandages, and must remain so for a couple of weeks to "train" the newly sculpted ear to stand erect. Worse, this occurs during a critical period in the young puppy's life, when he is forming impressions about the world. He should be out and about and enjoying only positive experiences.

The origins of cropping are threefold: (1) to give guarding breeds a satanic look; (2) to remove a potential handhold that intruders, predatory animals, or other dogs might latch on to during a fight; and (3) to prevent ear infections by exposing more of the ear to light and air. However, Rottweilers and Bullmastiffs are magnificent guard dogs whose natural hanging ears don't interfere with their ability to deter and confront intruders. And breeders and veterinarians who own and treat both cropped and uncropped individuals report no difference whatsoever in the occurrence of ear infections.

So we come to the real reason why certain breeds are still being cropped: appearance. Cropped Dobermans look sleeker and more alert than their uncropped brothers. Breeders say, "Their head is too narrow for long hanging ears." In other words, cropping takes place for aesthetic reasons. It is cosmetic surgery, performed for fashion purposes.

Attitudes about the ethics of this practice in a civilized society are changing. Owners across America are discovering, just as their European and Australian counterparts already have, that Dobermans and Boxers look just as handsome and will protect them just as earnestly when their natural ears are left alone. More and more veterinarians are refusing to crop ears, and eventually the procedure will probably be declared illegal in the United States, as it already is in much of the rest of the world. For the time being, the choice is yours—unless the breeder has already had it done or refuses to sell a puppy without a guarantee that it will be cropped. In the latter case, I would go to another breeder, but that is your choice.

Type of Tail

Let's turn our attention to the other end. A *natural* tail may hang down, rising when the dog becomes alert or begins to wag, as in a Golden Retriever. Or it may tuck between the hind legs, which denotes fear in most breeds, but is perfectly normal carriage for a Whippet. Or it may be curled over the back, either loosely or tightly, as in a Siberian Husky or Alaskan Malamute. All of these tail carriages are natural.

A *docked* tail is man-made. Docked tails are those that have been cut short, either by the breeder or by a veterinarian, a few days after birth. In most breeds, about 60 percent of the tail is removed. In a few breeds, only the tip is taken, while some are docked down to little more than a stump, as in an Old English Sheepdog or Pembroke Welsh Corgi.

Why are some breeds docked and not others? Some guarding breeds, such as Boxers and Rottweilers, were docked to provide intruders one less appendage to grab. Some herding dogs, such as Old English Sheepdogs, were docked to prove their working status, which made them exempt from taxation in Old England. Some hunting dogs, such as English Springer Spaniels, were docked to protect their tails from thwacking against thickets and fences and possibly breaking.

But today docking, like cropping, is done for aesthetic reasons. Our eye has become accustomed to the shape, proportions, and "balance" of docked Boxers and Rottweilers. Yet we have no difficulty admiring a Great Dane or Labrador with his natural tail.

As with ear cropping, docking may well become illegal in the United States, as it already is in some countries. For now, if you don't want it done to your dog, you'll have to work it out with the breeder before the litter is born, because the procedure is done only a few days after birth. Be prepared for resistance. Many breeders are willing to forgo ear cropping upon request, but fewer will allow a long tail to stay on a docked breed. Fortunately, newborn puppies have little pain sensation, and though they do wriggle and squeal a bit when the tail is snipped, they recover within a few minutes. Dogs with docked tails do seem to enjoy the sensation of wagging just as much as dogs with long tails, and certainly fewer breakables go flying off the coffee table. So, although tail docking is just as cosmetic a surgery as ear cropping, my opinion is that it is not as inhumane.

HEALTH ISSUES

This paragraph lists the health clearances that the breeder should have obtained for both parents before breeding. Health problems are a huge issue in purebred dogs today and one that sets off sparks in many breeders. You will encounter many individuals who are not testing their dogs and who will minimize or emphatically deny that a particular health problem is a concern in their breed,

especially in *their* line. Their heads are buried firmly in the sand, and if you allow yourself to be reassured by their "guarantees," in lieu of the specific genetic testing and clearance certificates recommended in the profiles, you may well end up with an unhealthy puppy.

Stand firm on health issues. If a profile says, "Both parents should have OFA certificates (hips and elbows)," don't buy a pup whose parents don't have them. And don't take the breeder's word for it: See those certificates and make sure the registered names on them match the registered names of the parents. Sad to say, breeders can and do lie about health clearances.

The most common health clearances are:

OFA (Hips)

Hip dysplasia, where the ball of the hip does not fit properly into its socket, results in lameness of varying degrees and leads to degenerative joint disorder (arthritis). Its origin is a hot subject for debate, with some researchers insisting it is entirely hereditary, some declaring it a nutritional problem that can be avoided with natural feeding and vitamin C, and some blaming environment: too much exercise being forced on growing pups, along with high-protein "puppy" kibble that encourages rapid growth.

Whatever its origin, it is a serious problem in purebred dogs. All breeds are susceptible, but it is most common in large and giant breeds. Hip dysplasia is a developmental disease, meaning that it is not present at birth. Severe cases manifest themselves between five and twelve months of age, while moderate to mild cases may not show up until eighteen months or even later. That means you can't look at a three-month-old puppy and determine that just because he can play vigorously *now*, he won't develop hip dysplasia later. Similarly, an adult may have only a mild form, virtually undetectable by watching him run and jump, yet can pass on a more severe form to his offspring.

Until we have other answers, the best preventive (though not a guarantee) is buying a puppy whose parents and grandparents have had their hips X-rayed by a veterinarian. The X rays are then sent to the Orthopedic Foundation for Animals (OFA), the University of Pennsylvania Hip Improvement Program (PennHIP), the Institute for Genetic Disease Control in Animals (GDC), or the Canadian Ontario Veterinary College (OVC) for evaluation, an official rating, and a clearance certificate.

OFA (Elbows)

Elbow dysplasia is an umbrella term encompassing several orthopedic disorders: osteochondritis dissecans (OCD), fragmented coronoid process (FCP), and ununited anconeal process (UAP) are the most common forms. Breeds prone to elbow dysplasia should have X rays and certifications done on their elbows at the same time their hips are done.

OFA (Patellas)

Luxating patella, also referred to as slipping stifle, or more colloquially "bad knees," is a chronic or sporadic dislocation of the kneecap from its socket. It is most common in little and small breeds, but can occur in all sizes. In breeds prone to luxating patella, both parents should have their knees palpated by an experienced veterinarian. Patella certification programs are a fairly recent development, so not all breeders are going the extra step of sending their vet's report in for an official clearance certificate. But they should have something from their vet stating that the parents' knees are sound.

OFA (Heart)

Cardiomyopathy and subaortic stenosis (SAS) are two common heart defects that can be screened for with an EKG. As with patella certification, cardiac certification programs have been available for only a short time, so not all breeders will send their vet's report in for an official clearance certificate. But they should have something from their vet stating that the parents' hearts are sound.

CERF (Eyes)

Progressive retinal atrophy (PRA), retinal dysplasia, and juvenile cataracts are serious eye diseases that eventually cause blindness. Some forms of eye disease can be detected in six-week-old puppies, while others do not appear until middle age.

The best preventive (though not a guarantee) is buying a puppy whose parents and grandparents have had their eyes examined by a board-certified (American College of Veterinary Ophthalmologists) ophthalmologist, not a general veterinarian. The breeder then sends the results to the Canine Eye Registration Foundation (CERF) for evaluation and an official clearance certificate. Note that eye diseases, because of their variable age of onset, must be screened for every year, so CERF certificates are good for only one year. *Make sure the certificate you're looking at is current.*

In a few breeds, a DNA test has been developed for PRA that can tell with 100 percent accuracy whether a dog is affected, a carrier (unaffected, but carrying the gene to pass on to offspring), or clear (unaffected and not a a carrier). The list of breeds to whom this test is applicable will expand as researchers learn more about DNA markers.

BAER Tested (Hearing)

Congenital deafness can be detected by the BAER (Brainstem Auditory Evoked Response) test starting at six weeks of age. Puppies who can hear with both ears have bilateral hearing. Puppies who can hear with only one ear have unilateral hearing. Deafness is a major problem in some breeds: In the Dalmatian, for example, it is estimated that 66 percent have bilateral hearing, 22 percent have unilateral hearing, and 12 percent are born deaf. Unfortunately, a source for BAER testing is unavailable in some areas of the country, and in those areas you must decide if an untested puppy is worth the risk or if you should choose a different breed.

vWD Clear

Von Willebrand's disease is a blood-clotting disorder that can produce hemorrhaging (external or internal) from a small cut or minor surgery. As with PRA, a DNA test has been developed for a few breeds that can tell with 100 percent accuracy whether a dog is affected, a carrier (unaffected, but carrying the gene to pass on to offspring), or clear (unaffected and not a carrier). Until the list of applicable breeds expands, breeders of most vWD-prone breeds must rely on a simple blood test (the ELISA assay), which is often not reliable. Thus, clear blood test results are nice to see, but not conclusive.

Normal Thyroid

Thyroid abnormalities are almost an epidemic in purebred dogs today. When the thyroid gland doesn't produce enough hormones to maintain a dog's metabolism, the result is hypothyroidism (low thyroid), which tends to cause skin and hair abnormalities, weight gain, and lethargy. All breeds are susceptible, but some are more prone to it than others. In these breeds, a complete blood panel (testing for T3, T4, free T3, and free T4) should be run to determine thyroid function. Testing only for T4 is cheaper, but the results are not conclusive.

Passing all of the recommended genetic health tests doesn't prove that a dog is free of unhealthy genes. Most tests reveal only whether a dog is affected, not whether he is carrying a hidden gene for that disorder. DNA tests *do* reveal whether a dog is affected, a carrier, or clear; thus, they are our best weapon in the fight to eradicate genetic diseases. But until more of these DNA tests are established, we can only rely on the tests we have.

So passing these tests is not a guarantee that puppies from these parents will be perfect. However, it is currently the best way to reduce your risks. More important, it is a major indicator that the breeder is serious about his responsibility to do the best he can. Testing, then, gives you as much valuable knowledge about the breeder as about the dogs, and it is precisely these responsible breeders that we, as prospective owners, want to support.

There are hundreds of other genetic disorders that cannot be detected by testing. All you can do is ask the breeder about the occurrence of these conditions in his line and hope that he will be honest with you. The disorders are listed in each profile and explained in the glossary at the end of the book.

CAUTIONS WHEN BUYING

The final paragraph of the profile offers miscellaneous advice and warnings. You may learn that you need to be extra cautious because a breed is being mass-produced by unknowledgeable breeders who are out to make a buck. You may learn that the breed has branched into show types and field types and you'll need to decide which one appeals to you. You may learn that the breed is similar to another breed that you may also want to consider.

Keep in mind that the profiles are for mature dogs. A dog is physically mature when he has attained his adult height, weight, coat, and color. He is sexually mature when he is capable of breeding. He is emotionally mature when he loses most of his silliness and consistently acts as indicated in the temperament paragraph. Just as with people, physical and sexual maturity usually occur before emotional maturity. And just as with people, dogs are not puppies one day and adults the next; they go through awkward, gangly, adolescent stages, physically, sexually, and emotionally.

Small breeds are usually mature at six to twelve months, medium breeds at twelve to eighteen months, and large breeds at eighteen to thirty-six months. An eleven-month-old Rottweiler is not going to have the solid build, self-confidence, or protectiveness of a three-year-old Rottweiler. Be especially patient with breeds whose profiles indicate they mature more slowly than other breeds.

Now that you understand how to read the five paragraphs of the bottom section, how should you use them to narrow your list of suitable breeds?

Let's suppose the Brittany is one of your suitable breeds. Look first at his temperament, which includes "He loves an athletic lifestyle of hiking, biking, running, and ball playing. If left alone too much and not given outlets for his energy, you're likely to see hyperactivity and destructive chewing."

Now if you're an outdoors enthusiast, these traits present no problems. But if you're a couch potato living in a Manhattan studio apartment, you should eliminate the Brittany from further consideration.

Another example: "Most are sensitive, rather 'soft' dogs, willing to please and responsive to a calm voice and a light hand on the leash. He does not do well in an environment with frequent tension or loud voices." In other words, only gentle owners need apply. If you pride yourself on your booming voice and firm hand, or if you envision yourself the master of a macho dog, cross off the Brittany.

Notice that he is described as being "peaceful with other animals." If you had other pets, you would feel reassured by this Brittany characteristic. Indeed, if you had a cat or rabbit, you would probably want to eliminate a breed described as suspect with these small pets. You might even extend your caution to breeds described as being aggressive with other dogs, as they should be introduced to smaller pets with extra vigilance and supervision. Do keep in mind that all dogs should be properly introduced to small pets, and that an individual who constantly pesters the family cat has not been clearly taught that this behavior is unacceptable.

Read through the rest of the profile. If you see anything that makes you shake your head, wrinkle your nose, or otherwise feel doubtful about having this dog in your home, eliminate him from further consideration. Remember, based on ten important traits, these breeds are all potentially good matches for you, so you can base further narrowing on attractiveness, if you like. You may prefer a pudgy, low-slung, or streamlined build—or not. You may like or dislike a long, narrow face or a short, pushed-in face. You may prefer a wide range of color choices. You may admire the alert expression that pricked ears tend to enhance, or you may be partial to the softer expression associated with hanging ears.

Try not to get too hung up on appearance, though. Remember that beauty is only skin deep. If you choose an attractive breed whose personality and behavior don't suit you, you're going to spend a lot of time disliking the dog and you'll find his beauty fading in your eyes. If, on the other hand, you choose a breed with a personality that appeals to you but an appearance that you could take or leave, you'll be astonished, as time goes by, at how gorgeous he becomes in your eyes.

If you find yourself wavering between several breeds that pique your interest, try to find more photos. Check bookstores, libraries, and pet supply stores for picture books such as *The Complete Borzoi* and *How to Raise and Train a Puli*. Don't pay much attention to the text, as most of these books tend to glorify a breed while glossing over any negative traits. Primarily you are interested in the photos, especially color photos.

If you have Internet access, visit as many Web sites as you can find on the breeds you're interested in. Some Web sites are included in the Appendix, National Clubs and Contacts. Others you can find through search engines such as www.yahoo.com.

Finally, you may need to see your favorite breeds up close (perhaps ensconced in your lap!) before you can make a final decision. Visiting breeders' homes and attending a dog show are the two best ways to become personally acquainted with a breed. We'll be doing just that in Step Three.

◆ ◆ ◆

The Breed Profiles

Affenpinscher (AFF-en-pin-sher)

Fine for Novice Owners
Good with Older, Considerate Children
Little in Size
Wiry Coat

EXERCISE REQUIRED — LOW

TRIMMING/CLIPPING REQUIRED — MEDIUM

AMOUNT OF SHEDDING — LOW

ACTIVITY INDOORS — HIGH

EASE OF TRAINING — LOW

SOCIABILITY WITH STRANGERS — LOW

TEMPERAMENT

The AKC Standard says the Affenpinscher "is generally quiet but can become vehemently excited when threatened or attacked and is fearless toward any aggressor." This inquisitive toy terrier is often described as comically serious. Certainly he is spunkier and more spirited than most toys. He is a busybody who dashes around checking out new sights and sounds. His playful antics are delightfully entertaining, and he often clutches toys with his agile paws. An extremely keen watchdog, the Affen may maintain his suspicious attitude even after a guest has been welcomed in. Most are fine with other family pets, especially when raised with them, but this breed is somewhat high-strung, tends to tremble when excited, and if he perceives an invasion of his space by an approaching stranger or strange dog, he can become raucous and blustery. Affens seem to have little fear of heights and must be held firmly lest they leap from your arms. They have a mind of their own and without a firm hand can be obstinate and demanding, tossing tantrums or sulking when they don't get their own way. Spoiling is not recommended for this breed, especially since he is so bright and does respond well to calm, patient training. Like most terrier types, the Affenpinscher is proud and sensitive and does not take kindly to being jerked around or teased. He can be possessive of his food and toys, quick to bark, and hard to housebreak.

HISTORY

In his native Germany, he was dubbed *affen* (monkey) *pinscher* (terrier) because of his bushy black face and large eyes. AKC popularity: 121st of 146 (the rarest of all the toy breeds).

PHYSICAL FEATURES

He stands 9–12 inches and weighs 7–10 pounds. Larger individuals are common; these are not suitable for showing, but make sturdy pets. Brush and comb his harsh, rough coat once a week and keep his bottom trimmed for cleanliness. Show dogs are "stripped" (dead coat plucked out) every few months; pet owners may opt for more convenient clipping. He is usually black, but may also be black-and-tan, red, silver, or gray. His ears may be cropped or left natural (either dropped, semi-erect, or erect). Likewise, his tail may be docked or left natural.

HEALTH ISSUES

Both parents should be screened for luxating patella. Also ask about heart problems and Legg-Perthes in the lines. He doesn't like cold or rainy weather and should wear a sweater in inclement conditions. Lifespan: 12–14 years.

CAUTIONS WHEN BUYING

With only about two hundred puppies registered each year, difficult births, and tiny litters, Affens are very difficult to find. Expect a waiting list.

Afghan Hound

Best for Experienced Owners
Good with Older, Considerate Children
Large in Size
Long Coat

EXERCISE REQUIRED — HIGH MEDIUM

TRIMMING/CLIPPING REQUIRED — HIGH
MEDIUM LOW

AMOUNT OF SHEDDING — MEDIUM

ACTIVITY INDOORS — LOW

EASE OF TRAINING — LOW

SOCIABILITY WITH STRANGERS — LOW

TEMPERAMENT

The AKC Standard calls him "an aristocrat, his whole appearance one of dignity and aloofness . . . eyes gazing into the distance as if in memory of ages past." Some Afghans are indeed dignified, while others are silly clowns, and some alternate gleefully between the two. Though quiet indoors, he should not be left unsupervised for long periods of time without personal attention and running exercise, for he bores easily and can become destructive. Don't let this breed off-leash, for he is unbelievably fast and can gallop out of sight in seconds. His high hipbones make him one of the most agile of all breeds and one of the best jumpers. Fences must be high. Standoffish by nature, he needs extensive exposure to people and unusual sights and sounds so that his caution does not become timidity. He is sociable with other dogs, but may chase smaller pets. Obedience training will control his occasional bumptiousness and build his confidence, but you must be patient and persuasive, for sighthounds are extremely sensitive to leash jerking and may respond defensively if frightened. Independent and not particularly eager to please, their stubbornness takes the form of resistance rather than wild disobedience: They brace their legs and refuse to walk. Afghans can be finicky eaters and hard to housebreak.

HISTORY

The Afghan is a sighthound who relied on his keen vision and long legs to run down gazelles, hares, and leopards in the deserts and mountains of Afghanistan, while the huntsmen followed on horseback. His forte is not straightaway speed, like a Greyhound, but power and agility over rugged terrain. AKC popularity: 85th of 146.

PHYSICAL FEATURES

Males stand 26–28 inches; females stand 24–26 inches. Weight is 50–60 pounds. Brush and comb his long, silky coat every other day. Pet owners may choose to trim the coat short every few months. Keep his ear canals clean and dry and his bottom trimmed for cleanliness. Colors include black, cream, blue, brindle, black-and-tan, shaded solids, and exotic patterns such as "domino." His ears and tail are natural.

HEALTH ISSUES

Both parents should have OFA certificates (hips) and yearly CERF (eyes). Also ask about low thyroid and OCD in the lines. Afghans are sensitive to anesthetics, vaccines, and chemicals and should never be casually medicated or sedated. Lifespan: 12 years.

CAUTIONS WHEN BUYING

A neglected Afghan is a sorry sight, so be sure you're up for the grooming (three to four hours per week) or will keep the coat trimmed. Sighthounds have an unusual temperament—don't choose a member of this family if you want the instant obedience and fawning affection of a Golden Retriever.

Airedale Terrier

Best for Experienced Owners
Good with Older, Considerate Children
Medium to Large in Size
Wiry Coat

EXERCISE REQUIRED — HIGH MEDIUM
TRIMMING/CLIPPING REQUIRED — HIGH
AMOUNT OF SHEDDING — LOW
ACTIVITY INDOORS — HIGH MEDIUM
EASE OF TRAINING — MEDIUM
SOCIABILITY WITH STRANGERS — MEDIUM

TEMPERAMENT

A rowdy handful as a puppy, the Airedale matures into a dignified, self-assured, courageous adult. This athletic dog romps and plays hard. Without vigorous exercise and lots of personal interaction, he is easily bored and may become destructive as he seeks to entertain himself. Young Airedales are especially rambunctious and can turn your garden into a moonscape of excavated moles and tulip bulbs. Mental stimulation (hunting, fetching sticks, obedience, agility, playing games) is essential for this thinking breed. His attitude toward strangers varies from enthusiastically friendly to sensibly polite. He is a vigilant watchdog, and most are protective, though some are much more so than others. The Airedale can be bold and aggressive with other dogs, and with his strong hunting instincts must be exposed early to cats. Rabbits and rodents are not a wise addition to the household. This breed is very smart, but also independent. Unless you establish yourself as the alpha (number one), he can be headstrong. Yet assertive owners who know how to lead will find him eminently trainable. He has an innate sense of pride and fairness and will become exceedingly obstinate if handled harshly or jerked around. Positive training methods using praise and food rewards work much better.

HISTORY

"The King of the Terriers" was developed in the English river valley of Aire. He hunted river rats and badgers and helped his working-class owner poach game from wealthy estates. AKC popularity: 50th of 146 breeds.

PHYSICAL FEATURES

He stands 22–24 inches and weighs 50–70 pounds. (There are many oversize lines and individuals.) Brush and comb his hard wiry coat once a week. His beard should be combed daily for cleanliness. Likewise, keep his bottom trimmed for cleanliness. Show dogs are "stripped" (dead coat plucked out) every few months; pet owners may opt for more convenient clipping. His upper body (saddle) is black or grizzle (black mixed with gray); his head, chest, shoulders, and legs are tan. His ears are natural; his tail is docked.

HEALTH ISSUES

Both parents should have OFA certificates (hips). Also ask about low thyroid, vWD, and allergies or skin conditions in the lines. Lifespan: 11–14 years.

CAUTIONS WHEN BUYING

Warren Miller wrote, in *The American Hunting Dog*, "On the borderline between the bird dog and the fur dog stands the Airedale . . . being successfully trained to hunt everything alive." Some breeders advertise "Oorang line" Airedales, a larger strain than show lines. Just be sure to see the OFA certificates if you're considering this type.

Akita

Best for Experienced Owners
Good with Children If Raised with Children
Large to Giant in Size
Thick, Medium-Length Coat

EXERCISE REQUIRED — MEDIUM

TRIMMING/CLIPPING REQUIRED — LOW

AMOUNT OF SHEDDING — HIGH

ACTIVITY INDOORS — LOW

EASE OF TRAINING — LOW

SOCIABILITY WITH STRANGERS — LOW

TEMPERAMENT

The Akita is calm, dignified, and quiet (seldom barks), yet also has a dominant and challenging personality. Powerful, reserved with strangers, and protective, he must be accustomed to people at an early age so that his guarding instincts remain controlled rather than indiscriminate. He can be so aggressive with other dogs of the same sex that two males or two females should never be left alone together. He can be predatory toward smaller pets. Training can be a challenge, for he is assertive, strong-willed, and bores easily, and he may use his intelligence in ways that suit his own purposes. Yet owners who know how to lead will find him eminently trainable via praise and reward methods. He must be treated with respect and you must insist on respect in return. This rugged breed doesn't require hours of running, yet he enjoys vigorous exercise, especially in cold weather. Akitas can be very possessive of their food and do not accept teasing or mischief.

HISTORY

In the mountains of Akita Prefecture, Japan, he was used for bear hunting, guarding, and occasionally for dog-fighting. AKC popularity: 36th of 146.

PHYSICAL FEATURES

Males stand 26–28 inches and weigh 100–130 pounds. Females stand 24–26 inches and weigh 70–100 pounds. His coat is harsh, with a dense undercoat, and needs brushing once a week, daily during heavy seasonal shedding. Colors include fawn, brindle, pinto (white with colored patches), silver, red, and solid white, among others.

He often has a black mask and/or white blaze on his face. His ears and tail are natural.

HEALTH ISSUES

Both parents should have OFA certificates (hips and elbows) and yearly CERF (eyes). Screening for normal thyroid (full panel) is extra security. Also ask about bloat, sebaceous adenitis, cruciate ligament problems, allergies, skin conditions, and autoimmune problems in the lines. Lifespan: 10–13 years.

CAUTIONS WHEN BUYING

This demanding breed should not be purchased on a whim: He has become too popular for his own good, and unknowledgeable breeders abound. Buy only from a breeder who emphasizes sound temperament (observe both parents and preferably grandparents or other relatives). Plan on early training and socialization, and don't relegate your Akita to the backyard.

Alaskan Malamute

Best for Experienced Owners
Good with Children If Raised with Children
Large in Size
Thick, Medium-Length Coat

EXERCISE REQUIRED — HIGH MEDIUM

TRIMMING/CLIPPING REQUIRED — LOW

AMOUNT OF SHEDDING — HIGH

ACTIVITY INDOORS — MEDIUM

EASE OF TRAINING — LOW

SOCIABILITY WITH STRANGERS — HIGH

TEMPERAMENT

Some Malamutes remain playful puppies all their lives, while others mature into calm, dignified adults. This rugged breed is best suited to people who love the great outdoors. He plays vigorously and is most content when pulling or packing a load (sledding, ski-joring, weight pulling, backpacking), especially in cool weather. Without such exercise and lots of companionship, he can be boisterous and destructive—bored Mals are famous for chewing through drywall, ripping the stuffing out of sofas, and relandscaping backyards. Most individuals are friendly with everyone and make miserable watchdogs, but this is a substantial, powerful breed, so it is essential to socialize youngsters so they grow up to respect people. The Malamute can be so aggressive with other dogs of the same sex that two males or two females should never be kept together. With his Arctic heritage, he can be predatory with smaller pets and must be securely fenced when outdoors, for he is an explorer with strong hunting instincts. Once loose, he may run deer and molest livestock. This self-reliant breed will test for position in the family pecking order. Unless you establish yourself as the alpha (number one), he can be headstrong and demanding. Unneutered males, especially, can be very dominant and possessive of their food.

HISTORY

The Mahlemut tribe (note different spelling) used him as a freight dog to pull heavy sledges. A champion weight-puller can haul three thousand pounds. AKC popularity: 46th of 146.

PHYSICAL FEATURES

He stands 23–27 inches and weighs 75–110 pounds. Avoid "giant" lines, as there is a tendency to emphasize excessive weight at the expense of sound structure and athleticism. Brush his harsh coat twice a week, daily during heavy seasonal shedding. Along with his shedding great chunks of hair in the spring and fall, you'll find loose hair the rest of the year as well. Colors include wolf gray, black, Alaskan seal (black with a creamy undercoat), and red. Usually his face is white with mask markings. His ears and tail are natural.

HEALTH ISSUES

Both parents should have OFA certificates (hips) and be CHD-normal for chondrodysplasia (dwarfism). A yearly CERF certificate (eyes) is extra security. Also ask about bloat, low thyroid, and renal dysplasia in the lines. With their thick coat, Malamutes don't do well in extreme heat or high humidity. Lifespan: 10–12 years.

CAUTIONS WHEN BUYING

The so-called Eskimo tribes relied on the Malamute's natural instincts for survival, which included hunting for food and cleverly avoiding dangers along the trail. These instincts lead to independent, free-thinking behaviors that are not always appreciated in our more "civilized" environment. Malamutes are still a rather primitive breed; they live with you and not for you.

American Bulldog

Best for Experienced Owners
Good with Children
Medium to Large in Size
Smooth Coat

EXERCISE REQUIRED — HIGH

TRIMMING/CLIPPING REQUIRED — LOW

AMOUNT OF SHEDDING — MEDIUM

ACTIVITY INDOORS — MEDIUM LOW

EASE OF TRAINING — MEDIUM

SOCIABILITY WITH STRANGERS — MEDIUM

TEMPERAMENT

Described as "all the dog anyone could ever want, and too much dog for some," this muscular breed possesses great strength, tenacity, determination, and confidence. He is best owned by active people who are interested in developing his athletic abilities in weight pulling, obedience, agility, hunting, farmwork, or Schutzhund. Though usually calm and self-possessed, he must have vigorous exercise to stay fit and happy. His attitude toward strangers varies from friendly to standoffish, and even the friendly ones make vigilant guardians. Early socialization is an absolute requirement to promote a stable, discriminating temperament. The American Bulldog lives for his family and may become destructive if left alone too much. Dog aggression can be a problem; he should be thoroughly socialized with other dogs from an early age. Though strong-willed, he learns quickly and will respect an owner who is equally confident and consistent. Because of public/media prejudice toward any breed resembling a "pit bull," American Bulldogs should be kept on-leash outside their yard and trained through at least basic obedience.

HISTORY

His ancestors arrived in the United States with the first settlers. They were all-purpose working dogs used for catching unruly cattle, semi-wild hogs, and wild boar, and protecting their homestead and family. Registered by the UKC, ABA, NABA, and CKC.

HISTORY

Males stand 22–27 inches and weigh 70–120 pounds. Females stand 20–25 inches and weigh 60–100 pounds.

His short, stiff coat requires only an occasional quick brushing. The majority are solid white or pied (mostly white with brindle, red, tan, or brown patches), though other colors are allowed. His ears and tail are usually natural, but may be cropped/docked.

HEALTH ISSUES

Both parents should have OFA certificates (hips). Also ask about demodectic mange in the lines. Lifespan: 10 years.

CAUTIONS WHEN BUYING

In the 1980s, the movie *Homeward Bound* introduced the American Bulldog to the public. Since then, his popularity has skyrocketed. Big-talking breeders are preying on uninformed buyers, running flashy ads, representing dogs of dubious lineage as purebred, not testing temperament or working ability, and not certifying hips. Get references, double-check everything you're told, refuse to pay outrageous prices, and look for BST (Breed Suitability Test) titles and other performance and temperament titles in the pedigree. The best-known lines are the John D. Johnson ("Classic" or "Bully") line and the Alan Scott ("Standard") line. However, most ABs are hybrids of these. Currently, several American Bulldog clubs are vying to control the future of the breed, and politics and conflict abound.

American Cocker Spaniel

Fine for Novice Owners
Good with Children If Raised with Children
Small in Size
Feathered, Medium-Length Coat

EXERCISE REQUIRED — MEDIUM
TRIMMING/CLIPPING REQUIRED — HIGH
AMOUNT OF SHEDDING — MEDIUM
ACTIVITY INDOORS — MEDIUM
EASE OF TRAINING — HIGH MEDIUM
SOCIABILITY WITH STRANGERS — HIGH

TEMPERAMENT

The Cocker of good breeding is happy, gentle, and playful. The smallest of the sporting breeds, he does need regular exercise, but daily walks and romps will suffice. When well socialized, he is friendly and peaceful with strangers and other animals, though there is timidity and excessive submissiveness in some lines. This willing dog is responsive to persuasive, cheerful obedience training that includes praise and food rewards. However, he is extremely sensitive to harsh handling and may respond defensively if jerked around on the leash or teased. Housebreaking, submissive urination (sudden wetting when excited or frightened), and chronic barking can be problems. Unless taught to be independent, some individuals are so persistently affectionate that they become clingy and demanding of attention. Some are possessive of their food or toys.

HISTORY

This little bird dog originated in England, but was fully developed in the United States. *Cocker* is derived from the woodcock, an upland game bird. AKC popularity: 13th of 146.

PHYSICAL FEATURES

He stands 13–16 inches and weighs 20–28 pounds. Brush and comb his silky coat every other day and clip every eight weeks. Keep his ear canals clean and dry and his bottom trimmed for cleanliness. There are three color varieties: *Black* may be solid, or with tan trim; *ASCOB* (Any Solid Color Other than Black) may be buff (cream to red), brown (chocolate), or brown with tan trim; *Parti-color* may be a speckled roan pattern, white with patches of black, buff/red, or brown, or any of these with tan trim. His ears are natural; his tail is docked.

HEALTH ISSUES

Both parents should have OFA certificates (hips), yearly CERF (eyes), and be screened for luxating patella. Also ask about cataracts, glaucoma, PKD, low thyroid, disk disease, heart disease, renal dysplasia, Legg-Perthes, vWD, and seizures in the lines. Allergies and skin conditions are common, as are chronic ear infections. Lifespan: 10–14 years.

CAUTIONS WHEN BUYING

It's tough to find a good representative of this breed. There are at least as many poorly bred individuals as there are well-bred ones, and the Cocker from poor breeding can be a nasty creature brimming with health problems and unstable behaviors. Buy only from a breeder whose dogs are friendly and confident and who can show you all of the health clearances. If you're interested in hunting, stick with field-bred lines. Most show Cockers are not bred for hunting instinct, and most have such profuse coats they would likely become tangled in a thicket and need to be scissored free. Also see English Cocker Spaniel.

American Eskimo (Miniature)

Fine for Novice Owners
Good with Older, Considerate Children
Small in Size
Thick, Medium-Length Coat

EXERCISE REQUIRED — MEDIUM

TRIMMING/CLIPPING REQUIRED — LOW

AMOUNT OF SHEDDING — HIGH

ACTIVITY INDOORS — HIGH

EASE OF TRAINING — HIGH MEDIUM

SOCIABILITY WITH STRANGERS — MEDIUM
LOW

TEMPERAMENT

The Eskie is happy and high-spirited, a rowdy dog who plays hard and enjoys vigorous exercise, especially in the snow. He is very people-oriented and craves a lot of companionship. Without enough activity (physical and mental), this creative thinker becomes bored and mischievous, which translates to destructive and noisy. Most are conservative with strangers, keen of eye and acute of hearing, and serious about their watchdog responsibilities. Early and frequent socialization is required to ensure that their watchfulness does not become suspicion, sharpness, or shyness. Most are fine with other dogs, but some can be jealous when other animals get attention. Some can be predatory with pet rodents and birds. This breed learns very quickly, excels at performing tricks and complex stunts, and is one of the brightest problem-solvers in the canine world, but he is also independent and can be willful. If you don't consistently enforce the rules, he will use his intelligence in clever ways that suit his own purposes. Because he is proud and sensitive, obedience training must consist of positive methods (praise and food), as jerking on the leash only makes him obstinate or defensive. Eskies love to chew, dig, and bark, and some individuals have high-pitched, piercing voices.

HISTORY

You may hear this breed referred to as a "spitz"; however, spitz is simply a general type of dog with a thick furry coat, pricked ears, curly tail, and foxy muzzle. A "spitz" is not a breed any more than a "hound" or "retriever" is a breed. Spitz dogs originated in Germany and came to the United States with German immigrants. The white Eskie was eventually developed from these dogs, and some became popular as circus performers. AKC popularity: 96th of 146 (includes all three sizes and does not truly reflect this breed's popularity, as many are registered with the UKC).

PHYSICAL FEATURES

He stands 12–15 inches and weighs 10–20 pounds. Brush his harsh coat twice a week, daily when he is shedding. Along with heavy seasonal shedding, you'll see loose hair the rest of the year as well. He is solid white or white with biscuit cream shadings. Blue-eyed dogs have a high incidence of deafness and cannot be shown in conformation classes. His ears and tail are natural.

HEALTH ISSUES

Both parents should have OFA certificates (hips) and yearly CERF (eyes). Also ask about urinary stones, seizures, and luxating patella in the lines. Lifespan: 13–15 years.

CAUTIONS WHEN BUYING

Be sure you are up for this breed's high energy level, need for constant companionship (some breeders call them, affectionately, Peskies), and degree of shedding. Keep them busy with advanced obedience, agility, herding, and other activities. Watch out for unknowledgeable breeders: A poorly bred Eskie can be high-strung and nervous. Insist on those health certifications.

American Eskimo (Standard)

Fine for Novice Owners
Good with Older, Considerate Children
Medium in Size
Thick, Medium-Length Coat

EXERCISE REQUIRED — HIGH MEDIUM

TRIMMING/CLIPPING REQUIRED — LOW

AMOUNT OF SHEDDING — HIGH

ACTIVITY INDOORS — HIGH MEDIUM

EASE OF TRAINING — HIGH MEDIUM

SOCIABILITY WITH STRANGERS — MEDIUM
    LOW

TEMPERAMENT

The Eskie is happy and high-spirited, a rowdy dog who plays hard and enjoys vigorous exercise, especially in the snow. He is very people-oriented and craves a lot of companionship. Without enough activity (physical and mental), this creative thinker becomes bored and mischievous, which translates to destructive and noisy. Most are conservative with strangers, keen of eye and acute of hearing, and serious about their watchdog responsibilities. Early and frequent socialization is required to ensure that their watchfulness does not become suspicion, sharpness, or shyness. Most are fine with other dogs, but some can be jealous when other animals get attention. Some can be predatory with pet rodents and birds. This breed learns very quickly, excels at performing tricks and complex stunts, and is one of the brightest problem-solvers in the canine world, but he is also independent and can be willful. If you don't consistently enforce the rules, he will use his intelligence in clever ways that suit his own purposes. Because he is proud and sensitive, obedience training must consist of positive methods (praise and food), as jerking on the leash only makes him obstinate or defensive. Eskies love to chew, dig, and bark, and some individuals have high-pitched, piercing voices.

HISTORY

You may hear this breed referred to as a "spitz"; however, spitz is simply a general type of dog with a thick, furry coat, pricked ears, curly tail, and foxy muzzle. A "spitz" is not a breed any more than a "hound" or "retriever" is a breed. Spitz dogs originated in Germany and came to the United States with German immigrants. The white Eskie was eventually developed from these dogs, and some became popular as circus performers. AKC popularity: 96th of 146 (includes all three sizes and does not truly reflect this breed's popularity, as many are registered with the UKC).

PHYSICAL FEATURES

He stands 15–19 inches and weighs 25–35 pounds. Brush his harsh coat twice a week, daily when he is shedding. Along with heavy seasonal shedding, you'll see loose hair the rest of the year as well. He is solid white or white with biscuit cream shadings. Blue-eyed dogs have a high incidence of deafness and cannot be shown in conformation classes. His ears and tail are natural.

HEALTH ISSUES

Both parents should have OFA certificates (hips) and yearly CERF (eyes). Also ask about urinary stones, seizures, and luxating patella in the lines. Lifespan: 13–15 years.

CAUTIONS WHEN BUYING

Be sure you are up for this breed's high energy level, need for constant companionship (some breeders call them, affectionately, Peskies), and degree of shedding. Keep them busy with advanced obedience, agility, herding, and other activities. Watch out for unknowledgeable breeders: A poorly bred Eskie can be high-strung and nervous. Insist on those health certifications.

American Eskimo (Toy)

Fine for Novice Owners
Good with Older, Considerate Children
Little in Size
Thick, Medium-Length Coat

EXERCISE REQUIRED — MEDIUM
TRIMMING/CLIPPING REQUIRED — LOW
AMOUNT OF SHEDDING — HIGH
ACTIVITY INDOORS — HIGH
EASE OF TRAINING — HIGH MEDIUM
SOCIABILITY WITH STRANGERS — MEDIUM
    LOW

TEMPERAMENT

The Eskie is happy and high-spirited, a rowdy dog who plays hard and enjoys vigorous exercise, especially in the snow. He is very people-oriented and craves a lot of companionship. Without enough activity (physical and mental), this creative thinker becomes bored and mischievous, which translates to destructive and noisy. Most are conservative with strangers, keen of eye and acute of hearing, and serious about their watchdog responsibilities. Early and frequent socialization is required to ensure that their watchfulness does not become suspicion, sharpness, or shyness. Most are fine with other dogs, but some can be jealous when other animals get attention. Some can be predatory with pet rodents and birds. This breed learns very quickly, excels at performing tricks and complex stunts, and is one of the brightest problem-solvers in the canine world, but he is also independent and can be willful. If you don't consistently enforce the rules, he will use his intelligence in clever ways that suit his own purposes. Because he is proud and sensitive, obedience training must consist of positive methods (praise and food), as jerking on the leash only makes him obstinate or defensive. Eskies love to chew, dig, and bark, and some individuals have high-pitched, piercing voices.

HISTORY

You may hear this breed referred to as a "spitz"; however, spitz is simply a general type of dog with a thick furry coat, pricked ears, curly tail, and foxy muzzle. A "spitz" is not a breed any more than a "hound" or "retriever" is a breed. Spitz dogs originated in Germany and came to the United States with German immigrants. The white Eskie was eventually developed from these dogs, and some became popular as circus performers. AKC popularity: 96th of 146 (includes all three sizes and does not truly reflect this breed's popularity, as many are registered with the UKC).

PHYSICAL FEATURES

He stands 9–12 inches and weighs 6–10 pounds. Brush his harsh coat twice a week, daily when he is shedding. Along with heavy seasonal shedding, you'll see loose hair the rest of the year as well. He is solid white or white with biscuit cream shadings. Blue-eyed dogs have a high incidence of deafness and cannot be shown in conformation classes. His ears and tail are natural.

HEALTH ISSUES

Both parents should have OFA certificates (hips) and yearly CERF (eyes). Also ask about urinary stones, seizures, and luxating patella in the lines. Lifespan: 13–15 years.

CAUTIONS WHEN BUYING

Be sure you are up for this breed's high energy level, need for constant companionship (some breeders call them, affectionately, Peskies), and degree of shedding. Keep them busy with advanced obedience, agility, herding, and other activities. Watch out for unknowledgeable breeders: A poorly bred Eskie can be high-strung and nervous. Insist on those health certifications.

American Foxhound

Best for Experienced Owners
Good with Children
Large in Size
Smooth Coat

EXERCISE REQUIRED — HIGH

TRIMMING/CLIPPING REQUIRED — LOW

AMOUNT OF SHEDDING — MEDIUM

ACTIVITY INDOORS — HIGH MEDIUM

EASE OF TRAINING — LOW

SOCIABILITY WITH STRANGERS — MEDIUM

TEMPERAMENT

This stable, good-natured hound makes an amiable companion when vigorously exercised (jogging, biking, running), though some individuals seem to prefer living kenneled with other hunting hounds, rather than fulfilling the role of house pet. Without outlets for his energy, he is rambunctious and prone to destructive chewing. Unless trained for hunting, he should not be let off-leash, for he is an explorer who will drop his nose to the ground and take off. His reaction to strangers varies from friendly to reserved, and some are mildly protective. With other dogs, the Foxhound is sociable and gregarious (indeed, he is happiest when other dogs are present in the home), but he has a high prey drive and may chase smaller pets. As with other scenthounds, training takes a while, for he is independent and slow to obey. American Foxhounds are slow to mature and remain playfully puppy-like for many years, which does require patience and control. He bays a lot and can be hard to housebreak.

HISTORY

Descended from European scenthounds, he was developed by colonial settlers in Virginia and Maryland. Usually he hunts in packs, trailing foxes while the huntsmen follow on horseback. AKC popularity: 141st of 146.

PHYSICAL FEATURES

He stands 23–28 inches and weighs 60–90 pounds. His hard coat needs only an occasional quick brushing. Keep his ear canals clean and dry. He is usually tricolor (black, tan, and white), but may also be red and white, tan and white, or lemon and white. His ears and tail are natural.

HEALTH ISSUES

Both parents should have OFA certificates (hips). Also ask about deafness and bleeding disorders in the lines. Lifespan: 10–12 years.

CAUTIONS WHEN BUYING

Foxhounds are divided into show types and field types. Show lines usually retain hunting instincts, but don't expect the same serious hunting drive as a Foxhound from field lines. Field lines, on the other hand, may be too energetic and businesslike to be at their best as pets. Also see English Foxhound and Harrier.

American Hairless Terrier

Fine for Novice Owners
Good with Older, Considerate Children
Small in Size
Smooth Coat (Hairless)

EXERCISE REQUIRED — MEDIUM

TRIMMING/CLIPPING REQUIRED — LOW

AMOUNT OF SHEDDING — LOW

ACTIVITY INDOORS — HIGH

EASE OF TRAINING — MEDIUM

SOCIABILITY WITH STRANGERS — MEDIUM

TEMPERAMENT

The American Hairless Terrier carries himself with sleek, graceful, jaunty self-importance. This lively dog must be kept on-leash or in a fenced yard, for he is quick moving and busy and bred to chase things that run. He is also inquisitive and resourceful, so be sure your fence is secure enough to keep him in. This attentive, head-cocking little breed is always awake and aware and won't fail to sound the alarm when he sees or hears anything new. There is a potential for timidity, so early and ongoing socialization is required to build a confident temperament. Generally good with other dogs and cats, he does have quick reflexes and will dispatch squeaky creatures with little effort. Though he has a mild stubborn streak, he responds nicely to obedience training that utilizes food. Being a respectable terrier, the American Hairless enjoys digging and barking and doesn't tolerate teasing or mistreatment.

HISTORY

Initially a mutation in a litter of Rat Terriers, he was developed by the Scott family. He differs from other hairless breeds in that the AHT gene is not semi-lethal, so no coated variety is needed to safely obtain hairless pups. However, because the breed is descended from only four foundation dogs, genetic degradation is a concern. There is a program under way to infuse new genetic material (via outcrosses with Rat Terriers) and create a more diverse gene pool. Registered by the UKC (as "Rat Terrier—Hairless").

PHYSICAL FEATURES

Toys stand 7–10 inches and weigh 6–10 pounds. (There are tinier dogs, but they cannot regulate their body temperature well enough for sound health.) Miniatures stand 10–16 inches and weigh 10–16 pounds. Puppies are born with fuzzy down that diminishes over several months, though some dogs retain minimal eyebrows, whiskers, and guard hairs on the muzzle and very fine (vellus) hair on the body. Skin pigmentation is usually pink with spots and freckles of gray, black, chocolate, gold, or tan. His ears and tail are natural.

HEALTH ISSUES

Both parents should be screened for luxating patella. This breed doesn't like cold or rainy weather and should wear a sweater in inclement conditions. He sweats through the sebaceous glands in his skin and feet, so sponge daily and bathe weekly to keep the glands clean and open. Light-colored individuals sunburn easily, leaving them susceptible to skin cancer. On the plus side, AHTs do not have the dentition problems (weak and missing teeth) of other hairless breeds. Lifespan: 15 years.

CAUTIONS WHEN BUYING

The outcrossing program means that some coated AHTs will also be available to pet homes. Other hairless breeds include the Chinese Crested and Xoloitzcuintle.

American Pit Bull Terrier

Best for Experienced Owners
Good with Older, Considerate Children
Medium to Large in Size
Smooth Coat

EXERCISE REQUIRED — MEDIUM
TRIMMING/CLIPPING REQUIRED — LOW
AMOUNT OF SHEDDING — MEDIUM
ACTIVITY INDOORS — MEDIUM
EASE OF TRAINING — MEDIUM LOW
SOCIABILITY WITH STRANGERS — MEDIUM

TEMPERAMENT

It often surprises people to learn that this extremely muscular dog with the impressive, confident presence is so easygoing. A well-bred APBT is a dependable, good-natured, loyal companion. Athletic and agile, with finely tuned reflexes, he must have moderate daily exercise to maintain his splendid muscle tone. Companionship is even more important, and extensive ongoing socialization is paramount. His attitude toward strangers varies from exuberant face kissing to polite reserve, and guarding instincts vary from high to nil, with some lines being much stronger tempered than others. Some Pit Bulls are stolen right out of their yards because they are so amiable and trusting. His attitude toward other canines, however, is another story, with his ancestry dictating a strong-willed, no-nonsense kind of dog who does not take kindly to being challenged by other assertive dogs. If confronted, he will readily engage. Though many individuals live peacefully in a house full of pets, there is always the risk that dormant animal prey instincts may suddenly flare into deadly combat. He can be stubborn, yet he responds well to confident owners who know how to establish and enforce rules of expected behavior. Because of public/media prejudice, he should be trained through at least basic obedience and always leashed outside of his yard. Every well-behaved APBT seen on the street can help counteract antibreed sentiment.

HISTORY

This pit-fighting dog was developed from old-style bulldogs used for bull baiting and hunting, crossed with tough working terriers. In the United States, he was recog-nized first as the American Pit Bull Terrier (UKC and ADBA), then as the American Staffordshire Terrier (AKC).

PHYSICAL FEATURES

He stands 18–22 inches and weighs 40–80 pounds. His hard coat needs only an occasional quick brushing. Colors include red, blue, brindle, and white with colored patches, among others. His ears may be cropped to stand erect or left naturally folding on his head. His tail is natural.

HEALTH ISSUES

Both parents should have OFA certificates (hips). TT (Temperament Tested) or CGC (Canine Good Citizen) titles demonstrate stable temperament. Cardiac screening is also desirable. Ask about eye problems, low thyroid, and tumors/cancer in the lines. Lifespan: 12–15 years.

CAUTIONS WHEN BUYING

The responsibilities associated with owning this breed in today's society must be taken seriously. He is discriminated against, even banned in some areas. Homeowners' insurance policies may be refused. Well-bred, friendly individuals are unfortunately considered as guilty as the unsound, dangerous dogs produced by irresponsible breeders and/or raised improperly by irresponsible owners. It is imperative to buy an American Pit Bull Terrier only from a highly respected breeder who displays due caution in screening for responsible ownership.

American Staffordshire Terrier

Best for Experienced Owners
Good with Older, Considerate Children
Medium in Size
Smooth Coat

EXERCISE REQUIRED — MEDIUM

TRIMMING/CLIPPING REQUIRED — LOW

AMOUNT OF SHEDDING — MEDIUM

ACTIVITY INDOORS — MEDIUM

EASE OF TRAINING — MEDIUM

SOCIABILITY WITH STRANGERS — MEDIUM

TEMPERAMENT

It often surprises people to learn that this extremely muscular dog with the impressive, confident presence is so easygoing. A well-bred AmStaff is a dependable, good-natured, loyal companion. Athletic and agile, with finely tuned reflexes, he must have moderate daily exercise to maintain his splendid muscle tone. Companionship is even more important, and extensive ongoing socialization is paramount. His attitude toward strangers varies from exuberant face kissing to polite reserve, and guarding instincts vary from high to nil, with some lines being much stronger tempered than others. Some AmStaffs are stolen right out of their yards because they are so amiable and trusting. His attitude toward other canines, however, is another story, with his ancestry dictating a strong-willed, no-nonsense kind of dog who does not take kindly to being challenged by other assertive dogs. If confronted, he will readily engage. Though many individuals live peacefully in a house full of pets, there is always the risk that dormant animal prey instincts may suddenly flare into deadly combat. He can be stubborn, yet he responds well to confident owners who know how to establish and enforce rules of expected behavior. Because of public/media prejudice, he should be trained through at least basic obedience and always leashed outside of his yard. Every well-behaved AmStaff seen on the street can help counteract antibreed sentiment.

HISTORY

This pit-fighting dog was developed from old-style bulldogs used for bull baiting and hunting, crossed with tough working terriers. In the United States, he was rec-ognized first as the American Pit Bull Terrier (UKC and ADBA), then as the American Staffordshire Terrier (AKC). AKC popularity: 68th of 146.

PHYSICAL FEATURES

He stands 17–19 inches and weighs 55–75 pounds. His hard coat needs only an occasional quick brushing. Colors include red, blue, brindle, and white with colored patches, among others. His ears may be cropped to stand erect or left naturally folding on his head. His tail is natural.

HEALTH ISSUES

Both parents should have OFA certificates (hips). TT (Temperament Tested) or CGC (Canine Good Citizen) titles demonstrate stable temperament. Cardiac screening is also desirable. Ask about eye problems, low thyroid, and tumors/cancer in the lines. Lifespan: 12–15 years.

CAUTIONS WHEN BUYING

The responsibilities associated with owning this breed in today's society must be taken seriously. He is discriminated against, even banned in some areas. Homeowners' insurance policies may be refused. Well-bred, friendly individuals are unfortunately considered as guilty as the unsound, dangerous dogs produced by irresponsible breeders and/or raised improperly by irresponsible owners. It is imperative to buy an American Staffordshire Terrier only from a highly respected breeder who displays due caution in screening for responsible ownership.

American Water Spaniel

Fine for Novice Owners
Good with Children If Raised with Children
Small to Medium in Size
Curly Coat (sometimes more wavy than curly)

EXERCISE REQUIRED — HIGH

TRIMMING/CLIPPING REQUIRED — MEDIUM

AMOUNT OF SHEDDING — MEDIUM

ACTIVITY INDOORS — MEDIUM

EASE OF TRAINING — MEDIUM

SOCIABILITY WITH STRANGERS — MEDIUM

TEMPERAMENT

The AKC Standard says that he has "great energy and eagerness for the hunt." The solidly built American Water Spaniel is happy, hardy, and adaptable, but also energetic and in need of a good amount of daily exercise. Swimming and fetching are especially appreciated. Too much confinement or isolation can lead to hyperactivity and destructive behavior. The temperament of this breed is about midway between that of an ingratiating English Springer Spaniel and a self-reliant Irish Water Spaniel. Individuals who have been extensively socialized are friendly with everyone, but this breed makes an alert watchdog and may not always welcome strangers into his home. Most are fine with other family pets, though some can be dominant with strange dogs. Not as eager to please as some other spaniels, the AWS has a stubborn, assertive streak. Consistent leadership is a must, and obedience training must be persuasive rather than sharp, because he is sensitive and can become defensive if jerked around. He doesn't tolerate teasing, he can be possessive of his food and toys, and he tends to be vocal: barking, whining, and "yodeling."

HISTORY

Wisconsin hunters developed this durable little retriever, who will plunge readily into the icy bays of the Great Lakes and not tip the boat over when he climbs back in! He is the state dog of Wisconsin, yet not commonly seen outside of the Midwest. AKC popularity: 117th of 146.

PHYSICAL FEATURES

He stands 15–18 inches and weighs 30–45 pounds. His coat is a mass of crisp, coarse ringlets, which may be tightly curled or loosely waved in an undulating "marcel" pattern. His head and face are smooth. Brush once a week and occasionally trim straggly hairs. Keep his ear canals clean and dry and his bottom trimmed for cleanliness. His brown color ranges from liver to dark chocolate. His ears and tail are natural.

HEALTH ISSUES

Both parents should have OFA certificates (hips) and yearly CERF (eyes). Also ask about low thyroid and seizures in the lines. Lifespan: 10–15 years.

CAUTIONS WHEN BUYING

More American Water Spaniels are used for hunting than are shown in conformation classes. Yet it is a tribute to breeders that most dogs retain sound hunting instincts and that there is not a significant split between field types and show types. The American Water Spaniel is sometimes confused with the Irish Water Spaniel: The latter is larger and has a loose curly topknot on his head and a hairless "rat" tail.

Anatolian Shepherd Dog

Best for Experienced Owners
Good with Older, Considerate Children
Giant in Size
Thick, Medium-Length Coat

EXERCISE REQUIRED — HIGH MEDIUM
TRIMMING/CLIPPING REQUIRED — LOW
AMOUNT OF SHEDDING — HIGH
ACTIVITY INDOORS — MEDIUM LOW
EASE OF TRAINING — LOW
SOCIABILITY WITH STRANGERS — LOW

TEMPERAMENT

The rugged Anatolian is not inclined to play fetch or Frisbee, nor should you expect animated responsiveness. Developed strictly for utilitarian purposes, he appears serious and dignified, calm and quiet, unless challenged. Livestock guardians are bred to bond with flock animals and their own family with fierce possessiveness. They make their own decisions about who is a friend and who is a foe, what is a threat and what is not, and they react to every situation as they see fit. Potential owners who cannot understand and control these powerful instincts should look for another breed. Anatolians are dominant, self-reliant dogs who will try to manage everyone and everything unless you are an assertive leader who knows how to instill respect. This breed requires a formal introduction to strangers before being touched by them, and he will remain vigilant every moment they are on his territory. He is patient with his own children and with submissive family pets, but he should not be expected to welcome those outside the family. Despite his bulk, he is remarkably agile and reactive. He needs a spacious yard with a six-foot-high fence and often prefers to be outdoors where he can view and patrol his territory. Anatolians have a deep, impressive bark, which they tend to use freely, especially at night when they are most attentive. They often dig deep holes to lie in.

HISTORY

A native of Turkey, the Anatolian has survived in weather extremes from mountain snow to desert heat for thousands of years, protecting the flocks. AKC popularity: 126th of 146 (many others are registered only with the UKC).

PHYSICAL FEATURES

He stands 28–34 inches. Males weigh 100–160 pounds; females weigh 90–120 pounds. His harsh coat may be short (one inch) or rough (four inches). Brush once a week, daily during heavy seasonal shedding. Colors include fawn (ranging from cream to red and sometimes called "Kangal" when accompanied by black ears and black mask), white (sometimes called "Akbash"), pinto (patched), brindle, and wolf-sable, among others. His ears and tail are natural.

HEALTH ISSUES

Both parents should have OFA certificates (hips and elbows). Also ask about bloat and low thyroid in the lines. Eyelid disorders (entropion) can be a problem. With his low metabolism, he is sensitive to anesthetics, vaccines, and chemicals and should never be casually medicated or sedated. Lifespan: 13 years.

CAUTIONS WHEN BUYING

Though some lines are more tranquil than others, this breed requires more of a commitment than most others. In a home where he is allowed to do his job yet is kept under control by experienced hands, he is an impressive companion. However, without ongoing socialization and supervision, he is simply too much dog and will walk all over you. See also Great Pyrenees, Komondor, Kuvasz, and Tibetan Mastiff.

Appenzell Mountain Dog

Best for Experienced Owners
Good with Older, Considerate Children
Medium to Large in Size
Short Coat

EXERCISE REQUIRED — HIGH
TRIMMING/CLIPPING REQUIRED — LOW
AMOUNT OF SHEDDING — MEDIUM
ACTIVITY INDOORS — MEDIUM
EASE OF TRAINING — HIGH MEDIUM
SOCIABILITY WITH STRANGERS — MEDIUM

TEMPERAMENT

Steady and good-natured, yet bold and athletic, the Appenzeller enjoys romping and roughhousing. Pulling a cart or sled, herding, agility, fetching balls, playing Frisbee, and weight pulling are productive outlets for his boundless energy. This intelligent breed likes to keep busy and needs to have something to do; he is not an apartment dog. Appenzellers bond closely with their family and seek lots of attention. Their determination to jump up into your face or shove their body against your leg can be disconcerting to those who are not accustomed to an enthusiastic, vigorous dog. He likes children, but is likely to bowl over little ones. He makes a vigilant watchdog and will sound off in a loud, deep voice to announce visitors—or simply to let you know that your neighbor has stepped outdoors. Though polite with guests, he is the wariest of the Swiss mountain dogs. Early and ongoing socialization is essential to develop his stable, self-assured temperament. Most are companionable with other animals. The Appenzeller can be dominant and pushy—necessary traits for working with unruly cattle, but challenging for nonassertive owners to handle. During adolescence, his hormones will kick in and he may start to test his limits. Obedience training should start early. Heeling is an especially important lesson, for these powerful dogs can literally pull you off your feet. Appenzellers bark sharply while working, so be prepared to control excessive vocalizing from the beginning.

HISTORY

Descended from Roman mastiffs, he is the rarest of the four Swiss sennenhunds (dogs of the Alpine herdsmen) and the only one with a curled tail. In the Swiss canton of Appenzell, he guarded the farm, herded cattle, and pulled milk carts to the dairy. Registered by the UKC, FCI, and AKC-FSS.

PHYSICAL FEATURES

He stands 19–23 inches. Males weigh 60–75 pounds, females weigh 45–55 pounds. Brush his short, double coat once a week, more often when shedding. He is jet black with white markings on his face, chest, feet, and tail tip and rich rust markings over each eye, on his cheeks, chest, legs, and under his tail. His ears and tail are natural.

HEALTH ISSUES

Both parents should have OFA certificates (hips). Lifespan: 12–15 years.

CAUTIONS WHEN BUYING

Though many people are drawn to the Appenzeller's striking colors, wash-and-wear coat, and dependable, good-natured temperament, he is not a happy pet unless allowed to work and exercise. He is very rare in the United States and prices are high: up to $1,500 for a pet. See also the Bernese, Entlebucher, and Greater Swiss mountain dogs.

Australian Cattle Dog

Best for Experienced Owners
Good with Older, Considerate Children
Medium in Size
Short Coat

EXERCISE REQUIRED — HIGH
TRIMMING/CLIPPING REQUIRED — LOW
AMOUNT OF SHEDDING — HIGH MEDIUM
ACTIVITY INDOORS — MEDIUM
EASE OF TRAINING — MEDIUM
SOCIABILITY WITH STRANGERS — MEDIUM
     LOW

TEMPERAMENT

The AKC Standard says, "The Cattle Dog's loyalty and protective instincts make it a self-appointed guardian to the stockman." Steady in temperament, yet bold and athletic, this robust dog enjoys romping, roughhousing, and working. He is not an apartment dog. To stay in hard muscular condition and a satisfied frame of mind, he requires lots of exercise. Working stock, agility, jogging, biking, chasing balls, and playing Frisbee are productive outlets for his high energy. Cooping him up with nothing to do will lead to destructive behaviors and obsessive barking. With strangers, the ACD is watchful, often suspicious, and will defend his property fiercely if threatened. Early socialization is important so that he does not become too sharp. He can be dominant with other dogs, and with his strong chasing drives and tendency to nip at whatever he is pursuing, he is not recommended around cats unless raised with them. Herding dogs have ingrained instincts to gather things together, and in the absence of livestock, they will make do with toddlers, other pets, bicyclists, etc. A challenging combination of intelligence, cleverness, and hardheadedness, Cattle Dogs will test members of the family during adolescence and must be handled with firm, consistent leadership. They are exceptionally versatile in the right hands, but they will run right over hapless owners. Nippiness and barking need to be controlled—and some individuals have shrill, high-pitched voices.

HISTORY

Crosses between the Scottish Highland Collie, Dalmatian, Australian Kelpie, Bull Terrier, and the wild Dingo produced this hardworking driver of unruly cattle. He is often called Queensland Heeler, Blue Heeler, or Red Heeler. AKC popularity: 67th of 146.

PHYSICAL FEATURES

He stands 17–20 inches and weighs 35–50 pounds. Brush his short, double coat once a week, daily during heavy seasonal shedding. He is blue or red. Blue dogs are mottled or speckled, with tan markings on the jaw, chest, and legs, and often with darker blue, black, or tan patches on the head. Red dogs are speckled, often with darker red markings on the head and/or body. His ears and tail are natural. (This breed should *not* have a docked tail.)

HEALTH ISSUES

Both parents should have OFA certificates (hips) and yearly CERF (eyes). Puppies should come with a BAER printout that shows normal bilateral hearing. Lifespan: 12–15 years.

CAUTIONS WHEN BUYING

Because of the extreme levels of physical and mental stimulation that he requires, this breed is too much dog for most people. Be careful: Some "Queensland Heelers" are offered with dubious registration papers or with none at all; you cannot be sure of the true heritage of these dogs, or even if they are purebred.

Australian Kelpie

Best for Experienced Owners
Good with Older, Considerate Children
Medium in Size
Short Coat

EXERCISE REQUIRED — HIGH

TRIMMING/CLIPPING REQUIRED — LOW

AMOUNT OF SHEDDING — MEDIUM

ACTIVITY INDOORS — MEDIUM

EASE OF TRAINING — HIGH MEDIUM

SOCIABILITY WITH STRANGERS — MEDIUM

TEMPERAMENT

The lithe, hard-muscled Kelpie can work stock for many hours and cover long distances in heat and dust without giving in. One of the smartest of all breeds, he can also be one of the most challenging to live with. His superior intellect, combined with his independence, intensity, and passion for keeping busy, are his best features—and the ones that make him unsuitable for most homes. This sharp-eyed, quick-thinking, fanatical workaholic must be allowed to do his job with livestock, to learn advanced obedience or agility, to accompany you jogging or biking, or to chase balls or Frisbees. Without physical and mental stimulation, Kelpies become bored and hyperactive and will drive you crazy with obsessive, destructive behaviors as they seek creative outlets for their energy. High intelligence means they learn quickly—including how to do anything they set their mind to. They are master escape artists (going over and under fences) and zealous gatherers of cars, bikes, joggers, cats, other dogs, livestock, and running children—circling, poking, pushing, and nipping if the object/animal/person doesn't cooperate. You must stay one step ahead of this brilliant breed, and most people are simply not up to the task.

HISTORY

An estimated 200,000 Kelpies work sheep, cattle, goats, and poultry in Australia. They are often trusted to work unsupervised, using their hypnotic "eye" (a fixed, intimidating stare) to control livestock, along with barking and gripping (biting) when necessary. Registered by the UKC and FCI.

PHYSICAL FEATURES

He stands 17–21 inches and weighs 30–55 pounds. Brush his short coat once a week. He may be black, black-and-tan, red, red-and-tan, fawn, chocolate, or smoke blue. His ears and tail are natural.

HEALTH ISSUES

Both parents should have OFA certificates (hips) and yearly CERF (eyes). Lifespan: 13 years.

CAUTIONS WHEN BUYING

Kelpies who are able to work are mentally and physically fulfilled and have pleasant dispositions, with some lines being calmer than others. The rest are likely to be described as "hyper" and "neurotic" and turned over to rescue organizations. Compared to Border Collies, Kelpies are less excitable but a bit harder to train because they are less compliant and prefer to rely more on their own initiative. This is a working dog, not a casual pet.

Australian Shepherd

Best for Experienced Owners
Good with Children If Raised with Children
Medium in Size
Feathered, Medium-Length Coat

EXERCISE REQUIRED — HIGH

TRIMMING/CLIPPING REQUIRED — LOW

AMOUNT OF SHEDDING — HIGH MEDIUM

ACTIVITY INDOORS — MEDIUM

EASE OF TRAINING — HIGH

SOCIABILITY WITH STRANGERS — MEDIUM

TEMPERAMENT

The AKC Standard describes him as "attentive and animated, lithe and agile, solid and muscular." Exceptionally intelligent and versatile, this breed is quite variable in temperament. Some lines are extremely energetic, quick moving, and reflex responsive, while others tend toward a milder, calmer manner. Yet all Aussies need a great deal of physical exercise and mental stimulation. Herding, advanced obedience, agility, jogging or biking, chasing balls, and playing Frisbee are constructive outlets for their enthusiasm. Aussies are demanding of time and attention and want to be with you constantly. They can be polite to aloof with strangers; there is timidity in some lines, and early socialization is important so that he does not become shy or sharp. Some are dominant with other dogs and will chase cats, while others are good-natured with all living creatures. One of the most capable and trainable breeds in all of dogdom, he excels at the highest levels of competition, yet some individuals are more challenging to train than others. Aussies are uncomfortable when their charges (family members and other pets) are separated and may try to gather them together by circling, poking, and nipping, especially when young.

HISTORY

Named for his association with Basque sheepherders who came to the United States from Australia in the nineteenth century, he was fully developed by American ranchers. AKC popularity: 40th of 146 (many more are registered only with the original parent club, the ASCA).

PHYSICAL FEATURES

Males stand 20–23 inches and weigh 50–75 pounds. Females stand 18–21 inches and weigh 40–60 pounds. Herding lines tend toward the smaller side, while conformation lines tend to be larger and heavier boned. Some coats are shorter with less undercoat, making them easier to care for, while others have a heavy undercoat and feathering that requires frequent combing. Shedding is heavy twice a year. The four allowed colors are black, blue merle, red (light cinnamon to dark liver), and red merle. White markings and/or tan points are common. Eyes range from brown to glassy blue, including any combination. His ears are natural; his tail is docked.

HEALTH ISSUES

Both parents should have OFA certificates (hips and elbows) and yearly CERF (eyes). Each individual puppy must have his eyes examined by an AVCO-certified ophthalmologist (not just a regular vet) at six to eight weeks of age. Also ask about seizures, low thyroid, heart disease, allergies and skin conditions, and cancer in the lines. Lifespan: 12–15 years.

CAUTIONS WHEN BUYING

Aussies are often turned in to rescue organizations because their owners wouldn't or couldn't channel their high energy through obedience training. This brilliant canine must be respected, given lots of attention, and rigorously worked with on a regular basis.

Australian Shepherd (Miniature)

Best for Experienced Owners
Good with Children If Raised with Children
Small to Medium in Size
Feathered, Medium-Length Coat

EXERCISE REQUIRED — HIGH MEDIUM

TRIMMING/CLIPPING REQUIRED — LOW

AMOUNT OF SHEDDING — HIGH MEDIUM

ACTIVITY INDOORS — MEDIUM

EASE OF TRAINING — HIGH

SOCIABILITY WITH STRANGERS — MEDIUM

TEMPERAMENT

The Mini Aussie is exactly as its name implies: a small Australian Shepherd with the same attentive, energetic temperament, high intelligence, and need to have some purpose in life. Some lines are extremely spirited and quick moving, while others have a milder, calmer manner. Minis can get by with a bit less physical exercise than their full-size brothers, but need just as much mental stimulation. Boredom is the leading cause of destructive behavior and excessive barking. Herding, obedience, agility, chasing balls, and playing Frisbee are productive outlets for their enthusiasm. These dogs are demanding of time and attention and want to be with you constantly. They can be polite to aloof with strangers; there is timidity in some lines, and early socialization is important so that he does not become shy or sharp. Some are dominant with other dogs and will chase cats, while others are good-natured with all living creatures. One of the most capable and trainable of all breeds, he excels at the highest levels of competition. Aussies are uncomfortable when their charges (family members and other pets) are separated and may try to gather them together by circling, poking, and nipping, especially when young.

HISTORY

See Australian Shepherd. The smaller lines have been around since the beginning, but when the breed standard was drawn up, it accepted only the larger dogs. The Miniature Australian Shepherd Club of America (MASCA) would like to see their dogs eventually accepted as a variety of Australian Shepherd. Registered by the MASCA and the SKC.

PHYSICAL FEATURES

He stands 14–18 inches and weighs 20–40 pounds (most are 28–40 pounds). Some coats are shorter with less undercoat, making them easier to care for, while others have a heavy undercoat and feathering that requires frequent combing. Shedding is heavy twice a year. The four allowed colors are black, blue merle, red (light cinnamon to dark liver), and red merle. White markings and/or tan points are common. Eyes range from brown to glassy blue, including any combination. His ears are natural; his tail is docked, though some are born with natural bobtails.

HEALTH ISSUES

Both parents should have OFA certificates (hips and elbows) and yearly CERF (eyes). Each individual puppy must have his eyes examined by an AVCO-certified ophthalmologist (not just a regular vet) at six to eight weeks of age. Also ask about seizures, low thyroid, heart disease, allergies and skin conditions, and cancer in the lines. Lifespan: 12–15 years.

CAUTIONS WHEN BUYING

The Mini Aussie should not be regarded as an "easy" substitute for the Australian Shepherd, i.e., an Australian Shepherd Lite. Their smaller size may be easier to manage, but their high intelligence and energy level must be channeled through obedience training and regular activities, just as with their larger brothers.

Australian Terrier

Best for Experienced Owners
Good with Older, Considerate Children
Little in Size
Wiry Coat

EXERCISE REQUIRED — MEDIUM

TRIMMING/CLIPPING REQUIRED — MEDIUM

AMOUNT OF SHEDDING — LOW

ACTIVITY INDOORS — MEDIUM

EASE OF TRAINING — HIGH MEDIUM

SOCIABILITY WITH STRANGERS — MEDIUM

TEMPERAMENT

The AKC Standard calls him "spirited, alert, coura-geous, and self-confident, with the natural aggressiveness of a ratter and hedge hunter." One of the most sensible and least demanding of the terriers, the Aussie is nonethe-less as hardy and spunky as the rest. He is so adaptable that he's easy to live with in any home that understands the dynamic terrier temperament and provides enough com-panionship, outdoor walks, and vigorous play sessions. Though small, he is an alert watchdog with keen senses, reserved but polite with strangers. Though he can be scrappy with other dogs of the same sex, most Aussies are willing to coexist peacefully with other pets. But they can be bossy and they are chasers, bred to pursue anything that runs. Quick to learn and usually eager to please (though he definitely has his independent moments and must be taught who is in charge), he responds well to obedience training that utilizes food and praise more than jerking around. As befits their heritage, some are born diggers, and some can be barky, though in general this breed is quieter than most terriers.

HISTORY

He was developed in Australia from various rough-coated terriers, and once hunted rats and snakes. AKC popularity: 101st of 146.

PHYSICAL FEATURES

He stands 10–11 inches and weighs 12–18 pounds. Brush and comb his hard, wiry coat once a week. Keep his bottom trimmed for cleanliness. Show dogs are "stripped" (dead coat plucked out) every few months; pet owners may opt for more convenient clipping. Most commonly he is blue-and-tan, the blue ranging from steel to silver, the tan quite rich. He may also be solid sandy or red. His ears are natural; his tail is docked.

HEALTH ISSUES

Both parents should be screened for luxating patella. Also ask about Legg-Perthes, allergies, and skin conditions in the lines. Lifespan: 11–14 years.

CAUTIONS WHEN BUYING

If you admire the smaller, short-legged, nonsquare ter-riers, the Aussie makes an interesting alternative to the more popular Cairn or Westie. He is harder to find, but tends to be healthier and more consistently stable in tem-perament. However, terriers are not for everyone—take heed of the high energy level and independent spirit.

Basenji

Best for Experienced Owners
Good with Older, Considerate Children
Small in Size
Smooth Coat

EXERCISE REQUIRED — MEDIUM

TRIMMING/CLIPPING REQUIRED — LOW

AMOUNT OF SHEDDING — LOW

ACTIVITY INDOORS — HIGH

EASE OF TRAINING — LOW

SOCIABILITY WITH STRANGERS — LOW

TEMPERAMENT

The AKC Standard says, "Elegant and graceful, his whole demeanor is one of poise and inquiring alertness." High-spirited and endlessly curious, the dapper, light-footed Basenji demands to be in on everything. Without enough physical and mental activity, he will become bored and then he may chew up your home or scale fences (sometimes trees) in search of a more interesting life. Crate training is a must: This dog is too busy and inquisitive to be left loose and unsupervised in your house or yard. Don't let him off the leash, for he is a swift, agile chaser who is impossible to catch. He can be dominant and scrappy with other animals. You must stay one step ahead of this thinking breed, for he uses his keen intelligence in clever, sometimes manipulative ways that suit his own purposes. Consistent leadership is a must. Training must be upbeat and persuasive rather than sharp, because this proud dog may react defensively if jerked around or teased. Basenjis are intriguing in that they are physically unable to bark. Yet their wariness of strangers, inherent distrust of anything new or different, territorial instincts, acute senses, and canny intuition all combine to make them vigilant watchdogs. And they do whine, growl, chortle, yodel, and scream, so they are far from soundless.

HISTORY

Once called the Congo Dog, the Basenji dashed through the woods of Africa driving small game into the tribal huntsmen's nets. AKC popularity: 70th of 146.

PHYSICAL FEATURES

He stands 16–17 inches and weighs 20–25 pounds. His soft coat needs only an occasional quick brushing. He is chestnut red, black, or brindle, always with white markings; or tricolor (black with tan trim and white markings). His ears and tail are natural.

HEALTH ISSUES

Both parents should have yearly CERF certificates (eyes). Also ask about Fanconi syndrome, digestive problems, hemolytic anemia, low thyroid, hip dysplasia, and PKD in the lines. Females usually come into heat once a year, rather than twice. Lifespan: 13 years.

CAUTIONS WHEN BUYING

Cat lovers may appreciate the independence of this breed, and indeed they are clean, compact dogs who groom themselves much like a cat. But too many Basenjis are turned over to rescue organizations because owners saw only their convenient size, ease of housebreaking, and nonbarking. Therefore it should be emphasized that they are a rather primitive breed with strong instincts to run, chew, and climb. They require activity, training, and supervision to be happy and well-mannered. Pleasing you is not their goal in life.

Basset Hound

Fine for Novice Owners
Good with Children
Medium in Size
Smooth Coat

EXERCISE REQUIRED — MEDIUM

TRIMMING/CLIPPING REQUIRED — LOW

AMOUNT OF SHEDDING — HIGH MEDIUM

ACTIVITY INDOORS — LOW

EASE OF TRAINING — MEDIUM

SOCIABILITY WITH STRANGERS — HIGH
     MEDIUM

TEMPERAMENT

Bassets are among the most easygoing and mildest mannered of all breeds. Some are dignified, most are clownish, almost all are reliably good-natured and peaceful. At a dog show, one can count on seeing cheerfully wagging tails in the Basset ring. Stronger and heavier than you might think, he needs daily exercise to stay fit, even if he appears to be content snoring in front of the fireplace. Lazy owners have fat Bassets with concurrent health problems. Outdoors, keep him on-leash or in a fenced area, for if he finds an interesting scent and launches himself, your shouting and arm waving will fall on deaf ears. His reaction to strangers varies from friendly to polite, and he is usually sociable with other animals. Stubborn and slow to obey (expect thoughtful, deliberate responses), he can exhibit an amusing sense of humor while doing his own thing. Yet he responds amiably to patient obedience training that includes praise and especially food rewards. Bassets live for food, are champion beggers, and will steal any tidbit within reach—which includes countertops when they stand up on their hind legs. He is notoriously hard to housebreak, and he bays and howls in a deep, soulful voice.

HISTORY

A French scenthound descended from the Bloodhound, he trails rabbits, baying as he goes. His name comes from the French *bas*, meaning "low to the ground." There are several varieties of Basset in Europe, some with less crooked legs. AKC popularity: 21st of 146.

PHYSICAL FEATURES

He stands 11–15 inches and weighs 45–75 pounds. His hard coat needs only an occasional quick brushing. Keep his ear canals clean and dry. He is usually tricolor (black, tan, and white), red with white markings, or white with tan patches. His ears and tail are natural.

HEALTH ISSUES

Both parents should have OFA certificates (hips) and yearly CERF (eyes). Also ask about bloat, bleeding disorders, disk problems, seizures, OCD, luxating patella, low thyroid, panosteitis, and Addison's disease in the lines. Eyelid disorders (entropion) and chronic ear infections are common problems. Bassets do have a distinctive houndy odor. Lifespan: 12 years.

CAUTIONS WHEN BUYING

Generally stick with show lines, though there are a few field lines that are leggier, faster, and less loose-skinned than show lines.

Beagle

Fine for Novice Owners
Good with Children
Small in Size
Smooth Coat

EXERCISE REQUIRED — MEDIUM

TRIMMING/CLIPPING REQUIRED — LOW

AMOUNT OF SHEDDING — MEDIUM

ACTIVITY INDOORS — HIGH MEDIUM

EASE OF TRAINING — MEDIUM LOW

SOCIABILITY WITH STRANGERS — HIGH
    MEDIUM

TEMPERAMENT

The Beagle of good breeding is happy, good-natured, and playful. Though adaptable to a city lifestyle of daily walks, he is fast and athletic and really needs regular running. However, unless trained for hunting, he should not be allowed off-leash, for he is an obsessive explorer who will follow his nose right across the freeway if that's where that fascinating smell went. Your fences need to be secure, for he is prone to wanderlust and can be an adept climber. Friendly with people and other pets, he does better in a home with another dog, for he is a sociable pack animal. His stubbornness and tendency to gaze around at all the interesting sights and sounds call for early, consistent obedience training, but don't jerk this breed around or he may become defensive. Use food rewards to motivate him, but don't indulge too much or you'll end up with a portly Beagle. He is often found with his head buried in the garbage and he will cheerfully steal whatever morsels you leave within reach. He bays and howls a lot, especially if left alone too much, and he is notoriously hard to housebreak. Youngsters (up to age two) can be serious chewers.

HISTORY

A scenthound from England, he trails rabbits either singly or in packs, baying as he goes. His name comes from a group of old hunting hounds called *begles*. AKC popularity: 6th of 146.

PHYSICAL FEATURES

He comes in two size varieties: A 13-inch Beagle stands 10–13 inches and weighs 16–20 pounds. A 15-inch Beagle stands 13–15 inches and weighs 20–30 pounds. His hard coat needs only an occasional quick brushing. Keep his ear canals clean and dry. Usually he is tricolor (black, tan, and white). Blue-shaded (or liver-shaded) tricolor, where the black is diluted to blue or liver, is less common. Other colors include red-and-white, tan-and-white, and lemon-and-white. His ears and tail are natural.

HEALTH ISSUES

Both parents should have yearly CERF certificates (eyes). Also ask about glaucoma, seizures, low thyroid, hip dysplasia, heart disease, disk problems, PKD, and bleeding disorders in the lines. Chronic ear infections and allergies are common. Lifespan: 11–14 years.

CAUTIONS WHEN BUYING

It's tough to find a good Beagle. There are at least as many poorly bred individuals as there are well-bred ones, and the Beagle from poor breeding can be a nasty, neurotic creature with numerous health problems and unstable, shy, or aggressive behaviors. In addition, most of these dogs are a conglomeration of generic houndy features that are out of proportion for true Beagle type. A Beagle from a knowledgeable show breeder is compact and solidly muscled, with a lovely chiseled head, a hard coat, and a merry temperament. However, if you want a serious hunter, stick with field-bred lines.

Bearded Collie

Fine for Novice Owners
Good with Children
Medium in Size
Long Coat

EXERCISE REQUIRED — HIGH MEDIUM

TRIMMING/CLIPPING REQUIRED — HIGH
  MEDIUM LOW

AMOUNT OF SHEDDING — MEDIUM

ACTIVITY INDOORS — MEDIUM

EASE OF TRAINING — MEDIUM

SOCIABILITY WITH STRANGERS — HIGH
  MEDIUM

TEMPERAMENT

Lively and playful, good-natured and stable, this animated breed is famous for the "Beardie Bounce" that represents his happy, carefree attitude about the world. Some are rowdier than others, but most tend to jump up into your face unless taught otherwise. This athletic dog needs a good amount of exercise to satisfy his high energy, especially when young. More urgently, he needs constructive activities (herding, hiking, agility, pet therapy, watching over other pets) to occupy his inquisitive mind. Beardies are very sociable dogs who can become unhappy and destructive if left for long periods of time without the companionship of people or other pets. Most individuals love everyone to the point where their "watchdog" bark is more welcome than warning. As with most sweet-natured tail-waggers, there is potential for timidity, and socialization is necessary to develop the buoyant temperament. This independent thinker can be stubborn and requires a confident owner who will establish and enforce the rules. Sensitive to correction, he responds best to praise and food rewards; jerking the leash only makes him more obstinate. You also need patience and a sense of humor, for this mischievous, whimsical breed often thinks up novel variations on what you're attempting to teach. Some will herd children and other pets by poking and nipping.

HISTORY

The Beardie originated in Scotland as a sheepherder and cattle drover (driving cattle to market) and was once called the Highland Collie. AKC popularity: 90th of 146.

PHYSICAL FEATURES

He stands 20–22 inches and weighs 40–60 pounds. Brush his harsh, shaggy coat twice a week, daily during seasonal shedding. Pet owners may choose to trim/clip the coat short every few months. He may be black (ranging from black to slate), blue (steel to silver), brown (chocolate to ginger), or fawn (cinnamon to champagne), and the shade may change and shift throughout his life. White markings and/or tan points are common. His ears and tail are natural.

HEALTH ISSUES

Both parents should have OFA certificates (hips). Also ask about cataracts, low thyroid, allergies and skin conditions, and Addison's disease in the lines. Lifespan: 12–14 years.

CAUTIONS WHEN BUYING

The happy-go-lucky, casual Beardie is not for fastidious households—he tracks in mud, splashes in his water bowl, and affectionately thrusts his wet and/or dirty beard into your lap. Grooming is a serious commitment unless you decide to clip the coat short.

Beauceron (BO-ser-on)

Best for Experienced Owners
Good with Children If Raised with Children
Large in Size
Short Coat

EXERCISE REQUIRED — HIGH
TRIMMING/CLIPPING REQUIRED — LOW
AMOUNT OF SHEDDING — HIGH MEDIUM
ACTIVITY INDOORS — MEDIUM
EASE OF TRAINING — MEDIUM
SOCIABILITY WITH STRANGERS — MEDIUM

TEMPERAMENT

The Beauce is a confident, steady-tempered, usually serious dog. Athletic and agile, he needs hard exercise (running, hiking, biking, fetching)—a walk around the block is most assuredly not enough, and too much confinement can lead to rambunctiousness and destructive behaviors, especially in youngsters. Mental exercise (advanced obedience, agility, herding, Schutzhund) is just as important to this highly intelligent breed. Naturally watchful and keen-eyed, he often lies in the corner of his yard, front paws crossed, head up, observing. Or he may wear out a path through the grass as he paces back and forth patrolling his domain. Matching his stern appearance, he is aloof and discriminating with strangers, intensely loyal to and protective of his family. Socialization must be early and frequent so that his watchfulness doesn't shade into aggression. Shyness and spookiness are unfortunately present in some lines. Most Beaucerons are territorial with other animals, but usually good with the pets in their own family, if raised with them. You must discourage their habit of poking or pushing people and other animals in an attempt to move them along or gather them together. Beaucerons like to control everyone and everything and require a confident, consistent owner who knows how to lead. However, they are also sensitive and must be treated with respect. When his needs for exercise and work are met, this dependable breed can learn and do virtually anything.

HISTORY

Arbitrarily named for the Beauce region of France, this shepherd dog is cousin to the Briard. Registered by the UKC, SKC, and FCI.

PHYSICAL FEATURES

He stands 24–28 inches and weighs 70–105 pounds. Some lines are more heavily built, while others are more elegant and refined. Brush his short, double coat once a week. Usually he is bicolor (mostly black with red/rust trim). Less common is harlequin (blue merle with red/rust trim). His ears may be cropped or left hanging naturally. His tail is natural. It is a peculiarity of this breed that he must have one dewclaw on each front leg and double dewclaws on each hind leg.

HEALTH ISSUES

Both parents should have OFA certificates (hips). Also ask about vWD and OCD in the lines. Lifespan: 10–12 years.

CAUTIONS WHEN BUYING

This is a versatile working breed, so along with Ch. (beauty champion) titles in the pedigree, look for temperament and performance titles: obedience, tracking, herding, Schutzhund, Ringsport, TT, CGC. Some lines are "harder" and have more drive and intensity than others.

Bedlington Terrier

Best for Experienced Owners
Good with Older, Considerate Children
Small in Size
Curly Coat

EXERCISE REQUIRED — MEDIUM

TRIMMING/CLIPPING REQUIRED — HIGH

AMOUNT OF SHEDDING — LOW

ACTIVITY INDOORS — MEDIUM

EASE OF TRAINING — MEDIUM LOW

SOCIABILITY WITH STRANGERS — MEDIUM

TEMPERAMENT

The Bedlington is milder-mannered, less rowdy, and calmer indoors than some terriers, but more athletic than you might imagine if all you're looking at is the elegant, lamblike coat. Agile and graceful, with a unique lightness of movement and a springy gait, he needs access to a safe area where he can play and dodge and gallop at the breathtaking speeds clearly suggested by his lithe build. Once outdoors and aroused, he changes from docile couch potato to dauntless explorer. Bright and clownish with his own family, his reaction to strangers varies from inquisitive to reserved; he needs early socialization so that any caution does not become timidity. He is generally peaceful with other pets, though some can be scrappy with strange dogs, and with his terrier heritage, one should expect that running animals will be chased. Bedlingtons can be demanding and stubborn, but do respond well to obedience training that is upbeat and persuasive, preferably with food rewards. This sensitive breed should not be handled harshly or jerked around, nor does he respond well to being teased. He barks a lot and loves to dig.

HISTORY

His name comes from Bedlington, England, where he was used by miners as a rat hunter and fighting dog. He can either "go to ground" or run his prey down. AKC popularity: 124th of 146.

PHYSICAL FEATURES

He stands 15–17½ inches and weighs 17–23 pounds. His coat is a mixture of hard and soft hair, crisp to the touch and tending to curl. He should be brushed twice a week, and to look like the dog in the photo above, he requires expert scissoring every two months. Pet owners may opt for a slightly shaggier look that is easier to maintain. Keep his ear canals clean and dry. He may be blue, sandy, or liver, or any of these colors with tan trim. His ears and tail are natural.

HEALTH ISSUES

Both parents should have yearly CERF certificates (eyes) and be diagnosed negative for copper toxicosis (CT). The breeder may be able to guarantee that your puppy will not be affected with CT because of knowledge of the parents' genetic status gained through DNA analysis and test mating. Those pups will never need a surgical biopsy to determine their status. Also ask about luxating patella and allergies in the lines. Lifespan: 12–15 years.

CAUTIONS WHEN BUYING

Fortunately, this breed has not been singled out for mass production by unknowledgeable breeders, so quality is high. However, fewer than two hundred Bedlington puppies are registered in the United States each year, so you may need to search a bit. Keep in mind that terriers are high-spirited and stubborn and must be taught that they are not the rulers of the world.

Belgian Groenendael (GRO-en-en-doll)

Best for Experienced Owners
Good with Older, Considerate Children
Large in Size
Thick, Medium-Length Coat

EXERCISE REQUIRED — HIGH
TRIMMING/CLIPPING REQUIRED — LOW
AMOUNT OF SHEDDING — HIGH
ACTIVITY INDOORS — MEDIUM
EASE OF TRAINING — HIGH
SOCIABILITY WITH STRANGERS — MEDIUM

TEMPERAMENT

Athletic, agile, lithe, elegant—the graceful Groenendael is frequently in motion, often moving in quick, light-footed, seemingly tireless circles. This working dog needs a lot of exercise (running, hiking, biking, fetching) to stay in hard condition. Even more important is personal interaction and mental stimulation (advanced obedience, agility, herding, Schutzhund, tracking). Responsible and eager to learn, he becomes bored, frustrated, and prone to obsessive behaviors without something to do. Sometimes playing the mischievous clown, yet more often serious, he is observant, often reserved with strangers, and has strong protective instincts. He needs more extensive socialization than most breeds so that his watchfulness doesn't become suspicion or sharpness. Shyness and spookiness are present in some lines. Most are okay with other pets if raised together, but he has a high prey drive, so small animals (cats, rabbits, ferrets, birds) should be introduced with care and supervision. He often pokes (or nips) people and other animals in an attempt to move them along or gather them together. Attentive and responsive to the direction of a confident owner, he requires a light hand on the leash, for he is extremely sensitive to correction. This intelligent dog must be owned and handled by someone who is as smart and capable as he is and who will provide for his exercise and working needs.

HISTORY

Most of the world (but not the AKC) considers the four Belgian shepherd dogs to be varieties of the same breed, with different coats and colors. The AKC confuses this further by calling the Groenendael the Belgian Sheep-dog, when all *four* varieties are Belgian sheepdogs. The Groenendael takes his name from Chateau Groenendael, a restaurant owned by a prominent breeder. AKC popularity: 106th of 146.

PHYSICAL FEATURES

Males stand 24–26 inches and weigh 55–75 pounds. Females stand 22–24 inches and weigh 45–60 pounds. Brush and comb his abundant double coat twice a week, daily during heavy seasonal shedding. Along with his shedding great chunks of hair in the spring and fall, you'll find loose hair the rest of the year as well. He is solid black. His ears and tail are natural.

HEALTH ISSUES

Both parents should have OFA certificates (hips and elbows) and yearly CERF (eyes). Also ask about seizures and low thyroid in the lines. Lifespan: 12–14 years.

CAUTIONS WHEN BUYING

Most show breeders are also interested in preserving working instincts—look for Ch. (beauty champion) titles and performance titles (obedience, herding, Schutzhund, TT, CGC) in the pedigree. Indeed, you shouldn't choose any of the Belgians if you have no interest in pursuing a canine sport or activity.

Belgian Laikenois (LAK-en-wah)

Best for Experienced Owners
Good with Older, Considerate Children
Large in Size
Wiry Coat

EXERCISE REQUIRED — HIGH

TRIMMING/CLIPPING REQUIRED — HIGH

AMOUNT OF SHEDDING — MEDIUM

ACTIVITY INDOORS — MEDIUM

EASE OF TRAINING — HIGH

SOCIABILITY WITH STRANGERS — MEDIUM

TEMPERAMENT

Rustic and natural in appearance, yet athletic and agile, the Laeken is frequently in motion, often moving in quick, light-footed, seemingly tireless circles. This working dog needs a lot of exercise (running, hiking, biking, fetching) to stay in hard condition. Even more important are personal interaction and mental stimulation (advanced obedience, agility, herding, Schutzhund, tracking). Responsible and eager to learn, he becomes bored, frustrated, and prone to obsessive behaviors without something to do. Sometimes playing the mischievous clown, yet more often serious, he is observant, often reserved with strangers, and has strong protective instincts. He needs more extensive socialization than most breeds so that his watchfulness doesn't become suspicion or sharpness. Shyness and spookiness are present in some lines. Most are okay with other pets if raised together, but he has a high prey drive, so small animals (cats, rabbits, ferrets, birds) should be introduced with care and supervision. He often pokes (or nips) people and other animals in an attempt to move them along or gather them together. Attentive and responsive to the direction of a confident owner, he requires a light hand on the leash, for he is extremely sensitive to correction. This intelligent dog must be owned and handled by someone who is as smart and capable as he is and who will provide for his exercise and working needs.

HISTORY

Most of the world (but not the AKC) considers the four Belgian shepherd dogs to be varieties of the same breed, with different coats and colors. The Laekenois takes his name from Castle Laeken, home of Queen Marie Henriette, who admired the rough-coated working dogs used by local shepherds. Often dubbed "the other Belgian," the Laeken is both the oldest variety and the only one not yet accorded recognition by the AKC. Registered by the FCI and UKC.

PHYSICAL FEATURES

Males stand 24–26 inches and weigh 55–75 pounds. Females stand 22–24 inches and weigh 45–60 pounds. Brush and comb his harsh, tousled coat twice a week. His beard should be combed daily for cleanliness. Likewise, keep his bottom trimmed for cleanliness. Show dogs are "stripped" (dead coat plucked out) every few months; pet owners may opt for more convenient clipping. He is fawn to mahogany, with black-tipped hairs. His ears and tail are natural.

HEALTH ISSUES

Both parents should have OFA certificates (hips and elbows) and yearly CERF (eyes). Also ask about seizures and OCD in the lines. Lifespan: 12–14 years.

CAUTIONS WHEN BUYING

The number of Laekenois in the United States is slowly growing, but litters are not numerous, so be prepared to wait up to a year for a pet puppy.

Belgian Malinois (MAL-in-wah)

Best for Experienced Owners
Good with Older, Considerate Children
Medium to Large in Size
Short Coat

EXERCISE REQUIRED — HIGH

TRIMMING/CLIPPING REQUIRED — LOW

AMOUNT OF SHEDDING — HIGH

ACTIVITY INDOORS — MEDIUM

EASE OF TRAINING — HIGH MEDIUM

SOCIABILITY WITH STRANGERS — MEDIUM

TEMPERAMENT

Athletic, agile, lithe, elegant—the graceful Malinois is frequently in motion, often moving in quick, light-footed, seemingly tireless circles. This working dog needs a lot of exercise (running, hiking, biking, fetching) to stay in hard condition. Even more important is personal inter-action and mental stimulation (advanced obedience, agility, herding, Schutzhund, tracking). Responsible and eager to learn, he becomes bored, frustrated, and prone to obsessive behaviors without something to do. Sometimes playing the mischievous clown, yet more often serious, he is observant, often reserved with strangers, and has strong protective instincts. He needs more extensive socialization than most breeds so that his watchfulness doesn't become suspicion or sharpness. Shyness and spookiness are present in some lines. Most are okay with other pets if raised together, but he has a high prey drive, so small animals (cats, rabbits, ferrets, birds) should be introduced with care and supervision. He often pokes (or nips) people and other animals in an attempt to move them along or gather them together. Most are attentive to confident owners. Some are extremely sensitive and require a light hand on the leash, while others are "harder" and more stubborn. This intelligent dog must be owned and handled by some-one who is as smart and capable as he is and who will pro-vide for his exercise and working needs.

HISTORY

Most of the world (but not the AKC) considers the four Belgian shepherd dogs to be varieties of the same breed, with different coats and colors. The Malinois, from the Malines region of Belgium, reigns supreme in work-ing trials. AKC popularity: 92nd of 146.

PHYSICAL FEATURES

Males stand 24–26 inches and weigh 55–75 pounds. Females stand 21–24 inches and weigh 45–60 pounds. Brush his dense, double coat once a week, daily during heavy seasonal shedding. Along with his shedding great chunks of hair in the spring and fall, you'll find loose hair the rest of the year as well. He is fawn to mahogany, with black-tipped hairs and a black mask. His ears and tail are natural.

HEALTH ISSUES

Both parents should have OFA certificates (hips and elbows) and yearly CERF (eyes). Also ask about seizures and low thyroid in the lines. Lifespan: 12–14 years.

CAUTIONS WHEN BUYING

Malinois are somewhat divided into working lines (energetic, quick moving, intense, lots of drive) and show lines (more easygoing). However, many show breeders are also interested in preserving working instincts—look for both Ch. (beauty champion) titles and performance titles (obedience, herding, Schutzhund, TT, CGC) in the pedi-gree. Indeed, you shouldn't choose this breed if you have no interest in pursuing any canine sport or outdoor activ-ity. The Malinois is one of the finest working dogs in the world and belongs with an owner who will develop his potential to the fullest.

Belgian Tervuren (ter-VER-en)

Best for Experienced Owners
Good with Older, Considerate Children
Large in Size
Thick, Medium-Length Coat

EXERCISE REQUIRED — HIGH

TRIMMING/CLIPPING REQUIRED — LOW

AMOUNT OF SHEDDING — HIGH

ACTIVITY INDOORS — MEDIUM

EASE OF TRAINING — HIGH

SOCIABILITY WITH STRANGERS — MEDIUM

TEMPERAMENT

Athletic, agile, lithe, elegant—the graceful Tervuren is frequently in motion, often moving in quick, light-footed, seemingly tireless circles. This working dog needs a lot of exercise (running, hiking, biking, fetching) to stay in hard condition. Even more important is personal interaction and mental stimulation (advanced obedience, agility, herding, Schutzhund, tracking). Responsible and eager to learn, he becomes bored, frustrated, and prone to obsessive behaviors without something to do. Sometimes playing the mischievous clown, yet more often serious, he is observant, often reserved with strangers, and has strong protective instincts. He needs more extensive socialization than most breeds so that his watchfulness doesn't become suspicion or sharpness. Shyness and spookiness are present in some lines. Most are okay with other pets if raised together, but he has a high prey drive, so small animals (cats, rabbits, ferrets, birds) should be introduced with care and supervision. He often pokes (or nips) people and other animals in an attempt to move them along or gather them together. Attentive and responsive to the direction of a confident owner, he requires a light hand on the leash, for he is extremely sensitive to correction. This intelligent dog muct be owned and handled by someone who is as smart and capable as he is and who will provide for his exercise and working needs.

HISTORY

Most of the world (but not the AKC) considers the four Belgian shepherd dogs to be varieties of the same breed, with different coats and colors. The Tervuren takes his name from the Belgian town of Tervueren (note different spelling). AKC popularity: 100th of 146.

PHYSICAL FEATURES

Males stand 24–26 inches and weigh 55–75 pounds. Females stand 22–24 inches and weigh 45–60 pounds. Brush and comb his abundant double coat twice a week, daily during heavy seasonal shedding. Along with his shedding great chunks of hair in the spring and fall, you'll find loose hair the rest of the year as well. He is fawn to mahogany, with black-tipped hairs and a black mask. His ears and tail are natural.

HEALTH ISSUES

Both parents should have OFA certificates (hips and elbows) and yearly CERF (eyes). Also ask about seizures and low thyroid in the lines. Lifespan: 12–14 years.

CAUTIONS WHEN BUYING

Most show breeders are also interested in preserving working instincts—look for Ch. (beauty champion) titles and performance titles (obedience, herding, Schutzhund, TT, CGC) in the pedigree. Indeed, you shouldn't choose this breed if you have no interest in pursuing any canine sport or activity.

Bernese Mountain Dog

Fine for Novice Owners
Good with Children
Large to Giant in Size
Thick, Medium-Length Coat

EXERCISE REQUIRED — MEDIUM

TRIMMING/CLIPPING REQUIRED — LOW

AMOUNT OF SHEDDING — HIGH MEDIUM

ACTIVITY INDOORS — LOW

EASE OF TRAINING — HIGH MEDIUM

SOCIABILITY WITH STRANGERS — HIGH
    MEDIUM

TEMPERAMENT

The Bernese is steady-tempered, gentle, and easygoing. Though calm indoors, he does love getting out, especially in cool weather. Romping in the snow is a favorite form of recreation for this Alpine breed. Pulling carts and sleds is a wonderful source of exercise, especially if it involves children of any age. Attitude toward strangers varies from friendly to aloof, but he should remain poised and hold his ground. The most common temperament fault is excessive shyness, sometimes toward everyone and sometimes focused on one group of people, such as men with beards. A Berner puppy needs lots of socialization so that his natural caution does not become timidity. Most individuals are peaceful and sociable with other animals. Responsive to obedience training in a good-natured way, this sweet, sensitive breed should be handled kindly, with much praise and encouragement. Some males may become dominant during adolescence and will require more leadership on your part. Females have a stronger tendency to attach themselves to one person.

HISTORY

He is one of four Swiss sennenhunds (dogs of the Alpine herdsmen). His name comes from the Swiss canton of Berne, where he guarded the farm, drove cows to and from pasture, and pulled milk carts to the dairy. AKC popularity: 63rd of 146.

PHYSICAL FEATURES

Males stand 25–28 inches and weigh 80–120 pounds. Females stand 23–26 inches and weigh 65–90 pounds. Brush his thick coat twice a week, daily during seasonal shedding. He is jet black with white markings on his face, chest, feet, and tail tip and rich rust markings over each eye, on his cheeks, chest, legs, and under his tail. His ears and tail are natural.

HEALTH ISSUES

Both parents should have OFA certificates (hips and elbows) and yearly CERF (eyes). Screening for normal thyroid (full panel) is extra security. Also ask about bloat and OCD in the lines. The major life-threatening problem is cancer, which is causing the premature death of a dismaying number of Berners. Some autoimmune problems and allergic skin conditions are reported. With his thick black coat, he is uncomfortable in excessive heat and humidity. Lifespan: 8–10 years (search for long-lived lines).

CAUTIONS WHEN BUYING

Some lines are huge and some are more medium in size. This breed is becoming more popular, which means more unknowledgeable breeders are producing litters. Make sure puppies and parents (and grandparents and other relatives, if you can see them) are outgoing and confident, and insist on seeing those health clearances.

Bichon Frise (BEE-shon free-ZAY)

Fine for Novice Owners
Good with Older, Considerate Children
Small in Size
Curly Coat

EXERCISE REQUIRED — LOW

TRIMMING/CLIPPING REQUIRED — HIGH

AMOUNT OF SHEDDING — LOW

ACTIVITY INDOORS — HIGH MEDIUM

EASE OF TRAINING — MEDIUM

SOCIABILITY WITH STRANGERS — HIGH

TEMPERAMENT

The AKC Standard calls the Bichon "a white powder puff of a dog whose merry temperament is evidenced by his plumed tail carried jauntily over the back and his dark-eyed inquisitive expression." Cheerful and playful, he enjoys dashing around the house and yard and accompanying you for walks. Bichons are so sociable and dependent that they don't do well when left for long periods of time without companionship. Though cheerful and gentle with everyone (humans and other pets), he likes to sit perched on the back of a sofa or chair, looking out the window so he can announce visitors. There is timidity in some lines, so early socialization is important. Though he does have an independent streak, he is not a dominant dog and responds well to nonforceful training. He prefers learning tricks to formal obedience and is especially bright-eyed when food treats are offered as rewards. Harshness only makes him spiteful. Bichons can be barkers and often have a shrill, piercing voice. Housebreaking is notoriously difficult and some individuals are never completely housebroken.

HISTORY

Originating on the island of Tenerife in the Canaries, he was favored by Italian and French nobility and also played the role of common street dog, organ grinder's dog, and circus dog. His name translates to "curly lap dog." AKC popularity: 25th of 146.

PHYSICAL FEATURES

He stands 9–12 inches and weighs 12–18 pounds. His plush velvety coat, when scissored and shaped for the show ring, resembles a white powder puff that springs back when patted. It requires daily brushing; thus, most pet owners opt to trim/clip the coat short every four to six weeks. Keep his ear canals clean and dry and his bottom trimmed for cleanliness. He is white, often with a few shadings of buff, cream, or apricot. His ears and tail are natural.

HEALTH ISSUES

Both parents should have OFA certificates (hips and patellas) and yearly CERF (eyes). Also ask about bladder stones, seizures, and allergies in the lines. Breeders report that Bichons are tremendously allergic to flea bites and will chew themselves to pieces when bitten, causing massive hot spots. Lifespan: 14–15 years.

CAUTIONS WHEN BUYING

Similar breeds in the bichon family include the Bolognese, Coton de Tulear, Havanese, and Maltese. If you're not going to keep the coat short, a daily commitment to grooming is a must. Most Bichons turned in to shelters and rescue organizations are there because of housebreaking difficulties—crate training or a doggy door are musts, as are patience and consistency.

Black and Tan Coonhound

Best for Experienced Owners
Good with Children
Large in Size
Smooth Coat

EXERCISE REQUIRED — HIGH MEDIUM

TRIMMING/CLIPPING REQUIRED — LOW

AMOUNT OF SHEDDING — MEDIUM

ACTIVITY INDOORS — LOW

EASE OF TRAINING — LOW

SOCIABILITY WITH STRANGERS — MEDIUM

TEMPERAMENT

The AKC Standard says the Black and Tan is "first and fundamentally a working dog, a trail and tree hound." Though good-natured and easygoing, this hardy hound is so in need of exercise that he belongs with an owner who will take him jogging, biking, hiking, and/or swimming. Unless trained for hunting, he must not be let off-leash, for he is an explorer who will follow his nose over hill, over dale, through the woods . . . and onto the highway. When well exercised, he is calm and undemanding, apt to sprawl and snore in front of the fire. Without exercise, he can be a rambunctious handful. He may be friendly or politely reserved with strangers. Some are territorial and their booming bark and muscular, confident stature may give an intruder pause. He can be dominant with strange dogs and may stalk smaller pets. Black and Tans are among the most intelligent of the coonhound breeds, but because they use that intelligence to figure out ways to outwit their prey, they may do the same with people. Following commands blindly is not part of their genetic makeup. Consistent leadership is a must, and obedience training must be upbeat and persuasive (include food rewards). Leash jerking will bring out their stubbornness. Not surprisingly, they bay and howl, especially when bored.

HISTORY

Descended from British scenthounds, he was developed in the American Deep South. AKC popularity: 116th of 146 (many, many more are registered only with the UKC).

PHYSICAL FEATURES

He stands 21–27 inches and weighs 65–100 pounds. His hard coat needs only an occasional quick brushing. Keep his ear canals clean and dry. Not surprisingly, he is black with tan markings over the eyes, on the muzzle, cheeks, legs and feet, and under the tail. His ears and tail are natural.

HEALTH ISSUES

Both parents should have OFA certificates (hips and elbows) and yearly CERF (eyes). Also ask about bleeding disorders in the lines. Eyelid disorders (entropion) can be a problem. Lifespan: 10–12 years.

CAUTIONS WHEN BUYING

Black and Tans are divided into show types and field types. Show lines are heavier boned and longer eared. For a serious hunting dog, choose an individual from performance-titled or hunting stock.

Bloodhound

Best for Experienced Owners
Good with Children If Raised with Children
Large to Giant in Size
Smooth Coat

EXERCISE REQUIRED — HIGH

TRIMMING/CLIPPING REQUIRED — LOW

AMOUNT OF SHEDDING — MEDIUM

ACTIVITY INDOORS — LOW

EASE OF TRAINING — LOW

SOCIABILITY WITH STRANGERS — MEDIUM

TEMPERAMENT

The AKC Standard says, "The expression is noble and dignified, and characterized by solemnity, wisdom, and power." Though gentle and easygoing, even somewhat bumbling, the Bloodhound is not the lazy, lie-around dog he is often portrayed to be on TV. This big breed requires plenty of space and safe areas where he can romp and ramble every day. A leash and/or fence is mandatory, because if his tremendous nose locks on to a fascinating scent, his ears turn off and it is almost impossible to regain his attention. Bloodhounds will trail scents for miles and miles, until they are hit by a car. Though generally good-natured and gregarious with people and other animals, some individuals can be aggressive with other dogs of the same sex. His great strength and stubbornness call for a confident owner who knows how to enforce rules in an assertive (yet not harsh) manner. This kindly, sensitive breed should never be treated roughly. He is slow to mature, so your patience and firmness need to extend over several years. His tendency to chew and swallow anything that fits in his mouth may send you both to the veterinary emergency room at some point. He can be possessive of his food and toys, a potential problem around children and other pets. If bored, he may bay in his deep, soulful voice or excavate impressive caverns in your yard. With those great wrinkled jowls, he drools profusely.

HISTORY

This ancient scenthound originated in Europe, where he was kept "of pure blood" and owned only by aristocratic bluebloods, hence the name "blooded hound." AKC popularity: 51st of 146.

PHYSICAL FEATURES

Males stand 25–29 inches; females stand 24–27 inches. He weighs 90–130 pounds. His hard coat needs only an occasional quick brushing. Keep his ear canals clean and dry. He is black-and-tan, liver-and-tan (red-and-tan), or red (tawny). His ears and tail are natural.

HEALTH ISSUES

Both parents should have OFA certificates (hips). Also ask about bloat, low thyroid, OCD, and cardiomyopathy in the lines. Eyelid disorders (entropion) are common. Lifespan: 7–9 years.

CAUTIONS WHEN BUYING

Bloodhounds are so valuable in a community emergency that all owners should involve their hounds in local tracking clubs. Whether trailing lost children, disoriented elderly people, or escaped criminals, this face-kisser only tracks—never attacks. He is almost impossible to shake off a trail, and documented tracks one hundred miles long and one hundred hours old have made his olfactory evidence admissible in a court of law. Mind his huge size and power, though, and be prepared to socialize and train while he is still young and easy to manage.

Bolognese (bolo-NEESE)

Fine for Novice Owners
Good with Older, Considerate Children
Little in Size
Long, Curly Coat

EXERCISE REQUIRED — LOW
TRIMMING/CLIPPING REQUIRED — HIGH
      MEDIUM LOW
AMOUNT OF SHEDDING — LOW
ACTIVITY INDOORS — HIGH
EASE OF TRAINING — HIGH
SOCIABILITY WITH STRANGERS — MEDIUM

TEMPERAMENT

Some breeders believe that of all the breeds in the bichon family (Maltese, Havanese, Bolognese, and Bichon Frise), the Bolognese is the most intelligent and trainable, the best thinker and problem solver. Devoted and attentive, he shadows his owner possessively and is such a skilled reader of body language and expression that he often appears telepathic. This sturdy dog is happy and playful, even rough-and-tumble. Most are friendly with strangers, though there is some potential for watchfulness and timidity, so early socialization is important. He gets along well with other animals. Indeed, this breed is so sociable and interactive that he doesn't do well without companionship (either human or other pets) for long periods of time. Quick to learn and very responsive to nonforceful training, quite a few individuals excel in competitive obedience and agility. Housebreaking may take a while.

HISTORY

Originating in the Mediterranean, he was the household pet of wealthy noble families in Bologna, Italy. Registered by the Bolognese Club of America, UKC, and FCI.

PHYSICAL FEATURES

He stands 9–12 inches and weighs 8–14 pounds. His dense double coat is a soft mass of fluffy, frocky ringlets that should be brushed and combed every other day. Pet owners may choose to have the coat trimmed/clipped short every four to six weeks. Keep his ear canals clean and dry. He is white, sometimes with champagne shadings. His ears and tail are natural.

HEALTH ISSUES

Both parents should have yearly CERF certificates (eyes) and be screened for luxating patella. Lifespan: 13–15 years.

CAUTIONS WHEN BUYING

Larger and sturdier than his Maltese cousin, the Bolognese is easier to raise and care for. However, his coat, if left long, requires a commitment to grooming. Because he is less popular and has not been exploited by unknowledgeable breeders, he is a safer bet to be healthy and good-natured.

Border Collie

Best for Experienced Owners
Good with Older, Considerate Children
Medium in Size
Feathered, Medium-Length Coat or Short Coat

EXERCISE REQUIRED — HIGH

TRIMMING/CLIPPING REQUIRED — LOW

AMOUNT OF SHEDDING — MEDIUM

ACTIVITY INDOORS — HIGH

EASE OF TRAINING — HIGH MEDIUM

SOCIABILITY WITH STRANGERS — MEDIUM

TEMPERAMENT

Probably the smartest of all breeds, the Border Collie is also one of the most challenging to live with. His superior intellect, combined with his intensity and zeal for working, are his best features—and the ones that make him unsuitable for most homes. This sharp-eyed, quick-thinking, fanatical workaholic has been bred for endless miles of running and sprinting and stop-and-go action. If it isn't possible for him to work livestock, you must substitute advanced obedience, agility, jogging or biking, chasing balls, and playing Frisbee—lots and lots of it. Without physical and mental stimulation, Border Collies become hyperactive and will drive you up the wall with obsessive and destructive behaviors as they seek creative outlets for their boundless energy. Trying to train an intelligent Border Collie can be frustrating, because they are constantly thinking, analyzing, and reacting to every tiny movement you make. High intelligence does mean they learn quickly—but that includes how to do anything they set their minds to. They are master escape artists who can virtually pick the lock on your gate. They are passionate gatherers of cars, bikes, joggers, cats, other dogs, livestock, deer, and running children—poking, pushing, and nipping if the object/animal/person doesn't cooperate. They can be a bit high-strung and oversensitive to sound and touch. You must stay one step ahead of this brilliant breed, and most people are simply not up to the task.

HISTORY

Originating on the border between England and Scotland, he is famous for his intimidating "eye": a fixed, hypnotic stare as he crouches low and creeps up on the sheep (or a tennis ball). AKC popularity: 71st of 146 (many more are registered only with working organizations).

PHYSICAL FEATURES

He stands 17–21 inches and weighs 30–55 pounds. Herding lines tend toward the smaller side, while conformation lines tend to be larger and heavier boned. Some coats are short and easy to care for, while others have light to moderate feathering that requires combing. Shedding is heavy twice a year. Black-and-white is the most common color, but others are allowed. Eyes range from brown to glassy blue, or any combination. His ears and tail are natural.

HEALTH ISSUES

Both parents should have OFA certificates (hips) and yearly CERF (eyes). Each individual puppy must have his eyes examined by an AVCO-certified ophthalmologist (not just a regular vet) at six to eight weeks of age. Also ask about seizures, deafness, OCD, and allergies in the lines. Lifespan: 12–15 years.

CAUTIONS WHEN BUYING

Border Collies who are able to work are mentally and physically fulfilled and can be terrific companions, albeit a bit quirky. The rest are likely to be labeled hyper or neurotic and turned in to rescue organizations.

Border Terrier

Best for Experienced Owners
Good with Older, Considerate Children
Small in Size
Wiry Coat

EXERCISE REQUIRED — HIGH MEDIUM

TRIMMING/CLIPPING REQUIRED — MEDIUM

AMOUNT OF SHEDDING — LOW

ACTIVITY INDOORS — MEDIUM

EASE OF TRAINING — HIGH MEDIUM

SOCIABILITY WITH STRANGERS — HIGH

TEMPERAMENT

The AKC Standard says, "The characteristic 'otter' head with its keen eye, combined with a body poise which is 'at the alert,' gives a look of fearless and implacable determination." In the home, the Border is milder mannered, more laid-back, and more sensible than most terriers, yet in the field he is "hard as nails, game as they come, and driving in attack." Some individuals are more work-oriented, while some are mellower, but in general he is energetic and athletic. He tends to play rough and prefers vigorous exercise and interactive games. He must not be let off-leash, for there is no terrier more determined to explore and pursue anything that runs (except, perhaps, for the Jack Russell). Borders are so inquisitive they often get themselves wedged into tight holes or crawl spaces. A secure yard, kennel run, crate, or personal supervision is essential at all times. Most individuals who have been extensively socialized are bouncy and kissy with strangers, though there is timidity in some lines. Unlike most terriers, he is sociable with other dogs and not given to fiery posturing. He may or may not live peacefully with the family cat, and he is a businesslike hunter of anything else. Pet rodents are out of the question. Generally willing to please and very sensitive to harsh correction, he responds nicely to motivational obedience training, especially if it includes food. But in moderation: Borders live for food and can become pudgy if indulged. It goes without saying that this breed is a tireless digger, and some like to bark.

HISTORY

This hardy hunter of fox, badger, and barnyard varmints originated in the Cheviot Hills on the border between England and Scotland. AKC popularity: 87th of 146.

PHYSICAL FEATURES

He stands 12–15 inches and weighs 12–18 pounds. Brush and comb his harsh double coat once a week. Show dogs are "stripped" (dead coat plucked out) every few months; pet owners may opt for more convenient clipping. He may be red, blue with tan markings, or grizzle (dark-tipped hairs on a red/tan coat) with tan markings. Wheaten is less common. His ears and tail are natural.

HEALTH ISSUES

Both parents should have OFA certificates (hips) and yearly CERF (eyes). Also ask about heart defects, low thyroid, seizures, luxating patella, and allergies in the lines. Lifespan: 12–15 years.

CAUTIONS WHEN BUYING

The Border is an unexaggerated workmanlike terrier. Where other terriers in the show ring are coiffed and fiery, up on their toes sparring with one another, the plain brown Border looks like he belongs in a Disney movie, alongside Benji. This is just as his admirers want him to remain.

Borzoi

Best for Experienced Owners
Good with Older, Considerate Children
Large to Giant in Size
Feathered, Medium-Length Coat

EXERCISE REQUIRED — HIGH MEDIUM

TRIMMING/CLIPPING REQUIRED — LOW

AMOUNT OF SHEDDING — MEDIUM

ACTIVITY INDOORS — LOW

EASE OF TRAINING — MEDIUM LOW

SOCIABILITY WITH STRANGERS — MEDIUM
 LOW

TEMPERAMENT

Possessed of a quiet dignity and independence, the Borzoi is sometimes compared to a cat. Once past the puppy stage, he is calm and quiet indoors, gliding through the living room with light-footed grace. Off-leash, though, he explodes into a powerful, driving, floating gallop, so the space where he is loosed to run must be safe and enclosed, else he will be out of sight in seconds. Breeders say the leading cause of death in their breed is being hit by a car. Most Borzoi (also the plural) are polite but reserved with strangers, and because of their great size and strength, they require early socialization to avoid either shyness or aggression. Usually sociable with other dogs, he is a deadly serious chaser of anything that runs, including cats and tiny dogs. Like all sighthounds, Borzoi are independent and not inclined to obey slavishly. They must be trained with praise and food rewards and never jerked around. Though usually sweet and docile, they can be touch-sensitive and may react with lightning reflexes if grabbed unexpectedly or startled. This is a not a breed to be taken lightly or teased.

HISTORY

In Czarist Russia, the Borzoi was owned by the aristocracy and hunted in packs, running down wolves across open terrain while the huntsmen followed on horseback. He was originally known as the Russian Wolfhound. AKC popularity: 81st of 146.

PHYSICAL FEATURES

Males stand 28–33 inches and weigh 75–105 pounds. Females stand 26–31 inches and weigh 55–90 pounds. Brush and comb his silky coat twice a week, daily during seasonal shedding. Colors include white, white with colored markings, red, red sable, black, black-and-tan, and brindle, among others. His ears and tail are natural.

HEALTH ISSUES

Both parents should have OFA certificates (hips) and yearly CERF (eyes). Also ask about bloat and cardiomyopathy in the lines. He is sensitive to anesthetics, vaccines, and chemicals and should never be casually medicated or sedated. Lifespan: 9–12 years.

CAUTIONS WHEN BUYING

Fortunately Borzoi have not been singled out for mass production by unknowledgeable breeders, so quality is high, but remain cautious. This is an extremely agile and powerful breed with marked instincts to pursue and seize fleeing creatures. You must buy from a breeder who has emphasized sound temperament and then raise your pup with consistent leadership and control.

Boston Terrier

Fine for Novice Owners
Good with Children If Raised with Children
Small in Size
Smooth Coat

EXERCISE REQUIRED — LOW
TRIMMING/CLIPPING REQUIRED — LOW
AMOUNT OF SHEDDING — MEDIUM
ACTIVITY INDOORS — HIGH MEDIUM
EASE OF TRAINING — MEDIUM
SOCIABILITY WITH STRANGERS — HIGH
  MEDIUM

TEMPERAMENT

Usually high-spirited and clownish, sometimes calm and dignified, always sturdy and stable, the Boston Terrier is an altogether dapper and charming little dog. Playing games and chasing balls are two of his passions. Seeking companionship is another, for he always wants to be with people. His large, expressive eyes, attentively cocked head, and snorting/snuffling sounds tend to bring out parental feelings. Extremely sensitive to his owner's moods, some are one-person dogs (with a special affinity for the elderly), but most are outgoing with everyone. Yet he is a dependable watchdog who will let you know when someone is at the door. Usually fine with other pets, he may put on a blustery show upon spying a larger dog across the street. Bostons are very individualistic: Some have super high energy, while others are more placid; some are stubborn characters, while others are sweet and gentle. Positive training methods that focus on praise and food are a must. Bostons are sensitive and neither require nor respond well to being jerked around. Gassiness can be an embarrassing problem, and housebreaking can be difficult.

HISTORY

One of the few breeds developed in America, he is a blend of English Bulldog and the now extinct Old English White Terrier. AKC popularity: 19th of 146.

PHYSICAL FEATURES

He stands 12–16 inches and usually weighs 14–18 pounds, though some individuals may weigh up to 25 pounds. His shiny coat needs only an occasional quick brushing. He is preferably brindle, but may also be black or seal, always with a white blaze and chest. Proportionate markings are essential for show; "mismarked" Bostons with excessive white are sold as pets. His ears may stand up naturally or be cropped. His tail is naturally straight or kinked.

HEALTH ISSUES

Both parents should have yearly CERF certificates (eyes) and be screened for luxating patella. Also ask about cataracts, elongated palate, low thyroid, seizures, demodectic mange, and allergies in the lines. Blue-eyed puppies and those with excessive white markings should come with a BAER printout that shows normal bilateral hearing. His large eyes are susceptible to lacerations, infections, and eyelid/eyelash defects. Select a puppy whose eyes are not bulging or showing too much white around the iris, whose facial features show no signs of crowding, and whose nostrils are wide open. He is prone to heatstroke in hot, humid, and/or stuffy conditions. He loves air-conditioning in the summer and a sweater in the winter. Bostons are sensitive to anesthetics, vaccine, and chemicals and should never be casually medicated or sedated. Lifespan: 11–13 years.

CAUTIONS WHEN BUYING

This breed has been exploited by unknowledgeable breeders, and individuals from such lines are often unsound, hyperactive, and neurotic. Stick with show breeders who emphasize temperament.

Bouvier Des Flandres

(BOO-vee-ay day FLAHN-dra)

Best for Experienced Owners
Good with Children If Raised with Children
Large in Size
Unusual Coat (see Physical Features below)

EXERCISE REQUIRED — HIGH

TRIMMING/CLIPPING REQUIRED — HIGH

AMOUNT OF SHEDDING — MEDIUM LOW

ACTIVITY INDOORS — LOW

EASE OF TRAINING — MEDIUM

SOCIABILITY WITH STRANGERS — MEDIUM

TEMPERAMENT

The AKC Standard calls him "equable, steady, resolute, rugged." The Bouvier is sober and thoughtful, rather than clownish. Though he can be athletic and agile, he is often a bit lazy unless deliberately taken out and encouraged to move. Brisk walks are a must to keep him in hard condition. Mental stimulation in the form of advanced obedience, agility, tracking, herding, carting, or Schutzhund is even more important to this highly intelligent breed. Though he is not overly demonstrative—he shows his loyalty in deeper, more subtle ways—he must live closely with his family, his "flock." When these needs are met, he is laid-back and serene. Matching his stern appearance, he is often aloof with strangers and assertive when challenged. His air of calm appraisal can be intimidating, and he may use his big body to control people, rather than biting. Socialization must be early and frequent so that he learns to discriminate between friend and foe. Most are dominant with other dogs, especially of the same sex, and those with a high prey drive are not reliable with cats and other creatures that run or flutter. He may poke or nudge people and other animals in an attempt to gather them or move them along. Bouviers are pushy, strong-willed dogs who require confident owners, especially during the challenging adolescent period. This shaggy dog is not for the immaculate household. Mud, snow, and leaves cling to his tousled coat, and his beard collects water like a sponge and can mat and smell. A drink of water is likely to leave a sopping wet trail across your floors and rugs. On a more delicate note, Bouviers are one of the more flatulent breeds.

HISTORY

The "Cow Dog of Flanders" was a Belgian farm dog who herded cattle and pulled milk carts. During World War I, many Belgians were able to flee when their Bouviers protected them against the invading Germans. AKC popularity: 72nd of 146.

PHYSICAL FEATURES

He stands 24–28 inches and weighs 65–100 pounds. His harsh double coat should be brushed and combed thoroughly twice a week, his beard combed daily for cleanliness. Regular trimming or clipping is required for neatness. He may be black, salt-and-pepper, brindle, or fawn. His ears may be cropped or left naturally hanging. His tail is docked.

HEALTH ISSUES

Both parents should have OFA certificates (hips and heart), yearly CERF (eyes), and normal thyroid (full panel). Also ask about SAS, glaucoma, cataracts, bloat, and cancer in the lines. Lifespan: 10–12 years.

CAUTIONS WHEN BUYING

Along with Ch. (beauty champion) titles in the pedigree, look for performance titles: obedience, tracking, herding, Schutzhund, Ringsport, CGC. Strict working lines have more drive and intensity and are best suited to active working homes.

Boxer

Fine for Novice Owners
Good with Children
Large in Size
Smooth Coat

EXERCISE REQUIRED — MEDIUM

TRIMMING/CLIPPING REQUIRED — LOW

AMOUNT OF SHEDDING — MEDIUM

ACTIVITY INDOORS — MEDIUM

EASE OF TRAINING — MEDIUM LOW

SOCIABILITY WITH STRANGERS — MEDIUM

TEMPERAMENT

The Boxer has been called an "honest" dog because his face expresses his emotions. This steadfast, good-natured dog is usually animated and playful, though some adults are more deliberate and dignified. Exercise needs vary from vigorous romping for high-energy individuals to long daily walks for more sedentary Boxers. Most make vigilant watchdogs, though guarding and territorial instincts vary. Reaction to strangers varies from "Hi there! Come on in!" (often accompanied by enthusiastic jumping), to sensible and polite, to wary, even challenging. Early socialization is important to develop a stable attitude. Most Boxers love children, though some are too exuberant for toddlers, and while his reputation for stoicism is deserved, some can be grumpy in response to mischievous kids. Some love to play with other dogs, while others can be dominant with those of the same sex. Consistent leadership is a must, as the Boxer is a strong-minded working dog, but obedience training must be upbeat and persuasive rather than sharp. This breed is stubborn, but also sensitive and proud, and may shut down if jerked around. Some individuals wheeze and/or drool. With his short face, he gulps air, which often leads to flatulence.

HISTORY

Descended from European bulldogs, the Boxer was developed in Germany as a dogfighter, bull-baiter, and police dog. AKC popularity: 12th of 146.

PHYSICAL FEATURES

He stands 21–26 inches. Males weigh 65–85 pounds; females weigh 50–70 pounds. His hard coat needs only an occasional quick brushing. He may be fawn (tan to mahogany) or brindle. White markings on his face, chest, neck, and feet are considered "flashy" and desirable for the show ring. Boxers who are solid white or mostly white cannot be shown in conformation classes, and deafness is a problem in these colors. His ears may be cropped or left naturally hanging; his tail is docked. He is one of the few breeds whose teeth must meet in an undershot bite.

HEALTH ISSUES

Both parents should have OFA certificates (hips), yearly CERF (eyes), and be cardiac-clear for cardiomyopathy and other heart defects. Also ask about low thyroid, bloat, colitis, and especially tumors and cancer in the lines. He is susceptible to respiratory difficulties and heatstroke in hot, humid, and/or stuffy conditions. Boxers love shade and air conditioning. Lifespan: 8–12 years.

CAUTIONS WHEN BUYING

Compared to American show lines, German-bred lines focus on performance sports such as Schutzhund (protection, obedience, and tracking). Working lines are generally stockier (as opposed to more elegant and stylish) and temperaments are "harder."

Briard (BREE-ard)

Best for Experienced Owners
Good with Children If Raised with Children
Large in Size
Long Coat

EXERCISE REQUIRED — HIGH

TRIMMING/CLIPPING REQUIRED — LOW

AMOUNT OF SHEDDING — MEDIUM

ACTIVITY INDOORS — MEDIUM

EASE OF TRAINING — LOW

SOCIABILITY WITH STRANGERS — MEDIUM
    LOW

TEMPERAMENT

Vigorous and spirited in body, independent and purposeful in mind, the Briard can be serious ("a reserved philosopher") or a humorous clown. His light, supple gait, like that of a large feline, has been described as "quicksilver," permitting him to make the springing starts, abrupt turns, and sudden stops required of a shepherd dog. Athletic and agile under that long coat, he needs some hard exercise each day. Mental exercise (herding, agility, tracking, watching over his home) is just as important to this thinking breed. Naturally watchful, with acute hearing, he often lies in the corner of his yard, front paws crossed, head up, observing. Matching his stern appearance, he is aloof with strangers, intensely loyal to and protective of his family. Socialization must be early and frequent so that his watchfulness does not shade into aggression or reticence. Sharp-shyness and spookiness are unfortunately present in some lines. Most are territorial with other animals, but usually good with pets in their own family, if raised with them. You must discourage his habit of poking or pushing people and other pets with his huge, powerful head in an attempt to keep them within boundaries. Briards like to control situations and require a confident, consistent owner who knows how to lead. However, they are very sensitive (sometimes overly so) and must be treated with respect and a light hand. This breed has a long memory and doesn't easily forgive or forget harsh handling.

HISTORY

Arbitrarily named for the Brie region of France, he was both a herding dog and flock guardian. He was also the official dog of the French army, serving as messenger, sentry dog, and in search and rescue for the medical corps. AKC popularity: 110th of 146.

PHYSICAL FEATURES

He stands 22–27 inches and weighs 55–100 pounds. Some lines are more heavily built than others. Brush and comb his hard, double coat twice a week, more often during seasonal shedding. He is shades of tawny (wheaten to red), gray, or black. His ears may be cropped or left naturally hanging. His tail is natural. It is a peculiarity of this breed that he must have one dewclaw on each front leg and double dewclaws on each hind leg.

HEALTH ISSUES

Both parents should have OFA certificates (hips) and yearly CERF (eyes). Also ask about low thyroid and bloat in the lines. Lifespan: 12 years.

CAUTIONS WHEN BUYING

The Briard's coarse "goat's coat" will stay handsome and rustic-looking only if you commit to grooming. Sound genetic temperament is important—carefully evaluate parents and other relatives.

Brittany

Fine for Novice Owners
Good with Children
Medium in Size
Feathered, Medium-Length Coat

EXERCISE REQUIRED — HIGH

TRIMMING/CLIPPING REQUIRED — MEDIUM

AMOUNT OF SHEDDING — MEDIUM

ACTIVITY INDOORS — MEDIUM

EASE OF TRAINING — HIGH

SOCIABILITY WITH STRANGERS — MEDIUM

TEMPERAMENT

The Brittany is usually happy, playful, quick moving, and light on his feet. He loves an athletic lifestyle of hiking, biking, running, and ball playing. If left alone too much and not given outlets for his energy, you're likely to see hyperactivity and destructive chewing. When well socialized, most are polite and gentle with everyone and peaceful with other animals. There is timidity and excessive submissiveness in some lines, so early socialization is a must to promote a confident temperament. Most are sensitive, rather "soft" dogs, willing to please and responsive to a calm voice and a light hand on the leash. He does not do well in an environment with frequent tension or loud voices. When excited or nervous, some are prone to submissive urination (sudden wetting), while others will whine persistently.

HISTORY

Once called the Brittany Spaniel, the "spaniel" was dropped in the United States because he hunts more like a pointer or setter—freezing into a point upon scenting a hiding bird. "Spaniel" has been retained in Canada and in his native France, where he was the favorite hunting dog of the peasants in the province of Brittany. AKC popularity: 32nd of 146.

PHYSICAL FEATURES

He stands 17½–20½ inches and weighs 30–45 pounds. Brush and comb his soft coat twice a week, and trim straggly hairs when necessary. Some coats have longer feathering and require more maintenance. He is orange and white or liver and white. Less common is tricolor: liver and white with orange trim. His ears are natural; his tail is docked or naturally bobtailed.

HEALTH ISSUES

Both parents should have OFA certificates (hips) and yearly CERF (eyes). Also ask about glaucoma and seizures in the lines. Lifespan: 12 years.

CAUTIONS WHEN BUYING

It is a tribute to Brittany breeders that virtually all Britts have some hunting instinct. There are more Dual Champion Brittanys (champions in both conformation and field trials) than in all other sporting breeds combined. Look for a pedigree balanced with Ch. titles and performance (field, obedience, agility) titles.

Brussels Griffon (Rough) (griff-ON)

Best for Experienced Owners
Good with Older, Considerate Children
Little in Size
Wiry Coat

EXERCISE REQUIRED — LOW
TRIMMING/CLIPPING REQUIRED — HIGH
AMOUNT OF SHEDDING — LOW
ACTIVITY INDOORS — HIGH
EASE OF TRAINING — MEDIUM LOW
SOCIABILITY WITH STRANGERS — MEDIUM

TEMPERAMENT

Described as "full of self-importance," the thickset, terrier-like Griffon is spunky, spirited, and comical. His adept climbing skills, coupled with his curiosity and imagination, can get him into trouble. An alert watchdog, he may become quite friendly with guests or remain cautious or even shy with new people and new situations. Socialization is a must to promote a confident, stable temperament. Most are fine with other family pets, but if he perceives an invasion of his space by a strange dog, he can display great ferocity, though it is mostly bluff and bluster. He has a clever mind of his own and without a firm hand can be demanding and manipulative. Training him to walk calmly on a leash may take time and patience, for he can be obstinate and may pitch a fit of acrobatic leaping and flinging himself about. If you can chuckle at some of his eccentricities yet remain firm about the general rules of the household, the Griffon (never call him a "Brussels") is very pleasant to live with. Like most breeds of terrier heritage, he is proud and sensitive and may become defensive if handled harshly or teased. He can be possessive of his food and toys, and he is hard to housebreak.

HISTORY

He originated in Brussels, Belgium, a cross of ratting terriers, Affenpinschers, Pugs, and English Toy Spaniels. He hunted vermin in the stables and accompanied the livery drivers on their horse-drawn carriages. AKC popularity: 88th of 146 (includes both Rough and Smooth varieties).

PHYSICAL FEATURES

He stands 8–12 inches and weighs 8–12 pounds. Brush his hard, wiry coat once a week and keep his bottom trimmed for cleanliness. Show dogs are "stripped" (dead coat plucked out) every few months; pet owners may opt for more convenient clipping. He may be clear red, "belge" (hairs banded with both black and red), black-and-tan, or solid black. His ears may be cropped or left naturally semi-erect; his tail is docked.

HEALTH ISSUES

Both parents should have yearly CERF certificates (eyes) and be screened for luxating patella. Also ask about cataracts, Legg-Perthes, seizures, and heart murmurs in the lines. Griffons do not like cold or rainy weather and should wear a sweater in inclement conditions. They are susceptible to respiratory difficulties and heatstroke in hot, humid, and/or stuffy conditions. Lifespan: 12–15 years.

CAUTIONS WHEN BUYING

Be careful. Since 1997, when a Griffon appeared in the movie *As Good as It Gets*, there has been an alarming increase in queries about the breed. Due to difficult (often C-section) births, tiny litters, and a high puppy mortality rate, Griffons have always been hard to find. Now with increased demand, unknowledgeable breeders have stepped in, hoping to make a quick buck.

Brussels Griffon (Smooth) (griff-ON)

Best for Experienced Owners
Good with Older, Considerate Children
Little in Size
Short Coat

EXERCISE REQUIRED — LOW
TRIMMING/CLIPPING REQUIRED — LOW
AMOUNT OF SHEDDING — LOW
ACTIVITY INDOORS — HIGH
EASE OF TRAINING — MEDIUM LOW
SOCIABILITY WITH STRANGERS — MEDIUM

TEMPERAMENT

Described as "full of self-importance," the thickset, terrier-like Griffon is spunky, spirited, and comical. His adept climbing skills, coupled with his curiosity and imagination, can get him into trouble. An alert watchdog, he may become quite friendly with guests or remain cautious or even shy with new people and new situations. Socialization is a must to promote a confident, stable temperament. Most are fine with other family pets, but if he perceives an invasion of his space by a strange dog, he can display great ferocity, though it is mostly bluff and bluster. He has a clever mind of his own and without a firm hand can be demanding and manipulative. Training him to walk calmly on a leash may take time and patience, for he can be obstinate and may pitch a fit of acrobatic leaping and flinging himself about. If you can chuckle at some of his eccentricities yet remain firm about the general rules of the household, the Griffon (never call him a "Brussels") is very pleasant to live with. Like most breeds of terrier heritage, he is proud and sensitive and may become defensive if handled harshly or teased. He can be possessive of his food and toys, and he is hard to housebreak.

HISTORY

He originated in Brussels, Belgium, a cross of ratting terriers, Affenpinschers, Pugs, and English Toy Spaniels. He hunted vermin in the stables and accompanied the livery drivers on their horse-drawn carriages. AKC popularity: 88th of 146 (includes both Rough and Smooth varieties).

PHYSICAL FEATURES

He stands 8–12 inches and weighs 8–12 pounds. His short coat needs only an occasional quick brushing. He may be clear red, "belge" (hairs banded with both black and red), black-and-tan, or solid black. His ears may be cropped or left naturally semi-erect; his tail is docked.

HEALTH ISSUES

Both parents should have yearly CERF certificates (eyes) and be screened for luxating patella. Also ask about cataracts, Legg-Perthes, seizures, and heart murmurs in the lines. Griffons do not like cold or rainy weather and should wear a sweater in inclement conditions. They are susceptible to respiratory difficulties and heatstroke in hot, humid, and/or stuffy conditions. Lifespan: 12–15 years.

CAUTIONS WHEN BUYING

Be careful. Since 1997, when a Griffon appeared in the movie *As Good as It Gets*, there has been an alarming increase in queries about the breed. Due to difficult (often C-section) births, tiny litters, and a high puppy mortality rate, Griffons have always been hard to find. Now with increased demand, unknowledgeable breeders have stepped in, hoping to make a quick buck.

Bulldog

Fine for Novice Owners
Good with Children
Medium in Size
Smooth Coat

EXERCISE REQUIRED — LOW
TRIMMING/CLIPPING REQUIRED — LOW
AMOUNT OF SHEDDING — MEDIUM
ACTIVITY INDOORS — LOW
EASE OF TRAINING — MEDIUM
SOCIABILITY WITH STRANGERS — MEDIUM

TEMPERAMENT

The AKC Standard says his disposition should be "equable and kind, resolute and courageous . . . demeanor should be pacific and dignified." Despite his gloomy mug, the Bulldog is one of the most amiable and dependable of all breeds. Puppies are frisky, but adults are quiet and rather phlegmatic, spending much of the day snoring on the sofa. They do need some exercise to stay fit, preferably walks in cool weather. Some are friendly with strangers, while others are politely reserved. Though not a barking watchdog, his blocky build and odd, rolling, shuffling gait give intruders pause. It takes a tremendous amount of serious teasing or threatening to provoke this sweet-natured breed, but once aroused, he can be a force to reckon with. His tenacity and resolve mean that it's difficult to change his mind once he decides to do something. Usually peaceful with other pets, some males may engage in a battle of wills (or jaws) with other males. Though stubborn, he is surprisingly sensitive, remembers what he learns, and responds well to patient, persistent training that utilizes food motivation. Jerking this breed around accomplishes absolutely nothing. Bulldogs are food fanatics: They can be extremely possessive and should be fed by themselves. Snorting, snuffling, wheezing, grunting, slobbering water, and flatulence go with the territory of short-faced breeds.

HISTORY

He originated in England as a bull-baiter, but today the ferocity has been bred out of him, replaced by an exceptionally docile nature. AKC popularity: 23rd of 146.

PHYSICAL FEATURES

He stands 14–15 inches and weighs 40–55 pounds. His glossy coat needs only an occasional quick brushing, but facial wrinkles must be cleaned daily. Colors include brindle, white, red, fawn, fallow, or piebald. His ears and tail are natural.

HEALTH ISSUES

Both parents should be screened for heart defects and low thyroid. Also ask about elongated soft palate, demodectic mange, and eyelid/eyelash defects such as entropion. Bulldogs cannot regulate their temperature very well, must be protected from extreme heat and cold, and are at great risk in humid or stuffy conditions. Especially after exertion, they should have access to water, shade, ventilation, and/or air-conditioning. He is sensitive to anesthetics and should never be casually sedated. Lifespan: 8–10 years.

CAUTIONS WHEN BUYING

Some lines are less extreme (more athletic build, slightly longer muzzle) and may provide a healthier pet. Due to the expenses of artificial insemination, C-sections, and high puppy mortality rates, Bulldogs are expensive ($1,000 and up). It cannot be stressed enough that this breed has special needs in hot weather and must be carefully supervised.

Bullmastiff

Best for Experienced Owners
Good with Children If Raised with Children
Giant in Size
Smooth Coat

EXERCISE REQUIRED — MEDIUM

TRIMMING/CLIPPING REQUIRED — LOW

AMOUNT OF SHEDDING — MEDIUM

ACTIVITY INDOORS — LOW

EASE OF TRAINING — LOW

SOCIABILITY WITH STRANGERS — MEDIUM
LOW

TEMPERAMENT

The AKC Standard describes him as "fearless and confident, yet docile . . . showing great strength, endurance, and alertness." Though usually mild-mannered, the powerful Bullmastiff is also serious and self-assured. He is afraid of nothing, and once aroused will seldom back down. Bullmastiff puppies (up to two or three years old) can be rambunctious and have an aversion to keeping all four feet on the ground at the same time. Fortunately, adults are calm and quiet and need only moderate exercise to maintain their impressive muscle tone. This breed is intensely loyal to his family and doesn't like being left outside. If he doesn't get enough companionship or personal attention, he may walk through fences just to be with people. Though sensible with strangers, he does have well-established protective and territorial instincts. He must be thoroughly socialized at an early age so that he learns to distinguish friend from foe. He can be aggressive with other dogs of the same sex, and though he may be fine with the family cat, strange animals will not be accepted onto his property. Tremendously strong and stubborn, Bullmastiffs are inclined to do things their own way and will test members of the family. However, he learns quickly and will respond to early, consistent obedience training that includes leadership, cheerful praise, and food rewards. Overall, he's a splendid, capable companion for assertive owners, but without ongoing time and effort, socialization and supervision, he can be too much to handle. Some individuals drool.

HISTORY

He was developed in England by gamekeepers (the gamekeeper's "night dog") as protection against poachers. The foundation breeding was 60 percent Mastiff and 40 percent Bulldog. AKC popularity: 52nd of 146.

PHYSICAL FEATURES

He stands 24–27 inches and weighs 100–130 pounds. His hard coat needs only an occasional quick brushing. He may be red, fawn, red-fawn, or brindle. His ears and tail are natural.

HEALTH ISSUES

Both parents should have OFA certificates (hips and elbows). Also ask about low thyroid, bloat, and tumors and cancer in the lines. Eyelid disorders (entropion) can be a problem. He is susceptible to respiratory difficulties and heatstroke in hot, humid, and/or stuffy conditions. Bullmastiffs love shade and air-conditioning. Lifespan: 7–9 years.

CAUTIONS WHEN BUYING

Compared to the Mastiff, the Bullmastiff is smaller and stockier, more active and agile, more confident, more of a thinking dog, and potentially more aggressive.

Bull Terrier

Best for Experienced Owners
Good with Older, Considerate Children
Medium in Size
Smooth Coat

EXERCISE REQUIRED — MEDIUM
TRIMMING/CLIPPING REQUIRED — LOW
AMOUNT OF SHEDDING — MEDIUM
ACTIVITY INDOORS — HIGH MEDIUM
EASE OF TRAINING — LOW
SOCIABILITY WITH STRANGERS — HIGH
    MEDIUM

TEMPERAMENT

The "White Cavalier" is sweet-tempered, yet also rowdy and clownish, full of fire and determination. This muscular, forceful dog does best with active families, for he has a high energy level that comes in spurts and bursts. He needs frequent, brisk walks, occasional vigorous games of ball, and total immersion in the family—i.e., lots of companionship and interactive play sessions. If ignored, he will become bored, and mischief will surely follow. Youngsters who are neglected can be especially rambunctious: happily devouring your furniture, excavating great caverns in your yard, and spinning in dizzy circles, chasing their tails obsessively. Most Bullies greet strangers with enthusiastic bounding (often knocking the guest about!) and face kissing. Aggression and timidity are present in some lines, and early socialization is important to develop a stable attitude. Most individuals play too roughly for small children, especially when egged on. A Bull Terrier should not be kept with another dog of the same sex, and cats may or may not be safe. Bullies can be very possessive of their food. At some point, if you have not raised this breed with consistent leadership, he will likely challenge your ability to control his actions. Such dominance attempts must be met with calm assertiveness. Keep training sessions brief, and use food as motivation. Some are "talkers" who grunt and mumble to themselves.

HISTORY

Developed in England from crosses of various bulldogs with an extinct white terrier, he was matched against other dogs in the fighting arena (or "pit"). AKC popularity: 84th of 146.

PHYSICAL FEATURES

He stands 15–22 inches; weight varies greatly, from 35–80 pounds. His hard coat requires only an occasional quick brushing. (People with sensitive skin may react adversely to the "pokes" of the harsh hair.) He comes in two color varieties: White may be solid white, or mostly white with a few colored patches on his head; colored may be brindle, fawn, or black-and-tan, all of which usually include white markings. His ears and tail are natural.

HEALTH ISSUES

Both parents should have OFA certificates (patellas) and be cardiac-clear for heart disease and screened every year (by urine test and ultrasound) for kidney disease. Each puppy should come with a BAER printout showing normal bilateral hearing. Also ask about low thyroid, seizures, allergies, and skin conditions in the lines. White coats are sensitive to sunburn; provide shade when outdoors for long periods. Lifespan: 12 years.

CAUTIONS WHEN BUYING

With his distinctive egg-shaped head, large erect ears, and tiny, sunken, triangular eyes, it should be evident that this breed is not a "Pit Bull." Nonetheless, public/media prejudice has slopped over onto him and you should be prepared for the moral and legal responsibilities. See American Pit Bull Terrier for more information.

Cairn Terrier

Best for Experienced Owners
Good with Older, Considerate Children
Small in Size
Wiry Coat

EXERCISE REQUIRED — MEDIUM
TRIMMING/CLIPPING REQUIRED — HIGH
    MEDIUM
AMOUNT OF SHEDDING — LOW
ACTIVITY INDOORS — HIGH
EASE OF TRAINING — MEDIUM
SOCIABILITY WITH STRANGERS — MEDIUM

TEMPERAMENT

Toto, the Cairn Terrier in *The Wizard of Oz*, is what many people picture when they hear "terrier." This sturdy little dog is everything a terrier was designed to be: game and hardy, up on his toes, confident, plucky, and spirited. The Cairn loves to play and needs his daily walks, but is adaptable to any home in which he can be a full participant and busybody and where his bold terrier traits are kept under control. Adults may be friendly or reserved with strangers, but are always alert and quick to announce guests. He can be scrappy and bossy with other pets, but will coexist with them more readily than some other terriers. However, strange animals may be a different story, as the Cairn was bred to hunt and will chase anything that moves. He is inquisitive, so a leash or fenced yard is essential at all times. Assertive but cheerful, with typical terrier stubbornness, he must be shown that you are in charge. He does respond well to consistent discipline and to obedience training that focuses on treats and praise. Cairns can be possessive of their food and toys, and being respectable terriers, they are enthusiastic diggers and barkers.

HISTORY

He was developed in Scotland to hunt fox, otter, and weasel, and he takes his name from the piles of rocks (cairns) where his prey took refuge. AKC popularity: 44th of 146.

PHYSICAL FEATURES

He stands 10–11 inches and weighs 13–16 pounds. Brush and comb his harsh coat twice a week. Keep his bottom trimmed for cleanliness. Show dogs are "stripped" (dead coat plucked out) every few months; pet owners may opt for more convenient clipping. Colors include wheaten, red, and various shades of brindle. His ears and tail are natural.

HEALTH ISSUES

Both parents should have yearly CERF certificates (eyes), and GDC certificates showing they are clear of GCL (globoid cell leukodystrophy) and Legg-Perthes. OFA or GDC certificates showing they are clear of luxating patella are also desirable. Also ask about CMO, heart disease, low thyroid, glaucoma, liver shunt, seizures, vWD, and allergies in the lines. Lifespan: 13–15 years.

CAUTIONS WHEN BUYING

Exploitation by unknowledgeable breeders has created a gene pool with a considerable number of genetic health problems. The Cairn Terrier Club of America has been instrumental in encouraging its breeders to screen rigorously for these genetic defects. Your hardy, healthy Cairn should come only from these careful breeders. Breeders who offer only a general health certificate and vaccination records are *not* what you're looking for.

Canaan Dog (CAY-nen)

Best for Experienced Owners
Good with Children If Raised with Children
Medium in Size
Short Coat

EXERCISE REQUIRED — MEDIUM
TRIMMING/CLIPPING REQUIRED — LOW
AMOUNT OF SHEDDING — HIGH MEDIUM
ACTIVITY INDOORS — MEDIUM
EASE OF TRAINING — MEDIUM
SOCIABILITY WITH STRANGERS — LOW

TEMPERAMENT

The AKC Standard says, "The Canaan Dog moves with athletic agility and grace in a quick, brisk, ground-covering trot." He is light-footed and can turn on a dime and will take as much exercise as you can offer, yet adults are calm enough to curl up on the sofa when the day's work or fun is over. This independent dog is self-reliant and doesn't need constant petting. However, he is also highly intelligent and an excellent problem-solver and needs plenty of mental stimulation (obedience, agility, tracking, herding, playing games) to prevent boredom, which can lead to destructiveness. His wariness of strangers, inherent distrust of anything new or different, territorial instincts, keen senses and canny intuition all combine to make him a vigilant watchdog. This primitive breed is 100 percent aware of his surroundings, constantly observing and listening. He will sound the alarm at every perceived threat. However, this is not an aggressive dog—rather, he reacts to intrusions into his territory by retreating just out of reach and barking continuously. Because caution can easily shade into fearfulness, early and extensive socialization is required to build a confident, stable temperament. Dog aggression can be a problem, and these dogs do have a strong prey drive and may stalk smaller animals. Canaans resist repetitive training and jerking on the leash. Motivate them with variation, praise, and food. Yet they may also test you for pack leadership, so they require a confident, consistent owner. They love to dig and they are very vocal—barking and whining need to be controlled.

HISTORY

A "pariah" (feral) dog whose cleverness and defensive instincts enabled him to survive in the harsh Israeli desert, he was by and large shaped by natural selection and eventually domesticated by the Israelites. AKC popularity: 135th of 146.

PHYSICAL FEATURES

He stands 19–24 inches. Males weigh 45–55 pounds; females weigh 35–45 pounds. Brush his double coat once a week, daily during heavy seasonal shedding. He may be white with colored patches and a colored mask, or a solid color such as white, cream, sandy, red-brown, or black, sometimes with white trim and/or sabling (black-tipped hairs). His ears and tail are natural.

HEALTH ISSUES

Both parents should have OFA certificates (hips) and yearly CERF (eyes). Also ask about low thyroid and seizures in the lines. Lifespan: 12–15 years.

CAUTIONS WHEN BUYING

The Canaan Dog is a survivor because of his instincts. He appeals to those who have respect for a natural dog, who can admire his resourcefulness, inquisitiveness, and independent character. There are two physical types: a lighter build with a shorter coat (favored by the CDCA) and a heavier-boned build with a thicker coat (favored by the ICDCA).

Cane Corso (CAH-nay COR-so)

Best for Experienced Owners
Good with Children If Raised with Children
Large in Size
Smooth Coat

EXERCISE REQUIRED — HIGH

TRIMMING/CLIPPING REQUIRED — LOW

AMOUNT OF SHEDDING — MEDIUM

ACTIVITY INDOORS — MEDIUM LOW

EASE OF TRAINING — MEDIUM

SOCIABILITY WITH STRANGERS — MEDIUM
LOW

TEMPERAMENT

Often described as a "coursing mastiff," the Corso outdoes the other mastiff breeds in athleticism, agility, speed, energy level, and sense of adventure. This robust dog needs his share of exercise, but above all he requires companionship and personal interaction. He lives for his family and may become destructive if left alone too much. Puppies should be friendly and trusting and with proper socialization become more aloof and discerning as they mature. As with all mastiffs, socialization is an absolute requirement to promote the correct temperament, which is protective, but in a calm, stable, discriminating way. Though the Corso was not used for fighting, dog aggression can be a problem; he should be thoroughly socialized with other dogs from an early age. He is more attentive and responsive to training than other mastiffs, and though quite dominant, will respect an owner who is confident and consistent. Corsos have tighter skin than other mastiffs and drool much less. Some love to dig, and most enjoy splashing in water, whether it be the pond, a mudhole, the lawn sprinkler, or their water bowl. These are not dainty dogs.

HISTORY

Descended from the now extinct Roman Molosser, war dog of ancient Rome who also fought in the Roman Colosseum for sport, the Cane Corso hunted big game, caught unruly cattle, and protected his home. Registered by the FCI, ICCF, and AKC-FSS.

PHYSICAL FEATURES

Size is controversial. The FCI Standard, in conformity with the Italian Cane Corso club (SACC), calls for males at 24–28 inches, 90–110 pounds, and females at 22–26 inches, 85–100 pounds. However, the largest CC club in the United States, the ICCF, which espouses the original conformation standard for the breed, is promoting dogs that match the wider varieties of size and weight that are actually being bred in Italy: males at 100–140 pounds, females at 80–115 pounds. His short, dense coat requires only an occasional quick brushing. Colors include black, blue, chestnut (red), tawny (fawn), and brindle. His ears may be cropped or left naturally hanging; his tail is docked.

HEALTH ISSUES

Both parents should have OFA certificates (hips). Also ask about demodectic mange in the lines. Lifespan: 10 years.

CAUTIONS WHEN BUYING

The first Cane Corsos brought to the United States in 1988 were large, with a moderate-length muzzle and scissors bite. The ICCF believes this is the average type and contends that the FCI Standard, which was drawn up later in cooperation with the SACC of Italy, is an attempt to conform the breed to one particular line of smaller dogs with a shorter muzzle and undershot bite. ENCI/SACC enthusiasts, for their part, insist that the ICCF dogs are too ponderous to be athletic working dogs. In any case, insist on the hip certificates—many breeders are not X-raying hips.

Cavalier King Charles Spaniel

(CAV-ah-leer)

Fine for Novice Owners
Good with Older, Considerate Children
Small in Size
Feathered, Medium-Length Coat

EXERCISE REQUIRED — MEDIUM

TRIMMING/CLIPPING REQUIRED — LOW

AMOUNT OF SHEDDING — MEDIUM

ACTIVITY INDOORS — MEDIUM

EASE OF TRAINING — HIGH MEDIUM

SOCIABILITY WITH STRANGERS — HIGH
      MEDIUM

TEMPERAMENT

Often called a sporting toy because of his combination of spaniel and toy traits, the Cavalier is sweet-tempered, gentle, happy, and playful. This comfort-loving breed adores cuddling in laps and snuggling on soft pillows, but he has more field instincts than you might think. He can be a runner. A fenced yard or a leash are musts, because he will pursue squirrels, chipmunks, low-flying birds, even butterflies, right into the street. One Cavalier chased a seagull into the ocean and was swimming determinedly seaward before his owner managed to rescue him. He is people-oriented and friendly, though there is potential for timidity. He needs plenty of early socialization to build a confident, outgoing temperament. With other dogs and cats, he is peaceful, but as mentioned, he'll chase little creatures that run or flutter. Cavs are willing to please and respond well to praise and encouragement. This sociable breed does not enjoy being left alone and should have companionship (either human or other pets) most of the day. He may whine or chew destructively if not given enough attention.

HISTORY

Developed in England, his primary job was to warm laps (especially those of the sick) in drafty castles and on chilly carriage rides. AKC popularity: 56th of 146.

PHYSICAL FEATURES

He stands 12–13 inches and weighs 13–18 pounds, though quite a few are oversized. Brush and comb his silky coat twice a week, more often when he is shedding. Keep his ear canals clean and dry, and keep his bottom trimmed for cleanliness. There are four color varieties: Blenheim (most common) is white with chestnut red markings; Ruby is solid rich red; Black-and-Tan is mostly black with red trim; Tricolor is white with black markings and red trim. His ears are natural; his tail may be natural or slightly docked.

HEALTH ISSUES

Both parents should have OFA certificates (hips and patellas), yearly CERF (eyes), and most important be evaluated cardiac-clear (via auscultation and preferably Doppler ultrasound) for mitral valve disease. MVD is the number-one killer of Cavaliers, with up to 50 percent of the breed likely to be affected. Try to choose parents who show clear of MVD at older ages (three to five), as their puppies seem to have the best chance to be clear or less severely affected. Lifespan: 7–12 years.

CAUTIONS WHEN BUYING

This lovely, graceful breed is a dream come true for many families and senior citizens, but the companionship and grooming must be kept up, and the health clearances are mandatory.

Cesky Terrier (CHESS-kee)

Fine for Novice Owners
Good with Children
Small in Size
Unusual Coat (see Physical Features below)

EXERCISE REQUIRED — MEDIUM

TRIMMING/CLIPPING REQUIRED — HIGH
    MEDIUM

AMOUNT OF SHEDDING — LOW

ACTIVITY INDOORS — MEDIUM

EASE OF TRAINING — MEDIUM

SOCIABILITY WITH STRANGERS — MEDIUM

TEMPERAMENT

In the field, the rugged, persistent Cesky has more working instincts than some other terriers. But in the home, he possesses a sweeter, more laid-back disposition; indeed, he may be the mildest and easiest to handle of all the terriers. Given moderate exercise and lots of personal attention (he doesn't like being left alone for long periods), he adapts to virtually any household, city or country, apartment or estate. Though playful and inquisitive outdoors—his large nose is usually glued to the ground—he is calm indoors. With strangers, he is usually reserved but polite, though early socialization is a must to develop this attitude. With other dogs and cats, he is more sociable and less aggressive than most terriers. Rodents, however, will be chased with enthusiasm and determination. Though he has his stubborn, independent streak, he responds well to obedience training that includes praise and food. Just go easy on the food so that he doesn't pack on the weight. This may be easier said than done, as he tends to be a food thief whose long reach, when standing on his hind legs, can result in the birthday cake vanishing off the kitchen countertop. And unfortunately, it isn't only food that Ceskys like to eat—they are noted for swallowing inedible objects, which may lead to some frantic evenings in the veterinary emergency room.

HISTORY

Also called the Czech or Bohemian Terrier, he is the deliberate creation of a geneticist who crossed the Scottish Terrier with the Sealyham in the 1950s. The Cesky came to the United States in the late 1980s. Registered by the FCI, UKC, and CKC.

PHYSICAL FEATURES

He stands 10–12 inches and weighs 16–22 pounds. His silky, wavy coat should be brushed and combed twice a week. Unlike most terriers, the Cesky is never "stripped" (dead coat plucked out), but rather every eight to ten weeks he is clipped short on his neck, back, and sides, with the hair left long on his face, chest, stomach, and legs. Adults are shades of blue-gray, ranging from silver to slate to dark charcoal (almost black), usually with off-white (platinum), buff, lighter gray, or tan furnishings. Light brown is an allowed color, but almost never seen. His ears and tail are natural.

HEALTH ISSUES

Females have a tendency toward ovarian cysts and infertility. Long-backed breeds are susceptible to disk disease that can be exacerbated by excessive high-jumping, dashing down stairs, being picked up without proper support, and obesity. Lifespan: 12–15 years.

CAUTIONS WHEN BUYING

The Cesky is an intriguing alternative to other short-legged terriers such as the Dandie Dinmont, Sealyham, and Skye. Just remember that his lustrous coat needs frequent brushing and clipping to look nice. There are only about four hundred individuals in the United States, and a high percentage of pups, especially female, are kept for showing and breeding, so be prepared to wait for a pet.

Chesapeake Bay Retriever

Best for Experienced Owners
Good with Children
Large in Size
Short Coat

EXERCISE REQUIRED — MEDIUM

TRIMMING/CLIPPING REQUIRED — LOW

AMOUNT OF SHEDDING — MEDIUM

ACTIVITY INDOORS — LOW

EASE OF TRAINING — MEDIUM

SOCIABILITY WITH STRANGERS — LOW

TEMPERAMENT

The Chessie is the most powerful of the retrievers, with the strongest personality, yet possessed of quiet good sense. This rugged dog should be taken hiking, biking, jogging, and swimming as often as possible. A walk around the block is not enough to maintain his muscle tone or to satisfy his working instincts. This breed needs a job (learning obedience exercises, fetching a stick or ball, field work), else he will find his own ways to keep himself busy, and you may not appreciate his choices. The most protective of the retrievers, typically he is reserved with strangers and intensely loyal to his family. Most are fine with the pets in their own family, but some are territorial with strange dogs and cats. You must control his tendency to chew on objects and to mouth your hands—provide a box filled with toys so he can carry something around in his mouth. Confident leadership and obedience training are required to develop respect. This breed will test members of the family to find his place in the pecking order, and if you don't take the top position, the Chessie will do so.

HISTORY

One of the few breeds developed in the United States, along the icy bays of Maryland, he is the supreme retriever of ducks and geese in rough, frigid waters. AKC popularity: 43rd of 146.

PHYSICAL FEATURES

Males stand 23–26 inches and weigh 65–80 pounds. Females stand 21–24 inches and weigh 55–70 pounds. His coat is thick, harsh, and kinky and should be brushed deeply only when shedding, as too much brushing will alter the texture. Earth shades range from wheaten (called deadgrass), to reddish gold (sedge), to light brown, to rich chocolate brown. His ears and tail are natural. His feet are webbed.

HEALTH ISSUES

Both parents should have OFA certificates (hips), yearly CERF (eyes), and a DNA certificate that shows whether they are affected, carriers, or clear of PRA (at least one parent must be clear). Also ask about OCD and vWD in the lines. Lifespan: 12 years.

CAUTIONS WHEN BUYING

Don't choose a Chesapeake if you are more attracted to the temperament of Labradors and Goldens. Chessies are not happy-go-lucky dogs who will greet all of your friends with enthusiasm; they are more serious, more discriminating, and more dominant.

Chihuahua (Long Coat)

(chih-WAH-wah)

Best for Experienced Owners
Good with Older, Considerate Children
Little in Size
Feathered, Medium-Length Coat

EXERCISE REQUIRED — LOW

TRIMMING/CLIPPING REQUIRED — LOW

AMOUNT OF SHEDDING — MEDIUM LOW

ACTIVITY INDOORS — MEDIUM

EASE OF TRAINING — LOW

SOCIABILITY WITH STRANGERS — LOW

TEMPERAMENT

Chihuahuas are comical and entertaining. Other than that generalization, they are extremely variable: You can find individuals who are lively or placid, bold or timid, feisty or mellow, confident or nervous, stubborn or eager to please. Some Chis (*cheez*) are friendly with all the world, while others loathe every person on the planet other than their owner. Most live peacefully with other pets, though they usually raise a ruckus when they spy a strange dog. They do recognize and tend to prefer their own breed, and it's a good idea to keep them in pairs so they can play together and keep warm by sleeping on top of each other. Chihuahuas are very difficult to housebreak, especially in bad weather; consider an indoor litter box. Barking must be controlled from day one. More than most other breeds, how a Chihuahua turns out depends mightily on the genetic temperament of parents and grandparents (entire lines are social or antisocial), how thoroughly he was socialized by the breeder, and how you raise him (continued socialization and training) when you bring him home.

HISTORY

Legends connect him with the Mayan, Toltec, and Aztec civilizations; he takes his name from the Mexican state of Chihuahua. AKC popularity: 8th of 146 (includes both coat varieties).

PHYSICAL FEATURES

He stands 5–8 inches and weighs 2–6 pounds; however, those under 3 pounds are often not sound or healthy.

Larger individuals (6–12 pounds) are common; though not suitable for show, they make sturdy pets. His soft coat may be single (no undercoat, which means little shedding) or double (top coat plus undercoat equals more shedding). Some coats are longer/thicker than others and require more maintenance. Colors include white, fawn, red, cream, black, chocolate, or blue (gray). White markings and/or tan trim are common. His ears and tail are natural.

HEALTH ISSUES

Both parents should be screened for luxating patella. Check parents' teeth for soundness—poor teeth run through some lines. He is sensitive to anesthetics, vaccines, and chemicals and should never be casually medicated or sedated. Chis tremble a lot from cold, excitement, and/or a high metabolism. They do not like cold or rain and should wear a sweater in inclement conditions. Blues may have skin/coat problems. An open molera (soft spot on the head) and honking sounds after eating or drinking are common breed traits, not health problems. Individuals under four pounds are more susceptible to hypoglycemia (low blood sugar). Lifespan: 15 years.

CAUTIONS WHEN BUYING

This breed has special needs that require extra vigilance and occasional indulgence, yet they must be raised with consistent rules and not spoiled. Avoid breeders producing "deer-headed" Chihuahuas with flat heads and long, pointy muzzles. They are not adhering to the AKC Chihuahua Standard, which calls for a distinctive domed head. Also run from any breeder who uses the made-up terms "teacup" or "tiny toy" or who places his puppies before twelve weeks.

Chihuahua (Smooth) (chih-WAH-wah)

Best for Experienced Owners
Good with Older, Considerate Children
Little in Size
Smooth Coat

EXERCISE REQUIRED — LOW

TRIMMING/CLIPPING REQUIRED — LOW

AMOUNT OF SHEDDING — MEDIUM LOW

ACTIVITY INDOORS — MEDIUM

EASE OF TRAINING — LOW

SOCIABILITY WITH STRANGERS — LOW

TEMPERAMENT

Chihuahuas are comical and entertaining. Other than that generalization, they are extremely variable: You can find individuals who are lively or placid, bold or timid, feisty or mellow, confident or nervous, stubborn or eager to please. Some Chis (*cheez*) are friendly with all the world, while others loathe every person on the planet other than their owner. Most live peacefully with other pets, though they usually raise a ruckus when they spy a strange dog. They do recognize and tend to prefer their own breed, and it's a good idea to keep them in pairs so they can play together and keep warm by sleeping on top of each other. Chihuahuas are very difficult to house-break, especially in bad weather; consider an indoor litter box. Barking must be controlled from day one. More than most other breeds, how a Chihuahua turns out depends mightily on the genetic temperament of parents and grandparents (entire lines are social or antisocial), how thoroughly he was socialized by the breeder, and how you raise him (continued socialization and training) when you bring him home.

HISTORY

Legends connect him with the Mayan, Toltec, and Aztec civilizations; he takes his name from the Mexican state of Chihuahua. AKC popularity: 8th of 146 (includes both coat varieties).

PHYSICAL FEATURES

He stands 5–8 inches and weighs 2–6 pounds; however, those under 3 pounds are often not sound or healthy. Larger individuals (6–12 pounds) are common; though not suitable for show, they make sturdy pets. His soft coat may be single (no undercoat, which means little shedding) or double (top coat plus undercoat equals more shedding). Some coats are longer/thicker than others and require more maintenance. Colors include white, fawn, red, cream, black, chocolate, or blue (gray). White markings and/or tan trim are common. His ears and tail are natural.

HEALTH ISSUES

Both parents should be screened for luxating patella. Check parents' teeth for soundness—poor teeth run through some lines. He is sensitive to anesthetics, vaccines, and chemicals and should never be casually medicated or sedated. Chis tremble a lot from cold, excitement, and/or a high metabolism. They do not like cold or rain and should wear a sweater in inclement conditions. Blues may have skin/coat problems. An open molera (soft spot on the head) and honking sounds after eating or drinking are common breed traits, not health problems. Individuals under four pounds are more susceptible to hypoglycemia (low blood sugar). Lifespan: 15 years.

CAUTIONS WHEN BUYING

This breed has special needs that require extra vigilance and occasional indulgence, yet they must be raised with consistent rules and not spoiled. Avoid breeders producing "deer-headed" Chihuahuas with flat heads and long, pointy muzzles. They are not adhering to the AKC Chihuahua Standard, which calls for a distinctive domed head. Also run from any breeder who uses the made-up terms "teacup" or "tiny toy" or who places his puppies before twelve weeks.

Chinese Crested (Hairless)

Fine for Novice Owners
Good with Older, Considerate Children
Little to Small in Size
Mostly Hairless Coat

EXERCISE REQUIRED — MEDIUM
TRIMMING/CLIPPING REQUIRED — LOW
AMOUNT OF SHEDDING — LOW
ACTIVITY INDOORS — HIGH
EASE OF TRAINING — MEDIUM LOW
SOCIABILITY WITH STRANGERS — MEDIUM
     LOW

TEMPERAMENT

The unique Chinese Crested is fine-boned, elegant, and graceful. High-spirited and happy, animated and agile, he is an adept climber and jumper who can grip his toys (or his owner's neck) tightly with his paws. This people-oriented "Velcro" dog depends emotionally on his owner and demands a lot of personal interaction, stroking, and rubbing. He doesn't like being left for long without companionship. Reserved with strangers, some lines or individuals are high-strung and/or timid with new people and new situations. Early and frequent socialization will help build a confident, stable temperament. He is playful with (though sometimes jealous of) other pets. Though independent and somewhat willful, he is also bright and responds well to the obedience training he needs to control his inquisitive activities. Use reward-based methods. Some will bark (or howl), and some are clever escape artists who can scale high fences or dig under them. Housebreaking is very difficult, especially when a dog is not neutered, as this somewhat primitive breed is inclined to excessive marking of his territory.

HISTORY

He was discovered by Chinese traders either in Mexico or Africa. There are two coat varieties: hairless and powderpuff. There is a lethal gene involved with the hairless mutation, so every surviving hairless dog carries one gene for hairless and one gene for puff. Both hairless and puff varieties show up in the same litter and are occasionally interbred. AKC popularity: 69th of 146.

PHYSICAL FEATURES

He stands 11–15 inches and weighs 8–15 pounds. He is supposed to be hairless except for a tuft of hair on the head (the crest), the tail (plume), and the feet (socks), but some do have a sparse coating of body hair, which is shaved off for the show ring. He sweats through the sebaceous glands in his skin and feet, so sponge daily and bathe weekly to keep the glands clean and open. Colors (really skin pigmentation) include white, black, brown, blue, golden, even pink or lilac. Exotic spotted patterns are common. His ears and tail are natural.

HEALTH ISSUES

Both parents should have yearly CERF certificates (eyes) and be screened for luxating patella. He is sensitive to anesthetics, vaccines, and chemicals and should never be casually medicated or sedated. Most are prone to acne and allergic to wool and lanolin lotion. He doesn't like cold or rainy weather and should wear a sweater in inclement conditions. The lighter colors sunburn easily, which leaves them susceptible to skin cancer. Most have missing teeth, and those teeth they do have are soft and must be carefully maintained. Lifespan: 13–15 years.

CAUTIONS WHEN BUYING

Sadly, this breed is often chosen for his lack of shedding and his exotic appearance (like that of a tiny deer or pony), without the owner realizing the high energy level, need for companionship, and commitment to skin care.

Chinese Crested (Powderpuff)

Fine for Novice Owners
Good with Older, Considerate Children
Little to Small in Size
Long Coat

EXERCISE REQUIRED — MEDIUM

TRIMMING/CLIPPING REQUIRED — HIGH
   MEDIUM LOW

AMOUNT OF SHEDDING — LOW

ACTIVITY INDOORS — HIGH

EASE OF TRAINING — MEDIUM

SOCIABILITY WITH STRANGERS — MEDIUM
   LOW

TEMPERAMENT

The unique Chinese Crested is fine-boned, elegant, and graceful. High-spirited and happy, animated and agile, he is an adept climber and jumper who can grip his toys (or his owner's neck) tightly with his paws. This people-oriented "Velcro" dog depends emotionally on his owner and demands a lot of personal interaction, stroking, and rubbing. He doesn't like being left for long without companionship. Reserved with strangers, some lines or individuals are high-strung and/or timid with new people and new situations. Early and frequent socialization will help build a confident, stable temperament. He is playful with (though sometimes jealous of) other pets. Though independent and somewhat willful, he is also bright and responds well to the obedience training he needs to control his inquisitive activities. Use reward-based methods. Some will bark (or howl), and some are clever escape artists who can scale high fences or dig under them. Housebreaking is very difficult, especially when a dog is not neutered, as this somewhat primitive breed is inclined to excessive marking of his territory.

HISTORY

He was discovered by Chinese traders either in Mexico or Africa. There are two coat varieties: hairless and powderpuff. There is a lethal gene involved with the hairless mutation, so every surviving hairless dog carries one gene for hairless and one gene for puff. Both hairless and puff varieties show up in the same litter and are occasionally interbred. AKC popularity: 69th of 146.

PHYSICAL FEATURES

He stands 11–15 inches and weighs 8–15 pounds. Brush and comb his long, silky coat twice a week. Pet owners may choose to have the coat trimmed/clipped short every four to six weeks. Colors include white, black, brown, blue, golden, sable, and spotted, among others. His ears and tail are natural.

HEALTH ISSUES

Both parents should have yearly CERF certificates (eyes) and be screened for luxating patella. He is sensitive to anesthetics, vaccines, and chemicals and should never be casually medicated or sedated. Lifespan: 13–15 years.

CAUTIONS WHEN BUYING

Most breeders say the Powderpuff variety is calmer and quieter than his Hairless brother—more content to sit beside you or curled into your lap, rather than wrapped around your neck or batting at you with his paws, demanding attention.

Chinese Shar-Pei (Shar-PAY)

Best for Experienced Owners
Good with Children If Raised with Children
Medium in Size
Smooth or Short Coat

EXERCISE REQUIRED — MEDIUM
TRIMMING/CLIPPING REQUIRED — LOW
AMOUNT OF SHEDDING — MEDIUM
ACTIVITY INDOORS — MEDIUM LOW
EASE OF TRAINING — MEDIUM LOW
SOCIABILITY WITH STRANGERS — LOW

TEMPERAMENT

This sober, dignified dog with the wrinkled skin, hippopotamus head, and scowling expression stands firmly on the ground with a calm, confident stature. Naturally clean and easy to housebreak, quiet and mannerly in the home, the Shar-Pei is an impressive companion if you can establish a relationship of mutual respect—i.e., admiring his independent character while consistently enforcing household rules so that he respects *you* as well. He does well with brisk daily walks. Unless securely fenced, he is not the best choice for a farm or rural setting, for he has strong hunting instincts: He can be predatory with cats and may run deer and molest livestock. Aloof (but not hostile) with strangers, he should be accustomed to people at an early age so that his territorial instincts are properly discriminatory. Though he usually minds his own business unless provoked, some can be aggressive with other dogs. Obedience training should emphasize praise and food—"jerking" methods will only make this proud breed more obstinate. Some snort and snore.

HISTORY

The loose skin of this Chinese hunting/fighting dog enabled him to twist and fight even when gripped by an opponent. *Shar-pei* means "sandpaper-like skin." AKC popularity: 35th of 146.

PHYSICAL FEATURES

He stands 18–20 inches and weighs 40–60 pounds. His extremely harsh coat may be smooth (horse coat) or one inch long (brush coat). Horse coats are prickly and may cause people with sensitive skin to itch. Colors include cream, fawn, silver, red, chocolate, black, and sable, as well as "dilute" versions where eyes, nose, and toenails are light-colored. Spotted ("flowered") dogs may not be shown in conformation. His tongue is blue-black (lavender in dilute colors). Pink tongues are a disqualification; spotted tongues are a major fault. His ears and tail are natural.

HEALTH ISSUES

Both parents should have OFA certificates (hips). Also ask about amyloidosis and FSF (familial Shar-Pei fever), low thyroid, demodectic mange, luxating patella, inflammatory bowel disease, and cancer in the lines. This breed is notorious for allergies and skin conditions and for eyelid disorders (entropion and ectropion). Some puppies are so wrinkled they must have their eyelids "tacked" until they grow into their skin. He is sensitive to anesthetics and chemicals and should never be casually medicated or sedated. Ears must be kept clean and dry to prevent infections. It is imperative to find an excellent vet who is familiar with Shar-Pei. Lifespan: 8–12 years.

CAUTIONS WHEN BUYING

The Shar-Pei is still recovering from its fad status of the 1980s, when exploitation by unknowledgeable breeders flooded the gene pool with health problems. Some lines have heavier, more jowly heads than others. The loose skin and wrinkles that are superabundant in puppies usually smooth out a great deal with maturity, though some lines maintain adult body wrinkling.

Chinook

Fine for Novice Owners
Good with Children
Medium to Large in Size
Thick, Medium-Length Coat

EXERCISE REQUIRED — HIGH MEDIUM
TRIMMING/CLIPPING REQUIRED — LOW
AMOUNT OF SHEDDING — MEDIUM
ACTIVITY INDOORS — MEDIUM LOW
EASE OF TRAINING — MEDIUM
SOCIABILITY WITH STRANGERS — HIGH
    MEDIUM

TEMPERAMENT

Characterized by his dependable nature, sensible energy level, and sound working ability, the versatile Chinook is both frisky and dignified. He enjoys vigorous outdoor exercise such as jogging, backpacking, carting, agility, weight pulling, herding, and especially recreational sledding and ski-joring. However, he is not a workaholic, and given enough physical and mental outlets for his enthusiasm, he is happy to settle on the sofa during quiet times. Very people-oriented and especially attuned to children, he requires daily companionship (either by humans or other dogs) and can become bored and destructive if left alone too much. Gentleness and nonaggression are his hallmarks. Most will bark to announce visitors, but that's the extent of their guarding inclination. All sweet-natured, slightly reserved breeds have the potential for submissiveness and shyness, and early socialization is required to build a confident temperament. Usually peaceful with other animals, he can be a chaser of furry rodents or trespassing cats. Chinooks are independent thinkers who may use their problem-solving skills to open gates and cupboards. You must stay one step ahead of this intelligent dog. They are also slow to mature, acting like big puppies for several years. Some enjoy digging, and in groups they may point their noses into the air and harmonize in beautiful song.

HISTORY

A blend of Greenland Husky, Saint Bernard, and German/Belgian shepherds, he was developed in New Hampshire and takes his name from the foundation sire of the breed, one of the greatest lead dogs of all time. Chinooks are most famous for forming the backbone of Admiral Byrd's Antarctic expedition in 1928. They might be considered "the gentleman's carriage horse" of the sledding breeds. Registered by the UKC.

PHYSICAL FEATURES

Males stand 23–27 inches and weigh 60–90 pounds. Females stand 21–25 inches and weigh 45–70 pounds. His double coat (some are longer and thicker than others) should be brushed once a week, daily during heavy seasonal shedding. He is usually tawny, ranging from light honey to reddish gold, though other colors are accepted. His ears and tail are natural.

HEALTH ISSUES

Both parents should have OFA certificates (hips) and yearly CERF (eyes). Also ask about seizures and genetic shyness. Lifespan: 12–14 years.

CAUTIONS WHEN BUYING

The modern rebuilding of the breed has focused on temperament, health, and working ability. Thus there is still wide variation in build, size, coat, and especially ear set (pricked, dropped, or "helicoptered" to the side). To promote genetic health and create diversity in the gene pool, crossbreeding is being done with other healthy working breeds, under strict UKC regulations. These Chinook crosses are often available as pets.

Chow Chow (Rough)

Best for Experienced Owners
Good with Older, Considerate Children
Medium in Size
Thick, Medium-Length Coat

EXERCISE REQUIRED — MEDIUM

TRIMMING/CLIPPING REQUIRED — LOW

AMOUNT OF SHEDDING — HIGH

ACTIVITY INDOORS — LOW

EASE OF TRAINING — LOW

SOCIABILITY WITH STRANGERS — LOW

TEMPERAMENT

This dignified, serious dog with the lion-like ruff and scowling expression is a true introvert. Naturally clean and easy to housebreak, quiet and mannerly in the home, he is an impressive companion if you can establish a relationship of mutual respect—i.e., admiring his strong-willed independent character while consistently enforcing household rules so that he respects *you* as well. He does well with daily walks; with his stilted gait, he is not built for strenuous jogging. However, the Smooth Chow is often more active (and more outgoing with strangers) than his Rough brother. He should be accustomed to people at an early age so that his territorial instincts are properly discriminatory. Though he usually minds his own business unless provoked, some can be aggressive with other dogs of the same sex. Some have hunting instincts and can be predatory with cats and tiny dogs. Obedience training will go nowhere if you use old-fashioned "jerking" methods—this proud breed will either shut down or retaliate. Chows cannot be forced to do anything. Modern methods that emphasize food and praise are more productive.

HISTORY

In northern China, he was used for hunting, herding, pulling, and protection and also served as a source of meat and fur. "Chow chow" was a slang term for Oriental curios (including dogs) transported in European trading ships. AKC popularity: 39th of 146 (includes both coats).

PHYSICAL FEATURES

He stands 17–21 inches and weighs 45–75 pounds. His harsh coat with its dense undercoat stands well off his body.

Brush twice a week, daily when he is shedding. Along with heavy seasonal shedding, you'll see loose hair the rest of the year as well. The most common colors are red and black. "Dilute" colors are cinnamon and blue. Creams usually have a light-colored nose, so cannot be shown. His tongue is blue-black. Individuals with pink or spotted tongues are disqualified from show competition. His ears and tail are natural.

HEALTH ISSUES

Both parents should have OFA certificates (hips and elbows). Also ask about luxating patella, low thyroid, allergies and skin conditions, and renal dysplasia in the lines. Eyelid disorders (entropion and ectropion) are a common problem. Avoid puppies with extremely small or deep-set eyes and excessive loose skin on the head. Chows don't do well in extreme heat or high humidity. He is sensitive to anesthetics and should never be casually medicated or sedated. Lifespan: 8–12 years.

CAUTIONS WHEN BUYING

Many people buy Chow puppies because they are adorable teddy bears, then discover that they have a very different personality than other breeds. If a breeder has not emphasized stable temperament, and/or if you don't socialize thoroughly in the first year, you could end up with an intractable, antisocial Chow. Buy the most outgoing puppy you can find and insist on that hip/elbow certification: As many as 50 percent of this breed are dysplastic.

Chow Chow (Smooth)

Best for Experienced Owners
Good with Older, Considerate Children
Medium in Size
Thick, Medium-Length Coat

EXERCISE REQUIRED — MEDIUM

TRIMMING/CLIPPING REQUIRED — LOW

AMOUNT OF SHEDDING — HIGH

ACTIVITY INDOORS — LOW

EASE OF TRAINING — LOW

SOCIABILITY WITH STRANGERS — LOW

TEMPERAMENT

This dignified, serious dog with the lion-like ruff and scowling expression is a true introvert. Naturally clean and easy to housebreak, quiet and mannerly in the home, he is an impressive companion if you can establish a relationship of mutual respect—i.e., admiring his strong-willed independent character while consistently enforcing household rules so that he respects *you* as well. He does well with daily walks; with his stilted gait, he is not built for strenuous jogging. However, the Smooth Chow is often more active (and more outgoing with strangers) than his Rough brother. Still, he should be accustomed to people at an early age so that his territorial instincts are properly discriminatory. Though he usually minds his own business unless provoked, some can be aggressive with other dogs of the same sex. Some have hunting instincts and can be predatory with cats and tiny dogs. Obedience training will go nowhere if you use old-fashioned "jerking" methods—this proud breed will either shut down or retaliate. Chows cannot be forced to do anything. Modern methods that emphasize food and praise are more productive.

HISTORY

In northern China, he was used for hunting, herding, pulling, and protection and also served as a source of meat and fur. "Chow chow" was a slang term for Oriental curios (including dogs) transported in European trading ships. AKC popularity: 39th of 146 (includes both coats).

PHYSICAL FEATURES

He stands 17–21 inches and weighs 45–75 pounds. His harsh coat with its dense undercoat should be brushed twice a week, daily when he is shedding. Along with heavy seasonal shedding, you'll see loose hair the rest of the year as well. The most common colors are red and black. "Dilute" colors are cinnamon and blue. Creams usually have a light-colored nose, so cannot be shown. His tongue is blue-black. Individuals with pink or spotted tongues are disqualified from show competition. His ears and tail are natural.

HEALTH ISSUES

Both parents should have OFA certificates (hips and elbows). Also ask about luxating patella, low thyroid, allergies and skin conditions, and renal dysplasia in the lines. Eyelid disorders (entropion and ectropion) are a common problem. Avoid puppies with extremely small or deep-set eyes and excessive loose skin on the head. Chows don't do well in extreme heat or high humidity. He is sensitive to anesthetics and should never be casually medicated or sedated. Lifespan: 8–12 years.

CAUTIONS WHEN BUYING

Many people buy Chow puppies because they are adorable teddy bears, then discover that they have a very different personality than other breeds. If a breeder has not emphasized stable temperament, and/or if you don't socialize thoroughly in the first year, you could end up with an intractable, antisocial Chow. Buy the most outgoing puppy you can find and insist on that hip/elbow certification: As many as 50 percent of this breed are dysplastic.

Clumber Spaniel

Fine for Novice Owners
Good with Children
Medium in Size
Feathered, Medium-Length Coat

EXERCISE REQUIRED — MEDIUM

TRIMMING/CLIPPING REQUIRED — MEDIUM

AMOUNT OF SHEDDING — HIGH

ACTIVITY INDOORS — LOW

EASE OF TRAINING — MEDIUM

SOCIABILITY WITH STRANGERS — MEDIUM

TEMPERAMENT

The AKC Standard says, "His stature is dignified, his expression pensive, but at the same time, he shows great enthusiasm for work and play." The mild-mannered, almost imperturbable Clumber sometimes puts on aristocratic airs, yet he also plays the clown, greeting people with two tennis balls stuffed into his mouth and his entire rear end wagging. Adults spend much of their time lying around and looking sleepy, but this massive dog needs regular exercise to stay fit. Outdoors he comes alive and moves with great determination—he has been called "a great bustling creature." Fetching and ball playing are good sources of exercise, though too much twisting and jumping could injure a disk in his long back. Most are friendly with everyone, strangers and other animals included. This is not a guard dog. Though stubborn, he does respond to persuasive, persistent, motivational obedience training, especially if it includes food. He resists harshness or force by refusing to move. He does have a mischievous streak, but because of his easygoing approach to life, he is seldom a problem even when he doesn't obey very quickly.

HISTORY

This dependable hunter, named after England's Clumber Park, has been called "the portly gentleman's shooting dog" and "the ideal choice for the man who doesn't like to hunt in a hurry." AKC popularity: 115th of 146.

PHYSICAL FEATURES

Males stand 19–20 inches and weigh 70–85 pounds. Females stand 17–19 inches and weigh 55–70 pounds. Brush and comb his silky coat every other day, and occa-sionally trim straggly hairs. Keep his ear canals clean and dry and his bottom trimmed for cleanliness. Be prepared for a good amount of shedding, more than other spaniels. He is mostly white with a few lemon or orange markings. His ears are natural; his tail is usually docked, though some breeders are no longer doing so.

HEALTH ISSUES

Both parents should have OFA certificates (hips) and yearly CERF (eyes). However, the hip certification may be hard to find. Hip dysplasia is so common in this breed, and breeding stock so limited, that dysplastic dogs are being bred. Fortunately, because of their unusual rolling gait, some members of this breed can show up dysplastic on X ray yet not be affected much in day-to-day living. Eyelid disorders (entropion) are a common problem. Lifespan: 10 years.

CAUTIONS WHEN BUYING

There are only about two thousand Clumbers in the United States and Canada. Litters are not numerous, and a high percentage of pups are kept for showing and breeding, so be prepared to wait up to a year for a pet puppy and to pay $1,000 or more.

Collie (Rough)

Fine for Novice Owners
Good with Children If Raised with Children
Large in Size
Long Coat

EXERCISE REQUIRED — MEDIUM

TRIMMING/CLIPPING REQUIRED — LOW

AMOUNT OF SHEDDING — HIGH

ACTIVITY INDOORS — MEDIUM LOW

EASE OF TRAINING — MEDIUM

SOCIABILITY WITH STRANGERS — MEDIUM

TEMPERAMENT

Proud and animated, sensitive and gentle, the Collie needs moderate exercise and a great deal of personal attention. Some lines are more active than others and enjoy activities such as herding, hiking, and chasing balls, but in general, the Rough Collie is often less athletic and more laid-back than his Smooth brother. Collies are sociable and can become unhappy, noisy, or destructive if left for long periods of time without the companionship of people or other pets. Most are polite with strangers—they say hello, then go lie down—and make sensible watchdogs, but as with most sweet-natured breeds, there is potential for timidity. Young Collies need to be thoroughly socialized in order to build a confident temperament. Most are peaceful with other animals. Thriving on praise and extremely sensitive to correction, a Collie should be trained with positive methods: praise and food rewards. Roughness or jerking on the leash only make him confused and skittish. He is more reactive to loud noises than some other breeds and does not do well in an environment with frequent tension or loud voices. Some are barky, and some may try to herd people and other animals by circling, poking, and nipping.

HISTORY

The Collie originated in Scotland as a plain shepherd dog. Today, with his heavy coat and long, refined head, he looks very different from his working ancestor. AKC popularity: 31st of 146 (includes both Rough and Smooth varieties, which can occur in the same litter).

PHYSICAL FEATURES

Males stand 24–26 inches; females stand 22–24 inches. Weight is 50–75 pounds. Brush and comb his harsh, double coat twice a week, daily during heavy seasonal shedding. Along with his shedding great chunks of hair in the spring and fall, you'll find loose hair the rest of the year as well. Four colors are allowed: sable (gold to mahogany with black-tipped hairs and white markings), tricolor (mostly black, with white markings and tan trim), blue merle (mottled blue/gray/black with white markings and tan trim), and white (mostly white with a few sable, tricolor, or blue merle patches). His ears are natural, but unless weighted into a folding position for several months during adolescence, they may tend to prick up. His tail is natural.

HEALTH ISSUES

Both parents should have OFA certificates (hips) and yearly CERF (eyes). Each individual puppy must have his eyes examined by an AVCO-certified ophthalmologist (not just a regular vet) at six to eight weeks of age. Also ask about seizures, low thyroid, allergies and skin conditions, and bloat in the lines. Lifespan: 12–14 years.

CAUTIONS WHEN BUYING

There are some poorly bred, high-strung lines. Buy only from a breeder who emphasizes sound temperament and who can show you all of the health clearances, especially the puppy eye tests.

Collie (Smooth)

Fine for Novice Owners
Good with Children If Raised with Children
Large in Size
Short Coat

EXERCISE REQUIRED — MEDIUM

TRIMMING/CLIPPING REQUIRED — LOW

AMOUNT OF SHEDDING — HIGH

ACTIVITY INDOORS — MEDIUM LOW

EASE OF TRAINING — MEDIUM

SOCIABILITY WITH STRANGERS — MEDIUM

TEMPERAMENT

Proud and animated, sensitive and gentle, he needs moderate exercise and a great deal of personal attention. In general, the Smooth Collie tends to be more active and athletic than his Rough brother and retains more working instincts. Collies are sociable and can become unhappy, noisy, or destructive if left for long periods of time without the companionship of people or other pets. Most are polite with strangers—they say hello, then go lie down—and make sensible watchdogs, but as with most sweet-natured breeds, there is potential for timidity. Young Collies need to be thoroughly socialized in order to build a confident temperament. Most are peaceful with other animals. Thriving on praise and extremely sensitive to correction, a Collie should be trained with positive methods: praise and food rewards. Roughness or jerking on the leash only make him confused and skittish. He is more reactive to loud noises than some other breeds and does not do well in an environment with frequent tension or loud voices. Some are barky, and some may try to herd people and other animals by circling, poking, and nipping.

HISTORY

The Collie originated in Scotland and was used for herding and for driving livestock to market. Today, with his long, refined head, he looks very different from his working ancestor. AKC popularity: 31st of 146 (includes both Rough and Smooth varieties, which can occur in the same litter).

PHYSICAL FEATURES

Males stand 24–26 inches; females stand 22–24 inches. Weight is 50–75 pounds. Brush his dense double coat once a week, daily during heavy seasonal shedding. Along with his shedding great chunks of hair in the spring and fall, you'll find loose hair the rest of the year as well. Four colors are allowed: sable (gold to mahogany with black-tipped hairs and white markings), tricolor (mostly black, with white markings and tan trim), blue merle (mottled blue/gray/black with white markings and tan trim), and white (mostly white with a few sable, tricolor, or blue merle patches). His ears are natural, but unless weighted into a folding position for several months during adolescence, they may tend to prick up. His tail is natural.

HEALTH ISSUES

Both parents should have OFA certificates (hips) and yearly CERF (eyes). Each individual puppy must have his eyes examined by an AVCO-certified ophthalmologist (not just a regular vet) at six to eight weeks of age. Also ask about seizures, low thyroid, allergies and skin conditions, and bloat in the lines. Lifespan: 12–14 years.

CAUTIONS WHEN BUYING

There are some poorly bred, high-strung lines. Buy only from a breeder who emphasizes sound temperament and who can show you all of the health clearances, especially the puppy eye tests.

Coton de Tulear

(ca-TONE day too-lay-ARE)

Fine for Novice Owners
Good with Older, Considerate Children
Small in Size
Long Coat

EXERCISE REQUIRED — LOW

TRIMMING/CLIPPING REQUIRED — HIGH

MEDIUM LOW

AMOUNT OF SHEDDING — LOW

ACTIVITY INDOORS — MEDIUM

EASE OF TRAINING — MEDIUM

SOCIABILITY WITH STRANGERS — HIGH

TEMPERAMENT

Happy, clownish, and inquisitive, the Coton enjoys clever games of dexterity such as "pull the stale bit of fallen cheese from under the refrigerator with your paw." He is both boisterous and calm, dashing around the yard to play, then snuggling in your lap to snooze. Cotons are very people-oriented and will push for as much attention as they can get. They are so sociable that they don't do well when left for long periods without companionship. Though peaceful and gentle with everyone (humans and other pets), this breed forms a strong bond with his family and can be conservative with strangers. Socialization is important to build a confident, outgoing temperament, as there is a potential for excessive caution. Though he does have a mild stubborn streak, he is normally a "soft" dog and responds well to nonforceful training. He prefers learning tricks to formal obedience and is especially bright-eyed when food treats are offered as rewards. Harshness only makes him wilt.

HISTORY

Developed in Madagascar, an island off the coast of Africa, he was favored by royal families. *Coton* is French for "cotton," referring to the texture of his coat, while Tulear is the trading port where his ancestors were first introduced. Registered by the FCI, UKC, SKC, and AKC-FSS.

PHYSICAL FEATURES

He stands 10–13 inches and weighs 10–15 pounds. His soft, dry, cottony coat needs daily brushing. Pet owners may choose to trim/clip the coat short every four to six weeks. Keep his ear canals clean and dry and his bottom trimmed for cleanliness. Most American clubs and registries follow the breed's Madagascar standard in allowing only white dogs, with limited cream/biscuit shadings accepted. The CTCA also allows black-and-white and tricolor (white with cream/biscuit patches and sprinkled black hairs). His ears and tail are natural.

HEALTH ISSUES

Both parents should have OFA certificates (hips), yearly CERF (eyes), and be screened for luxating patella and low thyroid. Lifespan: 14–16 years.

CAUTIONS WHEN BUYING

There are several Coton clubs in the United States, each with differing opinions and each vying to become "the" national club. Make sure both parents of your puppy are properly registered with one of the registries listed above. Unfortunately, breeders seem to have a tacit agreement to keep prices extremely high—you may be asked to spend $1,500 for a pet puppy. Consider waiting until this fad status dies down or check out similar breeds in the bichon family: Bichon Frise, Bolognese, Havanese, and Maltese.

Curly-Coated Retriever

Fine for Novice Owners
Good with Children
Large in Size
Curly Coat

EXERCISE REQUIRED — HIGH

TRIMMING/CLIPPING REQUIRED — LOW

AMOUNT OF SHEDDING — MEDIUM

ACTIVITY INDOORS — MEDIUM

EASE OF TRAINING — MEDIUM

SOCIABILITY WITH STRANGERS — LOW

TEMPERAMENT

The AKC Standard says, "A correctly-built and tempered Curly will work as long as there is work to be done." This graceful, elegant dog is also strong and robust, quick and agile. His daily exercise requirement is such that he belongs with an athletic owner who will take him jogging, biking, hiking, and swimming. Though reserved and sometimes distrustful with strangers, he should remain poised and hold his ground. A Curly puppy needs more socialization than other retrievers to develop a confident temperament. Many have sensible protective instincts and may not welcome strangers into their homes as will a Golden or Labrador. He relates well to other animals and is playful and accepting. Sometimes described as "wickedly smart," he may use his intelligence in clever, independent ways that suit his own purposes; thus he needs early, consistent obedience training to establish that you are in charge. All retrievers are slow to mature, and the Curly remains playfully puppy-like for many years. This sounds delightful, but does require patience and control to live with.

HISTORY

The oldest of the retrievers, the Curly-Coat was developed in England. In the United States, he is seldom seen outside of the show ring, but in New Zealand, he is a popular duck and quail retriever. AKC popularity: 128th of 146.

PHYSICAL FEATURES

Males stand 25–27 inches; females stand 23–25 inches. Weight is 60–95 pounds. His coat is a mass of short, tight, crisp curls. Deep brushing frizzes the coat, so is done only during shedding seasons to remove dead undercoat. Be aware that this breed is not a hypoallergenic Poodle and does shed moderately. He is solid black or solid liver. His ears and tail are natural.

HEALTH ISSUES

Both parents should have OFA certificates (hips) and yearly CERF (eyes). Also ask about bloat, seizures, low thyroid, and autoimmune problems in the lines. Pattern baldness can occur and consists of hair loss on the neck and/or hind legs, uncurled hair on the sides of the body, or an overall thin, brittle coat. Lifespan: 12 years.

CAUTIONS WHEN BUYING

If you like the general build, robustness, and reputation of retrievers as dependable family dogs, consider this breed as an interesting (and overall healthier) alternative to the more common retrievers. Just remember that a Curly is *not* a ringleted Labrador, but a proud, observant, discriminating dog who requires extensive socialization and activity to be happy.

Dachshund, Longhaired

(DAHKS-hoond)

Fine for Novice Owners
Good with Older, Considerate Children
Little to Small in Size
Feathered, Medium-Length Coat

EXERCISE REQUIRED — LOW

TRIMMING/CLIPPING REQUIRED — MEDIUM

AMOUNT OF SHEDDING — MEDIUM

ACTIVITY INDOORS — MEDIUM

EASE OF TRAINING — MEDIUM

SOCIABILITY WITH STRANGERS — MEDIUM

TEMPERAMENT

Curious, lively, charming, and brave, the Dachshund is similar to a terrier in his demands to be in on everything. He becomes very attached to his owner and firmly believes that sleeping under the bedcovers is in the Dachshund Bill of Rights. Though adaptable to virtually any lifestyle, he does need his walks and plenty of companionship, either by humans or other pets, with whom he is quite sociable. He especially enjoys the company of other wiener dogs. This comical clown loves to play games and has a great sense of humor. He is bright and clever and likes to do things his own way. Cheerful, food-based training methods are recommended, as Dachsies are proud little dogs who will resist force. They may respond defensively if jerked around, handled harshly, or teased. Most are extremely alert watchdogs. They tend to bark sharply, and their hunting and tunneling instincts may result in holes in your garden. They can be possessive of their food and toys and are notoriously difficult to housebreak. The Longhaired variety has more of a gentle dignity and tends to be sweeter, more docile, and more obedient than the Smooth or Wirehaired.

HISTORY

The *dachs* (badger) *hund* (dog) or "Teckel" began as a twenty-five-pound hunter of the thirty-five-pound German badger. Eventually he was bred down in size to hunt rabbits. AKC popularity: 5th of 146.

PHYSICAL FEATURES

Miniatures are about 5 inches and 8–11 pounds. Standards are 8-9 inches and 16-32 pounds. "Tweenie" is an informal term for individuals who fall between the two sizes, though fanciers prefer "oversized miniature" or "small standard." Brush and comb twice a week and occasionally trim straggly hairs. Keep his ear canals clean and dry and his bottom trimmed for cleanliness. The most common colors are red, red sable, and black-and-tan. Other colors include blue, chocolate, Isabella, cream, piebald, brindle, dapple, and double dapple (dapple and white). His ears and tail are natural.

HEALTH ISSUES

Ask about low thyroid, urinary stones, seizures, and heart disease. Of all breeds, Dachshunds are the most susceptible to back problems (disk disease), which can be exacerbated by excessive high-jumping or sitting up and begging, dashing down stairs, being picked up without proper support, and obesity. Blues are susceptible to color mutant alopecia. Double dapples may have vision and hearing problems. Lifespan: 15 years.

CAUTIONS WHEN BUYING

Many unknowledgeable people are breeding Dachshunds for "cuteness," without regard for stable temperament or health. Be sure both parents (and preferably other relatives) are outgoing and confident. Be sure they have strong backs and move well. Then socialize your puppy extensively, immediately correct persistent barking or possessive aggression, and don't allow him to be sharp or nasty with anyone.

Dachshund, Smooth (DAHKS-hoond)

Fine for Novice Owners
Good with Older, Considerate Children
Little to Small in Size
Smooth Coat

EXERCISE REQUIRED — LOW
TRIMMING/CLIPPING REQUIRED — LOW
AMOUNT OF SHEDDING — MEDIUM
ACTIVITY INDOORS — HIGH
EASE OF TRAINING — MEDIUM LOW
SOCIABILITY WITH STRANGERS — MEDIUM
    LOW

TEMPERAMENT

Curious, lively, charming, and brave, the Dachshund is similar to a terrier in his demands to be in on everything. He becomes very attached to his owner and firmly believes that sleeping under the bedcovers is in the Dachshund Bill of Rights. Though adaptable to virtually any lifestyle, he does need his walks and plenty of companionship, either by humans or other pets, with whom he is quite sociable. He especially enjoys the company of other wiener dogs. This comical clown loves to play games and has a great sense of humor. He is bright and clever and likes to do things his own way. Cheerful, food-based training methods are recommended, as Dachsies are proud little dogs who will resist force. They may respond defensively if jerked around, handled harshly, or teased. Most are extremely alert watchdogs. They tend to bark sharply, and their hunting and tunneling instincts may result in holes in your garden. They can be possessive of their food and toys and are notoriously difficult to housebreak. The Smooth variety tends to be more active, mischievous, and obstinate than the Longhaired (though less so than the Wire). Smooths are more apt to attach themselves to one person and are often more aloof with strangers.

HISTORY

The *dachs* (badger) *hund* (dog) or "Teckel" began as a twenty-five-pound hunter of the thirty-five-pound German badger. Eventually he was bred down in size to hunt rabbits. AKC popularity: 5th of 146.

PHYSICAL FEATURES

Miniatures are about 5 inches and 8–11 pounds. Standards are 8–9 inches and 16–32 pounds. "Tweenie" is an informal term for individuals who fall between the two sizes, though fanciers prefer "oversized miniature" or "small standard." His hard coat needs only an occasional quick brushing. Keep his ear canals clean and dry. The most common colors are red, red sable, and black-and-tan. Other colors include blue, chocolate, Isabella, cream, piebald, brindle, dapple, and double dapple (dapple and white). His ears and tail are natural.

HEALTH ISSUES

Ask about low thyroid, urinary stones, seizures, and heart disease. Of all breeds, Dachshunds are the most susceptible to back problems (disk disease), which can be exacerbated by excessive high-jumping or sitting up and begging, dashing down stairs, being picked up without proper support, and obesity. Blues are susceptible to color mutant alopecia. Double dapples may have vision and hearing problems. Lifespan: 15 years.

CAUTIONS WHEN BUYING

Many unknowledgeable people are breeding Dachshunds for "cuteness," without regard for stable temperament or health. Be sure both parents (and preferably other relatives) are outgoing and confident. Be sure they have strong backs and move well. Then socialize your puppy extensively, immediately correct persistent barking or possessive aggression, and don't allow him to be sharp or nasty with anyone.

Dachshund, Wirehaired

(DAHKS-hoond)

Fine for Novice Owners
Good with Older, Considerate Children
Little to Small in Size
Wiry Coat

EXERCISE REQUIRED — LOW
TRIMMING/CLIPPING REQUIRED — MEDIUM
AMOUNT OF SHEDDING — LOW
ACTIVITY INDOORS — HIGH
EASE OF TRAINING — MEDIUM LOW
SOCIABILITY WITH STRANGERS — MEDIUM

TEMPERAMENT

Curious, lively, charming, and brave, the Dachshund is similar to a terrier in his demands to be in on everything. He becomes very attached to his owner and firmly believes that sleeping under the bedcovers is in the Dachshund Bill of Rights. Though adaptable to virtually any lifestyle, he does need his walks and plenty of companionship, either by humans or other pets, with whom he is quite sociable. He especially enjoys the company of other wiener dogs. This comical clown loves to play games and has a great sense of humor. He is bright and clever and likes to do things his own way. Cheerful, food-based training methods are recommended, as Dachsies are proud little dogs who will resist force. They may respond defensively if jerked around, handled harshly, or teased. Most are extremely alert watchdogs. They tend to bark sharply, and their hunting and tunneling instincts may result in holes in your garden. They can be possessive of their food and toys and are notoriously difficult to housebreak. The Wirehaired tends to be the most active and mischievous of the three coat varieties: a bold, extroverted clown.

HISTORY

The *dachs* (badger) *hund* (dog) or "Teckel" began as a twenty-five pound hunter of the thirty-five pound German badger. Eventually he was bred down in size to hunt rabbits. AKC popularity: 5th of 146.

PHYSICAL FEATURES

Miniatures are about 5 inches and 8-11 pounds. Standards are 8-9 inches and 16-32 pounds. "Tweenie" is an informal term for individuals who fall between the two sizes, though fanciers prefer "oversized miniature" or "small standard." Brush and comb twice a week. Show dogs are "stripped" (dead coat plucked out) every few months; pet owners may opt for more convenient clipping. Keep his ear canals clean and dry. The most common colors are "wild boar" (grizzled), red, red sable, and black-and-tan. Other colors include blue, chocolate, Isabella, cream, piebald, brindle, dapple, and double dapple (dapple and white). His ears and tail are natural.

HEALTH ISSUES

Ask about low thyroid, urinary stones, seizures, and heart disease. Of all breeds, Dachshunds are the most susceptible to back problems (disk disease), which can be exacerbated by excessive high-jumping or sitting up and begging, dashing down stairs, being picked up without proper support, and obesity. Blues are susceptible to color mutant alopecia. Double dapples may have vision and hearing problems. Lifespan: 15 years.

CAUTIONS WHEN BUYING

Many unknowledgeable people are breeding Dachshunds for "cuteness," without regard for stable temperament or health. Be sure both parents (and preferably other relatives) are outgoing and confident. Be sure they have strong backs and move well. Then socialize your puppy extensively, immediately correct persistent barking or possessive aggression, and don't allow him to be sharp or nasty with anyone.

DALMATIAN

Best for Experienced Owners
Good with Children If Raised with Children
Medium to Large in Size
Smooth Coat

EXERCISE REQUIRED — HIGH

TRIMMING/CLIPPING REQUIRED — LOW

AMOUNT OF SHEDDING — HIGH

ACTIVITY INDOORS — HIGH

EASE OF TRAINING — MEDIUM

SOCIABILITY WITH STRANGERS — MEDIUM

TEMPERAMENT

When well-bred, the Dalmatian is a dependable, dignified gentleman, yet high-spirited and playful. This athletic, vigorous dog has great endurance and a working heritage and should be taken jogging, hiking, or biking on a regular basis, or otherwise allowed to romp in a safe, enclosed area. Canine activities such as advanced obedience and agility (obstacle course) are highly recommended. Too much confinement (especially without the companionship of his family) and too little mental stimulation lead to boredom, hyperactivity, and destructive behaviors. Well-bred Dals love children but may be too exuberant for toddlers. Some greet strangers with enthusiastic jumping, while others are politely reserved. Some have sensible protective instincts. However, skittishness and/or aggression are seen in some lines, and socialization is required to promote a stable temperament. Usually good with other pets, the Dal is especially fond of horses. He is an independent thinker, but in the right hands is capable of learning and doing anything. Owners who don't understand the necessity of leadership or training will find him an impossible handful. Young Dals are especially rowdy and can excavate great holes in your yard.

HISTORY

"The Carriage Dog" has always been a versatile working dog: cart puller, sheepherder, vermin hunter, bird dog, circus performer, stable guardian, coach and carriage follower, and firehouse mascot. AKC popularity: 30th of 146.

PHYSICAL FEATURES

He stands 19–24 inches and weighs 40–70 pounds. His dense coat requires daily brushing to control his year-round shedding. He is white with black or liver spots. Individuals with patches rather than distinct spots may not be shown in conformation classes. His ears and tail are natural.

HEALTH PROBLEMS

Both parents should have OFA certificates (hips) and yearly CERF (eyes) and be screened for low thyroid. Also ask about seizures and allergies in the lines. Deafness is the major concern: Puppies should come with a BAER printout that shows normal bilateral hearing. An estimated 12 percent are born deaf, while another 22 percent can hear in only one ear. All Dalmatians excrete high levels of uric acid, which can form dangerous urinary stones. They should always have unlimited access to water and free access to the outside (a doggy door) or be taken out frequently to urinate. With their short coat, they are sensitive to extremes of heat and cold. Lifespan: 12–14 years.

CAUTIONS WHEN BUYING

The movie *101 Dalmatians* set this breed up for exploitation by unknowledgeable breeders, producing a host of genetic temperament and health problems that responsible breeders are still struggling with. To avoid a skittish or aggressive Dalmatian, buy only from a breeder who emphasizes stable temperament and intelligence (view both parents) and look for all of the health clearances. It should be emphasized that this breed sheds constantly—you'll find stiff white hairs everywhere.

Dandie Dinmont Terrier

Best for Experienced Owners
Good with Older, Considerate Children
Small in Size
Unusual Coat (see Physical Features below)

EXERCISE REQUIRED — MEDIUM LOW

TRIMMING/CLIPPING REQUIRED — HIGH
    MEDIUM

AMOUNT OF SHEDDING — LOW

ACTIVITY INDOORS — MEDIUM

EASE OF TRAINING — LOW

SOCIABILITY WITH STRANGERS — HIGH

TEMPERAMENT

The plucky Dandie is one of the brightest of the terriers, and also one of the most independent. Though undemanding, dignified, and relaxed in the home, he can become bold and tenacious in a working situation when his hunting instincts are aroused. One look at his long, low-slung body and it's obvious that he isn't built for long-distance jogging or running beside your bike. He is content with daily walks and regular opportunities to play. Though friendly and diplomatic with strangers, the Dandie is confident of his territory and makes a determined watchdog. He doesn't put on a macho posturing act with other animals, as some terriers do, but he is exceedingly tough and will not back down from a confrontation. Two adult males are definitely an unwise combination. Assertive and strong-willed, with a definite mind of his own, he requires consistent leadership. Obedience training should include food rewards and praise, for the Dandie is sensitive and proud and will become more obstinate and uncooperative with heavy-handed training. Like many terriers, he can be possessive of his food and toys and is a natural digger. Though not particularly noisy, he has a surprisingly deep bark.

HISTORY

He hunted otter and badger in the border country between England and Scotland. In Sir Walter Scott's novel about a farmer named Dandie Dinmont, hunting terriers were described, and these later became known as Dandie Dinmont's dogs. AKC popularity: 138th of 146.

PHYSICAL FEATURES

He stands 8–11 inches and weighs 24–28 pounds. His coat is a mixture of hard and soft hair, with a silky, bushy topknot. Brush and comb twice a week and keep his bottom trimmed for cleanliness. Keep his ear canals clean and dry. Show dogs are "stripped" (dead coat plucked out) every few months; pet owners may opt for more convenient clipping. By the age of ten months, black-and-tan puppies will turn pepper (silvery gray to bluish black), with tan legs and a silvery white topknot. Brown puppies will turn mustard (pale fawn to reddish brown) with darker legs and a creamy white topknot. His ears and tail are natural.

HEALTH ISSUES

Ask about glaucoma and low thyroid in the lines. Long-backed breeds are susceptible to disk disease, which can be exacerbated by excessive high-jumping, dashing down stairs, being picked up without proper support, and obesity. Lifespan: 12–15 years.

CAUTIONS WHEN BUYING

This distinctive-looking breed with the curvy outline and large top-knotted head is difficult to find, but quality is high. Time spent on a waiting list should be well worth it.

Doberman Pinscher

Best for Experienced Owners
Good with Children If Raised with Children
Large in Size
Smooth Coat

EXERCISE REQUIRED — HIGH MEDIUM
TRIMMING/CLIPPING REQUIRED — LOW
AMOUNT OF SHEDDING — MEDIUM
ACTIVITY INDOORS — MEDIUM
EASE OF TRAINING — HIGH MEDIUM
SOCIABILITY WITH STRANGERS — MEDIUM
LOW

TEMPERAMENT

The Doberman varies tremendously in personality: Some are bold and dominant, some are sweet and mellow, some are good-natured goofballs, and some are rather high-strung. This athletic dog can be busy and needs brisk walking every day and all-out running as often as possible. Too little exercise and too little companionship can lead to restlessness and other behavioral problems. Mental exercise (advanced obedience, agility, tracking, Schutzhund) is just as important to this thinking breed. Though some Dobermans are big softies who love everyone, most are reserved with strangers and intensely loyal to and protective of their family. Early and extensive socialization is mandatory to avoid either shyness or sharpness. Some are dominant with other dogs and some are confirmed cat chasers, while others love small animals. Some excel in advanced obedience competition, while others are hardheaded and will test to find their place in the pecking order. Calm, consistent leadership is a must, and obedience training must be upbeat and persuasive rather than sharp. A Dobe is extremely proud and sensitive and can become defensive if jerked around. This breed does not tolerate teasing or mischief.

HISTORY

He was developed in Germany by Louis Dobermann (note different spelling) as a guard and military dog. AKC popularity: 22nd of 146.

PHYSICAL FEATURES

Males stand 26–28 inches; females stand 24–26 inches. He weighs 60–85 pounds. His hard coat needs only an occasional quick brushing. He is black, red (dark brown), blue, or Isabella (fawn), always with rust trim. White Dobermans (actually cream, with blue eyes and a pink nose) cannot be shown in conformation classes and are susceptible to a number of health problems associated with their albinism. His ears may be cropped or left naturally hanging; his tail is docked.

HEALTH ISSUES

Both parents should have the following certificates: OFA (hips), cardiac-clear (cardiomyopathy), normal thyroid (full panel), and a DNA certificate that shows whether they are affected, carriers, or clear of vWD (at least one parent must be clear). Also ask about Wobbler's syndrome, renal dysplasia, autoimmune problems, and cancer in the lines. Lifespan: 10–12 years.

CAUTIONS WHEN BUYING

Compared to American show lines, German-bred lines focus on performance sports such as Schutzhund (protection, obedience, tracking). Working lines are generally stockier (as opposed to more elegant and refined) and temperaments are "harder" and more work-oriented. Know what you're looking for: Schutzhund, obedience competition, show dog, or couch potato. You must choose your lines appropriately.

Dogo Argentino

(DOE-go ar-jen-TEE-no)

Best for Experienced Owners
Good with Children If Raised with Children
Large in Size
Smooth Coat

EXERCISE REQUIRED — HIGH MEDIUM

TRIMMING/CLIPPING REQUIRED — LOW

AMOUNT OF SHEDDING — MEDIUM

ACTIVITY INDOORS — MEDIUM LOW

EASE OF TRAINING — MEDIUM

SOCIABILITY WITH STRANGERS — MEDIUM

TEMPERAMENT

Powerful yet possessed of an almost feline grace, the Dogo is fearless yet sensitive, vivacious yet calm. This impressive dog is best owned by active people who will develop his athletic abilities. He must have physical exercise to maintain his superb muscle structure and mental exercise to satisfy his desire to work and hunt. Despite his intimidating appearance, he is usually outgoing and friendly, yet is also a vigilant guardian with a thunderous bark when faced with a threat. Early socialization is an absolute requirement to build the stable, discriminating temperament this breed is known for. Though tough to the core, Dogos love to be petted. They crave close physical contact, leaning against you and lying on your feet. Dog aggression can be a problem; he should be thoroughly socialized with other dogs from an early age, and two of the same sex should not be kept together. With his strong prey drive, he should not be kept with cats or other small pets unless raised with them. Strong-willed and independent, but also highly intelligent, he will respect an owner who is equally confident and consistent. Because of his hound heritage, he is constantly intrigued by the exciting smells around him, so you must work to keep his attention. Use positive methods (praise and food incentives), as Dogos are proud dogs who do not understand forceful training.

HISTORY

A recent (mid–twentieth century) creation of two Argentinian brothers, the Dogo is a judicious blend of ten parent breeds. He is a magnificent big-game hunter (primarily boar and mountain lion) and also a guardian of his family and home. Registered by the FCI and AKC-FSS.

PHYSICAL FEATURES

He stands 24–27 inches and weighs 80–110 pounds. His thick, glossy coat needs only an occasional quick brushing. He is solid white, though some standards allow minimal body ticking. His ears may be left hanging naturally or cropped. His tail is natural.

HEALTH ISSUES

Both parents should have OFA certificates (hips). Each puppy should come with a BAER printout that shows normal bilateral hearing. Also ask about allergies and other skin and coat conditions. White coats are sensitive to sunburn; provide shade when outdoors for long periods. Lifespan: 12 years.

CAUTIONS WHEN BUYING

There are two Dogo clubs in the United States, each following different standards that vary significantly from the original FCI standard. Make sure both parents are registered with the FCI and that you see the hip certificates—health guarantees are essential but are *not* a substitute for hip X rays and certification. This is a working breed: Look for performance or temperament titles (obedience, CGC, TT, tracking, Schutzhund) in the pedigree or ask if the breeder hunts with his dogs. Prices are high: $1,000 for a pet.

Dogue de Bordeaux (dog duh bor-DOE)

Best for Experienced Owners
Good with Children If Raised with Children
Giant in Size
Smooth Coat

EXERCISE REQUIRED — MEDIUM

TRIMMING/CLIPPING REQUIRED — LOW

AMOUNT OF SHEDDING — MEDIUM

ACTIVITY INDOORS — LOW

EASE OF TRAINING — LOW

SOCIABILITY WITH STRANGERS — LOW

TEMPERAMENT

The Dogue (meaning mastiff) is quiet, calm, and relaxed . . . until aroused. Don't be lulled by his bulk—he can be surprisingly athletic and agile when necessary. This is not an apartment dog (to stay fit, he needs some space and moderate daily exercise), but more than anything else, he requires personal interaction. Picture that massive body trying to settle itself onto your lap and an enormous tongue swiping across your face. Dogues love to be an integral part of your family. Puppies should be friendly and trusting, and with proper socialization, become reserved and discriminating as they mature. As with all mastiffs, socialization is an absolute requirement to avoid either aggression or shyness. The Dogue likes children, but can be overprotective if he perceives a threat to "his" child—i.e., roughhousing with a friend. Animal aggression can be a problem; most will not start fights, but they will surely finish them. This stubborn breed is inclined to do things his own way, but he will respond to early, consistent training that includes firm leadership, cheerful praise, and food rewards. Dogues have an astonishing talent for snoring, sliming, and drooling. Slobber towels should be high on your list of canine accessories.

HISTORY

Descended from the ancient (now extinct) Molosser who fought in the Roman Colosseum, this French mastiff herded cattle, baited bulls and bears, and protected homes, butcher shops, and vineyards. Registered by the FCI and UKC.

PHYSICAL FEATURES

Males stand 25–27 inches and weigh 120–160 pounds. Females stand 23–25 inches and weigh 100–130 pounds. His hard coat requires only an occasional quick brushing. He is dark auburn or fawn, with a red mask or a black mask. His ears and tail are natural.

HEALTH ISSUES

Both parents should have OFA certificates (hips). Also ask about bloat, elbow dysplasia, low thyroid, demodectic mange, cardiomyopathy, OCD, panosteitis, and cancer in the lines. Eyelid disorders (entropion) can be a problem. He is sensitive to anesthetics, vaccines, and chemicals and should never be casually medicated or sedated. He is susceptible to respiratory difficulties and heatstroke in hot, humid, and/or stuffy conditions. Dogues love shade and air-conditioning. Lifespan: 8–10 years.

CAUTIONS WHEN BUYING

Most people first "met" the DdB when they saw the movie *Turner and Hooch*. All of the molossan (mastiff) breeds have exceedingly strong natural instincts to protect and defend their loved ones. Owners must understand these instincts and channel them properly through socialization and training, so that the adult dog turns out stable and not a menace to society. Make sure you see the hip clearance certificate—many breeders are still not certifying hips.

English Cocker Spaniel

Fine for Novice Owners
Good with Children
Small in Size
Feathered, Medium-Length Coat

EXERCISE REQUIRED — MEDIUM

TRIMMING/CLIPPING REQUIRED — HIGH

AMOUNT OF SHEDDING — MEDIUM

ACTIVITY INDOORS — MEDIUM

EASE OF TRAINING — HIGH

SOCIABILITY WITH STRANGERS — HIGH

TEMPERAMENT

The AKC Standard says, "His enthusiasm in the field and the incessant action of his tail while at work indicate how much he enjoys the hunting for which he was bred." With more sporting instincts than the American Cocker Spaniel, the lively English Cocker likes more exercise. When well socialized, he has a merry tail-wagging nature and is sweet and gentle with everyone. Some are on the reserved side, and there is timidity and excessive submissiveness in some lines. This equable dog is responsive to persuasive obedience training that includes praise and food rewards. However, he is sensitive to harsh handling and may respond defensively if jerked around on the leash or teased. Housebreaking, submissive urination (sudden wetting when excited or frightened), and chronic barking can be problems. Unless taught to be independent, some individuals are so persistently affectionate that they become clingy and demanding of attention.

HISTORY

This little English hunter specialized in the woodcock game bird—hence his name. AKC popularity: 77th of 146.

PHYSICAL FEATURES

He stands 14–17 inches and weighs 25–35 pounds. Brush and comb his silky coat every other day and clip every eight weeks. Keep his ear canals clean and dry and his bottom trimmed for cleanliness. More than half are blue roan. Other colors include black, liver, red, deep golden (not the creamy buff of the American Cocker), other roans (liver, red, orange), and particolor. Tan trim can occur on most colors. His ears are natural; his tail is docked.

HEALTH ISSUES

Both parents should have OFA certificates (hips) and yearly CERF (eyes). Particolor puppies should come with a BAER printout that shows normal bilateral hearing. Also ask about low thyroid, seizures, allergies, and skin conditions in the lines. Lifespan: 12–15 years.

CAUTIONS WHEN BUYING

English Cockers are divided into show types and field types. For a serious hunting dog, choose a shorter-coated, field-bred line. Though some show lines retain hunting instincts, most are too heavily coated for practical field work. If you're comparing the two Cocker breeds (American and English), the head and muzzle of the English is long and narrow (setter-like), contrasted with the round domed skull and short, broad muzzle of the American. The English has not been exploited as much by unknowledgeable breeders and is thus a safer bet as a friendly, sociable, healthy pet.

English Foxhound

Best for Experienced Owners
Good with Children
Large in Size
Smooth Coat

EXERCISE REQUIRED — HIGH

TRIMMING/CLIPPING REQUIRED — LOW

AMOUNT OF SHEDDING — MEDIUM

ACTIVITY INDOORS — MEDIUM

EASE OF TRAINING — LOW

SOCIABILITY WITH STRANGERS — MEDIUM

TEMPERAMENT

The stable, good-natured Foxhound makes an amiable companion when vigorously exercised (jogging, biking, running), though some individuals prefer living kenneled with other hunting hounds, rather than fulfilling the role of house pet. Without outlets for his energy, he is rambunctious and prone to destructive chewing. Unless trained for hunting, he should not be let off-leash except in a safe, enclosed area, for he is an explorer who will drop his nose to the ground and take off. His reaction to strangers varies from friendly to reserved, and some are mildly protective. With other dogs he is sociable and gregarious (indeed he is happiest when other dogs are present in the home), but he has a high prey drive and may chase smaller pets. As with other scenthounds, training takes a while, for he's independent and slow to obey. He is slow to mature and remains playfully puppy-like for many years, which does require patience and control. He bays a lot and can be hard to housebreak.

HISTORY

This British scenthound usually hunts in packs, trailing foxes while the huntsmen follow on horseback. AKC popularity: 145th of 146.

PHYSICAL FEATURES

He stands 21–25 inches and weighs 60–95 pounds. His hard coat needs only an occasional quick brushing. Keep his ear canals clean and dry. He is usually tricolor (black, tan, and white), red-and-white, tan-and-white, or lemon-and-white. His ears and tail are natural.

HEALTH ISSUES

Both parents should have OFA certificates (hips). Lifespan: 10–12 years.

CAUTIONS WHEN BUYING

Foxhounds are divided into show types and field types. Show lines usually retain hunting instincts, but don't expect the same serious hunting drive as a Foxhound from field lines. Field lines, on the other hand, may be too energetic and businesslike to be at their best as pets. See also American Foxhound.

English Setter (Bench Type)

Fine for Novice Owners
Good with Children
Large in Size
Feathered, Medium-Length Coat

EXERCISE REQUIRED — MEDIUM

TRIMMING/CLIPPING REQUIRED — MEDIUM

AMOUNT OF SHEDDING — MEDIUM

ACTIVITY INDOORS — LOW

EASE OF TRAINING — MEDIUM

SOCIABILITY WITH STRANGERS — HIGH

TEMPERAMENT

The English is the mildest-mannered, gentlest, most mellow of the setters. Puppies are energetic, but adults are content with long daily walks and occasional running and fetching games. The graceful, elegant English Setter is a sweet-natured, sociable dog who won't thrive if left alone all day without the companionship of people or other pets. Like all setters he has an obstinate streak that takes the form of resistance rather than wild disobedience: He'll simply brace his legs and refuse to walk. You must be persistent, but never heavy-handed. Setters also have long memories: Once they learn something (whether right or wrong), they'll remember it for a long time. On the negative side, this means bad habits can be difficult to break and that harsh handling is not easily forgotten. House-breaking may go slowly.

HISTORY

The oldest of the setter breeds, he was developed in England. AKC popularity: 91st of 146.

PHYSICAL FEATURES

Males stand 24–26 inches and weigh 60–80 pounds. Females stand 22–24 inches and weigh 45–55 pounds. Brush and comb his silky coat every other day and occasionally trim straggly hairs. Keep his ear canals clean and dry and his bottom trimmed for cleanliness. He may be blue belton (mostly white with black flecking), orange belton (tan flecking), or tricolor (blue belton with tan trim). Liver belton and lemon belton are less common. His ears and tail are natural.

HEALTH ISSUES

Both parents should have OFA certificates (hips) and yearly CERF (eyes). Puppies should come with a BAER printout that shows normal bilateral hearing. Also ask about low thyroid in the lines. Lifespan: 10–12 years.

CAUTIONS WHEN BUYING

English Setters are divided into two types: the bench or show type (AKC registered) is much calmer and more laid-back than the field or Llewellin type (see next profile). Field-bred setters are also smaller and lighter boned, with a broader head and much less hair. If you want your setter for hunting and choose to buy from a show line, make sure there are field titles or hunting test titles (JH, MH, SH) in the pedigree.

English Setter
(Field or Llewellin Type)

Fine for Novice Owners
Good with Children
Medium in Size
Feathered, Medium-Length Coat

EXERCISE REQUIRED — HIGH

TRIMMING/CLIPPING REQUIRED — LOW

AMOUNT OF SHEDDING — MEDIUM

ACTIVITY INDOORS — MEDIUM

EASE OF TRAINING — MEDIUM

SOCIABILITY WITH STRANGERS — HIGH

TEMPERAMENT

Though the gentlest and mildest-mannered of the setters, he is lively and needs enough running exercise (jogging, biking, hiking, field work) that he belongs with an athletic owner. This sweet-natured, sociable dog does not thrive when left alone all day without the companionship of people or other pets. Like all setters he has an obstinate streak that takes the form of resistance rather than wild disobedience: He'll simply brace his legs and refuse to walk. You must be persistent, but never heavy-handed. Setters also have long memories: Once they learn something (whether right or wrong), they'll remember it for a long time. On the negative side, this means bad habits can be difficult to break and that harsh handling is not easily forgotten. Housebreaking may go slowly.

HISTORY

The oldest of the setter breeds, he was developed in England. Fast working and wide ranging, the Llewellin Setter is a consistent winner at national pointing trials. Registered by FDSB.

PHYSICAL FEATURES

He stands 18–22 inches and weighs 35–45 pounds. Brush and comb his silky coat once or twice a week, depending on length and feathering. Keep his ear canals clean and dry and his bottom trimmed for cleanliness. He is mostly white with patches and ticking of black or tan (occasionally of liver or lemon). He may also be tricolor (white with black patches and tan trim). His ears and tail are natural.

HEALTH ISSUES

Both parents should have OFA certificates (hips) and yearly CERF (eyes). Puppies should come with a BAER printout that shows normal bilateral hearing. Also ask about low thyroid in the lines. Lifespan: 12 years.

CAUTIONS WHEN BUYING

English Setters are divided into two types: The field or Llewellin type (FDSB registered) is more energetic than the bench or show type (AKC registered). Bench Setters are also taller, with a longer, narrower head, longer ears, and much more hair.

English Shepherd

Best for Experienced Owners
Good with Children
Medium in Size
Feathered, Medium-Length Coat

EXERCISE REQUIRED — HIGH
TRIMMING/CLIPPING REQUIRED — LOW
AMOUNT OF SHEDDING — MEDIUM
ACTIVITY INDOORS — MEDIUM
EASE OF TRAINING — HIGH
SOCIABILITY WITH STRANGERS — MEDIUM

TEMPERAMENT

Active and athletic, yet gentle and steady, the English Shepherd is noted for his calm dependability and is content to curl up at your feet at the end of the day. However, that day should include a good amount of physical exercise and mental stimulation. Herding, advanced obedience, agility, jogging or biking, chasing balls, and playing Frisbee are productive outlets for this breed's enthusiasm. Most are polite with strangers and make sensible watchdogs, but extensive socialization is required when young to avoid shyness. Most are fine with other pets if raised with them, but they can be dominant with strange animals. This is an attentive, sensitive breed who likes to keep his eye on you. One of the most capable and trainable of all breeds, he is an all-purpose working and competition dog who learns quickly, yet he does have the independence and good judgment of a herding breed. This is not a "push-button" breed—you must have the confidence to establish and enforce rules, or he may make up his own. English Shepherds prefer their charges (family members and other pets) to be gathered together and may try to accomplish this by circling, poking, and nipping.

HISTORY

Brought to America by the first English settlers, he was developed by American farmers and ranchers and was informally known as a "farm collie" or "farm shepherd." Recognized by the UKC.

PHYSICAL FEATURES

Size is quite variable: 18–24 inches and 40–90 pounds, though medium-sized is preferred. Some coats are fairly short and easy to care for, while others have a heavier undercoat and feathering that requires frequent combing. Colors include black-and-tan, tricolor, black-and-white, and sable-and-white. Chocolate or red are less common. His ears and tail are natural, though an occasional dog is born with a bobtail.

HEALTH ISSUES

Both parents should have OFA certificates (hips) and yearly CERF (eyes). Lifespan: 12–15 years.

CAUTIONS WHEN BUYING

Not as high-powered or intense as a Border Collie or Australian Shepherd, the English Shepherd often makes a better family pet—as long as his energy is channeled through training and other activities. If you want an undemanding dog who lies around much of the time, the English Shepherd is not for you. This smart dog must be made part of the family, given attention, and worked with regularly.

English Springer Spaniel

Fine for Novice Owners
Good with Children If Raised with Children
Medium in Size
Feathered, Medium-Length Coat

EXERCISE REQUIRED — HIGH

TRIMMING/CLIPPING REQUIRED — HIGH
  MEDIUM

AMOUNT OF SHEDDING — MEDIUM

ACTIVITY INDOORS — MEDIUM

EASE OF TRAINING — HIGH MEDIUM

SOCIABILITY WITH STRANGERS — HIGH
  MEDIUM

TEMPERAMENT

This cheerful, playful, high-spirited tail-wagger needs at least one long, vigorous run every day. Without exercise an English Springer can be a handful, especially when young. His opinion of strangers varies from friendly to reserved; most are good watchdogs, but not guardians. There is serious dominance/aggression lurking in the background of some lines. Early socialization *outside of the home* is critical for stability, as is a sound genetic foundation (stable parents). Most individuals are gregarious with other animals, though there is some same-sex aggression. Springers can be boisterous, but are eager to please and respond well to positive methods of obedience training. Some can be so persistently affectionate that they become clingy or demanding, which can result in separation anxiety and destructiveness when left alone. Many individuals love getting into puddles and water bowls and tracking mud through the house.

HISTORY

The name of this English sporting dog is derived from his duties of "springing" pheasants into the air for the hunter to shoot. AKC popularity: 27th of 146.

PHYSICAL FEATURES

He stands 19–20 inches and weighs 40–55 pounds. Brush and comb his silky coat every other day and clip every twelve weeks. (Field-bred dogs have much shorter coats that are easier to care for.) Keep his ear canals clean and dry and his bottom trimmed for cleanliness. In show lines, the traditional color pattern is mostly liver or mostly black, with flashy white markings and occasionally tan trim. Field lines usually have more white, with the black or liver occurring as patching and ticking. His ears are natural; his tail is docked.

HEALTH ISSUES

Both parents should have the following certificates: OFA (hips), yearly CERF (eyes), and normal PFK (no phosphofructokinase deficiency). Ask about dominance/aggression, low thyroid, vWD, seizures, allergies, and skin conditions in the lines. Lifespan: 12 years.

CAUTIONS WHEN BUYING

This breed has been exploited by unknowledgeable breeders, and temperament/health problems abound in such lines. Buy only from a breeder who can show you all of the health clearances and whose dogs are exceedingly good-natured. Look for a balanced pedigree with Ch. titles and performance (obedience, agility, field) titles. TT or CGC titles, which test for stable temperament, are a plus. Springers are divided into show lines and field lines. Though some show lines retain hunting instincts, opt for the field strains for serious hunting.

English Toy Spaniel

Fine for Novice Owners
Good with Older, Considerate Children
Little in Size
Feathered, Medium-Length Coat

EXERCISE REQUIRED — LOW
TRIMMING/CLIPPING REQUIRED — LOW
AMOUNT OF SHEDDING — MEDIUM
ACTIVITY INDOORS — LOW
EASE OF TRAINING — MEDIUM
SOCIABILITY WITH STRANGERS — MEDIUM
     LOW

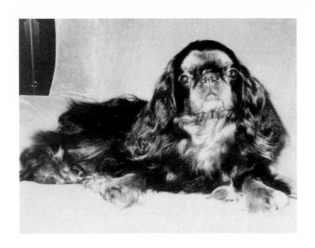

TEMPERAMENT

One of the most amiable and undemanding of the toys, the elegant English Toy Spaniel is easy to live with and easy to like. One breeder describes him as "quiet, intimate, dignified, funny, and sweet." Though he does love to play in the yard, he doesn't need or want much more exercise than that. The yard must be fenced, for he has just enough spaniel instincts that he will chase birds or butterflies into the street. Calm indoors, a lover of comfort and couches, he enjoys cuddling on laps and snuggling into soft pillows. His soulful eyes invite pampering, which he accepts graciously without taking nasty advantage. This docile yet merry breed is terrific for senior citizens. At the other end of the spectrum, he is easily overwhelmed by small children and cannot take rough handling or mischief. The "Charlie" (in honor of his European name, King Charles Spaniel) is somewhat reserved with strangers—his own family is enough for him, thank you very much. He gets along well with other pets. He is mildly stubborn, but the little training he needs will go well if you use praise and encouragement—and food rewards never hurt.

HISTORY

Developed in Great Britain, he was a favorite of the ruling class. His primary job was to warm laps (especially those of the sick) in drafty castles and on chilly carriage rides. AKC popularity: 120th of 146.

PHYSICAL FEATURES

He stands 9–10 inches and weighs 8–14 pounds, though many are larger. Brush and comb his silky coat twice a week, more often when he is shedding. Keep his ear canals clean and dry and his bottom trimmed for cleanliness. There are four color varieties: Blenheim (*blenum*) is white with rich red markings; Ruby is solid red; King Charles is black with red trim; Prince Charles is white with black patches and red trim. Prince Charles and King Charles tend to have the most profuse coats and ear fringes. His ears are natural. His tail may be docked (some are born with naturally short tails).

HEALTH ISSUES

Both parents should have yearly CERF certificates (eyes) and be screened for luxating patella and heart disease (PDA and MVD). He is sensitive to anesthetics, vaccines, and chemicals and should never be casually medicated or sedated. With his short face, he is susceptible to respiratory difficulties and heatstroke in hot, humid, and/or stuffy conditions. Charlies love air-conditioning. Lifespan: 10–12 years.

CAUTIONS WHEN BUYING

The English Toy Spaniel is a different breed than the Cavalier King Charles Spaniel. Charlies are smaller than Cavaliers, with a more domed head, shorter muzzle, and more placid temperament.

Entlebucher Mountain Dog
(EN-tell-boo-ker)

Best for Experienced Owners
Good with Older, Considerate Children
Medium in Size
Short Coat

EXERCISE REQUIRED — HIGH

TRIMMING/CLIPPING REQUIRED — LOW

AMOUNT OF SHEDDING — MEDIUM

ACTIVITY INDOORS — HIGH MEDIUM

EASE OF TRAINING — HIGH MEDIUM

SOCIABILITY WITH STRANGERS — HIGH
    MEDIUM

TEMPERAMENT

Steady and good-natured, yet bold and athletic, the stocky, muscular Entlebucher enjoys romping and rough-housing. Pulling a cart or sled, herding, agility, fetching balls, playing Frisbee, and weight pulling are productive outlets for his high energy. He likes to keep busy and needs to have something to do; he is not an apartment dog. Entlebuchers bond closely with their family and seek lots of attention. Their determination to jump up into your face or shove their body against your leg can be disconcerting to those who are not accustomed to an enthusiastic, vigorous dog. He likes children, but will bowl over little ones. He makes a vigilant watchdog and will sound off with a loud, deep voice to announce visitors—or simply to let you know that your neighbor has stepped outdoors. His attitude toward strangers varies from exuberantly friendly to polite to suspicious. Early and ongoing socialization is essential to develop the stable, self-assured temperament that all of the Swiss mountain dogs are known for. Most are companionable with other animals. The Entlebucher learns quickly but can be dominant and pushy—necessary traits for working with unruly cattle, but challenging for nonassertive owners to handle. During adolescence, his hormones will kick in and he may start to test limits. Obedience training should start early. Heeling is an especially imperative lesson, for these powerful dogs can literally pull you off your feet. Entlebuchers bark sharply while working, so be prepared to control excessive vocalization from the beginning.

HISTORY

Descended from Roman mastiffs, he is the smallest of the four Swiss sennenhunds (dogs of the Alpine herdsmen) and the only one with a short tail. In the Swiss canton of Entlebuch, he guarded the farm, drove cows to and from pasture, and pulled milk carts to the dairy. Registered by the FCI, UKC, and CKC.

PHYSICAL FEATURES

He stands 16–20 inches and weighs 50–65 pounds. Brush his short, double coat once a week, more often when shedding. He is jet black with white markings on his face, chest, feet, and tail tip and rich rust markings over each eye, on his cheeks, chest, legs, and under his tail. His ears are natural; his tail may or may not be docked.

HEALTH ISSUES

Both parents should have OFA certificates (hips) and yearly CERF (eyes). Lifespan: 12–13 years.

CAUTIONS WHEN BUYING

Though many people are drawn to his striking colors, wash-and-wear coat, and dependable, good-natured temperament, the Entlebucher is not a happy pet unless given plenty of work and exercise. He is very rare in the United States and prices are high: up to $2,000 for a pet. See also the Appenzell, Bernese, and Greater Swiss mountain dogs.

Field Spaniel

Fine for Novice Owners
Good with Children If Raised with Children
Medium in Size
Feathered, Medium-Length Coat

EXERCISE REQUIRED — MEDIUM
TRIMMING/CLIPPING REQUIRED — MEDIUM
AMOUNT OF SHEDDING — MEDIUM
ACTIVITY INDOORS – HIGH
EASE OF TRAINING — HIGH MEDIUM
SOCIABILITY WITH STRANGERS — MEDIUM

TEMPERAMENT

Levelheaded and mild-mannered, the Field Spaniel has more sporting instincts than most other spaniels and appreciates as much running, biking, hiking, or field work as you can provide. It isn't fair to keep this lively little hunter, bred for activity and endurance, in a small yard with only a walk around the block for exercise. When socialized early and extensively, he is accepting of strangers, though he seldom runs right up to people as might a Cocker or Springer. He is playful and docile with other animals. Field Spaniels do have an independent streak but respond well to light-handed, upbeat training methods. This sensitive breed cringes or withdraws when treated roughly or jerked around. Some enjoy hearing the sound of their own voices. The fun-loving Field Spaniel enjoys splashing in puddles and slobbering in water bowls and will track mud around the house with his oversize webbed feet.

HISTORY

Developed in England, he flushes birds from their hiding places, then retrieves them after the hunter shoots. AKC popularity: 127th of 146.

PHYSICAL FEATURES

He stands 17–18 inches and weighs 35–50 pounds. Brush and comb his silky coat every other day and occasionally trim straggly hairs. Keep his ear canals clean and dry and his bottom trimmed for cleanliness. Liver (ranging from golden to dark) is the most common color, followed by black, then the speckled roan pattern. Tan trim is some- times seen. His ears are natural; his tail is usually docked, though natural tails are allowed.

HEALTH ISSUES

Both parents should have OFA certificates (hips) and yearly CERF (eyes). Also ask about heart disease (SAS), low thyroid, and vWD in the lines. Lifespan: 12 years.

CAUTIONS WHEN BUYING

If you like the general appearance, silky coat, convenient size, and pleasant temperament of spaniels, this breed should be considered as an interesting (and overall healthier) alternative to the more common spaniels. He is larger than a cocker, smaller than a springer. His quality has remained high and his working instincts are dependable. You may be in for a wait, though, as litters are few and far between and most breeders are very selective about homes.

Fila Brasileiro (FEE-la bra-sill-YERO)

Best for Experienced Owners
Good with Children If Raised with Children
Giant in Size
Smooth Coat

EXERCISE REQUIRED — MEDIUM

TRIMMING/CLIPPING REQUIRED — LOW

AMOUNT OF SHEDDING — MEDIUM

ACTIVITY INDOORS — LOW

EASE OF TRAINING — MEDIUM

SOCIABILITY WITH STRANGERS — LOW

TEMPERAMENT

"Faithful as a Fila dog" is an old Brazilian proverb. The Fila has a temperament unlike that of any other breed. Sweet, gentle, and docile with his own family, he has an extreme distrust of and aversion to strangers and absolutely detests being touched by outsiders. Courageous, determined, and self-assured, he is one of the world's greatest instinctive guardians. One might take his bulk for laziness or clumsiness—and one would be terribly mistaken. Filas are calm and quiet, until aroused. They can shift into their fierce protector's role in an instant, moving with tremendous speed and athletic agility. Puppies should be friendly and trusting and with proper socialization become more discriminating as they mature. Their eventual degree of aggressiveness/defensiveness depends on genetics (parents and grandparents) and environment (socialization and training). Though this breed was not used for dogfighting (indeed, they were often worked and hunted in packs), dog aggression is a potential problem. The Fila may live peacefully with other pets in his own family, but won't back down from a challenge. This strong-willed breed is inclined to trust his own judgment, but will defer to confident leadership that includes consistent rules and cheerful praise. With his hindquarters raised slightly above his forequarters, the Fila often moves like a great feline, with a long, low, stalking stride. He tends to amble or pace and there is a rolling motion to his gait.

HISTORY

The national dog of Brazil, he was developed by Portuguese settlers to protect their plantations, track runaway slaves, work their cattle, and hunt jaguars and wild boar.

His ancestors include the English Mastiff, Bloodhound, and now extinct bulldogs. Registered by the FCI.

PHYSICAL FEATURES

Males stand 27–30 inches and weigh 120–140 pounds. Females stand 24–28 inches and weigh 90–120 pounds. His skin is loose and thick, and his tight coat requires only an occasional quick brushing. The most common colors are fawn or brindle. Black is sometimes seen. His ears and tail are natural.

HEALTH ISSUES

Both parents should have OFA certificates (hips) and yearly CERF (eyes). Also ask about bloat and OCD in the lines. Lifespan: 9–10 years.

CAUTIONS WHEN BUYING

Owning a dog who believes that his purpose in life is to defend you at any cost comes with the responsibility that you control his actions. The Fila requires early and ongoing socialization and obedience training and strong fences. He is always seeking the company of his master and must be made an integral part of your family and closely supervised with strangers.

Finnish Spitz

Fine for Novice Owners
Good with Children
Medium in Size
Thick, Medium-Length Coat

EXERCISE REQUIRED — HIGH MEDIUM
TRIMMING/CLIPPING REQUIRED — LOW
AMOUNT OF SHEDDING — HIGH MEDIUM
ACTIVITY INDOORS — MEDIUM
EASE OF TRAINING — MEDIUM LOW
SOCIABILITY WITH STRANGERS — MEDIUM
    LOW

TEMPERAMENT

The fox-like Finnish Spitz is lively and agile, quick moving and light on his feet. He plays hard and enjoys vigorous exercise, especially in the snow. Without enough activity (physical and mental), this creative thinker will become bored and perhaps destructive. He is very people-oriented and needs a great deal of companionship, especially from his favorite person. Because of his extremely sensitive nature, he doesn't do well in an environment with frequent tension or loud voices. The Finnish Spitz is sharp-eyed and keen of hearing and will immediately alert when he sees or hears anything unusual. Conservative with strangers, he requires early and frequent socialization to ensure that his caution does not become suspicion or shyness. He also needs early physical handling, as he often does not like being examined. Typically bold with other dogs, he can be jealous and scrappy with those of the same sex and predatory with rodents and birds. This breed learns quickly but is clever and independent and doesn't like too much repetition. Use positive training methods (praise and food), as jerking on the leash only makes him obstinate and skittish, and he has a very long memory for what he considers unjust treatment. These vocal dogs will greet you with throaty sounds of crooning, purring, and yodeling. They *love* to bark, and their barking pattern is high-pitched, piercing, and rapid (more than 150 barks per minute). If left outside unattended, they can drive neighbors up the wall.

HISTORY

He is the national dog of Finland, his ancestors the hunting companions of the ancient Finns. He flushes grouse into a tree, flicks his curled tail repeatedly to occupy the bird's attention, and barks virtually nonstop to alert his owner. AKC popularity: 142nd of 146.

PHYSICAL FEATURES

Males stand 17½–20 inches and weigh 25–33 pounds. Females stand 15½–18 inches and weigh 20–28 pounds. His harsh coat with its dense undercoat should be brushed once a week, daily when he is shedding. Along with heavy seasonal shedding, you'll see loose hair the rest of the year as well. He is clear golden red (pale honey to deep auburn). His ears and tail are natural.

HEALTH ISSUES

Both parents should have OFA certificates (hips) and yearly CERF (eyes). Also ask about luxating patella, seizures, and Addison's disease in the lines. Lifespan: 13–15 years.

CAUTIONS WHEN BUYING

Be sure you can provide the light-handed, reward-based training and peaceful home that this sensitive breed requires. Because of their vocalness and need for ongoing companionship, Finnish Spitz are happiest with a stay-at-home owner.

Flat-Coated Retriever

Fine for Novice Owners
Good with Children
Large in Size
Feathered, Medium-Length Coat

EXERCISE REQUIRED — HIGH

TRIMMING/CLIPPING REQUIRED — MEDIUM
LOW

AMOUNT OF SHEDDING — MEDIUM

ACTIVITY INDOORS — MEDIUM

EASE OF TRAINING — HIGH

SOCIABILITY WITH STRANGERS — HIGH

TEMPERAMENT

The AKC Standard says, "The Flat-Coat demonstrates stability and a desire to please with a confident, happy, and outgoing attitude characterized by a wagging tail." This cheerful, sweet-natured dog thrives on personal attention. He is athletic, not a couch potato, so he needs running exercise every day and, whenever possible, swimming and fetching. Otherwise he will find outlets for his energy through destructive chewing and digging. The gregarious Flat-Coat doesn't like being left for long periods of time without the companionship of people or other pets. Optimistic about everyone and everything, this breed is emphatically not a guardian. He is eternally lighthearted and playful, doesn't know his own strength, and can be an exuberant jumper. Supervision is important around toddlers and smaller pets. You must control his tendency to chew on objects and to mouth your hands—provide a box filled with toys so he can carry something around in his mouth. A Flat-Coat retains his youthfully good-humored outlook on life into old age, which sounds delightful but which does require patience and control to manage. Obedience training is a must to instill calmness and good manners. Fortunately, he is responsive and biddable, though not as "push-button" as a Golden Retriever; he has a willful streak.

HISTORY

Developed in England as both a land hunter and a water retriever, the Flat-Coat was immensely popular until the coming of flashier Goldens and Labs. AKC popularity: 97th of 146.

PHYSICAL FEATURES

He stands 22–24½ inches and weighs 60-75 pounds. His coat may be flat or wavy (he was once called the Wavy-Coated Retriever) and should be brushed and combed twice a week. Occasionally trim straggly hairs. Keep his ear canals clean and dry and his bottom trimmed for cleanliness. He is solid black or solid liver. Yellow or cream dogs cannot be shown in conformation classes. His ears and tail are natural.

HEALTH ISSUES

Both parents should have OFA certificates (hips) and yearly CERF (eyes). Also ask about low thyroid and especially cancer in the lines. Cancer is the major problem in this breed, resulting in the premature deaths of a dismaying number of Flat-Coats. Lifespan: 8–10 years.

CAUTIONS WHEN BUYING

If you like the general build, robustness, and reputation of retrievers as dependable family dogs, consider this breed as an interesting (and overall healthier) alternative to Labs and Goldens. Just be aware that Flat-Coat breeders are seriously interested in preserving working instincts. Most show dogs also have obedience and field titles, and breeders prefer owners who are interested in working their dogs. You shouldn't choose a Flat-Coat if you have no interest in pursuing canine sports or activities.

Fox Terrier (Smooth)

Best for Experienced Owners
Good with Older, Considerate Children
Small in Size
Smooth Coat

EXERCISE REQUIRED — HIGH MEDIUM

TRIMMING/CLIPPING REQUIRED — LOW

AMOUNT OF SHEDDING — MEDIUM

ACTIVITY INDOORS — HIGH

EASE OF TRAINING — LOW

SOCIABILITY WITH STRANGERS — HIGH
     MEDIUM

TEMPERAMENT

The Fox is one of the most curious, intense, and impulsive of the terriers—indeed of all breeds. Untiringly active and playful, he has a special passion for ball chasing and seldom walks when he can run. He loves the outdoors but must always be kept on-leash (he is a fast, agile, independent chaser) or in a secure yard, preferably supervised, because his ingenuity and relentless hunting instincts may drive him over or under the fence. This daredevil with the peppery personality does best with active owners who are firm, confident, consistent leaders. He has a marked stubborn streak, a mischievous sense of humor, and will take clever advantage if indulged. Positive training methods are a must—terriers do not react kindly to being jerked around. Fox Terriers are scrappy and fearless with other animals. They won't back down if challenged, and they may do much of the challenging themselves. They have a high prey drive and extremely quick reflexes, so little creatures that run won't get far. This breed has keen vision and acute hearing and can be counted on to sound the alert when anything is amiss—sometimes even when nothing is amiss, but *might* be in the future. Fox Terriers love to tunnel and dig and can be possessive of their food and cherished toys.

HISTORY

This breed was developed in England to bolt the fox from its den after it was chased in by the foxhounds. The Smooth Fox is an older breed than his Wirehaired cousin, but is currently not as popular. AKC popularity: 86th of 146.

PHYSICAL FEATURES

He stands 14-16 inches and weighs 18-22 pounds. His hard coat needs only an occasional quick brushing. He is mostly white with black and/or brown markings. His ears are natural, but unless "glued" into a folding position for several months during adolescence, they may tend to prick up rather than drop forward. His tail is docked.

HEALTH ISSUES

Both parents should have OFA certificates (hips) and yearly CERF (eyes). Also ask about Legg-Perthes, luxating patella, low thyroid, heart problems, seizures, and digestive problems in the lines. Lifespan: 12–15 years.

CAUTIONS WHEN BUYING

If you're looking for one of the most dynamic go-getters in the canine world, a cocky little dog who spends most of the day up on his tiptoes and happy to delight you with a vast repertoire of amusing antics, a Fox Terrier may be perfect for you. If you desire a peaceful household and a dog who lies quietly and obediently for much of the day, look elsewhere!

Fox Terrier (Wire)

Best for Experienced Owners
Good with Older, Considerate Children
Small in Size
Wiry Coat

EXERCISE REQUIRED — HIGH MEDIUM

TRIMMING/CLIPPING REQUIRED — HIGH

AMOUNT OF SHEDDING — LOW

ACTIVITY INDOORS — HIGH

EASE OF TRAINING — LOW

SOCIABILITY WITH STRANGERS — HIGH
MEDIUM

TEMPERAMENT

The Fox is one of the most curious, intense, and impulsive of the terriers—indeed of all breeds. Untiringly active and playful, he has a special passion for ball chasing and seldom walks when he can run. He loves the outdoors but must always be kept on-leash (he is a fast, agile, independent chaser) or in a secure yard, preferably supervised, because his ingenuity and relentless hunting instincts may drive him over or under the fence. This daredevil with the peppery personality does best with active owners who are firm, confident, consistent leaders. He has a marked stubborn streak, a mischievous sense of humor, and will take clever advantage if indulged. Positive training methods are a must—terriers do not react kindly to being jerked around. Fox Terriers are scrappy and fearless with other animals. They won't back down if challenged, and they may do much of the challenging themselves. They have a high prey drive and extremely quick reflexes, so little creatures that run won't get far. This breed has keen vision and acute hearing and can be counted on to sound the alert when anything is amiss—sometimes even when nothing is amiss, but *might* be in the future. Fox Terriers love to tunnel and dig and can be possessive of their food and cherished toys.

HISTORY

This breed was developed in England to bolt the fox from its den after it was chased in by the foxhounds. The Wire Fox is a newer breed than his Smooth cousin, but is currently more popular. AKC popularity: 62nd of 146.

PHYSICAL FEATURES

He stands 14-16 inches and weighs 15-20 pounds. Brush and comb his hard wiry coat once a week. Keep his bottom trimmed for cleanliness. Show dogs are "stripped" (dead coat plucked out) every few months; pet owners may opt for more convenient clipping. He is mostly white with black and tan markings, or just tan markings (called a "ginger"). His ears are natural, but unless "glued" into a folding position for several months during adolescence, they may prick up rather than drop forward. His tail is docked.

HEALTH ISSUES

Both parents should have OFA certificates (hips) and yearly CERF (eyes). Also ask about Legg-Perthes, luxating patella, low thyroid, heart problems, seizures, and digestive problems in the lines. Lifespan: 12–15 years.

CAUTIONS WHEN BUYING

If you're looking for one of the most dynamic go-getters in the canine world, a cocky little dog who spends most of the day up on his tiptoes and happy to delight you with a vast repertoire of amusing antics, a Fox Terrier may be perfect for you. If you desire a peaceful household and a dog who lies quietly and obediently for much of the day, look elsewhere!

French Bulldog

Fine for Novice Owners
Good with Children
Small in Size
Smooth Coat

EXERCISE REQUIRED — LOW
TRIMMING/CLIPPING REQUIRED — LOW
AMOUNT OF SHEDDING — MEDIUM
ACTIVITY INDOORS — MEDIUM
EASE OF TRAINING — MEDIUM
SOCIABILITY WITH STRANGERS — HIGH
        MEDIUM

TEMPERAMENT

Despite his glum expression, the Frenchie is one of the sweetest, most amusing, and dependably amiable of all breeds. As comfortable in an apartment as he is on a farm, he is livelier than you might suspect from his chunky appearance. Puppies are especially frisky; ball chasing is one of their passions. Adults are more dignified and can be champion couch potatoes, but also love to clown around and go for walks in cool weather. Most are friendly and outgoing with everyone; some are politely reserved. Frenchies will bark to announce visitors, but are otherwise quiet dogs. Usually peaceful and playful with other animals (some will hunt small rodents), males may bicker with other males. Though stubborn, he is surprisingly sensitive, remembers what he learns, and responds well to early, patient, persistent training that utilizes food motivation. Snorting, snuffling, and flatulence go with the territory of short-faced breeds. Swimming pool owners must exercise caution: Because of their squat build and heavy head, most Frenchies cannot swim and will drown if they fall into a pool.

HISTORY

When British lace workers sought work in France in the nineteenth century, they took undersized English Bulldogs ("culls") with them. The little Bulldogs became popular as ratters and fashionable favorites of the European artistic set and Parisian *belles de nuit*. AKC popularity: 76th of 146.

PHYSICAL FEATURES

He stands 11-14 inches and weighs 20-28 pounds. His glossy coat needs only an occasional quick brushing. The most common colors are black brindle, tiger brindle (striped), brindle pied (mostly white with brindle patches), cream, fawn with a black mask, and fawn pied. His ears and tail are natural.

HEALTH ISSUES

Both parents should have OFA certificates (hips, patellas, and heart) and yearly CERF (eyes). X rays for spinal defects are also desirable, as is screening for vWD and low thyroid. Also ask about elongated soft palate. He is susceptible to eye lacerations and eyelid/eyelash defects. He cannot regulate his temperature very well and must be protected from extreme heat and cold. In hot weather he should have free access to water and shade (and preferably air-conditioning), and in the winter he should wear a sweater outdoors. He is sensitive to anesthetics and should never be casually sedated. Lifespan: 10–12 years.

CAUTIONS WHEN BUYING

Frenchies (affectionately called "Frog Dogs") are easily distinguished from their English Bulldog cousins by their bat ears (rounded and erect), less exaggerated build (less undershot bite, straighter legs, tighter skin), and livelier nature. Due to artificial insemination, C-sections, small litters, and high puppy mortality rates, be prepared to spend $900 and up for a pet. Also be prepared for clever comments from passersby: "Say, is that a Vietnamese potbellied pig?"

German Pinscher

Best for Experienced Owners
Good with Older, Considerate Children
Medium in Size
Smooth Coat

EXERCISE REQUIRED — MEDIUM
TRIMMING/CLIPPING REQUIRED — LOW
AMOUNT OF SHEDDING — MEDIUM LOW
ACTIVITY INDOORS — HIGH
EASE OF TRAINING — MEDIUM LOW
SOCIABILITY WITH STRANGERS — LOW

TEMPERAMENT

The German Pinscher Club of America calls him "energetic, watchful, agile, fearless, determined." One might add "strong-willed, assertive, and manipulative." Both robust and elegant, the German Pinscher comes from a strong terrier background. This high-energy breed always seems to be observing, thinking, and planning. He makes direct eye contact, and unless you establish yourself as alpha (number one), he can be demanding and frequently in your face. Yet he is extremely smart, and owners who know how to lead will find him eminently trainable. Obedience training should consist of reward-based methods, because he is sensitive and proud and doesn't tolerate jerking around or other mistreatment or teasing. Highly territorial and keenly alert, he is very loyal and takes his watchdog role *very* seriously. He won't hesitate to back up his fierce bark with a bite. Early and frequent socialization is required so that his wariness does not become sharpness. Most are okay (though bossy) with other dogs if raised with them, but he has a high prey drive and extremely quick reflexes and is death on anything that runs. He can be overly possessive of objects (yours and his), and excessive barking can be a problem.

HISTORY

A vermin hunter and guardian, he originated in Germany, where both wire-coated and smooth-coated pups occurred in the same litters. The wires were developed into schnauzers and the smooths into pinschers. There are three separate breeds in the pinscher family: the oldest (and least known) is the German Pinscher, who was probably the midsized foundation breed used to develop the smaller Miniature Pinscher and the larger Doberman Pinscher. Registered by the FCI, UKC, SKC, and AKC-FSS.

PHYSICAL FEATURES

He stands 17-20 inches and weighs 25-35 pounds. His short, dense coat requires only an occasional quick brushing. He may be red, stag red (red intermingled with black hairs), black-and-rust, blue-and-rust, or fawn (Isabella). His ears may be cropped or left naturally folded. His tail is docked.

HEALTH ISSUES

Both parents should have OFA certificates (hips) and yearly CERF (eyes). Lifespan: 12–14 years.

CAUTIONS WHEN BUYING

The extreme quickness of this breed cannot be overemphasized. German Pinschers are very oriented to sight and motion, and most owners are simply not prepared for their instinctive reflexes and rapid reactions to stimuli. Leashes and secure fences are musts at all times. Buy only from a breeder who emphasizes temperament, then socialize and train thoroughly. This is not a couch potato breed.

German Shepherd

Best for Experienced Owners
Good with Children
Large in Size
Thick, Medium-Length Coat

EXERCISE REQUIRED — HIGH MEDIUM

TRIMMING/CLIPPING REQUIRED — LOW

AMOUNT OF SHEDDING – HIGH

ACTIVITY INDOORS — MEDIUM

EASE OF TRAINING — HIGH

SOCIABILITY WITH STRANGERS — MEDIUM

TEMPERAMENT

The AKC Standard says the German Shepherd "has a distinct personality marked by direct and fearless, but not hostile, expression, self-confidence and a certain aloofness that does not lend itself to immediate and indiscriminate friendships. The dog must be approachable, quietly standing its ground and showing confidence and willingness to meet overtures without itself making them." Some lines are "hard" and businesslike, while others tend toward a calmer, milder manner. Energy levels vary from vigorous to laid-back, but this athletic dog needs brisk walking every day and all-out running as often as possible. Mental exercise (advanced obedience, agility, Schutzhund, tracking, herding, fetching sticks or Frisbees) is even more important. There is skittishness in some lines, sharpness in others. Early socialization is a must to develop a stable, confident temperament. Some are dominant with strange dogs of the same sex, and some are confirmed cat chasers if not introduced when young. One of the most capable and trainable breeds in all of dogdom, exceedingly eager to learn and work, the German Shepherd excels at the highest levels of competition. Some can be chronic whiners.

HISTORY

He was developed in Germany as a herding dog, but eventually became the world's leading guardian, police and military dog, search and rescue dog, bomb and narcotics detection dog, and Seeing Eye dog. This breed can learn to do anything. AKC popularity: 3rd of 146.

PHYSICAL FEATURES

Males stand 24-26 inches and weigh 75-110 pounds. Females stand 22-24 inches and weigh 60-80 pounds. Brush his double coat every day or two to control shedding, which is constant all year and very heavy twice a year. He may be black with tan/red/cream/silver markings, either in the saddle-marked pattern or the bicolor (Doberman) pattern; sable (golden, red, or gray, with black-tipped hairs); or solid black. White dogs cannot be shown in conformation classes, but may be UKC registered and shown as White Shepherds (see profile). His ears and tail are natural.

HEALTH ISSUES

Both parents should have OFA certificates (hips and elbows) and be screened for cardiac problems. Also ask about bloat, vWD, seizures, low thyroid, sebaceous adenitis, OCD, panosteitis, and cancer. Allergies, skin conditions, autoimmune disorders, and digestive upsets are common. Lifespan: 12 years.

CAUTIONS WHEN BUYING

In both appearance and temperament, show lines and working lines appear to be two different breeds. Be very clear what you are looking for: Schutzhund dog, obedience competition dog, show dog, or couch potato. You must choose your lines appropriately. Health and temperament problems abound: Check those health certificates carefully and see parents and other relatives.

German Shorthaired Pointer

Best for Experienced Owners
Good with Children If Raised with Children
Large in Size
Smooth Coat

EXERCISE REQUIRED — HIGH

TRIMMING/CLIPPING REQUIRED — LOW

AMOUNT OF SHEDDING — MEDIUM

ACTIVITY INDOORS — MEDIUM

EASE OF TRAINING — MEDIUM

SOCIABILITY WITH STRANGERS — MEDIUM

TEMPERAMENT

Good-natured and adaptable, but primarily bred to be a hunting dog, the German Shorthair has a high activity level and belongs with an equally athletic owner who will take him running, biking, or hiking. A walk around the block is barely a warm-up for a vigorous German Shorthair, and too much confinement can lead to barking, hyperactivity, and destructive chewing. Exuberantly playful with children, he could accidentally knock a toddler down. Toward strangers he may be friendly or reserved, and his alarm bark may be protective or welcoming. Some can be aggressive with strange dogs, and some are determined cat chasers. Obedience training is a must for instilling self-discipline and control, for this breed can be a bundle of intense energy. Capable of learning anything and eminently trainable, the Shorthair can become focused when asked to do so, yet does know his own mind.

HISTORY

Developed in Germany as an all-purpose hunter of birds, small game, and large game, the Shorthair has both bird dogs and scenthounds in his ancestry. AKC popularity: 24th of 146.

PHYSICAL FEATURES

Males stand 23-25 inches and weigh 55-75 pounds. Females stand 21-23 inches and weigh 45-60 pounds. His hard coat needs only an occasional quick brushing. He is usually liver with white ticking and/or patches. Less common are solid liver, and mostly white with faint liver ticking and a liver head. Rarely, black may substitute for liver. His ears are natural; his tail is docked.

HEALTH ISSUES

Both parents should have OFA certificates (hips) and yearly CERF (eyes). Also ask about heart disease (SAS), vWD, OCD, seizures, Addison's disease, low thyroid, and cancer in the lines. Lifespan: 14–16 years.

CAUTIONS WHEN BUYING

The German Shorthaired Pointer is not as divided in type as the English Pointer. There are many Dual Champions (champions in both conformation and field trials), and a good breeder will breed with this in mind to ensure sound hunting instincts. For a well-balanced puppy, look for field titles or hunting test titles in the pedigree, along with obedience and Ch. titles.

German Wirehaired Pointer / Deutsch-Drahthaar (doych DROT-har)

Best for Experienced Owners
Good with Children If Raised with Children
Large in Size
Wiry Coat

EXERCISE REQUIRED — HIGH

TRIMMING/CLIPPING REQUIRED — MEDIUM

AMOUNT OF SHEDDING — MEDIUM

ACTIVITY INDOORS — HIGH

EASE OF TRAINING — LOW

SOCIABILITY WITH STRANGERS — MEDIUM

TEMPERAMENT

The AKC Standard says, "Typically Pointer in character and style . . . an intelligent, energetic, and determined hunter." The German Wirehair is steady and sensible, but also rugged and busy. He has a high energy level and belongs with an equally athletic owner who will take him running, biking, and hiking and preferably work him in the field. Too much confinement and too little attention can lead to barking, hyperactivity, and destructive chewing. Though some are outgoing, most are aloof with strangers and can be quite protective. He can be aggressive (or at least dominant and bold) with strange dogs, and with his strong hunting instincts, sharp with cats. Highly capable of learning anything, the German Wirehair is also strong-willed and determined and needs an owner who knows how to lead. Usually he is more serious and discriminating than his Shorthair cousin, though many do have a clownish side.

HISTORY

He was developed in Germany as a weather-resistant hunter of virtually any game in field, forest, thicket, and water. Because his ancestry does not include hounds, he is faster and more agile than his cousin, the German Shorthair. Recognized by AKC as German Wirehaired Pointer (popularity: 75th of 146) and by VDD (Verein Deutsch-Drahthaar) as Deutsch-Drahthaar.

PHYSICAL FEATURES

Males stand 24–26 inches; females stand 22–24 inches. Weight is 50–70 pounds. Brush his harsh coat once or twice a week. Show dogs are "stripped" (dead coat plucked out) every few months; pet owners may opt for more convenient clipping. Usually he is liver with white ticking and/or patches. Less common are solid liver, and mostly white with faint liver ticking and a liver head. Rarely, black may substitute for liver. His ears are natural; his tail is docked. His feet are webbed.

HEALTH ISSUES

Both parents should have OFA certificates (hips) and yearly CERF (eyes). Also ask about vWD, OCD, and low thyroid in the lines. Lifespan: 12 years.

CAUTIONS WHEN BUYING

AKC breeders consider the German Wirehaired Pointer and Deutsch-Drahthaar the same breed, while VDD breeders contend that their paths have diverged enough to warrant separate recognition. The latter seems more reasonable since, unlike the German Wirehair, the Drahthaar is bred to a strict standard that requires testing not only in conformation but also in hunting ability before dogs are allowed to be bred. Drahthaars are reliable "hunting machines." They generally have shorter, darker coats than German Wirehairs.

Giant Schnauzer (SHNOW-zer)

Best for Experienced Owners
Good with Older, Considerate Children
Large in Size
Wiry Coat

EXERCISE REQUIRED — HIGH

TRIMMING/CLIPPING REQUIRED — HIGH

AMOUNT OF SHEDDING — LOW

ACTIVITY INDOORS — MEDIUM

EASE OF TRAINING — MEDIUM

SOCIABILITY WITH STRANGERS — MEDIUM
 LOW

TEMPERAMENT

The AKC Standard calls him "a bold and valiant figure of a dog . . . amiable in repose and a commanding figure when aroused." Keen expression is what you may notice first about the Giant Schnauzer. Some are harder tempered, projecting boldness, seriousness, and vigor, while others are sweeter and more mellow. This athletic, energetic breed plays hard and needs a mile or two of walking and/or running each day. Mental exercise (advanced obedience, agility, Schutzhund) is just as important to this extremely intelligent dog. Most are watchful with strangers, reliable at determining friend or foe, and responsible about protecting their home. However, timidity, skittishness, and sharp-shyness are seen in some lines. To promote a stable, confident temperament, Giants need more socialization than many other breeds. Many are too spirited for small children, and some become overprotective of their own kids when a group is engaging in rough-and-tumble play. Other dogs may be challenged—males especially are dominant and aggressive with other males. Once you establish your leadership, the Giant responds very well to obedience training that is fair and consistent. This sensitive dog seems always aware of your moods and likes to be physically close to you and watching you.

HISTORY

He drove cattle in the German region of Bavaria, where all three Schnauzer breeds (Miniature, Standard, and Giant) originated. AKC popularity: 80th of 146.

PHYSICAL FEATURES

Males stand 26-28 inches; females stand 24-26 inches. Weight is 70-95 pounds. Brush his harsh coat twice a week, though compared to German lines, many American lines have a softer coat with heavier "furnishings" that require more maintenance. His beard should be combed daily for cleanliness. Likewise, keep his bottom trimmed for cleanliness. Show dogs are "stripped" (dead coat plucked out) every few months; pet owners may opt for more convenient clipping. He is usually black, but may also be pepper-and-salt (banded hairs of black and white, resulting in a gray appearance). His ears may be cropped or left naturally hanging; his tail is docked.

HEALTH ISSUES

Both parents should have OFA certificates (hips). Also ask about low thyroid, OCD, heart disease, cancer, seizures, allergies, and skin conditions in the lines. Lifespan: 10–12 years.

CAUTIONS WHEN BUYING

German-bred lines often focus on performance sports such as Schutzhund (protection, obedience, and tracking), so their temperaments tend to be "harder" and more work-oriented. Some breeders believe that pepper-and-salt dogs, in general, are more docile.

Glen of Imaal Terrier (E-MAHL)

Best for Experienced Owners
Good with Children If Raised with Children
Small to Medium in Size
Wiry Coat

EXERCISE REQUIRED — MEDIUM

TRIMMING/CLIPPING REQUIRED — MEDIUM

AMOUNT OF SHEDDING — MEDIUM LOW

ACTIVITY INDOORS — MEDIUM

EASE OF TRAINING — MEDIUM

SOCIABILITY WITH STRANGERS — MEDIUM

TEMPERAMENT

A sturdy, stoic dog with strong working instincts, the Glen has a rough-and-ready appearance that belies his calm, gentle, peaceful disposition. The heavily muscled Glen is surprisingly fast and agile, spirited and playful. He likes vigorous games and long walks and must be on-leash or loosed in a safe, enclosed area, because he is a hunter and chaser. Indoors he wants to be near you—resting his head on your lap or feet—so is often underfoot, yet his general nature is patient, laid-back, and undemanding, unusual for a terrier. He is polite with known visitors, but other dogs may be another matter. Early socialization and owner control and attentiveness are recommended. With his high prey drive, he must be carefully introduced to cats and should not be kept with rabbits or rodents. Glens have the stubborn character of a true terrier, but they are quite willing to work with you if you use praise and food to motivate them. With his enthusiasm, low center of gravity, and tremendous strength, he will tow you along the street unless you teach him how to walk on a leash. Glens are powerful diggers with a surprisingly deep bark.

HISTORY

From the rugged glen (valley) of Imaal in the Wicklow Mountains of Ireland comes this heavy-boned, crooked-legged hunter. He doesn't bark to worry his prey from its den, as most terriers do, but works silently and with great tenacity, relying on his powerful jaws, bowed front legs, and heavy shoulders to drag out his quarry—often a forty-pound badger fighting to the death. Some authorities say he was occasionally used for the dubious "sport" of dog-fighting. Registered by the FCI, UKC, SKC, CKC, and AKC-FSS.

PHYSICAL FEATURES

He stands 13-14 inches and weighs 35-45 pounds. People are often surprised at the great substance and strength of this dog. Brush and comb his harsh, shaggy double coat twice a week. His beard should be combed daily for cleanliness. Likewise, keep his bottom trimmed for cleanliness. Keep his ear canals clean and dry. Show dogs are "stripped" (dead coat plucked out) every few months; pet owners may opt for more convenient clipping. He is blue brindle, blue, or wheaten. His ears are natural; his tail is docked.

HEALTH ISSUES

Both parents should have OFA certificates (hips) and yearly CERF (eyes). Also ask about gastritis and allergies in the lines. Young Glens (under one year) should not be taken on very long walks and should not be allowed to jump off beds or sofas until the growth plates in their front legs have closed. Let puppies choose on their own when to attempt stairs. Lifespan: 13–14 years.

CAUTIONS WHEN BUYING

There are only about six hundred Glens in the United States, so you'll probably have to wait for a puppy. This very old breed has been ignored for a long time and has much to offer those who love terriers but who would prefer one without excessive fire or flash.

Golden Retriever

Fine for Novice Owners
Good with Children
Large in Size
Feathered, Medium-Length Coat

EXERCISE REQUIRED — MEDIUM

TRIMMING/CLIPPING REQUIRED — MEDIUM

AMOUNT OF SHEDDING — HIGH

ACTIVITY INDOORS — MEDIUM

EASE OF TRAINING — HIGH

SOCIABILITY WITH STRANGERS — HIGH

TEMPERAMENT

The Golden's kindly expression says it all. This is one of the finest family dogs in the world: cheerful, demonstrative, trustworthy, and forgiving of mistakes. If given two brisk walks each day and allowed to fetch balls and swim, he is adaptable to almost any lifestyle. Friendly with everyone (human and otherwise), his bark is welcoming rather than protective. You must control his tendency to chew on objects and to mouth your hands—provide a box filled with toys so he can carry things around in his mouth. A Golden remains enthusiastically puppy-like for many years, so early obedience training is required to instill calmness and good manners. Eager to please and wonderfully responsive, he is nonetheless distracted by exciting sights and sounds, so you must be both patient and persistent. The mind and heart of a Golden is sweet and gentle, but his body is robust—until he's taught not to pull on the leash, you'll need good biceps to walk him.

HISTORY

The Golden was developed in England and Scotland as both a land hunter and water retriever. He serves as a responsible guide dog for the blind and is one of the flashiest workers in advanced obedience and agility competition. AKC popularity: 2nd of 146.

PHYSICAL FEATURES

Males stand 23-24 inches and weigh 65-75 pounds. Females stand 21½–22½ inches and weigh 55-65 pounds. Avoid oversize Goldens. Brush and comb his silky coat twice a week and occasionally trim straggly hairs. Keep his ear canals clean and dry and his bottom trimmed for cleanliness. Goldens shed profusely and you'll see loose hair most of the year. Color ranges from fox red to medium gold to cream. Many individuals turn prematurely white around their eyes and muzzle. His ears and tail are natural.

HEALTH ISSUES

Both parents should have the following certificates: OFA (hips and elbows), yearly CERF (eyes), and cardiac-clear (for SAS). Also ask about low thyroid, OCD, vWD, seizures, and cancer in the lines. Allergies and skin conditions are common. Lifespan: 10–14 years.

CAUTIONS WHEN BUYING

With the extreme popularity of this breed, the glorious Golden temperament can no longer be taken for granted. You can help separate the wheat from the chaff by buying only from a breeder whose dogs are exceedingly good-natured and who can show you *all* of the health clearances. The best Golden pedigrees include obedience and/or field titles, as well as Ch. titles.

Gordon Setter

Fine for Novice Owners
Good with Children If Raised with Children
Large in Size
Feathered, Medium-Length Coat

EXERCISE REQUIRED — HIGH

TRIMMING/CLIPPING REQUIRED — MEDIUM

AMOUNT OF SHEDDING — MEDIUM

ACTIVITY INDOORS — MEDIUM

EASE OF TRAINING — MEDIUM

SOCIABILITY WITH STRANGERS — MEDIUM

TEMPERAMENT

The handsome, well-muscled Gordon is the most alert, serious, and sensible of the setters, a graceful yet powerful dog who enjoys hiking, biking, jogging, and field work as regular exercise. Though usually calm and dignified, with a wise and noble expression, he does have a silly side, and also a demanding side. He is loyal to his family, and some have protective instincts. He thrives on one-on-one attention and may become jealous of other pets and aggressive with strange dogs. His strong-mindedness calls for early training by someone who knows how to establish and stick to rules, but you must be patient and persuasive, never harsh—all setters are sensitive and will resist being jerked around by bracing themselves and refusing to move. Setters also have long memories: Once they learn something (whether right or wrong), they'll remember it for a long time. On the negative side, this means bad habits can be difficult to break and that harsh handling is not easily forgotten.

HISTORY

Developed in Scotland and first brought to the United States by Daniel Webster, the name of this breed was taken from the duke of Gordon. He hunts more methodically and closer to his owner than other setters. AKC popularity: 79th of 146.

PHYSICAL FEATURES

Males stand 24-27 inches and weigh 55-85 pounds. Females stand 23-26 inches and weigh 45-70 pounds. Brush and comb his silky coat twice a week and occasionally trim straggly hairs. Keep his ear canals clean and dry and his bottom trimmed for cleanliness. He is black with tan markings above his eyes, on his muzzle, throat, chest, legs, feet, and under his tail, and narrow black penciling (stripes) on his toes. Solid red, tan, or buff colors cannot be shown in conformation classes. His ears and tail are natural.

HEALTH ISSUES

Both parents should have OFA certificates (hips) and yearly CERF (eyes). Also ask about low thyroid, bloat, and OCD in the lines. Lifespan: 12 years.

CAUTIONS WHEN BUYING

Unlike Irish and English Setters, many Gordons are bred to be dual-purpose dogs (both field and show), which is most commendable. A Gordon from show-only lines is often heavier boned and has more hair than field-bred dogs.

Great Dane

Best for Experienced Owners
Good with Children If Raised with Children
Giant in Size
Smooth Coat

EXERCISE REQUIRED — MEDIUM

TRIMMING/CLIPPING REQUIRED — LOW

AMOUNT OF SHEDDING — MEDIUM

ACTIVITY INDOORS — LOW

EASE OF TRAINING — MEDIUM

SOCIABILITY WITH STRANGERS — MEDIUM

TEMPERAMENT

The AKC Standard says, "The Apollo of dogs . . . must be spirited and courageous, always friendly and dependable." The Great Dane is a gentle giant, usually easygoing and mild-mannered. He needs only moderate exercise, but does like some space and shouldn't be cramped into studio apartments and postage-stamp yards. Above all, this sociable breed needs companionship and doesn't do well when left alone for long periods of time. With his deep, resounding voice, he won't fail to announce visitors, but guarding and territorial instincts vary. Some lines and individuals are outgoing, some are responsibly protective, while others are standoffish or skittish. To build their confidence and promote a stable temperament, young Danes must be taken out into the world more frequently than some other breeds. Some are peaceful with other pets, while others are dominant. Because he is so huge and can be bossy if undisciplined, obedience training is essential, but Danes are also very sensitive and should be trained with cheerful methods. Leash jerking only confuses them and makes them distrustful. Great Danes drool and slobber and lumber around in a rather bumptious manner, so are not good choices for fastidious housekeepers or those with no sense of humor. Young Danes (up to three years old) can be boisterous and, unless supervised, will dismay you with the magnitude of their destructiveness.

HISTORY

This misnamed breed originated in Germany, not Denmark. In Europe he is correctly called German Mastiff. He hunted wild boar, guarded castles, and fought in battle as a fearsome dog of war. AKC popularity: 28th of 146.

PHYSICAL FEATURES

Males stand 32–37 inches and weigh 145–190 pounds. Females stand 30–35 inches and weigh 100–160 pounds. His hard coat requires only an occasional quick brushing. He may be fawn with a black muzzle, solid black, steel blue, brindle, harlequin (white with ragged black patches), or mantle (often called "Boston," mostly black with white markings). Merle (gray with black spots and white blaze/collar) is a mismarked harlequin and cannot be shown in conformation classes. His ears may be cropped or left naturally hanging. His tail is natural.

HEALTH ISSUES

Both parents should have the following certificates: CERF (eyes), OFA (hips), cardiac-normal, and normal thyroid (full panel). Also ask about bloat, vWD, Wobbler's syndrome, and especially bone cancer in the lines. Lifespan: 6–10 years.

CAUTIONS WHEN BUYING

The size and strength of this breed should not be underestimated: He fills up space in a hurry, and feeding expenses tend to be high, as do vet bills. He also requires more than the average amount of socialization and attention if he is to grow up to be a Dane with a sound temperament.

Greater Swiss Mountain Dog

Best for Experienced Owners
Good with Children
Giant in Size
Short Coat

EXERCISE REQUIRED — MEDIUM
TRIMMING/CLIPPING REQUIRED — LOW
AMOUNT OF SHEDDING — MEDIUM
ACTIVITY INDOORS — MEDIUM
EASE OF TRAINING — MEDIUM
SOCIABILITY WITH STRANGERS — HIGH
MEDIUM

TEMPERAMENT

Calm and steady, yet bold and athletic, the Swissy doesn't need hours of hard running, but he enjoys romping, roughhousing, and working. Pulling a cart or sled (or weight pulling) is a productive outlet for his high energy, especially when children are involved. However, don't expect him to be a baby-sitter. Swissies thrive on your companionship, though their determination to jump up into your face, shove their body against your leg, or slap a massive paw into your lap can be disconcerting. This vigilant watchdog will sound off in a loud, deep voice to announce visitors—or simply to let you know that your neighbor has stepped outdoors. Most are friendly with guests, some are warier, and some are shy, spooky, or aggressive. Early and ongoing socialization is essential to develop a stable Swissy. Some are peaceful with other animals, others have a high prey drive, while still others are aggressive with strange dogs. Obedience training should start at three months old and include praise and food. Heeling is imperative: These powerful dogs can literally pull you off your feet. During adolescence, his hormones will kick in and he will start to test his owner, who must respond with assertive, consistent leadership. Slower to mature (both physically and mentally) than many other breeds, he remains playfully puppy-like for many years. He drinks a lot of water and is slow to housebreak, often not gaining full control until a year of age. You must control his tendency to mouth your hands; similarly, he wants to ingest everything in his path, from sticks to gravel to paper.

HISTORY

Descended from Roman mastiffs, he is the eldest and largest of four Swiss sennenhunds (dogs of the Alpine herdsmen). Referred to as "Old Blaze," he was a farmer's cart dog, pack dog, and home guardian. AKC popularity: 108th of 146.

PHYSICAL FEATURES

Males stand 25–29 inches and weigh 105–140 pounds. Females stand 23–27 inches and weigh 85–110 pounds. Brush his short coat once a week, more often when shedding. Some shed more than others. He is jet black with white markings on his face, chest, feet, and tail tip and rich rust markings over each eye, on his cheeks, chest, legs, and under his tail. His ears and tail are natural.

HEALTH ISSUES

Both parents should have OFA certificates (hips, elbows, and patellas) and yearly CERF (eyes). A temperament-tested title (TT, CGC, or TDI) is also recommended. Ask about bloat, seizures, cancer, digestive problems, low thyroid, and OCD in the lines. Eyelid disorders (entropion) can be a problem. Lifespan: 6–10 years.

CAUTIONS WHEN BUYING

The Swissy is a lot of dog—more than most people realize until they get into the challenge of raising one. You must be committed to the responsibilities of socializing and training a powerful, giant breed with a strong-minded, exuberant personality. He should not be coddled or indulged.

Great Pyrenees

Best for Experienced Owners
Good with Children If Raised with Children
Giant in Size
Thick, Medium-Length Coat

EXERCISE REQUIRED — MEDIUM

TRIMMING/CLIPPING REQUIRED — LOW

AMOUNT OF SHEDDING — HIGH

ACTIVITY INDOORS — LOW

EASE OF TRAINING — LOW

SOCIABILITY WITH STRANGERS — MEDIUM
 LOW

TEMPERAMENT

The AKC Standard describes him as "strong willed, independent and somewhat reserved, yet attentive, fearless and loyal to his charges both human and animal." A majestic dog with a kindly, regal expression, the Great Pyrenees is calm, composed, and serious. He is quiet indoors and content with long daily walks and regular opportunities to stretch out. He does love to romp in the snow, and pulling a cart or carrying a backpack gives him a purpose in life. Aloof with strangers, he should be accustomed to many different people in his early months. He is patient with his own family's children, but some are overprotective when neighbors join in for rough-and-tumble play. Likewise, he may be protective of his own family's pets while aggressively driving off others. These characteristics stem from his background as a livestock guardian, where he was expected to keep watch over the flock, making his own decisions about friends and foes and appropriate actions. Unless you establish yourself as the alpha (number one), the Pyr will trust his own judgment. Obedience training requires consistent leadership; use food rewards rather than jerking this proud, dignified dog around. Pyrs have a deep, impressive bark, which they tend to use freely, especially at night when they are most vigilant. Fences must be high and secure, for they have a tendency to roam, and some produce "slime" (excessive saliva).

HISTORY

On the steep slopes of the Pyrenees Mountains between France and Spain, he guarded sheep flocks against wolves and bears. AKC popularity: 45th of 146.

PHYSICAL FEATURES

Males stand 27–32 inches; females stand 25–29 inches. Weight is 85–130 pounds. His coat is coarse with a dense undercoat and should be brushed twice a week, daily during heavy seasonal shedding. Along with his shedding great chunks of hair in the spring and fall, you'll find lots of loose hair the rest of the year as well. He is solid white, or mostly white with a few gray, badger, reddish brown, or tan shadings. His ears and tail are natural. It is a peculiarity of this breed that he must have one dewclaw on each front leg and double dewclaws on each hind leg.

HEALTH ISSUES

Both parents should have OFA certificates (hips). Also ask about luxating patella, bleeding disorders, bloat, and OCD in the lines. Eyelid disorders (entropion) can be a problem. With his low metabolism, he is sensitive to anesthetics, vaccines, and chemicals and should never be casually medicated or sedated. Lifespan: 8–12 years.

CAUTIONS WHEN BUYING

Because this breed is so powerful and self-reliant, it is essential to start with a genetically sound temperament. Observe both parents and preferably grandparents or other relatives. Some lines are stronger tempered and more work-oriented than others. For a family pet, look for a more easygoing, mellow Pyr.

Greyhound

Best for Experienced Owners
Good with Older, Considerate Children
Large in Size
Smooth Coat

EXERCISE REQUIRED — MEDIUM
TRIMMING/CLIPPING REQUIRED — LOW
AMOUNT OF SHEDDING — MEDIUM LOW
ACTIVITY INDOORS — LOW
EASE OF TRAINING — MEDIUM LOW
SOCIABILITY WITH STRANGERS — MEDIUM
  LOW

TEMPERAMENT

With his quiet dignity and independence, the Greyhound is often likened to a cat. Once past the puppy stage, he is calm and quiet indoors, moving lightly and gracefully, not toppling your lamps, and fulfilling his role as couch potato quite admirably. Though he needs a safe, enclosed area in which to sprint all-out a couple of times a week, he is built for sheer speed rather than endurance and doesn't require hours of exercise. The fastest of all breeds (he can outrun a horse in a sprint), once he has exploded into his powerful driving gallop for a short time, he is content to sleep for the rest of the day. This sensitive breed prefers peace and quiet and soft-spoken people. He does not do well in an environment with frequent tension or loud voices. He loves to lean against his owner, and most are politely reserved with strangers. He is peaceful with other dogs. Because of his heritage, he can be a serious chaser of cats and tiny dogs, but some individuals can learn to coexist with these smaller pets. Greyhounds are nonaggressive (tending to freeze when challenged or attacked) and can be touch-sensitive (tending to startle when touched unexpectedly). Because he is so gentle and docile, he must be trained with a very light hand and much more praise than correction and never jerked around. This quiet dog seldom barks, but many individuals take great delight in stealing and hoarding food and toys.

HISTORY

Developed in ancient Egypt, he used his keen eyesight to locate prey and run it down across open terrain. Today he is being exploited for racing, but fortunately this industry is slowly being eradicated in the United States. AKC popularity: 119th of 146 (though this doesn't reflect his true numbers, as many people adopt ex-racers that are not registered with the AKC).

PHYSICAL FEATURES

He stands 26–30 inches and weighs 55–90 pounds. His hard coat needs only an occasional quick brushing. Colors include brindle, white, white with colored markings, blue, fawn, cream, and black, among others. His ears and tail are natural.

HEALTH ISSUES

Both parents should have yearly CERF certificates (eyes). Also ask about bloat, low thyroid, and bone cancer in the lines. He is sensitive to anesthetics, vaccines, and chemicals and should never be casually medicated or sedated. He needs a sweater in cold weather, and to avoid pressure sores he requires soft blankets to sleep on. Lifespan: 10–14 years.

CAUTIONS WHEN BUYING

Rather than buying a puppy from a breeder, you may choose to save a life and adopt an adult ex-racer. An estimated twenty thousand are euthanized each year. When carefully screened by a responsible Greyhound rescue league, ex-racers make sweet-tempered, well-mannered companions.

Harrier

Best for Experienced Owners
Good with Children
Medium in Size
Smooth Coat

EXERCISE REQUIRED — HIGH MEDIUM

TRIMMING/CLIPPING REQUIRED — LOW

AMOUNT OF SHEDDING — MEDIUM

ACTIVITY INDOORS — MEDIUM

EASE OF TRAINING — MEDIUM LOW

SOCIABILITY WITH STRANGERS — HIGH
MEDIUM

TEMPERAMENT

The AKC Standard says he is "active, well-balanced, full of strength and quality . . . able to work tirelessly, no matter the terrain, for long periods." The Harrier is cheerful and stable and makes an amiable companion when vigorously exercised (jogging, biking, running, hiking). Though not hyperactive, without outlets for his energy he can be rambunctious and prone to destructive chewing and digging. Unless trained for hunting, he should not be let off-leash except in a safe, enclosed area, for he is an enthusiastic explorer who will drop his nose to the ground and head for the hills. Harriers are not known for their speedy response to a come command. He is usually friendly with everyone, sociable and gregarious with other dogs—indeed, he is happiest when other dogs are present in the home. With his hunting heritage, he may chase smaller pets if not taught otherwise. As with so many other scenthounds, training takes a while, for he is independent and self-willed. Harriers are "touchers" who like to lean against you or lie with their paw resting on your shoe. They will bay and howl if allowed to become bored, and some individuals can be hard to housebreak.

HISTORY

A scenthound from England, the Harrier trails hares or foxes while the huntsmen follow on horseback. AKC popularity: 143rd of 146.

PHYSICAL FEATURES

He stands 18–22 inches and weighs 45–60 pounds. His hard coat needs only an occasional quick brushing. Keep his ear canals clean and dry. He is usually tricolor (black, tan, and white), but may also be red-and-white, tan-and-white, or lemon-and-white. His ears and tail are natural.

HEALTH ISSUES

Both parents should have OFA certificates (hips) and yearly CERF (eyes). Also ask about genetic shyness in the lines. Lifespan: 10–12 years.

CAUTIONS WHEN BUYING

This breed is a good choice for those who love the classic hound shape, pleasant good nature, and outdoorsy inclinations of the scenthound family and who prefer something midway in size between a Beagle and a Foxhound. Be prepared to wait. Litters are not numerous (perhaps six per year in the United States), and a high percentage of pups are kept for showing and breeding. The good news is that he has not caught the attention of unknowledgeable breeders, so he is a far safer bet as a sound-tempered, healthy pet than his little cousin, the Beagle.

Havanese

Fine for Novice Owners
Good with Older, Considerate Children
Little in Size
Long Coat

EXERCISE REQUIRED — LOW
TRIMMING/CLIPPING REQUIRED — HIGH
     MEDIUM LOW
AMOUNT OF SHEDDING — LOW
ACTIVITY INDOORS — HIGH
EASE OF TRAINING — MEDIUM
SOCIABILITY WITH STRANGERS — MEDIUM

TEMPERAMENT

One of the brightest and sturdiest of the toys, the Havanese is happy and playful and enjoys clever games of dexterity such as "pull the hidden toy from under the cabinet with your paw." This curious, quick-moving sprite with the springy gait is a busy little dog who enjoys dashing around the yard and playing with other pets. Very people-oriented and a bit of a ham, he will seek attention by clowning around and showing off. He is peaceful and gentle with everyone, though he likes to sit perched on the back of a sofa or chair, looking out the window so he can announce visitors. The breed is attentive and responsive to nonforceful training, and many individuals excel in competitive obedience and agility. Some even have herding instincts. Housebreaking may take a while with some individuals.

HISTORY

Originating in the Mediterranean, he was the household pet of the wealthy ruling class in Havana, Cuba. AKC popularity: 98th of 146.

PHYSICAL FEATURES

He stands 8½–11½ inches and weighs 7–13 pounds. His soft double coat may be wavy (preferred), curly, or straight and needs to be brushed and combed every other day. Pet owners may choose to have the coat trimmed/clipped short every four to six weeks. Keep his ear canals clean and dry and his bottom trimmed for cleanliness. Colors include white, cream, champagne, gold, chocolate, silver, blue, black, particolor, and others. His ears and tail are natural.

HEALTH ISSUES

Both parents should have yearly CERF certificates (eyes) and be screened for luxating patella. Also ask about low thyroid, allergies, and skin conditions in the lines. Lifespan: 13–15 years.

CAUTIONS WHEN BUYING

Other breeds in the bichon family include the Bichon Frise, Bolognese, Coton de Tulear, and Maltese. Larger and sturdier than his Maltese cousin, the Havanese is easier to raise and care for, though his coat, if not trimmed or clipped, requires the same commitment to grooming. And because he is less popular and has not been exploited by unknowledgeable breeders, he is a safer bet in the genetic health and temperament departments.

Ibizan Hound (ah-BEETH-in)

Best for Experienced Owners
Good with Children
Medium to Large in Size
Smooth Coat or Wiry Coat

EXERCISE REQUIRED — HIGH MEDIUM
TRIMMING/CLIPPING REQUIRED — LOW
AMOUNT OF SHEDDING — MEDIUM
ACTIVITY INDOORS — MEDIUM LOW
EASE OF TRAINING — MEDIUM
SOCIABILITY WITH STRANGERS — MEDIUM

TEMPERAMENT

The AKC Standard says, "Lithe and racy, the Ibizan possesses a deerlike elegance combined with the power of a hunter." Once past the boisterous puppy stage, this sleek breed is quiet, gentle, and relaxed indoors and can be a couch potato. However, true to his heritage, he is also a swift and athletic dog who needs running exercise in a safe, enclosed area. He especially likes to leap, and he is incredibly graceful and light on his feet, without equal as a high-jumper and broad-jumper. Fences must be at least six feet high—the top of the refrigerator is not out of his reach. Polite but watchful with strangers, he does need early and extensive socialization to develop a confident, outgoing personality. Most are effective watchdogs and some have protective instincts, which is unusual for a sighthound. "Beezers" are good with other dogs, but likely to pursue (and catch!) smaller pets. He learns quickly and enjoys canine activities such as obedience and agility (when they are made interesting and challenging), but he is a freethinker who doesn't obey mindlessly. He must be handled calmly and persuasively and motivated with food and praise, for he is sensitive to sharp corrections. Sighthounds can be touch-sensitive, startling when touched unexpectedly or wrapped up in someone's arms. A verbal correction is more effective than a physical one, because it is less upsetting and distracting to the dog.

HISTORY

A statue of the canine god Anubis, uncovered in King Tut's tomb, is believed to be that of an Ibizan. However, this ancient breed did not come by his name until he became popular as a rabbit hunter on the Mediterranean island of Ibiza. AKC popularity: 137th of 146.

PHYSICAL FEATURES

He stands 24–28 inches and weighs 45–60 pounds. His coat may be smooth (most common) or wiry. Brush once a week. He is mostly red (ranging from deep red to tawny tan) with white markings, or mostly white with red patches (pinto). His ears and tail are natural.

HEALTH ISSUES

Do not buy a pup unless both parents have had an AD analysis to detect axonal dystrophy, a serious degenerative nerve disease. The following certificates are extra security: OFA (hips) and yearly CERF (eyes). Also ask about low thyroid, deafness, cardiomyopathy, seizures, and genetic shyness in the lines. He is sensitive to anesthetics, vaccines, and chemicals and should never be casually medicated or sedated. He needs a sweater in cold weather, and to avoid pressure sores he requires soft blankets to sleep on. Lifespan: 11–14 years.

CAUTIONS WHEN BUYING

Ibizans are the rarest of the sighthounds—expect to be put on a waiting list.

Irish Setter

Fine for Novice Owners
Good with Children
Large in Size
Feathered, Medium-Length Coat

EXERCISE REQUIRED — HIGH
TRIMMING/CLIPPING REQUIRED — MEDIUM
AMOUNT OF SHEDDING — MEDIUM
ACTIVITY INDOORS — HIGH MEDIUM
EASE OF TRAINING — MEDIUM
SOCIABILITY WITH STRANGERS — HIGH

TEMPERAMENT

The most popular of the setters, the elegant Irish has been described as rollicking, happy-go-lucky, clownish, impulsive, flighty, and demonstrative, though some individuals are more dignified and aristocratic. Without enough running exercise and obedience training to instill good manners, this lively dog can turn into a destructive handful, especially during the gawky adolescent stage—which lasts two or three years. The sociable Irish Setter gets along well with everyone and won't thrive if left alone all day without the companionship of either people or other pets. Though he has a willful streak and is easily distracted, he is more willing to please than the other setters and responds well to persistent—but never harsh—training. Setters are sensitive dogs with long memories: Once they learn something (whether right or wrong), they'll remember it for a long time. On the negative side, this means bad habits can be difficult to break and harsh handling is not easily forgotten.

HISTORY

He was developed in Ireland as a solid-color strain of the original Red and White Setter. AKC popularity: 60th of 146.

PHYSICAL FEATURES

Males stand 26–28 inches and weigh 70–80 pounds. Females stand 24–26 inches and weigh 60–70 pounds. Brush and comb his silky coat twice a week and occasionally trim straggly hairs. Keep his ear canals clean and dry and his bottom trimmed for cleanliness. His red color ranges from chestnut to mahogany. His ears and tail are natural.

HEALTH ISSUES

Both parents should have OFA certificates (hips), yearly CERF (eyes), and a DNA certificate that shows whether they are affected, carriers, or clear of PRA (at least one parent must be clear). Also ask about low thyroid, OCD, bloat, seizures, allergies, and skin conditions in the lines. Lifespan: 12–15 years.

CAUTIONS WHEN BUYING

If you want an Irish Setter for hunting, make sure the breeder can prove field ability with demonstrations and hunting test titles (JH, MH, SH) in the pedigree. Some lines are bred only for conformation, profuse coat, and extreme elegance.

Irish Terrier

Best for Experienced Owners
Good with Older, Considerate Children
Medium in Size
Wiry Coat

EXERCISE REQUIRED — HIGH MEDIUM

TRIMMING/CLIPPING REQUIRED — HIGH
   MEDIUM

AMOUNT OF SHEDDING — LOW

ACTIVITY INDOORS — MEDIUM

EASE OF TRAINING — LOW

SOCIABILITY WITH STRANGERS — HIGH
   MEDIUM

TEMPERAMENT

The AKC Standard says, "There is a heedless, reckless pluck about the Irish Terrier which . . . coupled with the headlong dash, blind to all consequences, with which he rushes at his adversary, has earned for the breed the proud epithet of Daredevil." One of the boldest and most animated of the terriers, this fearless breed, built on lines of speed with a graceful, racy outline, must often be protected from himself. Energetic and intense, he romps and plays with vigor and will take as much exercise as you can offer. Leashes and secure fences are compulsory, for he is exceedingly fast and agile, with strong chasing, digging, and jumping instincts. He does best with active families, for without such exercise and lots of companionship and personal interaction, he will become bored and seek to entertain himself—and his choices usually involve mischief and destructiveness. His reaction to strangers varies from polite to aloof, and even the polite ones are vigilant watchdogs. Early socialization is important for a stable, controlled temperament. The Irish can be exceedingly scrappy with other animals, whether canine or feline, and will make short shrift of rabbits and rodents. Stubborn and self-assured, he is inclined to test for position in the family pecking order. Some like to bark.

HISTORY

Developed in Ireland and England, the Irish Terrier was a versatile farm dog, vermin- and small-game hunter, and a messenger dog during World War I. AKC popularity: 113th of 146.

PHYSICAL FEATURES

He stands 18–19 inches and weighs 25–35 pounds. Brush and comb his hard, wiry coat once a week. Show dogs are "stripped" (dead coat plucked out) every few months; pet owners may opt for more convenient clipping. He is red, ranging from deep mahogany to wheaten. His ears are natural; his tail is docked.

HEALTH ISSUES

Ask about allergies and skin conditions in the lines. Lifespan: 12–16 years.

CAUTIONS WHEN BUYING

Be sure you are up for this breed's high energy level and rapidly shifting trains of thought. Terriers are determined, independent fellows who must be chosen only by owners who know what they're getting into.

Irish Water Spaniel

Best for Experienced Owners
Good with Children If Raised with Children
Large in Size
Curly Coat

EXERCISE REQUIRED — HIGH

TRIMMING/CLIPPING REQUIRED — MEDIUM

AMOUNT OF SHEDDING — LOW

ACTIVITY INDOORS — MEDIUM

EASE OF TRAINING — MEDIUM

SOCIABILITY WITH STRANGERS — LOW

TEMPERAMENT

The AKC Standard says, "Great intelligence is combined with rugged endurance and a bold, dashing eagerness." The tallest of the spaniels, with a unique quizzical expression, the Irish Water Spaniel has a distinct, purposeful presence. He varies in personality more than some other breeds, but most are bold, inquisitive, and eager to play. He needs plenty of vigorous exercise, including retrieving and swimming. He should be accustomed to a variety of people and new situations at an early age, as he tends to be reserved and often protective, and these traits could easily slide into shyness or sharpness. He can be aggressive with strange dogs, sometimes even with other pets. Most have strong opinions and are not hesitant about expressing them, yet he is capable of learning a great deal from an owner who knows how to lead. Obedience training must be persuasive rather than heavy-handed, because this breed is sensitive and can become defensive if jerked around. Handled properly and given outlets for his exuberance, he is a fun-loving, extremely perceptive dog. However, this is not a breed to be teased or ignored, nor one to be chosen by a nonassertive owner.

HISTORY

A very old breed from Ireland, he can work like a spaniel, flushing birds from thickets, but his curly coat burrs up quickly, so his responsibilities tend to focus on retrieving shot ducks from the water. AKC popularity: 131st of 146.

PHYSICAL FEATURES

Males stand 22–24 inches and weigh 55–65 pounds. Females stand 21–23 inches and weigh 45–60 pounds. His coat is a mass of short, crisp curls, with a hanging topknot of longer, looser curls on his head. His face is smooth, as is his tail except for a few inches of curls at the base. Brush twice a week and trim occasionally. Keep his ear canals clean and dry and his bottom trimmed for cleanliness. He is solid liver. His ears and tail are natural. His feet are webbed.

HEALTH ISSUES

Both parents should have OFA certificates (hips) and yearly CERF (eyes). Also ask about low thyroid and seizures in the lines. Some individuals are susceptible to a toenail disorder that may be related to allergies, skin conditions, and other immune system problems. Lifespan: 12 years.

CAUTIONS WHEN BUYING

Looks can be deceiving: The Irish Water Spaniel is not a brown, hypoallergenic, eager-to-obey Poodle. His strong personality must be appreciated and respected. Fortunately, he has never been popular enough to be heavily sought after by either show fanciers or field enthusiasts, so most breeders produce dogs who perform admirably in both arenas—truly a dual-purpose breed.

Irish Wolfhound

Best for Experienced Owners
Good with Children
Giant in Size
Wiry Coat

EXERCISE REQUIRED — MEDIUM

TRIMMING/CLIPPING REQUIRED — MEDIUM
LOW

AMOUNT OF SHEDDING — MEDIUM

ACTIVITY INDOORS — LOW

EASE OF TRAINING — MEDIUM

SOCIABILITY WITH STRANGERS — MEDIUM

TEMPERAMENT

The AKC Standard says, "Of great size and commanding appearance, the Irish Wolfhound is remarkable in combining power and swiftness with sight." This gentle giant is sometimes calm and dignified, sometimes playful and silly, always easygoing and reliable. He does best in a suburban or country home with lots of companionship and room to stretch out. He needs regular exercise to stay fit, whether he seems to want it or not. A daily one-hour walk/trot (on-leash) with twice-weekly gallops inside a safe enclosed area are necessary for proper development. However, young Wolfhounds (under eighteen months) shouldn't be heavily exercised (no jumping, biking, or jogging) because their growing bones can be overstressed. Sensible with strangers, most are friendly and expect to be petted, while some are warier. He does need early, frequent socialization to encourage an outgoing attitude. Few individuals are guardians; indeed, suspiciousness or aggressiveness should never be encouraged. With other animals he is amiable and peaceful, but he does love to chase, tackle, and pounce on anything that moves rapidly. A sweet and sensitive dog, he has his independent side but responds well (slowly and thoughtfully) to patient obedience training. Use positive rewards rather than heavy-handed jerking. Wolfhounds remain gawky, clumsy, and potentially destructive (in a big way!) for up to three years.

HISTORY

The tallest breed in the world was developed in feudal Ireland for hunting wolves and Irish elk. AKC popularity: 82nd of 146.

PHYSICAL FEATURES

Males stand 32–36 inches and weigh 120–160 pounds. Females stand 30–34 inches and weigh 105–130 pounds. Brush and comb his rough coat once a week and occasionally trim straggly hairs. Colors include fawn (cream to wheaten), red, gray, or brindle. His ears and tail are natural.

HEALTH ISSUES

Both parents should have OFA certificates (hips) and yearly CERF (eyes). Also ask about bone cancer, cardiomyopathy, OCD, vWD, liver shunt, and bloat in the lines. He is sensitive to anesthetics, vaccines, and chemicals and should never be casually medicated or sedated. Lifespan: 6-8 years (search for lines with longevity).

CAUTIONS WHEN BUYING

The size and strength of this breed should not be underestimated: He takes up considerable room sprawled on your sofa and bed, and your VW Beetle won't do for transporting him to the vet. Feeding and maintenance expenses are high. Ongoing socialization and obedience training are musts, as are patience and a sense of humor when he submerges his beard in his water bowl and comes up dripping. Wolfhounds are not the breed for impatient owners.

Italian Greyhound

Best for Experienced Owners
Good with Older, Considerate Children
Small in Size
Smooth Coat

EXERCISE REQUIRED — MEDIUM

TRIMMING/CLIPPING REQUIRED — LOW

AMOUNT OF SHEDDING — LOW

ACTIVITY INDOORS — MEDIUM

EASE OF TRAINING — MEDIUM LOW

SOCIABILITY WITH STRANGERS — MEDIUM
LOW

TEMPERAMENT

The Italian Greyhound is sweet-natured, gentle, and quiet (seldom barks), yet more playful and athletic than his racy appearance might suggest. This comfort-loving dog can usually be found on soft furniture, preferably hidden under a blanket, pillow, or jacket. However, the same dog will suddenly explode into a short burst of vigorous running and leaping, tearing pell-mell around the yard, darting and zigzagging without altering his pace, or bouncing off the sofa and beds. His yard must have a high fence, for he is an excellent jumper. Off-leash walks would be foolish; he can be out of sight in seconds and has no traffic sense. Polite (often a bit aloof) with strangers, there is a potential for timidity, so he should be socialized early and thoroughly. He is amiable with other dogs and cats, but some have a high prey drive and will run squeaky creatures into the ground. IGs (pronounced *eye-jees*) or Iggies are mildly stubborn and very sensitive. They respond favorably only to gentle, upbeat training methods that emphasize food rewards. Verbal corrections are less upsetting and distracting to them than physical corrections, because they can be touch-sensitive, startling when touched unexpectedly or grabbed for a hug. Yet they do love to be stroked and indeed demand affection and physical attention. Housebreaking is notoriously difficult; many refuse to go outside in the cold or rain.

HISTORY

Probably more than two thousand years old, he was especially popular with the Italians in the Middle Ages and was depicted in many Renaissance paintings. AKC popularity: 49th of 146.

PHYSICAL FEATURES

He stands 13–15 inches (though a good number are taller) and weighs 8–14 pounds. His soft, glossy coat needs only an occasional quick brushing. Colors include blue, fawn, red, black, and others, often with white markings. His ears and tail are natural.

HEALTH ISSUES

Both parents should have yearly CERF certificates (eyes) and be screened for luxating patella. Check parents' teeth for soundness—poor teeth run through some lines. Also ask about low thyroid, seizures, and Legg-Perthes. Blues are susceptible to color mutant alopecia. He is sensitive to anesthetics, vaccines, and chemicals and should never be casually medicated or sedated. His skin is exceedingly thin; he needs a sweater in cold weather, and to avoid pressure sores he requires soft blankets for sleeping. Leg fractures are common in adolescents, who believe they can fly and will launch themselves fearlessly into space from any height. Lifespan: 13–16 years.

CAUTIONS WHEN BUYING

Be sure you're not choosing this breed solely for his exotic deer-like build and chiseled head, his light, graceful, high-stepping gait, or his tendency to pose like an elegant porcelain statue. He does have special needs that must be met if he is to remain safe, healthy, and happy.

Italian Spinone (spin-O-nay)

Fine for Novice Owners
Good with Children
Large in Size
Wiry Coat

EXERCISE REQUIRED — HIGH

TRIMMING/CLIPPING REQUIRED — MEDIUM

AMOUNT OF SHEDDING — MEDIUM

ACTIVITY INDOORS — MEDIUM

EASE OF TRAINING — MEDIUM

SOCIABILITY WITH STRANGERS — MEDIUM

TEMPERAMENT

The Italian Spinone Club says: "Everything about this breed suggests great strength." Kind, patient, and gentle in the home, the Spinone is a serious, tireless hunting machine in the field. Though he looks gruff, rather like a wise old grandfather, he is happy and playful, even clownish. Youngsters can be restless and require lots of attention, but adults are calm and laid-back, as long as they are given sufficient daily exercise, including swimming if possible. Remember that this is a hunting breed, not an apartment decoration. This sweet-natured dog needs lots of early exposure to people and strange sights and sounds. When well socialized, he may turn out quite friendly or remain a bit cautious, yet poised. Most get along well with other animals. He has an independent mind and can be stubborn, but this is not a dominant dog who needs (or who can withstand) strong-arm training methods. Motivational methods work best with the sensitive Spinone. He can be a jumper and digger, so make sure fences are secure. Some drool.

HISTORY

The Italian Spinone, also called Spinone Italiano, is Italy's all-purpose hunting dog, a rather slow-footed, methodical, highly efficient pointing dog. Newly recognized by the AKC.

PHYSICAL FEATURES

He stands 22–27 inches and weighs 60–85 pounds. Brush his wiry coat once a week. Show dogs are "stripped" (dead coat plucked out) every few months; pet owners may opt for more convenient clipping. Keep his ear canals clean and dry and his bottom trimmed for cleanliness. He is solid white, mostly white with yellow or brown patches, orange roan, or brown roan. His ears are natural; his tail is docked.

HEALTH ISSUES

Both parents should have OFA certificates (hips and elbows). A yearly CERF certificate (eyes) is also desirable. Also ask about bloat and cerebellar ataxia in the lines. Lifespan: 12 years.

CAUTIONS WHEN BUYING

Most Spinoni (the plural) have strong hunting instincts. There is not a significant split between field types and show types, though more are used for hunting than are shown in conformation. Litters are not numerous, so be prepared to wait.

Jack Russell Terrier (Broken Coat)

Best for Experienced Owners
Good with Older, Considerate Children
Small in Size
Wiry Coat

EXERCISE REQUIRED — HIGH

TRIMMING/CLIPPING REQUIRED — MEDIUM
   LOW

AMOUNT OF SHEDDING — MEDIUM

ACTIVITY INDOORS — HIGH

EASE OF TRAINING — MEDIUM LOW

SOCIABILITY WITH STRANGERS — MEDIUM

TEMPERAMENT

If any dog can top the high energy level and daring of a Fox Terrier, it is a JRT. If any dog can top the hard-as-nails working ability of a Border Terrier, it is a JRT. And if any dog can top the strong prey drive, determination, tenacity, and intensity of a JRT . . . well, that could only be another JRT! This bright, clever, athletic breed is on top of everything that's going on. Nothing gets by him. A solitary or sedate lifestyle is not suited to a Jack Russell: He requires full participation in the family and vigorous daily play sessions, especially ball chasing. Too little exercise, companionship, and mental stimulation will quickly lead to boredom, which will in turn lead to destructive behaviors. Most are friendly with strangers, but in the presence of strange dogs, keep them close and under control. Some JRTs are so brash and fearless they will take on a Rottweiler if it looks cross-eyed at them. Two Jack Russells (regardless of sex or age) should never be left together, because a seemingly amiable relationship can suddenly flare into deadly combat over something as innocuous as possession of a chew toy. Small pets that run, squeak, or flutter probably won't last an hour. This breed must be kept on-leash or securely fenced at all times, for his exploratory instincts are legendary. He will "go to ground" after anything and will stay in or by the hole for days without food or water. Assertive but cheerful, with typical terrier stubbornness, he responds well to obedience training that utilizes food. He especially enjoys learning tricks. It is a foregone conclusion that JRTs are enthusiastic diggers and barkers.

HISTORY

Developed by Parson John Russell of England to run with the foxhounds, he was given the responsibility of bolting the fox from its den so the hunt could continue. AKC popularity: 78th of 146.

PHYSICAL FEATURES

He stands 12–15 inches (some organizations also allow 10–12 inches) and weighs 10–17 pounds. Brush and comb his harsh, broken coat once a week. Show dogs are "stripped" (dead coat plucked out) every few months; pet owners may opt for more convenient clipping. He is mostly white, with black, brown, and/or tan markings. His ears are natural; his tail is docked.

HEALTH ISSUES

Both parents should have yearly CERF certificates (eyes). Puppies should come with a BAER printout that shows normal bilateral hearing. Also ask about low thyroid, luxating patella, Legg-Perthes, vWD, heart disease, and cerebellar ataxia in the lines. Lifespan: 13–15 years.

CAUTIONS WHEN BUYING

Without an extraordinary amount of an owner's time and effort, this highly focused dog is challenging to live with. One breeder describes him as being reminiscent of a toddler at the "why" stage. Be sure you are buying a square "Parson Jack Russell," as some breeders are producing long-backed, short-legged dogs who would not even be recognized by the good parson today.

Jack Russell Terrier (Smooth)

Best for Experienced Owners
Good with Older, Considerate Children
Small in Size
Short Coat

EXERCISE REQUIRED — HIGH

TRIMMING/CLIPPING REQUIRED — LOW

AMOUNT OF SHEDDING — MEDIUM

ACTIVITY INDOORS — HIGH

EASE OF TRAINING — MEDIUM LOW

SOCIABILITY WITH STRANGERS — MEDIUM

TEMPERAMENT

If any dog can top the high energy level and daring of a Fox Terrier, it is a JRT. If any dog can top the hard-as-nails working ability of a Border Terrier, it is a JRT. And if any dog can top the strong prey drive, determination, tenacity, and intensity of a JRT . . . well, that could only be another JRT! This bright, clever, athletic breed is on top of everything that's going on. Nothing gets by him. A solitary or sedate lifestyle is not suited to a Jack Russell: He requires full participation in the family and vigorous daily play sessions, especially ball chasing. Too little exercise, companionship, and mental stimulation will quickly lead to boredom, which will in turn lead to destructive behaviors. Most are friendly with strangers, but in the presence of strange dogs, keep them close and under control. Some JRTs are so brash and fearless they will take on a Rottweiler if it looks cross-eyed at them. Two Jack Russells (regardless of sex or age) should never be left together, because a seemingly amiable relationship can suddenly flare into deadly combat over something as innocuous as possession of a chew toy. Small pets that run, squeak, or flutter probably won't last an hour. This breed must be kept on-leash or securely fenced at all times, for his exploratory instincts are legendary. He will "go to ground" after anything and will stay in or by the hole for days without food or water. Assertive but cheerful, with typical terrier stubbornness, he responds well to obedience training that utilizes food. He especially enjoys learning tricks. It is a foregone conclusion that JRTs are enthusiastic diggers and barkers.

HISTORY

Developed by Parson John Russell of England to run with the foxhounds, he was given the responsibility of bolting the fox from its den so the hunt could continue. AKC popularity: 78th of 146.

PHYSICAL FEATURES

He stands 12–15 inches (some organizations also allow 10–12 inches) and weighs 10–17 pounds. His short coat requires only an occasional quick brushing. He is mostly white, with black, brown, and/or tan markings. His ears are natural; his tail is docked.

HEALTH ISSUES

Both parents should have yearly CERF certificates (eyes). Puppies should come with a BAER printout that shows normal bilateral hearing. Also ask about low thyroid, luxating patella, Legg-Perthes, vWD, heart disease, and cerebellar ataxia in the lines. Lifespan: 13–15 years.

CAUTIONS WHEN BUYING

Without an extraordinary amount of time an owner's and effort, this highly focused dog is challenging to live with. One breeder describes him as being reminiscent of a toddler at the "why" stage. Be sure you are buying a square "Parson Jack Russell," as some breeders are producing long-backed, short-legged dogs who would not even be recognized by the good parson today.

Japanese Chin

Fine for Novice Owners
Good with Older, Considerate Children
Little in Size
Feathered, Medium-Length Coat

EXERCISE REQUIRED — LOW

TRIMMING/CLIPPING REQUIRED — LOW

AMOUNT OF SHEDDING — HIGH MEDIUM

ACTIVITY INDOORS — MEDIUM

EASE OF TRAINING — MEDIUM

SOCIABILITY WITH STRANGERS — HIGH
        MEDIUM

TEMPERAMENT

Perky, proud, and playful, the elegant Japanese Chin is less yappy than other toy breeds. Though he does love to play in the yard, he doesn't need much more exercise than that. The yard must be fenced, for he has just enough hunting instincts that he will chase birds or butterflies into the street. A lover of comfort, he enjoys cuddling on laps and snuggling into soft pillows, his soulful eyes inviting pampering, which he accepts graciously. However, you're just as apt to find him perched high on the back of the sofa, for he is a climber, light and graceful on his feet, much like a cat. This gentle yet merry breed insists on attention and interaction and is a terrific pet for senior citizens. At the other end of the spectrum, he is easily overwhelmed by small children and cannot take rough handling or mischief. Most are polite with strangers, though some are standoffish or timid, so socialization is important. He is peaceful with other pets. Though he has an aristocratic demeanor and definite likes and dislikes, he is also bright, sensitive, and responsive. The little obedience training he needs will go well if you rely on consistency, praise, and food rewards. He can be difficult to housebreak.

HISTORY

In Japan, there are Inu (dogs) and there are Chin (royalty). The Japanese Chin once warmed the laps of Chinese aristocracy and kept court with the ladies of the Japanese Imperial Palace. AKC popularity: 73rd of 146.

PHYSICAL FEATURES

He stands 8–11 inches and weighs about 7 pounds. Many individuals are larger; these are not suitable for showing, but make sturdy pets. Brush and comb his silky coat twice a week, more often when he is shedding. He does shed quite a lot, especially in warmer climates. Keep his ear canals clean and dry and his bottom trimmed for cleanliness. He is most commonly black-and-white, sometimes with tan trim. He may also be red-and-white, the red being any shade, including orange and lemon, sometimes with sabling (black-tipped hairs). His ears and tail are natural.

HEALTH ISSUES

Both parents should have yearly CERF certificates (eyes) and be screened for luxating patella. Also ask about heart disease in the lines. He is sensitive to anesthetics, vaccines, and chemicals and should never be casually medicated or sedated. With his short face, he is susceptible to respiratory difficulties and heatstroke in hot, humid, and/or stuffy conditions. Smaller individuals are more susceptible to hypoglycemia (low blood sugar). Lifespan: 12–14 years.

CAUTIONS WHEN BUYING

Because of similarities in size, coat, and build, some people find themselves comparing the Japanese Chin (once called the Japanese Spaniel) with the English Toy Spaniel. The Chin is lighter and finer in build, more agile and athletic, and usually more outgoing.

Keeshond (KAYZ-hawnd)

Fine for Novice Owners
Good with Children
Medium in Size
Thick, Medium-Length Coat

EXERCISE REQUIRED — MEDIUM
TRIMMING/CLIPPING REQUIRED — LOW
AMOUNT OF SHEDDING — HIGH
ACTIVITY INDOORS — MEDIUM
EASE OF TRAINING — MEDIUM
SOCIABILITY WITH STRANGERS — MEDIUM

TEMPERAMENT

Compared to other breeds in the spitz (northern breed) family, the Keeshond is more sensible and quiet and less dominant. Bright, cheerful, and lively, he needs moderate exercise, but more important, he needs companionship. He is very people-oriented, craves attention and petting, and needs to be fully involved in the family. Attitude toward strangers varies from friendly to polite; there is timidity in some lines, so early socialization is important to build an outgoing, confident temperament. With his acute hearing and emotional sensitivity, he is more reactive to loud noises than some other breeds and does not do well in an environment with frequent tension or loud voices. This is not a guard dog: Keeshonden (the plural) will bark, but it's usually welcoming rather than protective. Most are peaceful with other pets. He has an independent streak and can be a bit "clever" and mischievous, but forceful training only makes him obstinate and skittish. Focus on gentle, positive guidance and praise/food rewards. The Kees is known as the "Smiling Dutchman" because of his tendency to curl his lip and bare his teeth in a happy/submissive grin. It actually looks more like a grimace, but he thinks it's beautiful!

HISTORY

In Holland he began as a riverboat watchdog. When the country divided itself into two political camps, the leader of the Patriots, Kees de Gyselaar, had a little dog who became the mascot of the Patriots. Though they lost the party battle, Kees's *hond* (dog) was eventually designated the national dog of Holland. AKC popularity: 66th of 146.

PHYSICAL FEATURES

He stands 16–19 inches and weighs 35–45 pounds. His long, harsh coat with its dense undercoat stands well off his body. He should be brushed twice a week, daily when he is shedding. Along with heavy seasonal shedding, you'll see loose hair the rest of the year as well. Keep his bottom trimmed for cleanliness. He is a dramatic blend of gray, black, and cream, with dark "spectacles" around his eyes. His ears and tail are natural.

HEALTH ISSUES

Both parents should have OFA certificates (hips) and yearly CERF (eyes) and be screened for luxating patella. Also ask about low thyroid, seizures, vWD, allergies, and heart disease in the lines. With his thick coat, he doesn't do well in humid weather. Lifespan: 12–15 years.

CAUTIONS WHEN BUYING

Many people are not up for the shedding of northern breeds. Twice a year, these dogs "blow their coats," with the hair coming out in huge clumps and wafting through the house, under the furniture and appliances, even into your food. During this period, you'll be brushing and vacuuming constantly and using masking tape to pull the hair off your clothes.

Kerry Blue Terrier

Best for Experienced Owners
Good with Older, Considerate Children
Medium in Size
Unusual Coat (see Physical Features below)

EXERCISE REQUIRED — MEDIUM

TRIMMING/CLIPPING REQUIRED — HIGH

AMOUNT OF SHEDDING — LOW

ACTIVITY INDOORS — MEDIUM

EASE OF TRAINING — MEDIUM LOW

SOCIABILITY WITH STRANGERS — LOW

TEMPERAMENT

The Kerry Blue is extraordinarily bright and full of life, with a great sense of humor, but he can also be moody. He has a high energy level, is always ready to play, and wants to be wherever you are. When bored or ignored, he may get into mischief. Toward strangers he may be friendly or reserved, and even the friendly ones are sensibly protective. Some lines and individuals are warier, and some are over-protective. Socialization is imperative to develop a stable attitude. A Kerry may not be the best choice for multi-pet households—he may not go looking for a fight, but he won't walk away from one, and he can have a high prey drive with cats, birds, and other small animals. Kerries are one of the smartest breeds in dogdom, and one of the best problem-solvers, but that doesn't mean instant obedience. In other words, he is capable of learning anything, including how to get what *he* wants. Unless you establish your-self as a consistent leader, he may be headstrong and take clever advantage of those who indulge him. This proud, sensitive, self-assured dog doesn't meekly accept teasing, unfairness, or rough handling. He can be possessive of his food and toys, and some enjoy digging.

HISTORY

He originated in County Kerry, Ireland, as a versatile working dog, hunting birds and small game, herding sheep, and guarding the farm. AKC popularity: 107th of 146.

PHYSICAL FEATURES

He stands 17–20 inches and weighs 30–45 pounds. His coat is soft, dense, and wavy, with much facial hair, and requires brushing and combing twice a week. His beard should be combed daily for cleanliness. Likewise, keep his bottom trimmed for cleanliness. Keep his ear canals clean and dry. To look like the dog in the photo above, his coat needs expert shaping with scissors every four to six weeks; pet owners may choose to clip the coat rather than scissor. A puppy is born black, his coat gradually "clearing" to blue-gray (slate blue to silver gray) by eighteen months of age. His ears are natural; his tail is docked.

HEALTH ISSUES

Both parents should have OFA certificates (hips). Also ask about low thyroid, bleeding disorders, eye problems, tumors/cancer, and PNA (a fatal nerve disease of very young puppies) in the lines. Cysts and spiculosis (hard hairs), though usually not malignant, do require attention, so avoid lines covered with them. Many allergies and skin conditions are reported. Lifespan: 12–15 years.

CAUTIONS WHEN BUYING

Vigorous physical and mental exercise (advanced obedience, agility, interactive play sessions and games) are essential to the well-being of this highly intelligent breed. If you're looking for a dog you can safely spoil rotten and leave to his own devices, you are strongly advised to look elsewhere. The Kerry requires commitment and strong leadership.

Komondor (KOM-on-door)

Best for Experienced Owners
Good with Older, Considerate Children
Large to Giant in Size
Long Coat

EXERCISE REQUIRED — MEDIUM

TRIMMING/CLIPPING REQUIRED — HIGH
MEDIUM LOW

AMOUNT OF SHEDDING — LOW

ACTIVITY INDOORS — MEDIUM

EASE OF TRAINING — LOW

SOCIABILITY WITH STRANGERS — LOW

TEMPERAMENT

Although energetic and playful as a puppy, the Komondor matures into a serious, dignified, self-reliant adult at two or three years of age. Then he becomes calm and quiet indoors, yet he is not suited to an apartment. His ideal environment is set away from close neighbors, with a spacious, securely fenced yard. Selflessly devoted to his family and distrustful of strangers, some Komondorok (the plural) are never completely comfortable with any outsiders, including children. Most of these dogs must be carefully introduced to guests, then supervised while the guest is present in the home. Despite his bulk and heavy coat, this breed is remarkably agile and reacts very, very quickly. Early and ongoing socialization is essential if his territorial instincts are to remain controlled rather than indiscriminate. He is patient with his own family's children, but can be overprotective when neighborhood kids join in. Similarly, he may be protective of his own family's pets while aggressively attacking others. Livestock guardians were expected to keep watch and make their own decisions, and that is exactly what the Kom does. His instincts to trust his own judgment are very strong. Unless you establish yourself as the alpha (number one), no one will really have control over him. Komondorok have a deep, impressive bark, which they tend to use freely, especially at night when they are most attentive.

HISTORY

This imposing dog, described as a huge walking string mop, was developed on the Hungarian plains to guard large flocks of sheep. AKC popularity: 134th of 146.

PHYSICAL FEATURES

He stands 26–31 inches and weighs 80–130 pounds. By two years of age, the wiry hairs of his outercoat fuse with the wooly hairs of his undercoat to form felt cords, which must be separated every few weeks. Bathing takes an hour, for the cords must be rinsed well, and drying takes twenty-four to forty-eight hours with the dog in a crate surrounded by a dryer and box fans. Pet owners may choose to trim/clip the coat short every few months. He is solid white. His ears and tail are natural.

HEALTH ISSUES

Both parents should have OFA certificates (hips). Also ask about bloat in the lines. Eyelid disorders (entropion) can be a problem. With his low metabolism, he is sensitive to anesthetics, vaccines, and chemicals and should never be casually medicated or sedated. Lifespan: 12 years.

CAUTIONS WHEN BUYING

Though some lines are more tranquil than others, this imposing breed requires more of a commitment than most other breeds. He will respect an assertive owner who knows how to lead an equally strong-minded dog without resorting to harshness. But without ongoing time and effort, socialization and supervision, and regular grooming, he is just too much dog.

Kuvasz (KOO-vahz)

Best for Experienced Owners
Good with Older, Considerate Children
Giant in Size
Thick, Medium-Length Coat

EXERCISE REQUIRED — HIGH MEDIUM
TRIMMING/CLIPPING REQUIRED — LOW
AMOUNT OF SHEDDING — HIGH
ACTIVITY INDOORS — MEDIUM
EASE OF TRAINING — LOW
SOCIABILITY WITH STRANGERS — LOW

TEMPERAMENT

A cuddly white fluffball as a puppy, the Kuvasz matures into a bold, spirited dog, determined to protect those who are dear to him, even to the point of self-sacrifice. This rugged breed deserves a roomy home with a spacious, securely fenced yard in the suburbs or country. He is content with daily walks and regular opportunities to stretch out for a romp, but he does play hard and needs room to amble about and patrol his territory. Kuvaszok (the plural) are polite with accepted strangers, but rather suspicious and discriminating in making new friends. He needs early and ongoing socialization if his territorial instincts are to remain under control. He is gentle and patient with the children in his own family, but may become concerned and overprotective when neighborhood kids join in. Similarly, he may be amiable with the pets in his own family, yet think nothing of eradicating trespassing animals. Since they were livestock guardians, it is part of this breed's genetic makeup to lead. You must establish yourself as the alpha (number one) so that he will turn the decision-making over to you. He feels compelled to announce every strange person and sound, and his deep bark may disturb the neighbors, especially at night when he is most vigilant.

HISTORY

Hungarian rulers kept Kuvaszok as personal body-guards. His name comes from the Turkish word *kawasz,* which means "armed guard of the nobility." Later he was used by the village commoners as a livestock guardian. AKC popularity: 114th of 146.

PHYSICAL FEATURES

Males stand 28–30 inches and weigh 100–115 pounds. Females stand 26–28 inches and weigh 70–90 pounds. His coat may be straight or wavy, with shorter hair on his head and paws and a dense undercoat. He needs brushing twice a week, daily during heavy seasonal shedding. Along with his shedding great chunks of hair in the spring and fall, you'll find loose hair the rest of the year as well. He is solid white. His ears and tail are natural.

HEALTH ISSUES

Both parents should have OFA certificates (hips) and yearly CERF (eyes). Normal thyroid (full panel) is extra security. Also ask about deafness, OCD, and vWD in the lines. With his low metabolism, he is sensitive to anesthetics, vaccines, and chemicals and should never be casually medicated or sedated. Lifespan: 10–12 years.

CAUTIONS WHEN BUYING

Compared to the similar-looking Great Pyrenees, the Kuvasz is more alert and observant and more consistently standoffish with strangers, though some lines are more mellow than others.

Kyi-Leo (Ky LEO)

Fine for Novice Owners
Good with Older, Considerate Children
Little in Size
Long Coat

EXERCISE REQUIRED — LOW

TRIMMING/CLIPPING REQUIRED — HIGH
MEDIUM LOW

AMOUNT OF SHEDDING — MEDIUM LOW

ACTIVITY INDOORS — HIGH

EASE OF TRAINING — MEDIUM

SOCIABILITY WITH STRANGERS — MEDIUM
LOW

TEMPERAMENT

The sturdy Kyi-Leo is lively and playful and quite skilled at grasping toys with his paws or stretching flat out and batting a tidbit out from under the refrigerator. Devoted to his family and sociable with other pets, he is somewhat standoffish with strangers. Because it is so easy for caution to become reticence and timidity, it is important to take a Kyi-Leo out into the world and expose him to new people and unusual sights and sounds. In his own home, he is a bit of a ham, seeking attention and trying to con you out of treats by clowning around and showing off. His Maltese side is exemplified by his attentiveness and responsiveness to nonforceful training, while the Lhasa side is well represented by his stubbornness. Housebreaking may take a while with some individuals, and excessive barking may need to be controlled.

HISTORY

He was developed in the San Francisco Bay area from Lhasa Apso and Maltese crosses. *Kyi* is Tibetan (crediting the Lhasa) for "dog," while *Leo* is Latin (crediting the Maltese) for "lion." He is registered by the Kyi-Leo Club of America.

PHYSICAL FEATURES

He stands 9–12 inches and weighs 8–12 pounds. Brush and comb his silky coat every other day. Pet owners may choose to have the coat trimmed/clipped short every four to six weeks. Keep his ear canals clean and dry and his bottom trimmed for cleanliness. He is usually black-and-white, though the black often fades to silvery gray. Other colors are allowed. His ears and tail are natural.

HEALTH ISSUES

Both parents should be screened for luxating patella. Also ask about low thyroid, allergies, and skin conditions in the lines. Lifespan: 13–15 years.

CAUTIONS WHEN BUYING

This is still a breed in development and is very hard to find.

Labrador Retriever

Fine for Novice Owners
Good with Children
Large in Size
Short Coat

EXERCISE REQUIRED — MEDIUM
TRIMMING/CLIPPING REQUIRED — LOW
AMOUNT OF SHEDDING — MEDIUM
ACTIVITY INDOORS — MEDIUM
EASE OF TRAINING — HIGH
SOCIABILITY WITH STRANGERS — HIGH

TEMPERAMENT

The Lab is one terrific family dog, given enough vigorous exercise (jogging, biking, hiking, swimming, fetching) and not just a walk around the block once a day. He is kindly, good-natured, and tractable and takes most things in stride, but too much confinement and not enough companionship can lead to rambunctiousness and destructive chewing. Most are friendly with everyone and everything, though compared to Golden Retrievers, Labs tend to be more conservative. Also more independent—though quite biddable and responsive to obedience training, they can have a noticeable stubborn streak. Some have necks like bulls and barely notice tugs on the leash. You must control his tendency to chew on objects and to mouth your hands—provide a box filled with toys that he can choose from to carry around in his mouth. A Lab remains a spirited teenager for several years, requiring patience and training to manage.

HISTORY

His name to the contrary, he originated in the Canadian province of Newfoundland. With his speed and drive, he is the king of national retriever trials and has distinguished himself as a guide for the blind and a bomb/narcotics/arson dog. AKC popularity: 1st of 146.

PHYSICAL FEATURES

Males stand 22½–24½ inches and weigh 65–80 pounds. Females stand 21½–23½ inches and weigh 50–70 pounds. Avoid oversize Labs. Brush his dense coat once a week, more often when he is shedding. He is black, chocolate, or yellow (cream to reddish, and never called a

"golden Lab"). His ears and tail are natural, and his tail should be covered thickly with short hair (not feathering) to produce a rounded appearance described as an "otter tail."

HEALTH ISSUES

Both parents should have OFA certificates (hips and elbows) and yearly CERF (eyes). Also ask about low thyroid, heart disease, OCD, vWD, seizures, cancer, allergies, and skin conditions in the lines. Lifespan: 10–12 years.

CAUTIONS WHEN BUYING

Labs are a dime a dozen and definitely not equal. Buy only from a breeder who can show you both of the health clearances—that single stipulation will cut out the vast majority of breeders right there. This breed is also sharply divided between field and show types, with many current show dogs built like blocky Rottweilers. Look for a pedigree well balanced with champion titles, field or hunting test titles, and obedience titles.

Lakeland Terrier

Best for Experienced Owners
Good with Older, Considerate Children
Small in Size
Wiry Coat

EXERCISE REQUIRED — MEDIUM

TRIMMING/CLIPPING REQUIRED — HIGH
    MEDIUM

AMOUNT OF SHEDDING — LOW

ACTIVITY INDOORS — HIGH

EASE OF TRAINING — LOW

SOCIABILITY WITH STRANGERS — MEDIUM
    LOW

TEMPERAMENT

The AKC Standard describes him as "bold, gay and friendly, with a confident, cock-of-the-walk attitude." Though not as boisterous or argumentative as some terriers, the square, workmanlike Lakeland is still animated and intense. Always alert and ready to go, he has strong working instincts and loves to exercise outdoors, where his curiosity and tenacity can get him into tight spots (literally) unless your fences are secure and he is well supervised. He does best with active owners who are confident and consistent, for he has a marked independent streak and will take advantage if indulged too much. Positive training methods are a must—terriers do not react kindly to being jerked around. Lakelands are better with other dogs than some other terriers, but they won't back down if challenged. Little creatures that run will come to an untimely end. When well socialized, he is polite with strangers, yet he can be counted on to sound the alert when anything is amiss. As with most terriers, excessive barking may need to be controlled. Lakies love to tunnel and dig and can be possessive of their food and toys.

HISTORY

Originating in the rugged shale mountains of the Lake District of northern England, he was paired with Foxhounds to hunt foxes and with Otterhounds to hunt otters. AKC popularity: 123rd of 146.

PHYSICAL FEATURES

He stands 13–15 inches and weighs 15–20 pounds. Brush and comb his hard wiry coat once a week. His beard should be combed daily for cleanliness. Likewise, keep his bottom trimmed for cleanliness. Show dogs are "stripped" (dead coat plucked out) every few months; pet owners may opt for more convenient clipping. He may be reddish, wheaten, blue, black, or liver. He may also be saddle-marked, where one of the above colors or grizzle (a blend of the above colors) spreads over the back, while the head, shoulders, and legs are tan. His ears are natural; his tail is docked.

HEALTH ISSUES

Both parents should have yearly CERF certificates (eyes). Also ask about Legg-Perthes, luxating patella, low thyroid, and vWD in the lines. Lifespan: 12–15 years.

CAUTIONS WHEN BUYING

Too many people choose one of these small square terriers (Lakeland, Welsh, Fox) without realizing that they are *more* energetic and excitable and *more* of a training challenge than larger Airedales, Kerry Blues, and Soft-Coated Wheatens. The larger terriers were developed to be more multipurpose and more responsive to humans, while the smaller were bred specifically for hunting and killing prey underground, requiring a tough, independent mind-set. Though their convenient size does mean that you can pick them up to keep them out of trouble, their intense character is not for the faint of heart.

Leonberger

Best for Experienced Owners
Good with Children
Giant in Size
Thick, Medium-Length Coat

EXERCISE REQUIRED — HIGH MEDIUM
TRIMMING/CLIPPING REQUIRED — LOW
AMOUNT OF SHEDDING — HIGH
ACTIVITY INDOORS — MEDIUM
EASE OF TRAINING — MEDIUM
SOCIABILITY WITH STRANGERS — MEDIUM

TEMPERAMENT

Noble and powerful, a good Leonberger is calm and steady, yet bolder and more athletic than most giant breeds. The Leo enjoys swimming, tracking, agility, therapy work, pulling a cart or sled, and weight pulling—all productive outlets for his high energy. Fetching a ball or Frisbee, however, is not a natural activity. He is a loving, steadfast dog who thrives on being made an integral part of the family. Though protective instincts develop at maturity (three to four years) and he becomes more discriminating with strangers, he is never aggressive. His deep, imposing bark and confident presence should be enough to deter intruders. This stability, however, assumes early and ongoing socialization and a sound-tempered bloodline. Some individuals are unfortunately shy and/or sharp. Dog aggression can be a problem, and two individuals of the same sex should not be kept together. Obedience training should start at three months old; heeling is imperative, because these powerful dogs can literally pull you off your feet. His determination to jump up into your face and lean against your leg (leading to the affectionate nickname "Lean-on-berger") can be disconcerting. During adolescence, his hormones will kick in and he might start to test his owner, who must respond with consistent leadership and more training. Leos can be messy: Their huge paws track in mud; they may drool if stressed; and most play in their water bowls, dunking their heads and coming up slobbering. It is said that their natural look is slightly damp with leaves stuck to their coats.

HISTORY

The official crest of the city of Leonberg, Germany, included a lion, so the city's flamboyant mayor crossed Saint Bernards, Great Pyrenees, Newfoundlands, and perhaps other breeds to develop a massive dog who resembled a lion. Registered by the UKC and FCI.

PHYSICAL FEATURES

Males stand 28–31 inches and weigh 120–150 pounds. Females stand 26–28 inches and weigh 100–120 pounds. His profuse double coat should be brushed and combed twice a week, daily during heavy seasonal shedding. Along with his shedding great chunks of hair in the spring and fall, you'll find some loose hair the rest of the year as well. His "lion" color ranges from sandy to rich mahogany, accented by a black mask and often black-tipped hairs. His ears and tail are natural.

HEALTH ISSUES

Both parents should have OFA certificates (hips and elbows) and yearly CERF (eyes). Also ask about vWD, low thyroid, cardiomyopathy, bloat, panosteitis, Addison's disease, bone cancer, and OCD in the lines. Eyelid disorders (entropion) can be a problem. Lifespan: 6–10 years.

CAUTIONS WHEN BUYING

Make sure the breeder is a member of their national Leonberger Club and is on the current club list of approved breeders. Pet prices run about $1,000.

Lhasa Apso (LAH-sa AHP-so)

Best for Experienced Owners
Good with Older, Considerate Children
Small in Size
Long Coat

EXERCISE REQUIRED — LOW
TRIMMING/CLIPPING REQUIRED — HIGH
MEDIUM LOW
AMOUNT OF SHEDDING — MEDIUM LOW
ACTIVITY INDOORS — HIGH MEDIUM
EASE OF TRAINING — LOW
SOCIABILITY WITH STRANGERS — LOW

Apso means "longhaired dog." AKC popularity: 29th of 146.

TEMPERAMENT

Too many people buy a Lhasa puppy based on his friendly antics, envisioning a cuddly lapdog. In truth, the adult Lhasa is one of the hardiest, toughest, and strongest willed of all the small breeds. It is said, "When a Lhasa looks in the mirror he sees a lion." Though he can be playful, he also carries himself with regal dignity. Rather calm and deliberate in nature, he makes a mannerly house dog if you can establish a relationship of mutual respect—i.e., admiring his independent character while consistently enforcing your rules so that he respects *you* as well. The AKC Standard, showing great restraint, calls the Lhasa "chary with strangers." Indeed he is. With his acute senses, keen observation skills, and distrust of anything new or different, he takes his watchdog responsibilities seriously—some individuals are not just "all bark." Lhasas need early socialization with people to ensure that they don't become too sharp. He can be bossy and jealous with other animals. Very smart, but also dominant and manipulative, he is a challenge to train. Old-fashioned "jerking" methods will cause this proud breed either to shut down or to retaliate. Lhasas cannot be forced to do anything, nor will they meekly accept harshness or teasing. Modern methods that emphasize food and praise will be met with much more cooperation. Housebreaking may take a while.

HISTORY

In his native Tibet, he is called "Bark Lion Sentinel Dog." In monasteries and palaces around the sacred city of Lhasa, he barked vigorously when strangers approached.

PHYSICAL FEATURES

He stands 10–11 inches and weighs 12–18 pounds. Brush and comb his hard, heavy coat every other day. Pet owners may choose to trim/clip the coat short every four to six weeks. Keep his ear canals clean and dry and his bottom trimmed for cleanliness. The most common color is sable (red, gold, or cream, with dark-tipped hairs). Clear colors (red, gold, cream, white, black) are also popular, as are black-and-tan and particolor. His ears and tail are natural.

HEALTH ISSUES

Both parents should be screened for luxating patella and renal dysplasia (kidney disease). Renal dysplasia is the most serious hereditary problem in Lhasas—a DNA test for it is currently being developed. Also ask about hip dysplasia, bladder stones, allergies and skin conditions, diabetes, seizures, and heart murmurs. Lifespan: 12–15 years.

CAUTIONS WHEN BUYING

This breed originated in a culture quite different from ours and has a unique temperament that requires strong leadership and a firm hand. Many people cannot handle the willfulness and clever intelligence of the Lhasa.

Louisiana Catahoula Leopard Dog

Best for Experienced Owners
Good with Children If Raised with Children
Medium to Large in Size
Smooth Coat

EXERCISE REQUIRED — HIGH
TRIMMING/CLIPPING REQUIRED — LOW
AMOUNT OF SHEDDING — MEDIUM
ACTIVITY INDOORS — MEDIUM
EASE OF TRAINING — MEDIUM LOW
SOCIABILITY WITH STRANGERS — LOW

TEMPERAMENT

One breeder says, "The Catahoula will not let you forget that you own a dog." The "King of the Stock Dogs" really belongs on a farm or ranch, for he is a serious worker who goes about his business with tremendous focus and assertiveness. This athletic, rugged dog requires at least an hour of running exercise each day. Without sufficient outlets for his high energy, he will probably become destructive. Most are reserved with strangers and naturally protective. Skittishness and sharpness can be problems in some lines, and Catahoulas need extensive socialization to build the temperament required of city life. He can be dominant and pushy with other animals, especially with other dogs of the same sex, and doesn't always cohabit well in multi-pet homes. He can be possessive of his food. Catahoulas are independent and like to be in charge—you must be a confident leader or they will walk all over you. Overall, this is a capable, versatile companion when allowed to fulfill his working heritage. Otherwise, he can be too much dog to handle. Youngsters are especially rambunctious, bore easily, and can excavate caverns in your yard.

HISTORY

The state dog of Louisiana, sometimes called the Catahoula Cur, he was developed in the Catahoula Lakes region, possibly a blend of Louisiana red wolf, French Beauceron, and the Spanish Mastiffs and Greyhounds used by the explorer DeSoto to conquer the local Indians. Spread throughout the southern states, he was an all-around farm and ranch dog who excelled at controlling wild cattle, hunting wild boar, and treeing coons. Registered by the UKC, ARF, NALC, SKC, and AKC-FSS.

PHYSICAL FEATURES

Males stand 22–26 inches and weigh 65–85 pounds. Females stand 20–24 inches and weigh 50–65 pounds. His hard coat requires only a quick brushing once a week. The most striking colors are blue leopard (blue merle) and red leopard (red merle). However, caution must be exercised with merle genes: Breeding merle to merle often results in genetic defects (vision, hearing, and others). Other colors include solid, patched, and brindle. His eerie eyes can range from bright blue to translucent white ("glass" eyes) and are often "marbled" or "cracked" (different colors within the same eye). His ears and tail are natural. His feet are webbed.

HEALTH ISSUES

Both parents should have OFA certificates (hips) and yearly CERF (eyes). Puppies should come with a BAER printout that shows normal bilateral hearing. Lifespan: 12 years.

CAUTIONS WHEN BUYING

Another breeder says candidly, "Not everyone needs them, not everyone can handle them, and not everyone should have them." There is wide variation in size and build, with more individuals used for working purposes (hunting or stock work) than shown in conformation classes. That is exactly as it should be.

Löwchen (Little Lion Dog)

(LAOO-chen)

Fine for Novice Owners
Good with Older, Considerate Children
Small in Size
Long Coat

EXERCISE REQUIRED — MEDIUM LOW

TRIMMING/CLIPPING REQUIRED — HIGH

AMOUNT OF SHEDDING — LOW

ACTIVITY INDOORS — HIGH

EASE OF TRAINING — HIGH MEDIUM

SOCIABILITY WITH STRANGERS — MEDIUM

TEMPERAMENT

The bright, happy little Löwchen is lively and playful, yet sensible and low-key. A moderate breed in all respects and easy to care for, he will romp vigorously in the yard, trot gracefully beside you during walks (on-leash), then curl up in your lap to sleep. Very people-oriented and inquisitive, he needs a good amount of attention and interaction and doesn't like to be left alone for long periods of time. He is peaceful and gentle with everyone (humans and animals alike), though he often likes to sit perched on the back of a sofa or chair, looking out the window so he can announce visitors. As with most sweet-natured breeds, there is timidity in some lines; early socialization is important to build an outgoing, confident temperament. Attentive and responsive to nonforceful obedience training, many individuals do well in competitive obedience and agility. Some like to bark.

HISTORY

Originating in the Mediterranean, he was the household pet of Florentine nobility, groomed by the ladies of the court into the likeness of a small lion. He has been portrayed in tapestries, the woodcuttings of Albrecht Dürer, and the oil paintings of Goya. AKC popularity: 140th of 146.

PHYSICAL FEATURES

He stands 10–14 inches and weighs 10–18 pounds. His fine, silky, rather wavy coat should be brushed and combed every other day. Show dogs are sculpted into a rough lion pattern: shorn hindquarters and forelegs, leaving a mane around the neck, a cuff around each ankle, and a plume on the tail. Pets are usually clipped in a shorter, more uniform pattern every four to six weeks. Keep his ear canals clean and dry and his bottom trimmed for cleanliness. Colors include white, gold, cream, black, black-and-tan, chocolate-and-tan, particolor, and other solids and blends. His ears and tail are natural.

HEALTH ISSUES

Both parents should have yearly CERF certificates (eyes) and be screened for luxating patella. Also ask about allergies in the lines. Lifespan: 13–15 years.

CAUTIONS WHEN BUYING

Löwchen are not easy to find; expect to be put on a waiting list. Remember that the long coat, if not clipped short, must be brushed and combed frequently to prevent painful tangles.

Maltese

Fine for Novice Owners
Good with Older, Considerate Children
Little in Size
Long Coat

EXERCISE REQUIRED — LOW
TRIMMING/CLIPPING REQUIRED — HIGH
        MEDIUM LOW
AMOUNT OF SHEDDING — LOW
ACTIVITY INDOORS — HIGH
EASE OF TRAINING — MEDIUM
SOCIABILITY WITH STRANGERS — MEDIUM

TEMPERAMENT

One of the brightest and gentlest of the toys, he is exceedingly playful and enjoys clever games of dexterity such as "pull the hidden toy from under the cabinet with your paw." This curious, quick-moving sprite enjoys dashing around the yard and accompanying you for walks. Larger dogs may view him as a delicacy, so he must always be leashed for protection. He will bark to announce visitors, but he is generally peaceful with the world. Some lines are more confident and outgoing than others, and training and socialization also play key roles in how he turns out. If you treat him like a helpless baby or spoil/indulge him, he is likely to end up overdependent, insecure, or bratty and yappy. Treating him like an intelligent little dog will encourage him to strut out into the world with self-confidence. Attentive, sensitive, and responsive to non-forceful training, many individuals excel in competitive obedience and agility. Toy breeds do have special needs: Fences should be triple-checked for slight gaps through which he might wriggle. Hold him firmly in your arms and remember that falling objects can crush delicate bones. Maltese are notoriously difficult to housebreak, and excessive barking may need to be controlled.

HISTORY

On the Mediterranean island of Malta, he was the household pet of wealthy, cultured families. AKC popularity: 20th of 146.

PHYSICAL FEATURES

He stands about 8 inches and weighs 4–7 pounds. Larger individuals are common; though not suitable for the show ring, they make sturdy pets. Smaller individuals are often not sound or healthy. His straight, silky coat should be brushed and combed every day. Pet owners may choose to have the coat trimmed/clipped short every four to six weeks. Keep his ear canals clean and dry and his bottom trimmed for cleanliness. He should be solid white, but may have light tan or lemon shadings on his ears. His ears and tail are natural.

HEALTH ISSUES

Both parents should be screened for luxating patella and low thyroid. Also ask about eye problems, liver shunt, and white shaker dog syndrome in the lines. Check parents' teeth for soundness—poor teeth run through some lines. He is sensitive to anesthetics, vaccines, and chemicals and should never be casually medicated or sedated. Individuals under four pounds (often called extreme tinies) are more susceptible to hypoglycemia (low blood sugar). Lifespan: 13–15 years.

CAUTIONS WHEN BUYING

Other breeds in the bichon family include the Bichon Frise, Bolognese, Coton de Tulear, and Havanese. If you're not going to keep the coat trimmed or clipped, a daily commitment to grooming is a must. Look for confident, outgoing lines with healthy teeth. Run from breeders who use the term "teacup" or who place their puppies before ten to twelve weeks of age.

Manchester Terrier (Standard)

Best for Experienced Owners
Good with Older, Considerate Children
Small in Size
Smooth Coat

EXERCISE REQUIRED — MEDIUM

TRIMMING/CLIPPING REQUIRED — LOW

AMOUNT OF SHEDDING — MEDIUM

ACTIVITY INDOORS — HIGH MEDIUM

EASE OF TRAINING — MEDIUM

SOCIABILITY WITH STRANGERS — LOW

TEMPERAMENT

The AKC Standard says, "The Manchester presents a sleek, sturdy, yet elegant look . . . with a keen, bright, alert expression." This lively little dog, keenly observant and discerning, is more devoted to his owner, more responsive, and better mannered than some terriers. Athletic and agile, he is best suited to active families, as he enjoys brisk walking every day and all-out running whenever he can get it. However, he must be kept on-leash or in a securely fenced area at all times, for he is very curious, has strong hunting instincts, and will chase anything. Manchesters love to play—with you, with another dog, or by themselves (with or without a toy!). With his acute senses and wariness of strangers, he makes an excellent watchdog, but early socialization is imperative so that he does not become sharp or timid. Manchesters are not given to fiery posturing with other dogs and are generally accepting, but they will stand their ground and fight when challenged or when they feel their space has been invaded. Two adults of the same sex should not be kept together. Smaller creatures, including low-flying birds, will be pursued with determination. This breed is very smart and trainable if you are a confident, consistent leader who can smile at his antics, yet not allow him to outwit you. He is exceedingly sensitive to physical corrections, so use a light hand on the leash and rely more on praise and food rewards. (Food in moderation, please: He tends to pack on pounds quickly.) Manchesters are comfort-loving dogs who seek out soft beds and often tunnel under the covers. They can be possessive of their food and toys and some like to bark.

HISTORY

He was developed in Manchester, England, to hunt vermin. He especially excelled in rat-killing contests, a fashionable gambling activity in British pubs. There are two sizes: Standard and Toy. AKC popularity: 102nd of 146 (includes both varieties).

PHYSICAL FEATURES

He stands 15–17 inches and weighs 12–22 pounds. His hard coat requires only an occasional quick brushing. He is jet black with rich mahogany trim. There should be a black "thumbprint" on the front of each foreleg and a black "pencil mark" stripe on each toe on all four feet. His ears may fold forward naturally (button), stand up naturally (erect), or be cropped. His tail is natural.

HEALTH ISSUES

Both parents should have yearly CERF certificates (eyes) and a DNA certificate that shows whether they are affected, carriers, or clear of vWD (at least one parent should be clear). Also ask about Legg-Perthes, seizures, and low thyroid in the lines. He is sensitive to extremes of temperature, doesn't like the rain, and needs a sweater in cold weather. Lifespan: 15 years.

CAUTIONS WHEN BUYING

Compared to the Toy, the Standard has a calmer and more stable yet tougher and more independent temperament.

Manchester Terrier (Toy)

Fine for Novice Owners
Good with Older, Considerate Children
Little in Size
Smooth Coat

EXERCISE REQUIRED — MEDIUM

TRIMMING/CLIPPING REQUIRED — LOW

AMOUNT OF SHEDDING — MEDIUM

ACTIVITY INDOORS — HIGH MEDIUM

EASE OF TRAINING — MEDIUM

SOCIABILITY WITH STRANGERS — LOW

TEMPERAMENT

The AKC Standard says, "The Manchester presents a sleek, sturdy, yet elegant look . . . with a keen, bright, alert expression." This lively little dog, keenly observant and discerning, is more devoted to his owner, more responsive, and better mannered than some terriers. Athletic and agile, he is best suited to active families, as he enjoys brisk walking every day and all-out running whenever he can get it. However, he must be kept on-leash or in a securely fenced area at all times, for he is very curious, has strong hunting instincts, and will chase anything. Manchesters love to play—with you, with another dog, or by themselves (with or without a toy!). With his acute senses and wariness of strangers, he makes an excellent watchdog, but early socialization is imperative so that he does not become sharp or timid. Manchesters are not given to fiery posturing with other dogs and are generally accepting, but they will stand their ground and fight when challenged or when they feel their space has been invaded. Two adults of the same sex should not be kept together. Smaller creatures, including low-flying birds, will be pursued with determination. This breed is very smart and trainable if you are a confident, consistent leader who can smile at his antics, yet not allow him to outwit you. He is exceedingly sensitive to physical corrections, so use a light hand on the leash and rely more on praise and food rewards. (Food in moderation, please: He tends to pack on pounds quickly.) Manchesters are comfort-loving dogs who seek out soft beds and often tunnel under the covers. They can be possessive of their food and toys and some like to bark.

HISTORY

He was developed in Manchester, England, to hunt vermin. He especially excelled in rat-killing contests, a fashionable gambling activity in British pubs. There are two sizes: Standard and Toy. AKC popularity: 102nd of 146 (includes both varieties).

PHYSICAL FEATURES

He stands 8–13 inches and weighs up to 12 pounds. His hard coat requires only an occasional quick brushing. He is jet black with rich mahogany trim. There should be a black "thumbprint" on the front of each foreleg and a black "pencil mark" stripe on each toe on all four feet. His ears may fold forward naturally (button), stand up naturally (erect), or be cropped. His tail is natural.

HEALTH ISSUES

Both parents should have yearly CERF certificates (eyes) and a DNA certificate that shows whether they are affected, carriers, or clear of vWD (at least one parent should be clear). Also ask about Legg-Perthes, seizures, and low thyroid in the lines. He is sensitive to extremes of temperature, doesn't like the rain, and needs a sweater in cold weather. Lifespan: 15 years.

CAUTIONS WHEN BUYING

Compared to the Standard variety, the Toy is more companionable, more anxious to please, and less independent.

Mastiff

Best for Experienced Owners
Good with Children If Raised with Children
Giant in Size
Smooth Coat

EXERCISE REQUIRED — MEDIUM

TRIMMING/CLIPPING REQUIRED — LOW

AMOUNT OF SHEDDING — MEDIUM

ACTIVITY INDOORS — LOW

EASE OF TRAINING — MEDIUM

SOCIABILITY WITH STRANGERS — MEDIUM

TEMPERAMENT

The AKC Standard says, "A combination of grandeur and good nature, courage and docility. Dignity, rather than gaiety, is the Mastiff's correct demeanor." Indeed, he is calm and quiet (seldom barks), but he belongs in a roomy home with a spacious fenced yard so that his massive body has stretching room. To stay fit, he needs daily walks (whether he seems to want them or not), but he isn't a jogging partner. He also needs companionship—lots of it. To ensure a stable, confident temperament, Mastiffs need earlier and more frequent socialization than many other breeds, and it should continue throughout his life. Most are polite with everyone, but there is timidity and shyness in some lines and aggression in others. Watchfulness should be discouraged, as it is best for all concerned if the Mastiff intimidates by size alone, rather than by behavior. Some are peaceful with other animals, while others are dominant (even combative) with dogs of the same sex. Though mildly stubborn, this good-natured dog responds well to patient obedience training that consists of much praise and little physical correction. Mastiffs drool and slobber—big-time!—and are not for people who must have a tidy household.

HISTORY

He was a war dog with Caesar's Roman legions and a gladiator in the Roman arena, fighting bulls, lions, and other dogs. In England he served as village guardian, loosed at night to control prowling wolves. AKC popularity: 41st of 146.

PHYSICAL FEATURES

Males stand 30–34 inches and weigh 165–205 pounds. Females stand 28–32 inches and weigh 125–175 pounds. His hard coat requires only an occasional quick brushing. He is fawn, apricot, or brindle. His ears and tail are natural.

HEALTH ISSUES

Both parents should have OFA certificates (hips and elbows), yearly CERF (eyes), cardiac-clear for heart defects, and normal thyroid (full panel). Also ask about cystinuria (kidney disease), vWD, cancer, seizures, OCD, and bloat in the lines. Eyelid disorders (entropion) can be a problem. He is sensitive to anesthetics, vaccines, and chemicals and should never be casually medicated or sedated. Mastiffs love shade and air-conditioning and are susceptible to heatstroke in hot, humid, and/or stuffy conditions. Lifespan: 6–10 years.

CAUTIONS WHEN BUYING

Make sure parents, grandparents, and other relatives have their genetic health clearances and are sweet-natured. Poorly bred and/or poorly socialized Mastiffs can develop extreme aggression and shyness problems, and such a dog is a threat to society and a liability to his owner.

Miniature Bull Terrier

Best for Experienced Owners
Good with Older, Considerate Children
Small in Size
Smooth Coat

EXERCISE REQUIRED — MEDIUM

TRIMMING/CLIPPING REQUIRED — LOW

AMOUNT OF SHEDDING — MEDIUM

ACTIVITY INDOORS — HIGH

EASE OF TRAINING — LOW

SOCIABILITY WITH STRANGERS — HIGH

MEDIUM

TEMPERAMENT

Rowdy and clownish, full of fire and determination, this muscular, forceful dog does best with active families, for he has a high energy level that comes in spurts and bursts. He needs frequent, brisk walks, occasional vigorous games of ball, and total immersion in the family—i.e., lots of companionship and interactive play sessions. If ignored, he will become bored, and mischief will surely follow. Youngsters who are neglected can be especially rambunctious: happily devouring your furniture, excavating great caverns in your yard, and spinning in dizzy circles, chasing their tails obsessively. Most Mini Bulls greet strangers with enthusiastic bounding and face kissing. Aggression and timidity are present in some lines, and early socialization is important to develop a stable attitude. Most individuals play too roughly for small children, especially when egged on. A Bull Terrier should not be kept with another dog of the same sex, and cats may or may not be safe. Bullies can be very possessive of their food. At some point, if you have not raised this breed with consistent leadership, he will likely challenge your ability to control his actions. Such dominance attempts must be met with calm assertiveness. Keep training sessions brief, and use food as motivation. Keep your sense of humor handy, for this breed has a quick-witted imagination and likes to invent new variations on what you're trying to accomplish.

HISTORY

The full-size Bull Terrier was developed in England from bulldog/terrier crosses, then matched against other dogs in the fighting arena. The Miniature Bull is a smaller version, with more of a heritage as a vermin hunter than a dogfighter. AKC popularity: 133rd of 146.

PHYSICAL FEATURES

He stands 10–14 inches and weighs 18–28 pounds. He comes in two color varieties: White may be solid white, or mostly white with a few colored patches on his head. Colored may be brindle, fawn, red, or black-and-tan, all of which usually include white markings. People with sensitive skin may react adversely to the "pokes" of the harsh hair. His ears and tail are natural.

HEALTH ISSUES

Both parents should have OFA certificates (patellas) and be cardiac-clear for heart disease and screened every year (by urine test and ultrasound) for kidney disease. Each puppy should come with a BAER printout showing normal bilateral hearing. Also ask about low thyroid, seizures, allergies, and skin conditions in the lines. White coats are sensitive to sunburn; provide shade when outdoors for long periods. Lifespan: 12 years.

CAUTIONS WHEN BUYING

The Miniature Bull Terrier is a challenging dynamo with a natural ebullience and tenacity. With his distinctive egg-shaped head, large erect ears, and tiny, sunken, triangular eyes, it should be evident that he is not a "Pit Bull," but be prepared to explain this to the public.

Miniature Pinscher

Best for Experienced Owners
Good with Older, Considerate Children
Little in Size
Smooth Coat

EXERCISE REQUIRED — MEDIUM
TRIMMING/CLIPPING REQUIRED — LOW
AMOUNT OF SHEDDING — MEDIUM LOW
ACTIVITY INDOORS — HIGH
EASE OF TRAINING — LOW
SOCIABILITY WITH STRANGERS — LOW

TEMPERAMENT

The AKC Standard says that the Min Pin's characteristic traits are his "fearless animation, complete self-possession, and spirited presence." This sleek, elegant, deer-like breed with the quick, prancing gait is the "busiest" and most intense of the toy breeds, which is why his fanciers like him so much. Assertive and proud, athletic and agile, he is convinced that he's a big dog. He seems to be in perpetual motion and enjoys brisk, vigorous, interactive games. He also demands cuddling and often must be surgically removed from your lap or chest whenever you rise from the couch. He is a lover of comfort—usually that lump under the blanket is the resident Min Pin. Outdoors, he must be kept on-leash or in a securely fenced area at all times, for he is sharp-eyed, curious, and extremely quick. Unless exceptionally well trained, Min Pins don't come back when you call them, and often they don't stay where you leave them—they are artful climbers and clever escape artists. Keenly observant and territorial, this breed takes his watchdog role seriously, often showing strangers his backside, accompanied by defiant kicking of the ground with his rear feet. Early and frequent socialization is required so that he doesn't become sharp or shrill. Min Pins can be dominant with other dogs, and smaller creatures will be pursued with determination. In the right hands, this bright breed is very trainable, but he has a mind of his own and can be headstrong and demanding. Min Pins are tough on toys and will rip squeakers and stuffed animals to shreds. They love to bark, and housebreaking can be difficult.

HISTORY

This German breed, used for hunting vermin, was not bred down from the Doberman and is actually older than the Doberman, so *don't* call him a miniature Doberman. He is a Miniature *Pinscher,* which translates to "terrier-like" or "biter." AKC popularity: 16th of 146.

PHYSICAL FEATURES

He stands 10–12½ inches and weighs 8–12 pounds. His hard coat requires only an occasional quick brushing. He is clear red, stag red (sprinkled with black hairs), black-and-rust, or chocolate-and-rust. Blue-and-rust may not be shown in conformation classes. His ears may be left naturally hanging or cropped. Some will stand erect on their own. His tail is docked.

HEALTH ISSUES

Both parents should have yearly CERF certificates (eyes) and be screened for luxating patella. Also ask about demodectic mange and Legg-Perthes in the lines. He is sensitive to extremes of temperature, doesn't like the rain, and needs a sweater in cold weather. Lifespan: 13–15 years.

CAUTIONS WHEN BUYING

The extreme quickness of this dynamic little breed cannot be overemphasized. They are very oriented to sight and motion and spend most of the day up on their tiptoes, investigating everything that catches their interest.

Miniature Schnauzer

Fine for Novice Owners
Good with Children If Raised with Children
Small in Size
Wiry Coat

EXERCISE REQUIRED — MEDIUM
TRIMMING/CLIPPING REQUIRED — HIGH
AMOUNT OF SHEDDING — LOW
ACTIVITY INDOORS — HIGH MEDIUM
EASE OF TRAINING — HIGH MEDIUM
SOCIABILITY WITH STRANGERS — MEDIUM

TEMPERAMENT

Individuals vary in personality from merry and extroverted to serious and introspective, but generally the Miniature Schnauzer has a pleasant, playful, spunky temperament. He can be a busy dog and loves his walks, but mostly he wants to participate fully in the family. He makes an alert watchdog and may welcome strangers with enthusiasm or be a bit standoffish, even timid if not well socialized. Most are good with other family pets—though he may chase the family cat for fun, he's seldom serious about it. Some are scrappy with other dogs of the same sex, but it is a tribute to their overall amiability that Schnauzers can often be grouped together with little or no bickering. Although he knows his own mind and often displays an obstinate resistance to walking on the leash, he responds well to obedience training that includes motivational praise and food rewards. Many individuals win top awards in advanced obedience. This breed is adaptable, makes an excellent traveling companion, and even if slightly spoiled, doesn't take as much advantage of it as many other terriers. Schnauzers can be barky.

HISTORY

All three Schnauzers (Miniature, Standard, and Giant) originated in Germany, the Miniature being utilized as a vermin hunter. They are separate breeds—the Mini is the youngest (and most popular) of the three. AKC popularity: 14th of 146.

PHYSICAL FEATURES

He stands 12–14 inches and weighs 13–18 pounds. Brush and comb his wiry coat twice a week, though some coats have more "furnishings" than others and are harder to maintain. His beard should be combed daily for cleanliness. Likewise, keep his bottom trimmed for cleanliness. Show dogs are "stripped" (dead coat plucked out) every few months; pet owners may opt for more convenient clipping. He may be salt-and-pepper (banded hairs of black and white), solid black, or black-and-silver (black with silver trim). White individuals cannot be shown in conformation classes. His ears may be cropped or left naturally hanging; his tail is docked.

HEALTH ISSUES

Both parents should have yearly CERF certificates (eyes). Also ask about liver shunt, renal dysplasia, allergies, and skin conditions in the lines. Lifespan: 12–14 years.

CAUTIONS WHEN BUYING

This breed has been exploited by unknowledgeable breeders, so you must be careful. Pick up a well-bred Miniature Schnauzer and you'll be surprised at how muscular and substantial he is. Poorly bred individuals (of which there are many) tend to be lighter boned and more weedy.

Neapolitan Mastiff

Best for Experienced Owners
Good with Children If Raised with Children
Giant in Size
Smooth Coat

EXERCISE REQUIRED — MEDIUM

TRIMMING/CLIPPING REQUIRED — LOW

AMOUNT OF SHEDDING — MEDIUM

ACTIVITY INDOORS — LOW

EASE OF TRAINING — LOW

SOCIABILITY WITH STRANGERS — LOW

TEMPERAMENT

The Neo Standard says, "The essence of the Neapolitan is his bestial appearance, astounding head and imposing size and attitude." Once you're past the shock of your first impression, you'll be able to better appreciate how quiet, calm, and relaxed the Mastino is. Just don't mistake his bulk and ambling gait for laziness or clumsiness, for he can shift into his fierce protector's role on a moment's notice. He is not an apartment dog (to stay fit, he needs some space and moderate exercise), but more than anything else, he requires personal attention. He often attaches himself, shadow-like, to his favorite person. Puppies should be friendly and trusting and, with proper socialization, become more reserved and discriminating as they mature. As with all mastiffs, socialization is an absolute requirement to avoid either aggression or shyness. Neos can be overprotective if they perceive a threat to "their" child—i.e., roughhousing with a friend. Dog aggression can be a real problem; though many will not start fights, they will surely finish them. This massive, stubborn breed is inclined to do things his own way, but he will respond to early, consistent training that includes leadership, cheerful praise, and food rewards. Mastinos perform admirably in drooling, slobbering, and snoring competition.

HISTORY

Descended from the ancient (now extinct) Molosser who fought in the Roman Colosseum, he was refined into a guardian of Italian estates. Registered by the FCI, UKC, and SKC.

PHYSICAL FEATURES

Males stand 26–30 inches and weigh 135–170 pounds. Females stand 24–28 inches and weigh 110–135 pounds. His hard coat requires only an occasional quick brushing. He may be blue (gray), tawny (blond to fawn), mahogany (reddish brown), or black, sometimes with reverse brindling (tawny stripes). His ears may be cropped or left naturally hanging. His tail is docked.

HEALTH ISSUES

Both parents should have OFA certificates (hips and elbows) and yearly CERF (eyes). Also ask about low thyroid, cardiomyopathy, OCD, panosteitis, bloat, and cancer in the lines. Eyelid disorders (entropion) can be a problem, as can inflammation of the third eyelid (cherry eye). He is sensitive to anesthetics, vaccines, and chemicals and should never be casually medicated or sedated. Mastinos love shade and air-conditioning and are susceptible to heatstroke in hot, humid, and/or stuffy conditions. Lifespan: 8–11 years.

CAUTIONS WHEN BUYING

Owning a dog who believes that his purpose in life is to defend you at any cost comes with the responsibility that you understand the ancestry that made him what he is and take steps to keep him under control. You must provide ongoing socialization and obedience training, strong fences . . . and slobber-towels in every room.

Newfoundland

Fine for Novice Owners
Good with Children
Giant in Size
Thick, Medium-Length Coat

EXERCISE REQUIRED — MEDIUM

TRIMMING/CLIPPING REQUIRED — LOW

AMOUNT OF SHEDDING — HIGH

ACTIVITY INDOORS — LOW

EASE OF TRAINING — MEDIUM

SOCIABILITY WITH STRANGERS — HIGH

TEMPERAMENT

The AKC Standard says, "Sweetness of temperament is the hallmark of the Newfoundland." Calm, dignified, and generally quiet, he does best in a spacious home in the suburbs or country, preferably in a nonhumid climate, ideally with access to a lake or pond. To stay fit, he needs long daily walks, and swimming is much appreciated. He loves to romp in the snow, and pulling a cart or carrying a backpack gives him a purpose in life. This kindly breed is good-natured with everyone, especially children, though they should be as well-behaved as he is. He is very sociable and needs more companionship than many other breeds—he doesn't do well when left alone for long periods. Early socialization is critical in developing a stable temperament, for some males are aggressive with other male dogs, and a very few may be dominant-aggressive toward people. Excessive shyness is also seen. The Newf is not a pushover—he has an independent streak and must learn his manners—but he responds well to patient obedience training. Motivate him with praise and food rewards rather than jerking on the leash, for this breed may have a giant body, but his mind and heart are sensitive. Harshness only makes him skittish and distrustful. Females are most willing to please, while males may be more hardheaded. Newfs pant a lot, drink a lot (sometimes dunking half of their head into their water bucket), and are champion droolers.

HISTORY

In Newfoundland, Canada, he hauled fishermen's nets and carts and carried lifelines to shipwrecked vessels. AKC popularity: 53rd of 146.

PHYSICAL FEATURES

Males stand 28–32 inches and weigh 120–150 pounds. Females stand 26–28 inches and weigh 100–130 pounds. Brush his coarse, somewhat oily coat twice a week, daily during heavy seasonal shedding. Along with his shedding great chunks of hair in the spring and fall, you'll find loose hair the rest of the year as well. Usually he is solid black, or white with black markings (Landseer). Less common are solid brown and solid gray. His ears and tail are natural. His feet are webbed.

HEALTH ISSUES

Both parents should have OFA certificates (hips and elbows) and yearly CERF (eyes). Also ask about cystinuria, low thyroid, heart disease, vWD, seizures, bloat, OCD, panosteitis, and allergies and skin conditions in the lines. Eyelid disorders (entropion) can be a problem. Newfs love shade, air-conditioning, and wading pools and are susceptible to heatstroke in hot, humid, and/or stuffy conditions. Lifespan: 10 years.

CAUTIONS WHEN BUYING

Today the glorious Newfoundland temperament cannot be taken for granted. Buy only from a breeder whose dogs are exceedingly good-natured and who can show you the health clearances. Mind the tremendous quantities of slime (saliva) and dead hair and don't expect a home with a Newfoundland in it to ever qualify for *House Beautiful*.

Norfolk Terrier

Best for Experienced Owners
Good with Older, Considerate Children
Small in Size
Wiry Coat

EXERCISE REQUIRED — MEDIUM

TRIMMING/CLIPPING REQUIRED — MEDIUM

AMOUNT OF SHEDDING — LOW

ACTIVITY INDOORS — HIGH

EASE OF TRAINING — MEDIUM

SOCIABILITY WITH STRANGERS — MEDIUM

TEMPERAMENT

The AKC Standard calls him "game and hardy . . . a 'perfect demon' in the field . . . gregarious, fearless and loyal." A true representative of what a terrier is supposed to be, the Norfolk is full of fire and assertiveness, yet agreeable and thoroughly companionable. He can adapt to any home with moderate exercise (brisk walks and active play sessions). He is sociable, busy, and demands full participation in all activities. His reaction to strangers varies from friendly to reserved, but he should remain poised and hold his ground. He does need more socialization than some other terriers so that his caution does not become timidity. Many individuals are less scrappy with other dogs than many terriers, though they can be jealous of other pets, and trusting them around rabbits or rodents would be foolish. The Norfolk is inquisitive and independent, with strong chasing instincts, a combination that requires a leash or fence at all times. With typical terrier stubbornness, yet sensitive to harsh correction, he responds best to obedience training that utilizes food rather than jerking around. He can be possessive of his food and toys, and he can be a tireless digger and barker. Some have high-pitched, squeaky barks.

HISTORY

Beginning as a plain barnyard ratter, he was developed into a hunt terrier near the city of Norwich, riding in the saddlebag as the huntsmen on horseback followed the foxhounds. The hunt terrier was dropped from the saddle when the fox went to ground, it being his job to bolt the fox from the den so the chase could continue. Prick-eared dogs and drop-eared dogs were eventually developed into separate breeds, with only the prick-eared retaining the Norwich name. AKC popularity: 112th of 146.

PHYSICAL FEATURES

He stands 9–10 inches and weighs 12–15 pounds. Brush and comb his harsh coat once a week and keep his bottom trimmed for cleanliness. Show dogs are "stripped" (dead coat plucked out) every few months; pet owners may opt for more convenient clipping. He may be reddish, wheaten, black-and-tan, or grizzle (speckled). His ears are natural; his tail is docked.

HEALTH ISSUES

Both parents should be screened for luxating patella. Also ask about hip dysplasia and cardiomyopathy in the lines. Lifespan: 12–14 years.

CAUTIONS WHEN BUYING

To the casual eye, the Norfolk is virtually identical in appearance to his cousin, the Norwich, with the most obvious difference being ear carriage. Some terrier enthusiasts say the Norfolk is more emotionally sensitive, more prone to jealousy, and more independent than the Norwich.

Norwegian Buhund (BOO-hund)

Best for Experienced Owners
Good with Children
Medium in Size
Thick, Medium-Length Coat

EXERCISE REQUIRED — HIGH MEDIUM
TRIMMING/CLIPPING REQUIRED — LOW
AMOUNT OF SHEDDING — HIGH
ACTIVITY INDOORS — MEDIUM
EASE OF TRAINING — MEDIUM LOW
SOCIABILITY WITH STRANGERS — MEDIUM

TEMPERAMENT

The happy-go-lucky Buhund plays vigorously, yet is also light on his feet and very agile. More than some other spitz breeds, he likes to be at the center of his family, demanding (and offering) a great deal of companionship. Because he was bred to work all day, you must provide a good amount of physical exercise and mental stimulation. Herding, obedience, agility, jogging or biking, chasing balls, and playing Frisbee are productive outlets for his energy and enthusiasm. Most are friendly (or at least polite) with strangers, yet with their keen senses and watchful attitude, they make dependable alarm dogs. Buhunds are usually fine with other family pets if raised with them. Obedience training will go well if you use modern reward-based methods rather than jerking the leash. This breed is less headstrong and more willing to work with you than other spitzes, but he is still independent and may use his intelligence in clever ways that suit his own purposes. Yet owners who know how to lead will find him eminently trainable. Like most herding breeds, the Buhund is uncomfortable when his flock (family members and other pets) is scattered every which way; he may try to gather everyone together by circling, poking, and nipping. He barks *a lot* in a rapid, high-pitched voice.

HISTORY

This old spitz breed was the companion and herding dog of Scandinavian mountain shepherds. Both dog and man were transients, moving from one crude hut to another while their stock grazed on various pastures. *Buhund* means "homestead dog." Registered by the FCI, UKC, CKC, and AKC-FSS.

PHYSICAL FEATURES

He stands 16–19 inches and weighs 26–40 pounds. His coat is harsh and thick with a dense undercoat and should be brushed twice a week, daily when he is shedding. Along with heavy seasonal shedding, he'll lose hair the rest of the year as well. The most common color is wheaten (light to yellowish red), with or without sabling and/or a dark mask. Less common is black, often with limited white markings. His ears and tail are natural.

HEALTH ISSUES

Both parents should have OFA certificates (hips) and yearly CERF (eyes). Lifespan: 12–15 years.

CAUTIONS WHEN BUYING

Be sure you are up for the high energy level, and remember that this breed needs a job, a purpose in life, to feel satisfied and content. Try to hear a puppy bark—some are more shrill than others. This is a rare breed, so expect a waiting list.

Norwegian Elkhound

Best for Experienced Owners
Good with Children If Raised with Children
Medium in Size
Thick, Medium-Length Coat

EXERCISE REQUIRED — MEDIUM

TRIMMING/CLIPPING REQUIRED — LOW

AMOUNT OF SHEDDING — HIGH

ACTIVITY INDOORS — MEDIUM

EASE OF TRAINING — MEDIUM LOW

SOCIABILITY WITH STRANGERS — MEDIUM

TEMPERAMENT

The AKC Standard says, "Bold and energetic, an effective guardian yet normally friendly, with great dignity and independence of character." Definitely this is a capable, confident dog with a strong presence, whose self-reliance requires supervision and leadership. He's a bundle of energy just waiting for the signal to go, yet when well trained he can control himself. This rugged breed plays hard and enjoys vigorous exercise—on-lead or in a safe enclosed area, please, for some have strong hunting and chasing instincts. Most are friendly with strangers and must be taught not to jump up into their faces, while others are more restrained, but even the friendly ones are great watchdogs and can be protective when necessary. They seldom bite, however, preferring to corner intruders by barking nonstop and feinting to and fro, as they do when holding game animals at bay. Elkhounds can be aggressive with other dogs of the same sex and may be cat chasers unless raised with the family cat. Training can be a challenge, as this breed is dominant and headstrong and may use his intelligence in clever ways that suit his own purposes. Yet owners who know how to lead will find him eminently trainable. He barks *a lot*—and some individuals have extremely high-pitched, piercing voices.

HISTORY

This ancient comrade to the Vikings hunted bear and moose. His name comes from the Norwegian *elg* (moose or elk) *hund* (dog); American anglicized the *hund* into "hound," but this Nordic (spitz) breed bears no resemblance to scenthounds or sighthounds. AKC popularity: 74th of 146.

PHYSICAL FEATURES

He stands 20–21 inches and weighs 50–55 pounds. His coat is harsh with a dense undercoat and should be brushed twice a week, daily when he is shedding. Along with heavy seasonal shedding, you'll see loose hair the rest of the year as well. His coat is gray and silver, the hairs tipped with black. His ears and tail are natural.

HEALTH ISSUES

Both parents should have OFA certificates (hips) and yearly CERF (eyes). Also ask about renal (kidney) disease, cysts, and cancer in the lines. Lifespan: 12–15 years.

CAUTIONS WHEN BUYING

Be sure you're up for the vigorous, bouncing-ball character of this breed and the tufts of hair wafting everywhere during shedding seasons. For a family dog, best not to choose the boldest, most dominant pup in the litter. Try to hear the puppy bark—some are more shrill than others.

Norwegian Lundehund

(LOON-da-hoond)

Best for Experienced Owners
Good with Older, Considerate Children
Small in Size
Short Coat

EXERCISE REQUIRED — MEDIUM

TRIMMING/CLIPPING REQUIRED — LOW

AMOUNT OF SHEDDING — MEDIUM

ACTIVITY INDOORS — MEDIUM

EASE OF TRAINING — LOW

SOCIABILITY WITH STRANGERS — MEDIUM

TEMPERAMENT

Swift, graceful, and agile, the lively Lundehund moves with a light, springy gait and is a surefooted climber and jumper. He is an ancient breed who retains many primitive instincts: Happy and playful, he will pounce on his food and toys, grasping them with his toes and tossing them into the air like a cat or fox catching a mouse. He also hides food and toys, going to great lengths to find just the right place to stash his treasures. Though nonaggressive and gentle with everyone, he is extremely observant and 100 percent aware of his surroundings, quick to alert to anything out of the ordinary. Early and extensive socialization is required to build a confident temperament. He learns quickly and is an excellent, persistent problem-solver. If he outsmarts you once, he remembers. He can be obstinate, tending to use his intelligence in clever ways that suit his own purposes. Housebreaking is notoriously difficult—some individuals are never completely house-broken, and a doggy door to the outside is highly recommended.

HISTORY

Isolated for centuries on the Lofoten Islands off Norway, he hunted and caught the brightly colored puffin bird *(lunde),* providing the farmer with a source of meat and downy feathers. A good Lundehund was as valuable as a milk cow. His anatomy is unusual and leads some scientists to speculate that he may have survived the last Ice Age. With six toes (some grasping) on each foot, he can scale steep, slippery rock walls to reach the roosting dens. When squeezed into tight crevices, he can close his ears to protect the ear canals against dirt and moisture, flatten his flexible shoulders and front legs into a bearskin-rug position, and bend his neck backward until his nose touches his spine—the reindeer is the only other mammal with this neck structure. Today this rare breed is slowly being rebuilt. Registered by the FCI, UKC, and CKC.

PHYSICAL FEATURES

He stands 13–15 inches and weighs 13–16 pounds. Brush his dense, harsh coat once a week, more often during seasonal shedding. He is usually sable (reddish to fawn, with black-tipped hairs) with white markings. His ears and tail are natural.

HEALTH ISSUES

Serious intestinal diseases (protein losing enteropathy, intestinal bowel syndrome, malabsorption) are almost endemic in the Lundehund. They can begin at any age and recur as a frustrating chronic condition that may, depending on severity, end in euthanasia. Research is under way to determine the causes of these disorders, which are exacerbated by stress. Though not every Lundehund will be affected, each should have a fecal test and serum protein level test run at least twice a year. Lifespan: 12–15 years.

CAUTIONS WHEN BUYING

With only two hundred dogs in the United States, expect high prices and a waiting list. Be sure you feel comfortable handling the intestinal problems, house-breaking difficulties, and primitive behaviors.

Norwich Terrier

Best for Experienced Owners
Good with Older, Considerate Children
Small in Size
Wiry Coat

EXERCISE REQUIRED — MEDIUM

TRIMMING/CLIPPING REQUIRED — MEDIUM

AMOUNT OF SHEDDING — LOW

ACTIVITY INDOORS — HIGH

EASE OF TRAINING — MEDIUM

SOCIABILITY WITH STRANGERS — MEDIUM

TEMPERAMENT

The AKC Standard calls him "game and hardy . . . a 'perfect demon' in the field . . . gregarious, fearless and loyal." A true representative of what a terrier is supposed to be, the Norwich is full of fire and assertiveness, yet agreeable and thoroughly companionable. He can adapt to any home with moderate exercise (brisk walks and active play sessions). He is sociable, busy, and demands full participation in all activities. His reaction to strangers varies from friendly to reserved, but he should remain poised and hold his ground. He does need more socialization than some other terriers so that his caution does not become timidity. Many individuals are less scrappy with other dogs than many terriers, though they can be jealous of other pets, and trusting them around rabbits or rodents would be foolish. The Norwich is inquisitive and independent, with strong chasing instincts, a combination that requires a leash or fence at all times. With typical terrier stubbornness, yet sensitive to harsh correction, he responds best to obedience training that utilizes food rather than jerking around. He can be possessive of his food and toys, and he can be a tireless digger and barker.

HISTORY

Beginning as a plain barnyard ratter, he was developed into a hunt terrier near the city of Norwich, riding in the saddlebag as the huntsmen on horseback followed the foxhounds. The hunt terrier was dropped from the saddle when the fox went to ground, it being his job to bolt the fox from the den so the chase could continue. AKC popularity: 104th of 146.

PHYSICAL FEATURES

He stands 9–10 inches and weighs 11–14 pounds. Brush and comb his harsh coat once a week and keep his bottom trimmed for cleanliness. Show dogs are "stripped" (dead coat plucked out) every few months; pet owners may opt for more convenient clipping. He may be reddish, wheaten, black-and-tan, or grizzle (speckled). His ears are natural; his tail is docked.

HEALTH ISSUES

Both parents should be screened for luxating patella. Also ask about hip dysplasia, cardiomyopathy, seizures, and allergies in the lines. Lifespan: 12–14 years.

CAUTIONS WHEN BUYING

To the casual eye, the Norwich is virtually identical in appearance to his cousin, the Norfolk, with the most obvious difference being ear carriage. Some terrier enthusiasts say the Norwich is stronger-tempered, more stable in mood, and less independent than the Norfolk.

Nova Scotia Duck Tolling Retriever

Fine for Novice Owners
Good with Children If Raised with Children
Medium in Size
Feathered, Medium-Length Coat

EXERCISE REQUIRED — HIGH

TRIMMING/CLIPPING REQUIRED — MEDIUM
    LOW

AMOUNT OF SHEDDING — MEDIUM

ACTIVITY INDOORS — HIGH MEDIUM

EASE OF TRAINING — MEDIUM

SOCIABILITY WITH STRANGERS — MEDIUM
    LOW

TEMPERAMENT

This good-natured, high-energy breed is a joy in the right hands, but too much dog when mismatched with someone looking for a couch potato. Easygoing, but also high-spirited and playful, quick moving and agile, he is busy indoors and needs plenty of exercise, especially fetching and swimming. Mental exercise (advanced obedience, agility, tracking, field work) is just as important. His reaction to strangers varies from reserved to curious, but often includes some initial caution. He needs early and ongoing socialization to avoid suspiciousness or timidity. He's usually fine with other animals—he may chase the family cat for fun but seldom means any harm. Although bright and clever, most are easily distracted and easily bored, while some are strong-willed and dominant, testing the rules to see what they can get away with. You must demonstrate consistent leadership and keep training sessions short, upbeat, and challenging. As with all retrievers, you must control his tendency to chew on objects and to mouth your hands—provide a box filled with toys so he can carry something around in his mouth. When excited, he tends to whine and "whistle." Some are diggers and some youngsters chew destructively.

HISTORY

Tolling means "luring" or "enticing." The Toller's job is to run up and down the shoreline chasing sticks and waving his tail to lure curious ducks into gun range. Registered by the FCI, UKC, SKC, and CKC.

PHYSICAL FEATURES

He stands 17–21 inches and weighs 35–50 pounds. Brush and comb his silky coat twice a week, and occasionally trim straggly hairs. Keep his ear canals clean and dry and his bottom trimmed for cleanliness. He comes in shades of red or orange, usually with white markings on his face, chest, feet, and/or tail tip. His ears and tail are natural. His feet are webbed.

HEALTH ISSUES

Both parents should have OFA certificates (hips) and yearly CERF (eyes). Also ask about heart disease and low thyroid in the lines. Lifespan: 12–14 years.

CAUTIONS WHEN BUYING

If you like the general build, robustness, and reputation of retrievers as dependable family dogs, consider this breed. They are difficult to find (be prepared to go on a waiting list), but quality is high and health problems are minimal. Just remember that this is *not* a Golden Retriever, but a more alert, discriminating, somewhat demanding dog who requires extensive socialization and constructive direction of his energies.

Old English Sheepdog

Best for Experienced Owners
Good with Children
Large in Size
Long Coat

EXERCISE REQUIRED — MEDIUM

TRIMMING/CLIPPING REQUIRED — LOW

AMOUNT OF SHEDDING — HIGH

ACTIVITY INDOORS — MEDIUM

EASE OF TRAINING — MEDIUM LOW

SOCIABILITY WITH STRANGERS — MEDIUM

TEMPERAMENT

Good-natured and sociable, enthusiastic and bumptious, the Old English does best in the suburbs or country, with at least an hour of daily exercise and space to move. He loves people, can be quite the clown, and is demanding of attention. If left without the companionship of humans or other pets, he will become unhappy and destructive. Most individuals are polite with strangers and make sensible watchdogs with a deep, ringing bark, but they are not guard dogs. There is timidity and skittishness in some lines, sharpness in others; extensive socialization is important to develop a confident, stable temperament. Most are peaceful with other animals. Though very stubborn, he is also sensitive to correction and needs a light hand on the leash. You reach an OES through positive training methods that utilize praise and food rewards; roughness or jerking on the leash only make him obstinate and defensive. Some try to herd children and other pets by circling, poking, and nipping. However, compared to other herding breeds, Old English are more commonly show dogs and pets, rather than working sheepdogs. The happy-go-lucky, rustic OES is not for fastidious households—he tracks in mud, splashes in his water bowl, and affectionately thrusts his wet and/or dirty beard into your lap. Some drool.

HISTORY

In England he drove sheep and cattle to market. Since drover dogs were tax-exempt, their tails were commonly docked as proof of their occupation. AKC popularity: 65th of 146.

PHYSICAL FEATURES

He stands 21–26 inches and weighs 60–100 pounds. Brush and comb his profuse double coat twice a week (one to two hours per session). Pet owners may trim/clip the coat short every few months. Although OES do not shed seasonally, you'll find some loose hair all year round. He is blue, gray, grizzle, or blue merle, usually with white markings. His ears are natural; his tail is docked.

HEALTH ISSUES

Both parents should have OFA certificates (hips and elbows) and yearly CERF (eyes). Also ask about cerebellar ataxia, low thyroid, allergies, sebaceous adenitis, and other skin conditions in the lines. Full-coated dogs are very susceptible to heatstroke, and even clipped dogs must have protection from the heat. Lifespan: 12–14 years.

CAUTIONS WHEN BUYING

Unfortunately, the kind nature of this breed should no longer be taken for granted, as poorly bred lines can be high-strung and nasty. Buy only from a breeder who emphasizes sound temperament (make sure you see both parents) and who can show you the health clearances. If you're not going to shave the coat, you must commit to regular, frequent grooming because an unkempt, smelly OES is very hard to live with. Many are surrendered to rescue because neglect has made them undesirable as family members.

Otterhound

Best for Experienced Owners
Good with Children
Large in Size
Long Coat

EXERCISE REQUIRED — HIGH MEDIUM

TRIMMING/CLIPPING REQUIRED — LOW

AMOUNT OF SHEDDING — MEDIUM

ACTIVITY INDOORS — LOW

EASE OF TRAINING — LOW

SOCIABILITY WITH STRANGERS — MEDIUM

TEMPERAMENT

He has been described as a "big friendly dog with a mind of his own." Though amiable and easygoing, he is so rugged that he belongs in a rural area with an outdoorsy owner who can give him the exercise he loves. Swimming is an especially appreciated form of recreation, as these hounds were born to dive into water, whether it be a lake, a puddle, or simply submerging his shaggy head in his drinking bowl and coming up shaking. Unless he is well trained, a leash or secure fence is a must at all times, for the nose of this great hunter is exquisitely sensitive, always seeking out new and exciting scents. Once he's latched on to something, his perseverance, determination, and stamina (like those of his relative, the Bloodhound) are legendary. He tends to shamble along with a loose, shuffling gait, without lifting his feet high off the ground. His reaction to strangers varies from friendly to reserved; most are good watchdogs but not guard dogs. He can be clumsy with toddlers. Most are fine with other dogs, but with his powerful hunting instincts, small pets are not always safe. Obedience training takes time and effort, for he is stubborn and independent, yet "soft." In other words, though he'll be slow to obey, he'll be good-natured about it. With their propensity for slobbering water, lumbering around in a rather klutzy manner, and tracking in mud with their hairy webbed feet, Otterhounds are not good choices for fastidious housekeepers or those with no sense of humor. They have a loud, deep, distinctive bay that carries for amazingly long distances.

HISTORY

Large packs of Otterhounds were once used to dispatch otters preying on the trout in popular English fishing streams. He is related to the Bloodhound. AKC popularity: 144th of 146.

PHYSICAL FEATURES

Males stand 26–28 inches and weigh 95–115 pounds; females stand 24–26 inches and weigh 65–95 pounds. Brush and comb his shaggy coat twice a week. Pet owners may choose to trim/clip the coat short every few months. Colors include black-and-tan, black-and-tan grizzle (with gray flecking), liver-and-tan, wheaten, and tricolor (white with black-and-tan patches). His ears and tail are natural.

HEALTH ISSUES

Both parents should have OFA certificates (hips). Also ask about bloat and vWD in the lines. Lifespan: 10–13 years.

CAUTIONS WHEN BUYING

Fewer than fifty new Otterhounds are registered each year, so be prepared to wait for a puppy. However, most Otterhound breeders are good about referring "good homes" to other breeders who may have pups available or who are anticipating a breeding in the near future. Be prepared for a blank look when you tell people your dog is an Otterhound—this rustic, unassuming fellow is usually mistaken for a shaggy sheepdog mix.

Papillon (PAP-ee-yon)

Fine for Novice Owners
Good with Older, Considerate Children
Little in Size
Feathered, Medium-Length Coat

EXERCISE REQUIRED — MEDIUM LOW

TRIMMING/CLIPPING REQUIRED — LOW

AMOUNT OF SHEDDING — MEDIUM

ACTIVITY INDOORS — HIGH MEDIUM

EASE OF TRAINING — HIGH

SOCIABILITY WITH STRANGERS — HIGH MEDIUM

TEMPERAMENT

One of the brightest and most trainable of the toys, the fine-boned, elegant Papillon is commonly chosen by obedience or agility exhibitors who want a small top-notch competition dog. He learns very quickly and responds eagerly to positive training methods (praise and food). Papillons are also the master tracking dogs of the toy world. You do have to watch your lines: Some are dainty, even high-strung, while others are confident and outgoing. Much depends on genetics (parents' and grand-parents' temperaments and the breeder's goals) and the rest on socialization and training. When treated like an intelligent, capable fellow, he is likely to live up to these expectations. Indoors and out he is lively, happy, and playful, yet light-footed and graceful, not likely to topple lamps. Most are friendly or at least polite with strangers, but he is a gentle soul who can be overwhelmed by the roughhousing and mischief of small children. With other pets he is not as submissive as you might think. In fact, some are possessive and bossy, especially with larger dogs. This can be dangerous, as the quick-moving Pap may be viewed as prey. Some retain their own sporting instincts from their spaniel heritage and will stalk and pursue birds, mice, even flying insects. Housebreaking can be difficult, and barking may need to be controlled.

HISTORY

Papillon is French for "butterfly," an apt moniker for the large fringed ears that resemble wings. AKC popularity: 47th of 146.

PHYSICAL FEATURES

He stands 8–12 inches and weighs 5–10 pounds. Brush and comb his silky coat twice a week, more often when he is shedding. Keep his ear canals clean and dry and his bottom trimmed for cleanliness. He is mostly white with patches of black, black-and-tan, red, lemon, or sable. His ears are natural and may stand erect or droop down. His tail is natural.

HEALTH ISSUES

Both parents should have yearly CERF certificates (eyes) and be screened for luxating patella. He is sensitive to anesthetics, vaccines, and chemicals and should never be casually medicated or sedated. Papillons don't like cold or rain and should wear a sweater in inclement conditions. Lifespan: 14–16 years.

CAUTIONS WHEN BUYING

There are two types of ears in this breed. In most of Europe only the erect-eared dogs are called Papillons, while the drop-eared (the original variety) are considered a separate breed called Phalene (FAY-leen), which means "night moth." In the United States, both ear types are considered varieties of the same breed.

Pekingese (PEEK-in-ees)

Fine for Novice Owners
Good with Older, Considerate Children
Little in Size
Long Coat

EXERCISE REQUIRED — LOW

TRIMMING/CLIPPING REQUIRED — LOW

AMOUNT OF SHEDDING — HIGH

ACTIVITY INDOORS — LOW

EASE OF TRAINING — LOW

SOCIABILITY WITH STRANGERS — MEDIUM
        LOW

TEMPERAMENT

The AKC Standard says the Pekingese "should imply courage, boldness, and self-esteem rather than prettiness, daintiness, or delicacy." Indeed, the Peke is dignified, supremely confident, and one of the most independent (and stubborn) of the toy breeds. Clean, calm, and quiet indoors, he lies on the sofa cushions much of the time, observing his kingdom with his direct, inscrutable gaze. Yet he will also surprise you with sudden bursts of playfulness. Most are loyal to their owner without being cloying, undemonstrative (or polite) with strangers, and usually accepting of other animals. This proud, self-possessed dog won't meekly submit to mischief or rough handling from anyone whom he views as below himself in importance. He can be exasperatingly willful, but also sensitive, and resents being jerked around or even scolded. However, if he respects you, he will be well-mannered without much formal training required. Stick to positive training methods, using praise and treats. Make him feel that what you're asking him to do is what *he* wanted to do in the first place. He can be possessive of his food and toys. With his short face, he is a master of the four S's: snorting, snuffling, sneezing, and snoring.

HISTORY

Considered sacred by the Chinese Tang dynasty, he was one of the possessions looted by the British when they invaded the Peking Imperial Palace. AKC popularity: 26th of 146.

PHYSICAL FEATURES

He stands 8–9 inches and weighs 7–14 pounds. His coat is coarse and profuse, with a dense undercoat, and should be brushed twice a week, daily during heavy seasonal shedding. Keep his ear canals clean and dry and his bottom trimmed for cleanliness. Colors include red, fawn, white, black, black-and-tan, particolor, sable, and brindle. His ears and tail are natural.

HEALTH ISSUES

Both parents should be screened for luxating patella. His large eyes are susceptible to lacerations, infections, and eyelid/eyelash defects. Select a puppy whose eyes are not bulging or showing too much white around the iris, whose facial features show no signs of crowding, and whose nostrils are wide open. He is prone to heatstroke in hot, humid, and/or stuffy conditions. Pekes love shade and air-conditioning. Long-backed breeds are susceptible to disk disease that can be exacerbated by excessive high-jumping, dashing down stairs, being picked up without proper support, and obesity. Lifespan: 12–14 years.

CAUTIONS WHEN BUYING

Pekes are not a natural breed. Due to artificial insemination, C-sections, small litters, and a high puppy mortality rate, they are difficult to breed and whelp and tend to be expensive.

Petit Basset Griffon Vendeen
(Peh-TEE Bas-SAY Griff-ON Vahn-DAY-en)

Best for Experienced Owners
Good with Children
Small in Size
Wiry Coat

EXERCISE REQUIRED — MEDIUM

TRIMMING/CLIPPING REQUIRED — LOW

AMOUNT OF SHEDDING — LOW

ACTIVITY INDOORS — HIGH

EASE OF TRAINING — LOW

SOCIABILITY WITH STRANGERS — HIGH

TEMPERAMENT

The AKC Standard says, "Bold and vivacious in character . . . tough and robust in construction . . . an alert outlook, lively bearing, and a good voice freely used." The Petit Basset (or PBGV) is actually not basset-like, but terrier-like: curious, enthusiastic, reacting quickly to interesting scents and sudden movements, always looking for something to do. He plays vigorously and needs long daily walks and frequent romps, but this inquisitive sniffing machine should not be trusted off-leash, for he is a confirmed chaser who will follow his nose. He sounds off (in a surprisingly deep bass) when strangers enter his territory, then welcomes them with happy wags. Most are extroverted with other dogs and cats, but pet rabbits and rodents are not a wise addition to the household. This stubborn, clever little hound requires an owner who knows when to laugh at his appealing whiskery face and mischievous antics and when to be firm and in control. The PBGV demands attention and companionship and enjoys barking and digging. Some are escape artists who can go over, as well as under, fences.

HISTORY

The Petit (small) Basset (low to the ground) Griffon (rough-coated dog) is a native of the French province of Vendée, where he hunted rabbits through dense, brambly underbrush. There is also a Grand (large) version. AKC popularity: 111th of 146.

PHYSICAL FEATURES

He stands 13–15 inches and weighs 25–40 pounds. Brush his tousled coat twice a week. Keep his ear canals clean and dry and his bottom trimmed for cleanliness. He is mostly white, with lemon, orange, black, and/or grizzle markings. His ears and tail are natural.

HEALTH ISSUES

Both parents should have OFA certificates (hips) and yearly CERF (eyes). Also ask about luxating patella, heart disease, neck pain syndrome, and seizures in the lines. Lifespan: 14 years.

CAUTIONS WHEN BUYING

This breed has an intriguing and challenging combination of scenthound and terrier traits—be sure you are up for his high energy level (about that of an English Springer Spaniel) and general busyness. The rustic Petit is a robust, independent extrovert, not a docile lapdog.

Pharaoh Hound (FAIR-o)

Best for Experienced Owners
Good with Children
Medium to Large in Size
Smooth Coat

EXERCISE REQUIRED — HIGH MEDIUM
TRIMMING/CLIPPING REQUIRED — LOW
AMOUNT OF SHEDDING — MEDIUM LOW
ACTIVITY INDOORS — MEDIUM
EASE OF TRAINING — LOW
SOCIABILITY WITH STRANGERS — MEDIUM

TEMPERAMENT

The AKC Standard says, "Of noble bearing with hard clean-cut lines . . . very fast with a marked keenness for hunting." The Pharaoh Hound is athletic and playful, light on his feet and a jumper par excellence. Adults move gracefully through the house, though some sprinting and leaping should also be expected. This breed can be most entertaining if one has a sense of humor. He is fond of being comfortable and can curl himself into a surprisingly compact ball to fit whichever nook or cranny has the softest blankets. He needs a good deal of exercise, but is so swift and agile and has such powerful chasing instincts that he must be allowed to run only in a safe, enclosed area. Though extremely alert and quick to announce strangers, he is not a guard dog. Indeed, he is both curious and cautious, hesitantly investigating new people, places, sights, and sounds. Early and ongoing socialization is required to build confidence. Usually sociable with other dogs, he will pursue small animals that run. This independent thinker is sensitive to correction, so he should be handled calmly and motivated with food and praise. Sighthounds are touch-sensitive, tending to startle when touched unexpectedly and uncomfortable when cuddled excessively. A verbal correction is more effective than a physical one, because it is less distracting to the dog. Unlike most sighthounds, the Pharaoh Hound can be a barker.

HISTORY

Originally owned by Egyptian rulers, he was brought to the island of Malta and used to run down gazelles and hares. AKC popularity: 132nd of 146.

PHYSICAL FEATURES

He stands 21–25 inches and weighs 40–60 pounds. His hard coat needs only an occasional quick brushing. Color ranges from tan to chestnut. His ears and tail are natural.

HEALTH ISSUES

Both parents should have OFA certificates (hips) and yearly CERF (eyes). He is sensitive to anesthetics, vaccines, and chemicals and should never be casually medicated or sedated. Lifespan: 12–14 years.

CAUTIONS WHEN BUYING

Like most sighthounds, Pharaoh Hounds are fortunate in not being singled out for mass production by unknowledgeable breeders. Quality is high and health is excellent. However, their rarity (only 100 to 120 pups registered each year) means that you should expect a waiting list. Look for friendly, outgoing lines—be sure to see both parents (and grandparents, if possible).

Pointer

Best for Experienced Owners
Good with Children If Raised with Children
Large in Size
Smooth Coat

EXERCISE REQUIRED — HIGH

TRIMMING/CLIPPING REQUIRED — LOW

AMOUNT OF SHEDDING — MEDIUM

ACTIVITY INDOORS — MEDIUM

EASE OF TRAINING — MEDIUM

SOCIABILITY WITH STRANGERS — MEDIUM

TEMPERAMENT

The AKC Standard says, "Here is an animal whose every movement shows him to be a wide-awake, hard-driving hunting dog possessing stamina, courage, and the desire to go." Though dignified, sweet-natured, and gentle, the Pointer is bred primarily for sport afield. He is packed with energy and belongs with an active owner who will give him the running exercise he needs to feel satisfied. Pointers, especially youngsters, become restless and bored when confined too much and may resort to destructive chewing and barking. A walk around the block is barely a warm-up for this canine athlete. With strangers, most individuals are slightly reserved, but congenial. This is not a guard dog. He is amiable with other animals. A bit stubborn and easily distracted, but also kindly and sensitive, he responds well to patient obedience training that includes food rewards and praise rather than jerking around. Commands such as "down" and "stay" are important for instilling self-discipline and control.

HISTORY

Often called the English Pointer, he is one of the oldest of the pointing breeds. Spectacularly fast and wide ranging, with a concentration and competitiveness far surpassing those of other sporting dogs, he is the king of national pointing trials. AKC popularity: 93rd of 146.

PHYSICAL FEATURES

Males stand 25–28 inches and weigh 55–75 pounds. Females stand 23-26 inches and weigh 45–65 pounds. His hard coat needs only an occasional quick brushing. He is mostly white with black, orange, lemon, or liver patches or ticking. Solid colors are less common. His ears and tail are natural.

HEALTH ISSUES

Both parents should have OFA certificates (hips) and yearly CERF (eyes). Also ask about seizures and low thyroid in the lines. Lifespan: 11–14 years.

CAUTIONS WHEN BUYING

Pointers are divided into show lines and field lines. An individual from show lines tends to be more easygoing and willing to please, while strict field lines are often too work-oriented and energetic to be at their best as pets. If you want a pleasant companion who can double as a personal hunting dog, be sure a show-line pedigree includes field titles as well as Ch. titles.

Polish Lowland Sheepdog

Best for Experienced Owners
Good with Children If Raised with Children
Medium in Size
Long Coat

EXERCISE REQUIRED — HIGH MEDIUM

TRIMMING/CLIPPING REQUIRED — HIGH
  MEDIUM LOW

AMOUNT OF SHEDDING — MEDIUM LOW

ACTIVITY INDOORS — MEDIUM

EASE OF TRAINING — MEDIUM

SOCIABILITY WITH STRANGERS — MEDIUM
  LOW

TEMPERAMENT

The AKC Standard calls him "lively but self-controlled, clever and perceptive and endowed with an excellent memory." The PON (an affectionate acronym for his Polish name: Polish Owczarek Nizinny, pronounced *ov-CHA-rek nee-ZHEE-nee*) is a vigorous working dog. Strong and durable, athletic and agile, he requires daily exercise and does best with active owners. Mental stimulation in the form of obedience, agility, herding, or watching over his home is even more important to this highly intelligent breed. When these needs are met, he is calm and stable and settles down happily indoors. Somewhat aloof and suspicious of strangers, he makes a vigilant watchdog. In fact, socialization must be early and thorough so that his watchfulness does not become either skittishness or sharpness. Most are dominant with other dogs, especially of the same sex. Those with a high prey drive are not reliable around little creatures that run or flutter. Like most herding breeds, he often pokes or pushes people and other animals in an attempt to gather them or move them along. These confident dogs were bred to think independently and make their own decisions, and they will do exactly that unless you take charge and establish the rules. They are persistent problem-solvers ("If I can't get what I want this way, maybe I can get it this way . . .") and can be dominant and manipulative. This shaggy dog is not for the immaculate household. Mud, snow, and leaves cling to his tousled coat, and his beard collects water and food remnants and can then mat and smell.

HISTORY

The first Polish breed to be introduced to the United States, he is descended from the Hungarian Puli and sixteenth-century Hun herding breeds. Registered by the AKC, FCI, UKC, and SKC.

PHYSICAL FEATURES

He stands 17–20 inches and weighs 30–50 pounds. Brush and comb his thick, shaggy double coat every other day. Pet owners may choose to trim/clip the coat short every few months. The most common colors are white with black, gray, or sandy patches; gray with white markings; and chocolate. His ears are natural; his tail is docked, though some are born bobtailed.

HEALTH ISSUES

Both parents should have OFA certificates (hips) and yearly CERF (eyes). Also ask about low thyroid, digestive problems, and allergies in the lines. Lifespan: 12–14 years.

CAUTIONS WHEN BUYING

Litters are not numerous and many pups are kept for showing and breeding, so be prepared for a waiting list, especially for a female. If you're not going to clip the coat, you must commit to regular grooming because a neglected, unkempt PON will develop skin conditions and be undesirable to live with.

Pomeranian

Fine for Novice Owners
Good with Older, Considerate Children
Little in Size
Thick, Medium-Length Coat

EXERCISE REQUIRED — LOW

TRIMMING/CLIPPING REQUIRED — LOW

AMOUNT OF SHEDDING — HIGH

ACTIVITY INDOORS — HIGH

EASE OF TRAINING — MEDIUM

SOCIABILITY WITH STRANGERS — MEDIUM
LOW

TEMPERAMENT

The AKC Standard says he is "buoyant in deportment . . . inquisitive by nature . . . cocky, commanding, and animated." That he is. Vivacious and spirited, bold and brash, the Pom thinks he's "hot stuff." He is a sharp-eyed, extroverted busybody who must check out every sight, sound, and activity and preferably tell you what he thinks about it. He is delightfully alive and aware of everything going on around him. Keenly alert to approaching strangers, he requires early socialization so that he doesn't become sharp or shrill. Most are fine with other pets—it is a tribute to their amiability that male Poms can often run and play together with little or no bickering. Some individuals, though, are bossy and will attempt to chase strange dogs, regardless of size. This proud, self-possessed little dog won't meekly submit to mischief or rough handling. He is very bright and will look directly at you, cocking his head attentively, but he is not inclined to take orders from anyone whom he views as below himself in importance, and he resents being jerked around. Positive training methods (praise and treats) are the solution. Don't allow him to become possessive of his food or toys, and control barking from day one.

HISTORY

This little fellow is descended from Icelandic sled dogs and herding dogs, hence his "big dog" personality. He takes his name from Pomerania, Germany. AKC popularity: 10th of 146.

PHYSICAL FEATURES

He stands 6–7 inches and weighs 3–7 pounds. Many individuals are larger; these are not suitable for show, but make sturdy pets. Brush his harsh, upstanding coat twice a week, daily during heavy seasonal shedding. Along with his shedding great chunks of hair in the spring and fall, you'll find loose hair the rest of the year as well. Colors include red, orange, cream, white, blue, black, black-and-tan, particolor, sable, and brindle. His ears and tail are natural.

HEALTH ISSUES

Both parents should be screened for luxating patella. Check parents' teeth for soundness—poor teeth run through some lines. Ask about collapsing trachea, allergies and skin conditions, and heart disease (PDA) in the lines. The smaller Poms are susceptible to hypoglycemia (low blood sugar). Lifespan: 12–16 years.

CAUTIONS WHEN BUYING

Unfortunately, most Pomeranians are produced by unknowledgeable breeders, so virtually none of those you see on the street look the way they should. They have large pointy ears, a long pointy muzzle, a long back, and a soft, wooly, flat coat that mats by simply looking at it. Often they weigh 10–15 pounds and can have unstable temperaments. In sharp contrast, a Pom from a knowledgeable show breeder will be small and compact, with a short back, short muzzle, small furry ears, a harsh upstanding coat, and a spunky but sweet temperament.

Poodle (Miniature)

Fine for Novice Owners
Good with Older, Considerate Children
Small in Size
Curly Coat

EXERCISE REQUIRED — LOW

TRIMMING/CLIPPING REQUIRED — HIGH

AMOUNT OF SHEDDING — LOW

ACTIVITY INDOORS — HIGH MEDIUM

EASE OF TRAINING — HIGH

SOCIABILITY WITH STRANGERS — MEDIUM

TEMPERAMENT

One of the smartest, most sensitive, and most trainable of all breeds, the perky, proud Poodle is both elegant and athletic. Indoors and out he is lively and happy, carrying himself with pride and moving with a light, graceful, springy gait. Along with companionship, he requires mental stimulation such as advanced obedience, agility, and fetching toys; this intelligent breed cannot simply sit in the backyard and be ignored. He is a thinking dog who pays rapt attention to his owner, learns quickly, and responds eagerly to positive training methods. Most are polite with strangers and sociable with other animals. You do have to watch your lines: Some are rather dainty, even high-strung, while others are confident and outgoing. Excessive barking may need to be controlled.

HISTORY

He was bred down from the Standard Poodle, who was used as a retriever in Germany. *Pudelin* means "to splash in the water." France developed him into a circus and show dog. AKC popularity: 7th of 146 (but this includes all three size varieties).

PHYSICAL FEATURES

He stands 10–15 inches and weighs 14–20 pounds. Brush and comb twice a week. Show dogs are shorn into elaborately sculptured patterns, while pets are clipped more sensibly. Clipping must be repeated every four to six weeks. Keep his ear canals clean and dry. Colors include black, white, cream, silver, red, apricot, and brown. Parti-colors cannot be shown in conformation classes. His ears are natural; his tail is docked.

HEALTH ISSUES

Both parents should have OFA certificates (hips), yearly CERF (eyes), and be screened for luxating patella. A DNA certificate that shows whether they are affected, carriers, or clear of vWD (at least one parent must be clear) is extra security. Also ask about Legg-Perthes, low thyroid, seizures, allergies, and heart disease in the lines. Lifespan: 14–16 years.

CAUTIONS WHEN BUYING

Miniature Poodles are produced en masse by unknowledgeable breeders, and an individual from such lines is likely to end up with unsound structure, genetic health problems that weren't screened for, or a hyperactive, nervous temperament. Look for lines with performance titles in obedience, agility, or versatility, or temperament titles (TT, CGC, TDI).

Poodle (Standard)

Fine for Novice Owners
Good with Older, Considerate Children
Medium to Large in Size
Curly Coat

EXERCISE REQUIRED — MEDIUM

TRIMMING/CLIPPING REQUIRED — HIGH

AMOUNT OF SHEDDING — LOW

ACTIVITY INDOORS — MEDIUM

EASE OF TRAINING — HIGH

SOCIABILITY WITH STRANGERS — MEDIUM

TEMPERAMENT

One of the smartest, most capable, and most trainable of all breeds, the proud, sensible Poodle is both elegant and athletic. He is a thinking dog who pays rapt attention to his owner, learns quickly, and responds eagerly to positive training methods. He is so sensitive and intuitive, and such a skilled reader of body language and expression, that he often appears telepathic. Energy level varies from moderate to high, so a good amount of exercise (brisk walks, jogging, hiking, play sessions) is needed to keep him fit, satisfied, and calm indoors. Even more important is mental exercise: advanced obedience exercises, obstacle course, fieldwork, retrieving. This highly intelligent breed cannot simply sit in the backyard and be ignored. Most are polite with strangers and some have sensible protective instincts; early socialization is important to avoid excessive watchfulness or timidity. You do have to watch your lines: Some are rather dainty, even high-strung, while others are confident and outgoing. Most get along well with other pets.

HISTORY

The oldest and largest of the three Poodle varieties, he originated in Germany as a retriever of ducks. *Pudelin* means "to splash in the water." France developed him into a circus and show dog; thus, many people refer to him, incorrectly, as a "French" Poodle. AKC popularity: 7th of 146 (but this includes all three varieties).

PHYSICAL FEATURES

He stands over 15 inches (usually 22–27 inches) and weighs 45–80 pounds. "Royal Standard" is a made-up term for extra-large Poodles, who may or may not be structurally sound. Show dog coats are shorn into elaborate sculptured patterns, while pets are clipped more sensibly. Clipping must be repeated every four to six weeks. Keep his ear canals clean and dry. Colors include black, white, cream, silver, red, apricot, and brown. Particolors cannot be shown in conformation classes. His ears are natural; his tail is docked.

HEALTH ISSUES

Both parents should have OFA certificates (hips), yearly CERF (eyes), normal thyroid (full panel), a skin punch biopsy for sebaceous adenitis, and a DNA certificate that shows whether they are affected, carriers, or clear of vWD (at least one parent must be clear). Ask about bloat, Addison's disease, renal disease, seizures, and allergies in the lines. Lifespan: 10–12 years.

CAUTIONS WHEN BUYING

Buy only from a breeder who can show you all of the health clearances. Look for confident, outgoing lines with performance titles (obedience, agility, versatility, field) or temperament titles (TT, CGC).

Poodle (Toy)

Fine for Novice Owners
Good with Older, Considerate Children
Little in Size
Curly Coat

EXERCISE REQUIRED — LOW

TRIMMING/CLIPPING REQUIRED — HIGH

AMOUNT OF SHEDDING — LOW

ACTIVITY INDOORS — HIGH MEDIUM

EASE OF TRAINING — HIGH

SOCIABILITY WITH STRANGERS — MEDIUM

TEMPERAMENT

The smartest, most attentive, most trainable of the toys, the perky, elegant Poodle is commonly chosen by obedience and agility exhibitors who want a very small, top-notch competition dog. He learns faster than almost any other breed, is exceptionally sensitive to praise and correction, and responds eagerly to positive training methods. Indoors and out he is lively and happy, carrying himself with pride and moving with a light, graceful, springy gait. He loves to play and is especially fond of retrieving balls and toys. You do have to watch your lines: Some are dainty, even high-strung, while others are confident and outgoing. Much depends on socialization and training: When brought out to experience the world and treated like an intelligent, capable fellow, he is likely to live up to these expectations. Some are such gentle souls they are overwhelmed by the roughhousing and mischief of small children, while others simply won't put up with it. Toy Poodles are peaceful with other pets. Barking should be controlled.

HISTORY

He was bred down from the Standard Poodle, who was used as a retriever in Germany. *Pudelin* means "to splash in the water." France developed him into a circus and show dog. AKC popularity: 7th of 146 (but this includes all three size varieties).

PHYSICAL FEATURES

He stands 6–10 inches and weighs 4–7 pounds. Larger individuals make sturdy pets, while smaller individuals are often not sound or healthy. Brush and comb twice a week.

Show dogs are shorn into elaborately sculptured patterns, while pets are clipped more sensibly. Clipping must be repeated every four to six weeks. Keep his ear canals clean and dry. Colors include black, white, cream, silver, red, apricot, and brown. Particolors cannot be shown in conformation classes. His ears are natural; his tail is docked.

HEALTH ISSUES

Both parents should have yearly CERF certificates (eyes) and be screened for luxating patella. Check parents' teeth for soundness—poor teeth run through some lines. Also ask about low thyroid, Legg-Perthes, seizures, heart disease, hip dysplasia, and allergies. Toy Poodles do not like cold or rain and should wear a sweater in inclement conditions. The smaller individuals are prone to hypoglycemia (low blood sugar). Lifespan: 12–16 years.

CAUTIONS WHEN BUYING

Toy Poodles are produced en masse by unknowledgeable breeders, and an individual from such lines is likely to be unsound. Look for confident, outgoing lines with healthy teeth. Run from breeders who use the made-up term "teacup," who can't show you the health clearances, or who sell puppies before ten weeks of age.

Portuguese Water Dog

Best for Experienced Owners
Good with Children
Medium in Size
Curly Coat (but see Physical Features below)

EXERCISE REQUIRED — HIGH MEDIUM
TRIMMING/CLIPPING REQUIRED — HIGH
AMOUNT OF SHEDDING — LOW
ACTIVITY INDOORS — HIGH MEDIUM
EASE OF TRAINING — MEDIUM
SOCIABILITY WITH STRANGERS — MEDIUM

TEMPERAMENT

The AKC Standard calls him "an animal of spirited disposition, self-willed, brave, and very resistant to fatigue." Emotionally he's calm and sensible; physically he's lively and athletic, poised for any activity. The PWD loves to play and needs vigorous exercise: long walks, occasional runs, and swimming whenever possible, for he is a master swimmer and diver. Mental stimulation (agility, fetching, advanced obedience) is just as important to this clever, thinking breed. When well socialized, his reaction to strangers varies from friendly to polite, but he should always remain steadfast and hold his ground. This observant breed makes a fine watchdog, but not a guardian. Some are too bouncy for small children. Most are accepting of other pets when raised with them. PWDs are strong-minded, with an independent streak and a wicked sense of humor. Consistent leadership is a must. Obedience training must be upbeat and persuasive rather than sharp, because he is sensitive and proud and may become obstinate when jerked around. A natural retriever, he will pick up everything in his path, chew up both edible and inedible objects, and try to mouth your hands—provide a box filled with toys so he can satisfy his oral fixation by carrying something around in his mouth. Youngsters are especially rambunctious, bore easily, and without enough attention and structured activity can excavate vast chasms in your yard.

HISTORY

Called Cao de Agua (dog of the water) in his native Portugal, he worked along the coast, herding fish into the fishermen's nets, retrieving equipment that fell overboard, carrying messages from ship to ship, and riding trawlers out to sea. AKC popularity: 83rd of 146.

PHYSICAL FEATURES

Males stand 20–23 inches and weigh 45–60 pounds. Females stand 17–21 inches and weigh 35–50 pounds. His coat may be curly or wavy and needs brushing twice a week. He may be clipped into a lion style (forequarters left shaggy to resemble a lion's mane; hindquarters and face shaved) or a working retriever style (entire coat clipped to one inch long, tail left long and plume-like). Colors are black or brown (with or without white markings), or white (with or without black or brown markings). His ears and tail are natural. His feet are webbed.

HEALTH ISSUES

Both parents should have the following certificates: yearly CERF (eyes), a DNA certificate that shows whether they are affected, carriers, or clear of PRA (at least one parent must be clear), and normal for GM-1 storage disease. Also ask about Addison's disease, cardiomyopathy, and allergies in the lines. Lifespan: 12 years.

CAUTIONS WHEN BUYING

This intelligent breed can be both challenging and demanding. Be prepared to channel his high energy and enthusiasm into appropriate activities.

Pug

Fine for Novice Owners
Good with Children
Small in Size
Short Coat

EXERCISE REQUIRED — LOW
TRIMMING/CLIPPING REQUIRED — LOW
AMOUNT OF SHEDDING — HIGH
ACTIVITY INDOORS — MEDIUM
EASE OF TRAINING — MEDIUM
SOCIABILITY WITH STRANGERS — HIGH
MEDIUM

TEMPERAMENT

Sometimes playful and clownish, sometimes calm and dignified, always sturdy and stable, good-humored and amiable—this is the Pug. Peaceful with all the world, he is not a guard dog, though he will sound off with his rather odd bark when visitors arrive. Then he will welcome them inside with his snorts, snuffles, and grunts. Pugs are fine with other animals (cats are often fascinated with this breed), though they can be jealous of another pet sitting in your lap. A Pug is very childlike and always needs to be with you. He is easy to spoil, yet can be depended on to maintain his sweet, comical, charming personality. His large expressive eyes, wrinkled forehead, cocked head and innocent expression, and strange puggy sounds bring out parental feelings in many people. Though stubborn, Pugs seldom get into real mischief. Adults spend much of the day sleeping and snoring. Gassiness can be an embarrassing problem, and housebreaking can be a challenge, especially in the rain.

HISTORY

The beloved pet of Buddhist monks, he may have been named for his facial resemblance to marmoset (pug) monkeys. "Pug" is also an old term of endearment. AKC popularity: 17th of 146.

PHYSICAL FEATURES

He stands 10–11 inches and weighs 14–22 pounds. Brush his soft coat every day to minimize shedding, which is constant. He is apricot-fawn, black, or silver. His ears and tail are natural.

HEALTH ISSUES

Both parents should have OFA certificates (hips), yearly CERF (eyes), and be screened for luxating patella. Also ask about Legg-Perthes, seizures, allergies and skin conditions, and Pug Dog encephalitis (fatal inflammation of the brain). His large eyes are susceptible to lacerations, infections, prolapse (popping out of the socket from trauma), and eyelid/eyelash defects. Select a puppy whose eyes are not bulging or showing too much white around the iris, whose facial features show no signs of crowding, and whose nostrils are wide open. He is prone to heat-stroke in hot, humid, and/or stuffy conditions. Pugs love shade and air-conditioning. He is sensitive to anesthetics, vaccine, and chemicals and should never be casually medicated or sedated. Facial wrinkles must be kept clean and dry to prevent infections. Lifespan: 12 years.

CAUTIONS WHEN BUYING

Pugs are not a natural breed and can be high-maintenance dogs—i.e., high vet bills. Choose lines that are especially strong in health and longevity, and take care to monitor your Pug's physical condition and environment. Be aware of the shedding; many people are unpleasantly surprised to discover that these short-coated dogs shed so much.

Puli (POO-lee)

Best for Experienced Owners
Good with Older, Considerate Children
Small to Medium in Size
Long Coat

EXERCISE REQUIRED — MEDIUM

TRIMMING/CLIPPING REQUIRED — HIGH
    MEDIUM LOW

AMOUNT OF SHEDDING — LOW

ACTIVITY INDOORS — HIGH

EASE OF TRAINING — MEDIUM LOW

SOCIABILITY WITH STRANGERS — MEDIUM
    LOW

TEMPERAMENT

The acrobatic Puli has been likened to a bouncing spring. Happy and playful well into his teens, with boundless energy and insatiable curiosity, he bustles about with light-footed agility, checking out every new sight and sound and expressing his opinion about it. He is sturdy and durable, a superb athlete with quick reflexes who can turn on a dime and clear a six-foot fence from a standstill. With his keen eyesight, acute hearing, and suspicion of strangers, he is serious about his responsibility as a devoted watchdog. He will rush up to a stranger to take his measure and is willing to back up his loud warning bark if necessary. Extensive socialization is required to keep him from becoming too sharp. Some are playful with other dogs, while others are territorial. His high prey drive will send him in rollicking pursuit of small creatures that run. One of the smartest of all breeds, supremely self-confident and self-possessed, he is also one of the most demanding and manipulative, with (as one breeder puts it) "a capacity for causing mischief that is truly awesome." The Puli has an in-your-face personality and is accustomed to making his own decisions. He will continue to do so unless you take control with firm leadership and consistent rules. Positive training methods and fair handling are musts, for the proud, sensitive Puli won't tolerate harshness or teasing. He can be persistent in using his large nose and mouth to drive people and other animals along (or gather them together).

HISTORY

His name is Hungarian for "livestock drover." He is often entrusted with flocks of three hundred, keeping their attention with his vigorous bouncing and barking. AKC popularity: 129th of 146.

PHYSICAL FEATURES

He stands 15–18 inches and weighs 25–35 pounds. The wiry hairs of his outer coat tend to fuse with the wooly hairs of his undercoat to form felt cords. If you wish to keep this appearance, you must separate the cords every few weeks. Bathing takes a half hour, for the cords must be rinsed well, and drying takes twenty-four hours with the dog in a crate surrounded by a dryer and box fans. Your second option is to brush out the cords whenever they start to form. Finally, you may choose to trim/clip the coat short every few months. Most individuals are black (often fading to charcoal gray or salt-and-pepper and/or developing a rusty cast). Solid white is less common. His ears and tail are natural.

HEALTH ISSUES

Both parents should have OFA certificates (hips). Also ask about cataracts and urinary calculus in the lines. Lifespan: 14–16 years.

CAUTIONS WHEN BUYING

Though it can be hard to tell whether this "black tornado" is coming or going, you can count on him doing both in a forceful manner.

Rat Terrier

Fine for Novice Owners
Good with Older, Considerate Children
Small to Medium in Size
Smooth Coat

EXERCISE REQUIRED — MEDIUM
TRIMMING/CLIPPING REQUIRED — LOW
AMOUNT OF SHEDDING — MEDIUM
ACTIVITY INDOORS — HIGH MEDIUM
EASE OF TRAINING — MEDIUM
SOCIABILITY WITH STRANGERS — MEDIUM

TEMPERAMENT

Both sturdy and elegant, often described as having a dual personality, the Rat Terrier is a fearless, tenacious hunter in the field, yet a friendly, sensible companion at home. Untiringly active and playful, he has a special passion for ball chasing. He must always be kept in a fenced yard or on-leash, for he is agile and impulsive—also curious and clever, so be sure those fences are secure. The Rat Terrier craves companionship, often using his paws to demand attention, and most are somewhat vocal, "talking" and grumbling, especially when ignored. Generally good with other dogs and cats in his own family, he does have a high prey drive and quick reflexes and will dispatch squeaky creatures with little effort. Though he has a mild stubborn streak, this attentive, sensitive, head-cocking breed responds nicely to verbal discipline and to obedience training that utilizes food and praise. Being respectable terriers, Rats love to tunnel and dig.

HISTORY

An American-made breed, he descended from terriers brought over by English immigrants. His ancestry also includes scenthound and sighthound, and he is an outstanding ratter and squirrel hunter. Registered by the UKC and the National Rat Terrier Association. There is also a short-legged type, called the Teddy Roosevelt Terrier by the UKC (or Class B Rat Terrier by the NRTA). A hairless strain is called the American Hairless Terrier by some organizations.

PHYSICAL FEATURES

UKC calls for Miniature (up to 13 inches and 5–13 pounds) and Standard (13–18 inches and 13–36 pounds). NRTA calls for Toy (under 10 pounds), Mini (10–18 pounds), Standard (18–28 pounds), and Decker Giant (22–40 pounds). His smooth coat needs only an occasional quick brushing. Most are spotted tricolor: white with black and tan patches. He may also be bicolor: black, tan, sable, blue, red, chocolate, or lemon/apricot, with white markings and often tan trim. His ears are natural; his tail is usually docked, though some are born with bobtails.

HEALTH ISSUES

Ask about luxating patella, lens luxation, seizures, demodectic mange, and allergies in the lines. Lifespan: 15–18 years.

CAUTIONS WHEN BUYING

The Rat Terrier is quite variable in conformation. Depending on geographical region and hunting uses, various breed mixtures added different characteristics. Today you have a wide selection of sizes, colors, ear carriage, even tail. Make sure the breeder has either UKC or NRTA registration papers and belongs to one of the recognized clubs. Some unscrupulous breeders are crossing the smaller Rat Terriers with Chihuahuas or Toy Fox Terriers for decreased size.

Rhodesian Ridgeback

Best for Experienced Owners
Good with Children If Raised with Children
Large in Size
Smooth Coat

EXERCISE REQUIRED — HIGH MEDIUM

TRIMMING/CLIPPING REQUIRED — LOW

AMOUNT OF SHEDDING — MEDIUM

ACTIVITY INDOORS — LOW

EASE OF TRAINING — LOW

SOCIABILITY WITH STRANGERS — LOW

TEMPERAMENT

This dignified, muscular dog, a combination of scent-hound and sighthound, needs brisk walking every day and the chance to run as often as possible. The most territorial of the hounds, the Ridgeback is aloof with strangers, intensely loyal and protective of his family. He should be accustomed to people at an early age so that his guarding instinct remains controlled rather than indiscriminate. He can be dominant with other animals, especially with other dogs of the same sex. This serious, confident dog is independent, inclined to do things his own way, and will test members of the family to find his place in the pecking order. Consistent leadership and obedience training (using positive methods) is a must. Overall, he's a splendid, capable companion for assertive owners—calm and quiet in the home. However, without ongoing time and effort, exercise, socialization, and supervision, he can be too much dog. This is not a breed to sit quietly in your yard all day. Young Ridgebacks are especially rambunctious, bore easily, and can excavate vast holes.

HISTORY

The name of this South African native is derived from the peculiar ridge on his back, a raised strip of stiff hair that grows in the opposite direction from the rest of his coat. He has been used to hunt birds and small and large game, even lions. AKC popularity: 57th of 146.

PHYSICAL FEATURES

He stands 24–27 inches and weighs 70–85 pounds. His hard coat needs only an occasional quick brushing. He is light wheaten (golden tan) or dark wheaten (reddish tan). His ears and tail are natural.

HEALTH ISSUES

Both parents should have OFA certificates (hips and elbows). The most serious health problem is dermoid sinus (subcutaneous channels filled with serum), though affected pups are detected early. Also ask about low thyroid, bloat, and cancer in the lines. Lifespan: 12 years.

CAUTIONS WHEN BUYING

In a recent survey of national club members, excessive aggression was the most common behavioral problem, so it is essential to start with a genetically sound temperament. Observe both parents and preferably other relatives, then raise your puppy with consistent leadership and socialization. For a family dog, look for a more easygoing pup rather than a bold, dominant one.

Rottweiler (ROTT-why-ler)

Best for Experienced Owners
Good with Children If Raised with Children
Large in Size
Short Coat

EXERCISE REQUIRED — MEDIUM
TRIMMING/CLIPPING REQUIRED — LOW
AMOUNT OF SHEDDING — MEDIUM
ACTIVITY INDOORS — LOW
EASE OF TRAINING — HIGH MEDIUM
SOCIABILITY WITH STRANGERS — MEDIUM
    LOW

TEMPERAMENT

The AKC Standard describes him as "a calm, confident, and courageous dog with a self-assured aloofness that does not lend itself to immediate and indiscriminate friendships." Steadfast and usually serious, the Rottweiler tends to respond quietly and with a wait-and-see attitude to influences in his environment. This muscular dog needs some space and exercise: brisk daily walks, interactive romping sessions, and regular opportunities to stretch out and run. Mental exercise (advanced obedience, agility, retrieving a ball, Schutzhund) is even more important and appreciated. Intensely loyal to and protective of his family, he must be thoroughly socialized at an early age so that his territorial instincts are controlled rather than indiscriminate. He can be aggressive with other dogs of the same sex, and some individuals are predatory with cats. Rotts are inclined to test for position in the family pecking order, but they will respect an assertive owner who knows how to lead a strong-minded dog. Overall, he's a splendid, capable companion in the right hands, but without ongoing companionship, socialization, obedience training, and supervision, he is too much dog for many people.

HISTORY

Developed in Rottweil, Germany, he drove the butchers' cattle to and from market, pulled carts, and protected farm and family. AKC popularity: 4th of 146.

PHYSICAL FEATURES

Males stand 24–27 inches and weigh 95–130 pounds. Females stand 22–25 inches and weigh 80–100 pounds. Brush his short, dense coat once a week, daily when he is shedding. He is black with rust markings. His ears are natural; his tail is docked.

HEALTH ISSUES

Both parents should have OFA certificates (hips and elbows), yearly CERF (eyes), and be cardiac-clear for SAS (subaortic stenosis). Also ask about low thyroid, seizures, bloat, vWD, OCD, panosteitis, bone cancer, and allergies in the lines. Lifespan: 8–10 years.

CAUTIONS WHEN BUYING

The popularity of this breed has attracted swarms of unknowledgeable breeders who are producing dangerous, unsound, unhealthy dogs. Observe parents, grandparents, and other relatives and buy only from a breeder who can show you all of the health clearances. The health stipulation will eliminate most newspaper ads right there. Compared to American show lines, German-bred lines often focus on performance sports such as Schutzhund (protection, obedience, and tracking), and these dogs are often "harder" and more work-oriented. Because of breed prejudice and public/media hysteria, ownership of a Rottweiler comes with moral and legal responsibilities that must be considered; for instance, some insurance companies will not provide homeowners' insurance.

Saint Bernard (Longhaired)

Best for Experienced Owners
Good with Children
Giant in Size
Thick, Medium-Length Coat

EXERCISE REQUIRED — MEDIUM

TRIMMING/CLIPPING REQUIRED — LOW

AMOUNT OF SHEDDING — HIGH

ACTIVITY INDOORS — LOW

EASE OF TRAINING — MEDIUM

SOCIABILITY WITH STRANGERS — MEDIUM

TEMPERAMENT

A well-bred Saint Bernard is calm, sensible, and patient. Some are more outgoing, others more introspective. He's quiet indoors, but does need his space and deserves a roomy home with a spacious fenced yard in the suburbs or country. He needs daily exercise (whether he seems to want it or not) to stay fit, but long daily walks will do, along with regular opportunities to stretch out and lope around. He loves to romp in the snow, and pulling a cart or carrying a backpack gives him a purpose in life. Companionship is of prime importance to this sociable breed. Left alone too much, he becomes dispirited. Saints are generally relaxed and accepting of everyone, but because he is such a massive dog, he requires early, frequent excursions into the world so that he grows up to trust and respect people. Most are fine with other animals when raised with them, but there is some dog aggression, which can be frightening to experience because of this breed's sheer bulk and power. Saints have an independent streak, but they are willing to please if you can establish consistent rules through motivational training methods that include praise and food rewards. Saints are hard to beat as droolers, slobberers, and loud, contented snorers.

HISTORY

Near St. Bernard's Pass in the Swiss Alps, he served as a rescue dog for a hospice monastery, his sixth sense and keen hearing warning him of impending avalanches. There are two coat varieties: The Longhaired is the more recent and was found disadvantageous for rescue work because the hair collected chunks of ice. AKC popularity: 38th of 146.

PHYSICAL FEATURES

Males stand 27–32 inches; females stand 25–29 inches. Weight is 125–180 pounds. Brush his rough, longish coat twice a week, daily during heavy seasonal shedding. Along with his shedding great chunks of hair in the spring and fall, you'll find loose hair the rest of the year as well. He is red or brown-yellow with white markings, or white with red or brown-yellow markings. Brindling (black striping) may also occur in reddish/brownish areas. His ears and tail are natural.

HEALTH ISSUES

Both parents should have OFA certificates (hips and elbows). Also ask about bloat, heart problems, eye problems, seizures, OCD, and bone cancer in the lines. Eyelid disorders (entropion) can be a problem. Lifespan: 8–10 years.

CAUTIONS WHEN BUYING

This breed has been exploited by unknowledgeable breeders, and the result has been dangerous genetic shyness and aggression problems. Buy only from a breeder whose dogs are friendly and good-natured. Offer a polite "no thanks" to any breeder whose dogs haven't been X-rayed clear of hip dysplasia, regardless of the rationale they try to offer for not doing it. Beware of ads touting "pure Swiss lines"—there is no such thing.

Saint Bernard (Shorthaired)

Best for Experienced Owners
Good with Children
Giant in Size
Thick, Medium-Length Coat

EXERCISE REQUIRED — MEDIUM

TRIMMING/CLIPPING REQUIRED — LOW

AMOUNT OF SHEDDING — HIGH

ACTIVITY INDOORS — LOW

EASE OF TRAINING — MEDIUM

SOCIABILITY WITH STRANGERS — MEDIUM

TEMPERAMENT

A well-bred Saint Bernard is calm, sensible, and patient. Some are more outgoing, others more introspective. He's quiet indoors, but does need his space and deserves a roomy home with a spacious fenced yard in the suburbs or country. He needs daily exercise (whether he seems to want it or not) to stay fit, but long daily walks will do, along with regular opportunities to stretch out and lope around. He loves to romp in the snow, and pulling a cart or carrying a backpack gives him a purpose in life. Companionship is of prime importance to this sociable breed. Left alone too much, he becomes dispirited. Saints are generally relaxed and accepting of everyone, but because he is such a massive dog, he requires early, frequent excursions into the world so that he grows up to trust and respect people. Most are fine with other animals when raised with them, but there is some dog aggression, which can be frightening to experience because of this breed's sheer bulk and power. Saints have an independent streak, but they are willing to please if you can establish consistent rules through motivational training methods that include praise and food rewards. Saints are hard to beat as droolers, slobberers, and loud, contented snorers.

HISTORY

Near St. Bernard's Pass in the Swiss Alps, he served as a rescue dog for a hospice monastery, his sixth sense and keen hearing warning him of impending avalanches. There are two coat varieties: The Shorthaired is the original coat and the most suited to resisting snow and ice without tangling or matting. AKC popularity: 38th of 146.

PHYSICAL FEATURES

Males stand 27–32 inches; females stand 25–29 inches. Weight is 125–180 pounds. Brush his rough coat twice a week, daily during heavy seasonal shedding. Along with his shedding great chunks of hair in the spring and fall, you'll find loose hair the rest of the year as well. He is red or brown-yellow with white markings, or white with red or brown-yellow markings. Brindling (black striping) may also occur in reddish/brownish areas. His ears and tail are natural.

HEALTH ISSUES

Both parents should have OFA certificates (hips and elbows). Also ask about bloat, heart problems, eye problems, seizures, OCD, and bone cancer in the lines. Eyelid disorders (entropion) can be a problem. Lifespan: 8–10 years.

CAUTIONS WHEN BUYING

This breed has been exploited by unknowledgeable breeders, and the result has been dangerous genetic shyness and aggression problems. Buy only from a breeder whose dogs are friendly and good-natured. Offer a polite "no thanks" to any breeder whose dogs haven't been X-rayed clear of hip dysplasia, regardless of the rationale they try to offer for not doing it. Beware of ads touting "pure Swiss lines"—there is no such thing.

Saluki (sa-LOO-key)

Best for Experienced Owners
Good with Older, Considerate Children
Medium to Large in Size
Short Coat

EXERCISE REQUIRED — HIGH MEDIUM

TRIMMING/CLIPPING REQUIRED — LOW

AMOUNT OF SHEDDING — MEDIUM

ACTIVITY INDOORS — LOW

EASE OF TRAINING — LOW

SOCIABILITY WITH STRANGERS — LOW

TEMPERAMENT

One of the swiftest and most graceful of all breeds, the aristocratic Saluki is possessed of a quiet dignity and independence. Once past the destructive puppy stage, he is docile and quiet indoors, a creature of comfort who prefers soft beds and sofas on which he can lounge and survey his domain. However, his fragile appearance is deceiving: At full gallop he is so incredibly fast (up to forty-five miles per hour) and has such strong chasing instincts that he must not be let off-leash except in a safe, enclosed area. And he is an agile jumper, so fences should be at least six feet high. Salukis are aloof (often cautious) with strangers and require early socialization to encourage an outgoing attitude. Generally sociable with other dogs, he will pursue anything that runs, including small pets, and he can react with lightning reflexes. He is an independent thinker, yet sensitive to correction, so he should be trained calmly and coaxed with food and games. However, this breed does need firm boundaries or he will be quick to take advantage. Many sighthounds are touch-sensitive, tending to startle if touched unexpectedly and uncomfortable when cuddled excessively. A verbal correction is more effective than a physical one, because it is less upsetting and distracting to the dog.

HISTORY

An ancient breed from Egypt and Arabia, the Saluki ran down gazelles across open terrain, with trained falcons helping to distract the gazelle. The Mohammedans considered him the only sacred breed, and he was sometimes mummified along with his master. AKC popularity: 109th of 146.

PHYSICAL FEATURES

He stands 23–28 inches and weighs 40–65 pounds. There are larger "mountainous" types and more lightly built "desert" types. His soft coat comes in two varieties: the Smooth is uniformly short-coated, while the Feathered has longer hair on his legs, ears, and tail. Both coats need only an occasional brushing. Colors include white, cream, fawn, golden, red, and black-and-tan, among many others. His ears and tail are natural.

HEALTH ISSUES

Both parents should be screened for cardiac disease. Also ask about low thyroid in the lines. He is sensitive to anesthetics, vaccines, and chemicals and should never be casually medicated or sedated. Lifespan: 12–14 years.

CAUTIONS WHEN BUYING

Like most sighthounds, Salukis have deep, far-seeing eyes that appear to be gazing at something in the distant past. Indeed, they often seem to look right through or past their owners, which can be a blow to the ego if you're expecting adoration from your dog. If you like a more cat-like temperament, the Saluki might be for you. Lassie lovers should look elsewhere.

Samoyed (sa-MOY-ed or SAM-a-yed)

Best for Experienced Owners
Good with Children
Medium to Large in Size
Thick, Medium-Length Coat

EXERCISE REQUIRED — MEDIUM

TRIMMING/CLIPPING REQUIRED — LOW

AMOUNT OF SHEDDING — HIGH

ACTIVITY INDOORS — HIGH MEDIUM

EASE OF TRAINING — MEDIUM

SOCIABILITY WITH STRANGERS — HIGH
MEDIUM

TEMPERAMENT

The Samoyed is gentle and dependable in heart and mind, robust and spirited in body. This playful dog enjoys vigorous outdoor exercise, especially in cold weather. Without such outlets for his energy, and without sufficient companionship to satisfy his sociable nature, he can be boisterous and destructive. Bored Sams are famous for chewing through drywall, ripping the stuffing out of the sofa, and relandscaping the backyard. His attitude toward strangers varies from "Hi there! Come on in!" (often accompanied by enthusiastic jumping) to something more conservative, yet sensible and polite. Most will bark to announce visitors, but that's the extent of their guarding inclination. Samoyeds are usually good with other animals, but with strong chasing and herding instincts, they may take off after trespassing cats or wildlife. A securely fenced yard is a must. One of the brightest and most sensitive of the spitz (northern or sled dog) breeds, yet still demanding and independent, Sammies need consistent leadership and early obedience training, using persuasive methods such as food and praise. Jerking him around will only make him more obstinate. He has a jolly sense of humor and often exhibits it when disobeying. He barks *a lot,* and some individuals have high-pitched, extremely piercing voices.

HISTORY

He was invaluable to the nomadic Samoyed peoples of the Siberian tundra: herding their reindeer, pulling their sleds, and warming the huts at night. AKC popularity: 54th of 146.

PHYSICAL FEATURES

Males stand 21–24 inches and weigh 50–70 pounds. Females stand 19–21 inches and weigh 35–55 pounds. His harsh coat (some are longer than others) with its dense undercoat should be brushed twice a week, daily during heavy seasonal shedding. Along with his shedding great chunks of hair in the spring and fall, you'll find loose hair the rest of the year as well. He is solid white, cream, biscuit (beige), or white with biscuit shadings. His black lips curve upward at the corners in a perpetual "Sammy smile." His ears and tail are natural.

HEALTH ISSUES

Both parents should have OFA certificates (hips) and yearly CERF (eyes). Also ask about low thyroid, allergies, and skin conditions in the lines. With their thick coats, Samoyeds do not appreciate hot, humid weather. Lifespan: 12–14 years.

CAUTIONS WHEN BUYING

Poorly bred Samoyeds are often rangy, oversize, general spitz-type dogs with a long, pointy muzzle, large pointed ears, and a rather clumpy coat, while well-bred individuals are compact and solid, with a broad head and muzzle, thickly furred rounded ears, and a plush coat.

Schipperke (SKIP-er-key)

Best for Experienced Owners
Good with Older, Considerate Children
Small in Size
Thick, Medium-Length Coat

EXERCISE REQUIRED — MEDIUM
TRIMMING/CLIPPING REQUIRED — LOW
AMOUNT OF SHEDDING — HIGH MEDIUM
ACTIVITY INDOORS — HIGH
EASE OF TRAINING — MEDIUM LOW
SOCIABILITY WITH STRANGERS — LOW

TEMPERAMENT

The AKC Standard describes him as "questioning, mischievous, impudent . . . interested in everything around him." Indeed, he is one of the most intense, inquisitive, and impulsive of all breeds. The Schip is busy, busy, busy and seldom walks when he can trot or scamper. He must always be kept on-leash (he is an extremely fast, agile, independent chaser of anything that moves) or in a secure yard, preferably supervised, because his ingenuity and climbing/digging skills may send him over or under the fence. Possessed of extraordinary senses and an inherent suspicion of strangers, he sleeps lightly and makes a keen, vigilant watchdog. He is convinced that he is a big dog and may physically challenge an intruder foolish enough to ignore his sharp, penetrating bark. With dogs and cats in his own family, he is usually fine. With strange pets who invade his domain, he can be scrappy. He has a high prey drive and is likely to harass small caged pets, and with his quick reflexes and light-footed agility, creatures that run won't get far. This little rascal does best with owners who are firm, confident, and consistent. He has a marked stubborn streak, strong likes and dislikes, a mischievous sense of humor, and will take clever advantage if indulged. Positive training methods are a must—Schips are proud and sensitive and do not react kindly to being harshly handled or teased. Some can be hard to housebreak, and their barking must be kept under control.

HISTORY

In Belgium he was a ratter and riverboat watchdog, probably developed from the same roots as Belgian shepherd dogs. His name is Flemish for "little shepherd." AKC popularity: 55th of 146.

PHYSICAL FEATURES

He stands 10–13 inches and weighs 12–18 pounds. Brush his harsh, upstanding coat once a week, daily during heavy seasonal shedding. He is solid black. His ears are natural; his tail is docked, though a few are born with a natural bobtail.

HEALTH ISSUES

Both parents should have yearly CERF certificates (eyes). Also ask about low thyroid, seizures, and Legg-Perthes in the lines. Lifespan: 15 years.

CAUTIONS WHEN BUYING

If you're looking for one of the most dynamic go-getters in the canine world, a cocky little bundle of energy who will delight you with his busy antics and impress you with his serious devotion and watchfulness, a Schipperke may be perfect for you. If you desire a dog who lies quietly and obediently for much of the day, look elsewhere!

Scottish Deerhound

Best for Experienced Owners
Good with Children
Giant in Size
Wiry Coat

EXERCISE REQUIRED — HIGH MEDIUM
TRIMMING/CLIPPING REQUIRED — MEDIUM
    LOW
AMOUNT OF SHEDDING — MEDIUM
ACTIVITY INDOORS — LOW
EASE OF TRAINING — LOW
SOCIABILITY WITH STRANGERS — MEDIUM

TEMPERAMENT

Like all sighthounds, the quiet, dignified Deerhound doesn't behave like a Golden Retriever or German Shepherd. He is unlikely to fetch a ball or protect your family. Puppies and adolescents (up to two years old) can be as active and mischievous as any other breed, but adults are calm, graceful, and undemanding. They learn house rules well and spend much of their time sprawled blissfully on the softest sofa. It is outdoors where Deerhounds have such special needs: They require space for the long strides of their floating lope ("poetry in motion") and powerful, driving gallop, but it must be a safe, enclosed area, else they will be out of sight in seconds and end up dead on the freeway. Because of his great size, strength, and speed, the Deerhound does require early socialization, but he is almost unfailingly polite with strangers. This is not a guard dog, sometimes not even a watchdog—some easygoing individuals will remain comatose when the doorbell rings. He is amiable with other dogs, but is a serious chaser of anything that runs, including cats and tiny dogs. Though mildly stubborn and independent, this is a sweet and sensitive dog who is willing to respond (albeit in a slow, casual way, as though humoring you) to cheerful training that includes consistent guidance, verbal praise, and food rewards.

HISTORY

In the Middle Ages he was owned by Scottish Highland chieftains who set him on large deer about the size of an American elk. He can also take down coyotes and wolves. AKC popularity: 125th of 146.

PHYSICAL FEATURES

Males stand 30–33 inches and weigh 85–115 pounds. Females stand 28–31 inches and weigh 75–95 pounds. Brush his rough, shaggy coat twice a week and occasionally trim straggly hairs. Color ranges from light gray to blue-gray to black, with or without brindling. His ears and tail are natural.

HEALTH ISSUES

Ask about bloat, cardiomyopathy, and bone cancer in the lines. He is sensitive to anesthetics, vaccines, and chemicals and should never be casually medicated or sedated. Lifespan: 8–11 years.

CAUTIONS WHEN BUYING

The size of this breed should not be underestimated: He can fill up your sofa, bed, and the rear seat of most cars. He must be kept exercised whether he appears to want it or not. This fitness regime is particularly important with older dogs, as their rear muscles will weaken with age and they may have difficulty getting up and down. Scottish Deerhounds are much harder to find than Irish Wolfhounds, and you should expect to be questioned about a fenced yard and your commitment to exercise. Then you may be put on a waiting list.

Scottish Terrier

Best for Experienced Owners
Good with Older, Considerate Children
Small in Size
Wiry Coat

EXERCISE REQUIRED — MEDIUM
TRIMMING/CLIPPING REQUIRED — HIGH
AMOUNT OF SHEDDING — LOW
ACTIVITY INDOORS — MEDIUM
EASE OF TRAINING — LOW
SOCIABILITY WITH STRANGERS — LOW

TEMPERAMENT

The AKC Standard says, "The Scottish Terrier's bold, confident, dignified aspect exemplifies power in a small package . . . a determined and thoughtful dog whose 'heads up, tails up' attitude in the ring should convey both fire and control." Friendly and playful as a puppy, the Scottie matures into a bold, jaunty, yet steady and dignified adult, with greater independence than most terriers. He is staunchly self-reliant and fearless—also dour and crusty at times. He is content with daily walks and not built for long-distance jogging, but he will pursue squirrels and chipmunks with rollicking enthusiasm. Steadfastly loyal to his owner (some are one-person dogs) and reserved with strangers, he makes an intimidating watchdog. He should be socialized with lots of people at an early age and not allowed to be sharp. He can be scrappy with other dogs. Training is a challenge, for no breed has higher self-esteem or a stronger will—this is not a dog for permissive owners. Firm, consistent leadership is a must, and obedience training should be praise- and food-based, for the Scottie is proud, extremely sensitive, and easily insulted. He may retaliate or "go on strike" if jerked around or pushed too far with rough handling or teasing. He can be possessive of his food and toys. He loves to bark and may try to relandscape your garden.

HISTORY

Originally called the Aberdeen Terrier, he was developed in the rocky Scottish Highlands as a hunter of fox and vermin. AKC popularity: 42nd of 146.

PHYSICAL FEATURES

He stands about 10 inches and weighs 18–22 pounds. Brush and comb his hard, wiry coat twice a week. His beard should be combed daily for cleanliness. Likewise, keep his bottom trimmed for cleanliness. Show dogs are "stripped" (dead coat plucked out) every few months; pet owners may opt for more convenient clipping. He may be black, silver brindle (silver and black intermingled), red brindle, or wheaten. His ears and tail are natural.

HEALTH ISSUES

Both parents should have a DNA certificate that shows whether they are affected, carriers, or clear of vWD (at least one parent should be clear). Also ask about Scottie cramp, Cushing's syndrome, CMO, Legg-Perthes, luxating patella, seizures, disk problems, low thyroid, allergies and skin conditions, and cancer in the lines. Lifespan: 12–14 years.

CAUTIONS WHEN BUYING

Buy only from a breeder who emphasizes cheerful, steady temperament (observe both parents and preferably other relatives) and who has screened for all of the health problems.

Sealyham Terrier

Best for Experienced Owners
Good with Older, Considerate Children
Small in Size
Wiry Coat

EXERCISE REQUIRED — MEDIUM

TRIMMING/CLIPPING REQUIRED — HIGH

AMOUNT OF SHEDDING — LOW

ACTIVITY INDOORS — LOW

EASE OF TRAINING — LOW

SOCIABILITY WITH STRANGERS — MEDIUM

TEMPERAMENT

The AKC Standard says, "The Sealyham should be the embodiment of power and determination, ever keen and alert, of extraordinary substance." Though not as boisterous as some terriers, he is more independent and more self-willed. One of the few terriers who is calm, relaxed, and undemanding indoors (though he can play the entertaining clown), the Sealy does need his walks and an occasional romp—but only in a safe, enclosed area, for he has strong hunting instincts and will pursue whatever runs. He is devoted to his family, aloof with strangers, and can be scrappy with other animals. His great stubbornness calls for early obedience training, but use food and praise methods and don't jerk this proud breed around. Physical punishment doesn't work with terriers, only leading to greater obstinacy and/or retaliation. Teasing will produce the same results. Demonstrating consistent leadership so that a Sealy respects your decisions is more important than advanced obedience exercises. Possessiveness of food and toys is a potential behavioral trait that must be nipped in the bud. Sealys are powerful diggers with a surprisingly deep bark.

HISTORY

Developed in Wales, this hunter of fox, badger, and otter was named after his founder's Sealyham mansion, near the Sealy River. The rarest of all of the AKC-recognized terriers, the Sealyham was most popular during the 1920s and 30s, with famous owners including Gary Cooper, Cary Grant, Humphrey Bogart, Richard Burton, and Alfred Hitchcock. Hitchcock's own Sealyhams appeared in his films *The Birds* and *Suspicion*. AKC popularity: 139th of 146.

PHYSICAL FEATURES

He stands 10-11 inches and weighs 22–26 pounds. Brush and comb his hard wiry coat twice a week. His beard should be combed daily for cleanliness. Likewise, keep his bottom trimmed for cleanliness. Show dogs are "stripped" (dead coat plucked out) every few months; pet owners may opt for more convenient clipping. He is white with a few lemon, gray, tan, or badger (mix of gray/tan/white) markings on his head and ears. His ears are natural; his tail is docked.

HEALTH ISSUES

Both parents should have yearly CERF certificates (eyes). Individual puppies should come with a BAER printout that shows normal bilateral hearing. Also ask about glaucoma in the lines. Long-backed breeds are susceptible to disk disease that can be exacerbated by excessive high-jumping, dashing down stairs, being picked up without proper support, and obesity. Lifespan: 12–14 years.

CAUTIONS WHEN BUYING

Fewer than one hundred Sealy puppies are registered in the United States each year. A high percentage of pups (especially females) are kept for showing and breeding, so be prepared to wait and to pay at least $750.

Shetland Sheepdog

Fine for Novice Owners
Good with Older, Considerate Children
Small in Size
Long Coat

EXERCISE REQUIRED — MEDIUM

TRIMMING/CLIPPING REQUIRED — LOW

AMOUNT OF SHEDDING — HIGH

ACTIVITY INDOORS — MEDIUM

EASE OF TRAINING — HIGH

SOCIABILITY WITH STRANGERS — MEDIUM
    LOW

TEMPERAMENT

Proud and animated, sweet and gentle, the Sheltie is a swift, light-footed runner and graceful jumper. He needs and enjoys some physical exercise and mental stimulation such as obedience, agility, herding, or fetching a ball. Shelties are sociable and can become unhappy, noisy, or destructive if left for long periods of time without something to do or the companionship of people or other pets. Most are peaceful with everyone, though reserved and sometimes reticent with strangers. To build a confident temperament, he needs more extensive socialization than many other breeds. Exceptionally bright and attentive, he is easy to train if one has a quiet voice and a light hand on the leash, for Shelties are extremely sensitive, sometimes overly so. They respond beautifully to praise and food rewards and often need only verbal correction. More reactive to loud noises than some other breeds, he does not do well in an environment with frequent tension or loud voices. Many are a bit dainty and can be overwhelmed by the herky-jerky mannerisms of small children. Some may try to herd people and other pets by poking or nipping. Shelties tend to be barkers, and some have high-pitched, piercing voices.

HISTORY

Developed on the rugged Shetland Islands off Scotland, he was bred down from medium-size farm collies. Call him a Shetland Sheepdog or Sheltie, but never "Toy Collie" or "Miniature Collie," terms that annoy Sheltie fanciers. AKC popularity: 15th of 146.

PHYSICAL FEATURES

He stands 13–16 inches and weighs 15–25 pounds. Many individuals are oversize or undersize; these cannot be shown in conformation classes, but make fine pets. Brush and comb his harsh double coat twice a week, daily during heavy seasonal shedding. Along with his shedding great chunks of hair in the spring and fall, you'll find loose hair the rest of the year as well. He may be sable, tricolor, blue merle, bi-black (black-and-white), or bi-blue (blue merle and white). His ears are natural, but unless weighted into a folding position for several months during adolescence, they may tend to prick up. His tail is natural.

HEALTH ISSUES

Both parents should have OFA certificates (hips) and yearly CERF (eyes). Each individual puppy must have his eyes examined by an AVCO-certified ophthalmologist (not just a regular vet) at six to eight weeks of age. Also ask about seizures, low thyroid, luxating patella, heart disease, and allergies in the lines. Lifespan: 12–14 years.

CAUTIONS WHEN BUYING

Poorly bred lines can be high-strung and neurotic. Look for performance and/or temperament titles (obedience, agility, herding, TT, CGC) in the pedigree. The puppy eye clearances are mandatory and tend to separate the wheat from the chaff in this breed.

Shiba Inu (SHEE-ba E-new)

Best for Experienced Owners
Good with Children If Raised with Children
Small in Size
Thick, Medium-Length Coat

EXERCISE REQUIRED — MEDIUM

TRIMMING/CLIPPING REQUIRED — LOW

AMOUNT OF SHEDDING — MEDIUM

ACTIVITY INDOORS — MEDIUM

EASE OF TRAINING — MEDIUM LOW

SOCIABILITY WITH STRANGERS — LOW

TEMPERAMENT

Though clean and quiet indoors, and not a nuisance underfoot, the Shiba is not a lapdog, but a bold, high-spirited, hardy "big dog" in a compact body. He must always be kept on-leash, for he has a high prey drive and quick reflexes and will pursue anything that moves. He can outrun and outdodge any human. Your fences must be secure; indeed, if he is ever outdoors when unsupervised, he should have a covered run, for his ingenuity and jumping/climbing/digging skills may send him over or under an ordinary fence. Once he's loose, he's gone. You must stay one step ahead of this breed: He is both dominant and clever. He often tries to manipulate through intimidation and when displeased by something can emit a loud scream, which may catch you (and your vet!) totally unprepared. With his marked stubborn streak and mischievous sense of humor, he does best with owners who are firm, confident, and consistent. Positive training methods are a must—this proud, sensitive dog does not react kindly to harsh handling or teasing. Dog aggression is a common breed trait. Cats are iffy, and small caged pets will be stalked. Shibas are possessive; it is said that if they could utter one word, it would be "mine."

HISTORY

The *shiba* (little brushwood) *inu* (dog) hunted birds and small game through the dense low bushes of Japan. AKC popularity: 58th of 146.

PHYSICAL FEATURES

He stands 14–16 inches and weighs 18–30 pounds. Brush his plush coat once a week, daily during heavy sea-sonal shedding. He may be red, sesame (red with black-tipped hairs), or black-and-tan, always with creamy white markings. His ears and tail are natural.

HEALTH ISSUES

Both parents should have OFA certificates (hips) and yearly CERF (eyes) and be screened for luxating patella. Also ask about allergies and skin conditions in the lines. Lifespan: 12 years.

CAUTIONS WHEN BUYING

Cat lovers often appreciate the independence and graceful light-footedness of this breed. Indeed, they are clean, compact dogs who groom themselves much like a cat. But too many Shibas are turned in to rescue organizations because their owners were not aware of the typical fiery temperament. Therefore it should be reemphasized that these dogs are bold runners and chasers who need a great deal of activity, training, and supervision to remain happy and safe.

Shih Tzu (SHEET sue)

Fine for Novice Owners
Good with Older, Considerate Children
Little in Size
Long Coat

EXERCISE REQUIRED — LOW
TRIMMING/CLIPPING REQUIRED — ~~HIGH~~
    MEDIUM LOW
AMOUNT OF SHEDDING — MEDIUM LOW
ACTIVITY INDOORS — MEDIUM
EASE OF TRAINING — MEDIUM
SOCIABILITY WITH STRANGERS — ~~HIGH~~
    MEDIUM

TEMPERAMENT

Carrying himself with a proud, arrogant bearing, yet possessing a sweet-natured and docile temperament, the elegant Shih Tzu is less demanding and yappy than other toy breeds. Though he is solidly built and lively and loves to play in the yard, he doesn't need much more exercise than that. A lover of comfort, he enjoys cuddling on laps and snuggling into soft pillows, his soulful eyes inviting pampering, which he accepts graciously. This happy, gentle breed loves attention and is a terrific pet for senior citizens. However, he is easily overwhelmed by small children and cannot take rough handling or mischief. Most are friendly and trusting with strangers, though socialization is necessary to develop this outgoing temperament. He is peaceful with other pets. Though he has an aristocratic demeanor and definite likes and dislikes, he is also bright, sensitive, and responsive. The little training he needs will go well if you rely on consistency, praise, and food rewards. He can be hard to housebreak.

HISTORY

The Shih Tzu was cherished as the palace pet of the Tang and Ming dynasty imperial families. His name translates loosely to "lion." AKC popularity: 11th of 146.

PHYSICAL FEATURES

He stands 8–11 inches and weighs 9–16 pounds. His dense, flowing double coat should be brushed and combed every other day. Pet owners may choose to have the coat trimmed/clipped short every four to six weeks. Keep his ear canals clean and dry and his bottom trimmed for cleanliness. He comes in a rainbow of solid colors, particolors, and blends, with a solid white blaze over his forehead being highly prized. His ears and tail are natural.

HEALTH ISSUES

Both parents should have OFA certificates (hips), yearly CERF (eyes), and a urine screening for renal dysplasia. Also ask about luxating patella, bladder stones, vWD, low thyroid, allergies and skin conditions, portal systemic shunt, and autoimmune hemolytic anemia in the lines. His large eyes are susceptible to lacerations, infections, and eyelid/eyelash defects. Select a puppy whose eyes are not bulging or showing too much white around the iris, whose facial features show no signs of crowding, and whose nostrils are wide open. He is prone to heatstroke in hot, humid, and/or stuffy conditions. Long-backed breeds are susceptible to disk disease that can be exacerbated by excessive high-jumping, dashing down stairs, being picked up without proper support, and obesity. Lifespan: 10–14 years.

CAUTIONS WHEN BUYING

Run from breeders who use made-up terms such as "tiny," "imperial," or "standard size" in their ads. Some people confuse the Shih Tzu with the Lhasa Apso: Shih Tzus are smaller and sweeter natured, with a shorter muzzle, and are often groomed to include bows on their head.

Shiloh Shepherd

Best for Experienced Owners
Good with Children
Large to Giant in Size
Thick, Medium-Length Coat

EXERCISE REQUIRED — MEDIUM
TRIMMING/CLIPPING REQUIRED — LOW
AMOUNT OF SHEDDING — HIGH MEDIUM
ACTIVITY INDOORS — MEDIUM LOW
EASE OF TRAINING — HIGH
SOCIABILITY WITH STRANGERS — MEDIUM

TEMPERAMENT

Shiloh Shepherds are similar to German Shepherds, but most Shiloh lines have been bred with a calmer, softer, more easygoing personality. You seldom see the hard, businesslike, high-drive temperament present in many German Shepherds (especially those from German import lines). Though they need brisk daily walks to stay fit, they have stamina rather than high vigor—one breeder calls them "slow but steady." They enjoy swimming, carrying backpacks, and pulling carts or sleds. Early socialization and training are musts to develop a stable, confident temperament. Most are peaceful with other pets. Shilohs are one of the most capable and trainable breeds in all of dogdom, very eager to learn and work.

HISTORY

He was developed in the 1960s and 70s by breeder Tina Barber, who was seeking a more massive, steadier-tempered German Shepherd with sound hips. One Malamute line was crossed into selected German Shepherd lines. Registered by the International Shiloh Shepherd Registry and the International Shiloh Shepherd Dog Club Registry.

PHYSICAL FEATURES

Males stand 28–32 inches and weigh 120–140 pounds. Females stand 26–29 inches and weigh 80–120 pounds. The coat may be plush (silky, up to five inches long with a thick undercoat) or smooth (harsh, similar to that of a German Shepherd). Brush plush coats once or twice a week; brush smooth coats every day or two to control shedding. Smooth coats tend to shed all year, while plush coats shed heavily twice a year. He may be black with tan/red/cream/silver markings, either in the saddle-marked pattern or the bicolor (Doberman) pattern; sable (golden, red, or gray, with black-tipped hairs); solid black; or solid white. His ears and tail are natural.

HEALTH ISSUES

Both parents should have OFA certificates (hips and elbows). Also ask about cardiac problems (SAS), panosteitis, bloat, and low thyroid in the lines. Skin conditions, autoimmune disorders, and digestive upsets are common. Lifespan: 12–14 years.

CAUTIONS WHEN BUYING

There are two Shiloh Shepherd breed clubs, each with different ideas about the breed and its future. Insist on verification of registration. A DNA test that proves parentage is recommended. The hip clearance is mandatory. Look for temperament titles, performance titles, and conformation titles in the pedigree.

Siberian Husky

Best for Experienced Owners
Good with Children
Medium in Size
Thick, Medium-Length Coat

EXERCISE REQUIRED — HIGH MEDIUM
TRIMMING/CLIPPING REQUIRED — LOW
AMOUNT OF SHEDDING — HIGH
ACTIVITY INDOORS — HIGH
EASE OF TRAINING — LOW
SOCIABILITY WITH STRANGERS — HIGH

TEMPERAMENT

The AKC Standard says, "He does not display the possessive qualities of the guard dog, nor is he overly suspicious of strangers or aggressive with other dogs." The free-spirited Siberian is good-natured, demonstrative, and very playful. Athletic, agile, and light on his feet, he loves the great outdoors and enjoys vigorous exercise, especially in cool weather. He should be taken running, hiking, and/or biking every day, always on-leash, for he is independent and born to run. If something catches his interest, he'll be gone. Teaching him to pull carts and sleds gives him a purpose in life. Without such exercise, mental activity, and lots of companionship, he can be incredibly destructive—bored Siberians are famous for chewing through drywall, ripping the stuffing out of the sofa, and relandscaping the backyard. Most are friendly with everyone and sociable with other dogs, but he has a very high prey drive and may destroy cats if not raised with them. Siberians should not be kept around rabbits, ferrets, or birds. Fencing must be high and secure, for he can be an escape artist, and once loose, he may run deer and molest livestock. Training is a challenge because he is inclined to use his intelligence in clever ways that suit his own purposes. Use food rewards—jerking this breed results in melodramatic theatrics, including screaming. Digging and howling are favorite pastimes.

HISTORY

Developed by the Chukchi people of Siberia, his forte is traveling a great distance with a light load at a fast pace. AKC popularity: 18th of 146.

PHYSICAL FEATURES

Males stand 21–23½ inches and weigh 45–60 pounds. Females stand 20–22 inches and weigh 35–50 pounds. His coat is furry with a dense undercoat and should be brushed twice a week, daily during heavy seasonal shedding. Along with his shedding great chunks of hair in the spring and fall, you'll find loose hair the rest of the year as well. He is gray, silver, black, or red, always with white markings; or solid white. His ears and tail are natural.

HEALTH ISSUES

Both parents should have OFA certificates (hips) and yearly CERF (eyes). Also ask about low thyroid in the lines. Lifespan: 12–14 years.

CAUTIONS WHEN BUYING

Many Siberians are turned over to animal shelters because of their running and chasing instincts, escape attempts, destructiveness, demanding attitude, and shedding. Compared to the Alaskan Malamute, the Siberian Husky (which may be shortened to Siberian, but never to Husky) is smaller, lighter, and finer boned, built for racing rather than weight pulling. Whereas he can have either brown or blue eyes (or a combination of the two), the Malamute may have only brown eyes. Finally, his tail is more of a waving plume than the tightly curled tail of the Mal.

Silky Terrier

Fine for Novice Owners
Good with Older, Considerate Children
Little in Size
Long Coat

EXERCISE REQUIRED — MEDIUM LOW

TRIMMING/CLIPPING REQUIRED — MEDIUM LOW

AMOUNT OF SHEDDING — LOW

ACTIVITY INDOORS — HIGH

EASE OF TRAINING — MEDIUM

SOCIABILITY WITH STRANGERS — MEDIUM

TEMPERAMENT

The Silky is for people who love the sturdiness and hardiness of the short-legged terriers but who would prefer a finer-boned, graceful, elegant build covered by a lovely flowing coat. These cheerful, light-footed dogs like to keep busy—they are inquisitive, physically and mentally quick, and spend much time trotting (or dashing) around checking things out and inventing their own clever games. Keen of eye and sharp of tongue, he won't fail to announce strangers, often in a high-pitched voice that can set your teeth on edge. Early socialization is required so he doesn't become too sharp or suspicious. Though he can be bossy with other dogs and scrappy with those of the same sex, most Silkys (the plural) are willing to coexist with other pets. Squeaky pets, however, will be stalked, for he has a strong prey drive and can be an excitable chaser of anything that moves, including huge dogs. He must never be let off-leash except in a safe, enclosed area, and your fences must be secure, for he is an amazingly agile climber and an enthusiastic digger. Willful and opinionated, but quick to learn, he responds well to obedience training that utilizes food and praise rather than jerking around. Silkys are proud, sensitive dogs and may not put up with rough handling or mischief. They can be possessive of their food and toys, and housebreaking can be difficult.

HISTORY

Originating in Australia and once called the Sydney Silky, he is a blend of Australian and Yorkshire terriers. AKC popularity: 61st of 146.

PHYSICAL FEATURES

He stands 9–10 inches and weighs 8–11 pounds. His single, exceptionally shiny, silky coat must be brushed and combed every other day. Pet owners may trim the coat so that it doesn't drag on the ground. Keep his bottom trimmed for cleanliness. He is mostly blue (from silver to slate) with rich tan trim. His ears are natural; his tail is docked.

HEALTH ISSUES

Both parents should be screened for luxating patella. Also ask about allergies and skin conditions and Legg-Perthes in the lines. Lifespan: 13–15 years.

CAUTIONS WHEN BUYING

Be prepared for the high energy level and impulsiveness and the commitment to grooming. Many people confuse the Silky with the Yorkshire Terrier. Silkys are larger and more substantial than Yorkies, with a stronger, more terrier-like character. They have a flatter skull with a longer muzzle, and when groomed, they should never emerge with a bow on their head.

Skye Terrier

Best for Experienced Owners
Good with Older, Considerate Children
Small to Medium in Size
Long Coat

EXERCISE REQUIRED — MEDIUM

TRIMMING/CLIPPING REQUIRED — HIGH

MEDIUM LOW

AMOUNT OF SHEDDING — MEDIUM

ACTIVITY INDOORS — LOW

EASE OF TRAINING — LOW

SOCIABILITY WITH STRANGERS — LOW

TEMPERAMENT

More serious, dignified, and introspective than most terriers, the stylish Skye is much heavier and more powerful than you might imagine from just seeing a photo. One of the few terriers who is laid-back indoors, he is easy to exercise, requiring only walks and play sessions. However, he is a fearless, agile chaser with lightning reflexes and should never be let off-leash unless in a safe, enclosed area. Intensely loyal to his family (sometimes becoming deeply attached to a single person), he is keenly sensitive to moods and needs a lot of personal attention—he cannot be ignored. He is cautious with strangers and should be extensively socialized when young so his wariness does not become suspicion. He is dominant with other dogs and should not be trusted around smaller animals such as cats, rabbits, and rodents. Likewise, he can be dominant with family members who are wishy-washy. Skyes have great depth of character and prefer to make their own decisions, but they will respect an owner with an equally strong character and a firm voice who knows how to lead a proud, strong-minded dog. Skyes do not suffer fools gladly. They are highly sensitive to correction and likely to retaliate if handled harshly or teased.

HISTORY

One of the oldest of the terriers, he originated on the Isle of Skye off the coast of Scotland as a hunter of fox, badger, and otter. When his flowing coat became fashionable in the courts of London, he was cherished by the nobility. AKC popularity: 130th of 146.

PHYSICAL FEATURES

He stands 10–12 inches and weighs 25–35 pounds. His body length is twice his height—standing on his back legs, he'll reach your waist. Most folks who first see a Skye up close are surprised by his large bones and strength. His long coat (6–12 inches) requires brushing and combing every other day. Pet coats may be regularly trimmed short. He is shades of black, blue, gray, silver platinum, fawn, or cream. His ears are natural (either prick or drop), and his tail is also natural.

HEALTH ISSUES

Ask about hip and elbow dysplasia, allergies and autoimmune disease, low thyroid, and tumors/cancer (especially breast cancer, the number one health problem of Skyes). Long-backed breeds are susceptible to disk disease that can be exacerbated by excessive high-jumping, dashing down stairs, being picked up without proper support, and obesity. Excessive jumping, running, or climbing as a puppy can cause premature closure of the growth plates in the short legs, leading to arthritis as an adult. Lifespan: 12–14 years.

CAUTIONS WHEN BUYING

The motto of the Skye Club of Scotland fits this canny breed perfectly: "Wha daur meddle wi' me." Litters are not numerous, so be prepared to wait. The upside is that Skyes have not been exploited by unknowledgeable breeders, so quality remains high.

Sloughi (SLOOG-ee)

Best for Experienced Owners
Good with Older, Considerate Children
Medium to Large in Size
Smooth Coat

EXERCISE REQUIRED — HIGH MEDIUM

TRIMMING/CLIPPING REQUIRED — LOW

AMOUNT OF SHEDDING — MEDIUM

ACTIVITY INDOORS — LOW

EASE OF TRAINING — LOW

SOCIABILITY WITH STRANGERS — LOW

TEMPERAMENT

Possessed of a noble, melancholic expression, this elegant, graceful aristocrat is known for his quiet dignity, gentleness, and loyalty. The Sloughi bonds closely (in a subtle way) with his owner and doesn't change that allegiance easily. He is an alert watchdog, more territorial than most sighthounds—some should not be taken lightly if truly threatened. Aloof and cautious with strangers, he tends to hang back to observe and to avoid being touched. Early socialization is required to encourage a confident attitude. Generally he is sociable with other dogs. Indoors, he is a creature of comfort who prefers soft beds and sofas on which he can lounge and survey his domain. However, this composure assumes that he has had a good daily run, for he is a consummate athlete. You'll need a large fenced area—and Sloughis are agile jumpers, so fences should be six feet high—because he is otherwise too fast to be allowed off-leash. Another reason for leashes and fences is his deeply ingrained chasing instinct, which is triggered by the slightest movement, such as leaves blowing or little creatures scurrying. Sloughis are independent thinkers who need firm boundaries or they will take advantage, but they are extremely sensitive to correction. Train calmly and coax with food and games. Many sighthounds are touch-sensitive, startling when touched unexpectedly and uncomfortable when cuddled excessively, so a verbal correction is more effective than a physical one. Some Sloughis dig holes in hot weather.

HISTORY

An ancient breed from North Africa, he ran down hare, fox, gazelle, and jackal across open terrain, relying on his excellent vision, speed, and stamina to catch his prey. The native peoples kept him in their tents and treasured him as part of their family. Registered by the FCI, UKC, and AKC-FSS.

PHYSICAL FEATURES

He stands 24–29 inches and weighs 40–65 pounds. There are larger "mountainous" types and more lightly built "desert" types. His soft coat requires only an occasional quick brushing. The classic colors are sand and sand brindle, with a black mask. Red, red brindle, black brindle, and black mantle are less common. His ears and tail are natural.

HEALTH ISSUES

He is sensitive to anesthetics, vaccines, and chemicals and should never be casually medicated or sedated. Lifespan: 12–16 years.

CAUTIONS WHEN BUYING

The ascetic beauty (sleek build, chiseled features, deep, far-seeing eyes) and special needs of sighthounds appeal greatly to some people, not at all to others. Make sure you're prepared to address the special needs as well as admire the beauty.

Soft-Coated Wheaten Terrier

Best for Experienced Owners
Good with Older, Considerate Children
Medium in Size
Long Coat

EXERCISE REQUIRED — MEDIUM

TRIMMING/CLIPPING REQUIRED — HIGH

    MEDIUM

AMOUNT OF SHEDDING — LOW

ACTIVITY INDOORS — HIGH MEDIUM

EASE OF TRAINING — MEDIUM

SOCIABILITY WITH STRANGERS — HIGH

TEMPERAMENT

The AKC Standard says, "The Wheaten is a happy, steady dog and shows himself gaily with an air of self-confidence." More congenial than most terriers, he is cheerful, lively, and very sociable. He can adapt to any home if given enough companionship and exercise (he plays hard and vigorously) and allowed to participate in games and activities. This breed often acts like a joyful puppy throughout his life. Though he will bark to announce strangers, he welcomes them as long-lost friends, usually with exuberant jumping and face kissing. Early socialization is mandatory to develop this outgoing attitude, while training is necessary to control it! Fences should be high and secure or he may jump over to greet people on the other side, or to chase passing cats or squirrels. There is some aggression with other dogs of the same sex; otherwise he is usually gregarious with other family pets. Bright and sensitive, yet spunky and headstrong, he requires an assertive owner who can set consistent rules and follow through with reward-based obedience training. An occasional Wheaten may be more dominant and possessive of food and toys. Some individuals will bark and dig holes.

HISTORY

The Soft-Coated Wheaten originated in Ireland as an all-around farm dog, hunting small game, herding the flocks, and keeping watch over the family and property. AKC popularity: 59th of 146.

PHYSICAL FEATURES

He stands 17–19 inches and weighs 30–45 pounds. His silky, wavy coat should be brushed and combed every other day and trimmed or clipped every six to eight weeks. He is born black, his coat changing color as he grows. Up to one year it may be too dark, perhaps even with black-tipped hairs, and not yet wavy; up to two years, it may be too light; but by two years it should be properly wavy and wheaten. His ears are natural; his tail is docked.

HEALTH ISSUES

Both parents should have OFA certificates (hips) and yearly CERF (eyes). Also ask about renal disease (PLN, PLE, and renal dysplasia) and allergies and skin conditions in the lines. Wheatens are sensitive to anesthetics and should never be casually sedated. Lifespan: 12–14 years.

CAUTIONS WHEN BUYING

Too many people choose this breed for his luxurious coat and appealing expression, without understanding that he is a bouncy, very affectionate terrier who demands a great deal of personal interaction and sufficient outlets for his energy. Soft coat doesn't mean soft personality.

Staffordshire Bull Terrier

Best for Experienced Owners
Good with Older, Considerate Children
Small in Size
Smooth Coat

EXERCISE REQUIRED — MEDIUM

TRIMMING/CLIPPING REQUIRED — LOW

AMOUNT OF SHEDDING — MEDIUM

ACTIVITY INDOORS — HIGH

EASE OF TRAINING — MEDIUM LOW

SOCIABILITY WITH STRANGERS — HIGH
MEDIUM

TEMPERAMENT

The rugged Stafford is quiet (seldom barks), yet is also spirited, curious, and impulsive. "Why walk when you can run and play games?" is his motto. He requires rigorous exercise as an outlet for his energy and to maintain his splendid muscle tone. This people-oriented breed craves companionship and wants to be with you all the time. With proper socialization, he is friendly with everyone. Most individuals extend this "hail fellow well met" attitude to burglars, but would defend their family with their lives if that burglar attempted to harm a person in the household. As you might expect, the Stafford is not a pacifist with other dogs (especially those his own size or larger) and is more than willing to fight if challenged. This is not a breed who can run loose at the neighborhood dog park. However, with proper socialization, many will live peacefully with the dogs and cats in their own family. Stubborn and sometimes headstrong, he is inclined to test for position in the family pecking order. Confident leadership and obedience training are musts. Provide the strongest chew toys you can find to keep his powerful jaws busy and as an alternative to furniture. The athletic Stafford can scale a six-foot fence, and when inclined, he can dig his way under. This "buff little dude" is a stable, confident dog with excellent judgment, but he needs supervision and control from an owner who can match his intelligence.

HISTORY

Developed in England from crosses of old English bulldogs and terriers, he was used for dogfighting. AKC popularity: 95th of 146.

PHYSICAL FEATURES

He stands 14–16 inches and weighs 25–40 pounds. His hard coat requires only an occasional quick brushing. Colors include black, blue, red, fawn, or brindle, or any of these colors with white. His ears and tail are natural.

HEALTH ISSUES

Both parents should have OFA certificates (hips) and yearly CERF (eyes). Also ask about low thyroid and tumors/cancer in the lines. Staffords do not generally do well in extremes of temperature. Lifespan: 12-14 years.

CAUTIONS WHEN BUYING

This breed is a complex animal: He loves people and he loves to fight. Unfortunately, public/media prejudice has slopped over from the "Pit Bull" onto all bulldog-type breeds, and you should be prepared for the moral and legal responsibilities. See the American Pit Bull Terrier profile for more information.

Standard Schnauzer (SHNOW-zer)

Best for Experienced Owners
Good with Children If Raised with Children
Medium in Size
Wiry Coat

EXERCISE REQUIRED — MEDIUM

TRIMMING/CLIPPING REQUIRED — HIGH

AMOUNT OF SHEDDING — LOW

ACTIVITY INDOORS — MEDIUM

EASE OF TRAINING — MEDIUM

SOCIABILITY WITH STRANGERS — MEDIUM
     LOW

TEMPERAMENT

The AKC Standard says, "His nature combines high-spirited temperament with extreme reliability." As with the Giant Schnauzer, the Standard's keen expression is what you may notice first. Some are "harder tempered," projecting boldness, seriousness, and vigor, while others are sweeter and more mellow. Lively indoors and out, this agile, athletic dog loves to play games and needs brisk walking every day and a chance to run several times per week. Mental exercise (such as advanced obedience or agility) will satisfy his highly developed intelligence. Without structured activities, he will find his own amusements—and his choices may change the appearance of your house or yard. Most individuals are aloof with strangers, but with proper socialization are sensible and discriminating about who is a friend and who is not. Some are too spirited for toddlers and many are aggressive with other dogs of the same sex. One of the smartest of all breeds, and one of the best problem-solvers, the Standard Schnauzer is clever, strong-willed, and persistent. Unless you establish yourself as the alpha (number one), he can be demanding. Yet owners who know how to lead and who use upbeat training methods will find him eminently trainable. Schnauzers become obstinate when treated harshly or jerked around. This sensitive dog seems always aware of your moods and likes to be physically close to you and watching you.

HISTORY

All three breeds of Schnauzer (Miniature, Standard, and Giant) originated in Germany; the Standard is the oldest (and least popular) of the three. He served as a rat catcher and guardian of the marketplace produce stand. AKC popularity: 103rd of 146.

PHYSICAL FEATURES

He stands 18–20 inches and weighs 35–45 pounds. Brush his wiry coat twice a week and comb his beard every day for cleanliness. Likewise, keep his bottom trimmed for cleanliness. Show dogs are "stripped" (dead coat plucked out) every few months; pet owners may opt for more convenient clipping. He is usually pepper-and-salt (banded hairs of black and white, resulting in a gray appearance), but may also be black. His ears may be cropped or left naturally hanging; his tail is docked.

HEALTH ISSUES

Both parents should have OFA certificates (hips) and yearly CERF (eyes). Also ask about low thyroid and cancer in the lines. Lifespan: 12–14 years.

CAUTIONS WHEN BUYING

Unlike Miniature Schnauzers, Standards have not been singled out for mass production by unknowledgeable breeders, so quality is high. If you're wavering between the two breeds, the Standard is more rugged in physique, stronger in temperament, and more likely to take advantage of a wishy-washy owner.

Sussex Spaniel

Fine for Novice Owners
Good with Children If Raised with Children
Medium in Size
Feathered, Medium-Length Coat

EXERCISE REQUIRED — MEDIUM

TRIMMING/CLIPPING REQUIRED — MEDIUM

AMOUNT OF SHEDDING — MEDIUM

ACTIVITY INDOORS — MEDIUM LOW

EASE OF TRAINING — LOW

SOCIABILITY WITH STRANGERS — MEDIUM

TEMPERAMENT

Matching his somber, almost frowning expression, the Sussex is calmer and steadier than most other spaniels, though he does conceal a dry sense of humor. This long, low, heavyset dog is rather phlegmatic indoors, but loves the outdoors and will bound through the fields in search of lurking creatures. He is aloof with strangers and sometimes protective (unusual for a spaniel), but once guests are accepted, he is polite, even charming. He can be dominant with strange dogs. Early socialization with a variety of people and other animals is mandatory to develop his stable nature. His stubbornness requires obedience training from a consistent owner who knows how to lead and who will use positive, upbeat training methods. This proud dog will stand up for himself if handled sharply or teased. He tends to bark and howl, especially if left alone too much, and can be hard to housebreak. Many Sussex, especially when young, are finicky eaters, struggle to keep weight on, and even show little interest in treats.

HISTORY

Developed in Sussex County, England, he is unique in that he bays while he hunts. AKC popularity: 136th of 146 (rarest of the spaniels).

PHYSICAL FEATURES

He stands 13–15 inches and weighs 35–45 pounds. Brush and comb his silky coat twice a week and occasionally trim straggly hairs. Keep his ear canals clean and dry and his bottom trimmed for cleanliness. He is golden liver: liver hairs tipped with golden yellow (though this occurs only if exposed to sufficient sunlight). His ears are natural; his tail is docked.

HEALTH ISSUES

Both parents should have the following certificates: OFA (hips), yearly CERF (eyes), and cardiac-clear (for heart defects). Also ask about low thyroid in the lines. Lifespan: 12 years.

CAUTIONS WHEN BUYING

Be prepared to go onto a waiting list. Litters are few and far between, the puppy mortality rate is high, and since it is difficult to find quality breeding stock, the finest pups are kept by breeders.

Swedish Vallhund (VAHL-hoond)

Fine for Novice Owners
Good with Older, Considerate Children
Small to Medium in Size
Short Coat

EXERCISE REQUIRED — MEDIUM

TRIMMING/CLIPPING REQUIRED — LOW

AMOUNT OF SHEDDING — HIGH MEDIUM

ACTIVITY INDOORS — MEDIUM

EASE OF TRAINING — HIGH MEDIUM

SOCIABILITY WITH STRANGERS — HIGH

TEMPERAMENT

The FCI Standard calls him "watchful, alert, and energetic." Spirited and athletic, yet steady and dependable, the Swedish Vallhund is a true "big dog with short legs." Hiking, herding, obedience, agility, or chasing balls (with surprising speed) are enjoyable outlets (both physical and mental) for this breed's enthusiasm and desire to work. SVs love to be challenged with new tasks. If his days include such moderate exercise, along with the loving companionship of his family, he is adaptable and easy to live with. He is friendly (or at least polite) with everyone and makes a sensible, responsible watchdog. Most are fine with other animals and especially wonderful with livestock, including horses. This attentive breed learns quickly and responds well to obedience training, but he has the independent judgment and problem-solving abilities of a herding breed, coupled with the inquisitive, playful, persistent, sometimes manipulative nature of the spitz. You must have the confidence to establish and consistently enforce rules, or he may make up his own. Vallhunds prefer their flock (family members and other pets) to be gathered together and may try to accomplish this by poking or nipping. Barking needs to be controlled.

HISTORY

This rugged farm dog, skilled at herding cattle and sheep, probably descended from spitz breeds brought to Sweden by the Vikings. The Swedish name is Vastgotaspets, meaning "spitz from the province of Vastergotland." *Vallhund* means "herding dog." Registered by the FCI, UKC, CKC, and AKC-FSS.

PHYSICAL FEATURES

He stands 12–14 inches and weighs 20–35 pounds. Brush his harsh double coat once a week, daily when he is shedding. Along with heavy seasonal shedding, you'll see some loose hairs the rest of the year as well. His color pattern is sable (black-tipped hairs) in blended shades of gray, brown, yellow, and/or red. Light "harness" markings on his shoulders are essential. His ears are natural. His tail may be docked, a natural bobtail or stubtail, or a curled/curved spitz tail.

HEALTH ISSUES

Both parents should have OFA certificates (hips) and yearly CERF (eyes). Long-backed breeds are susceptible to disk disease that can be exacerbated by excessive high-jumping, dashing down stairs, being picked up without proper support, and obesity. However, the Vallhund's more moderate proportions of height to length give him more protection in this area than other breeds. Lifespan: 12–15 years.

CAUTIONS WHEN BUYING

Whether the Vallhund has crossed paths with the Pembroke Welsh Corgi is not known. The Vallhund is taller and longer-legged, with a steadier temperament; he is not as clownish as the Pem and not as bossy. Yet he is not as mellow as the Cardigan Welsh Corgi. This is a rare breed in the United States—expect a waiting list.

Teddy Roosevelt Terrier

Fine for Novice Owners
Good with Older, Considerate Children
Small in Size
Smooth Coat

EXERCISE REQUIRED — MEDIUM
TRIMMING/CLIPPING REQUIRED — LOW
AMOUNT OF SHEDDING — MEDIUM
ACTIVITY INDOORS — HIGH MEDIUM
EASE OF TRAINING — MEDIUM
SOCIABILITY WITH STRANGERS — MEDIUM

TEMPERAMENT

The sturdy Teddy Roosevelt Terrier is a fearless, tenacious hunter in the field, yet a friendly, sensible companion at home. Untiringly active and playful, he has a special passion for ball chasing. He must always be kept in a fenced yard or on-leash, for he is agile and impulsive—also curious and clever, so be sure those fences are secure. The Teddy Roosevelt Terrier craves companionship, often using his paws to demand attention, and most are somewhat vocal, "talking" and grumbling, especially when ignored. Generally good with other dogs and cats in his own family, he does have a high prey drive and quick reflexes and will dispatch squeaky creatures with little effort. Though he has a mild stubborn streak, this attentive, sensitive, head-cocking breed responds nicely to verbal discipline and to obedience training that utilizes food and praise. Being respectable terriers, Teddys love to tunnel and dig.

HISTORY

An American-made breed, the Teddy Roosevelt descended from terriers brought over by English immigrants. His ancestry also includes scenthound and sighthound and he is an outstanding ratter and squirrel hunter. Registered by the UKC and the National Rat Terrier Association. The original longer-legged type is called the Rat Terrier, while the shorter-legged type is called Class B Rat Terrier by the National Rat Terrier Association and Teddy Roosevelt Terrier by the UKC. (Ironically, Teddy Roosevelt hunted with the original, longer-legged type!)

PHYSICAL FEATURES

He stands 8–14 inches and weighs 12–24 pounds. His smooth coat needs only an occasional quick brushing. Most are spotted tricolor: white with black and tan patches. He may also be bicolor: black, tan, sable, blue, red, chocolate, or lemon/apricot, with white markings and often tan trim. His ears are natural; his tail is usually docked, though some are born with bobtails.

HEALTH ISSUES

Ask about luxating patella, lens luxation, seizures, demodectic mange, and allergies in the lines. Lifespan: 15–18 years.

CAUTIONS WHEN BUYING

Still in the early stages of standardization, the Teddy Roosevelt is quite variable in conformation. Make sure the breeder has either UKC or NRTA registration papers and belongs to one of the recognized clubs. Some unscrupulous breeders are trying to pass off mixed breeds as purebred.

Tibetan Mastiff

Best for Experienced Owners
Good with Older, Considerate Children
Large to Giant in Size
Thick, Medium-Length Coat

EXERCISE REQUIRED — MEDIUM

TRIMMING/CLIPPING REQUIRED — LOW

AMOUNT OF SHEDDING — MEDIUM

ACTIVITY INDOORS — MEDIUM LOW

EASE OF TRAINING — LOW

SOCIABILITY WITH STRANGERS — LOW

TEMPERAMENT

This powerful, rugged breed with the solemn expression is not inclined to play fetch or Frisbee. He was developed strictly for working purposes, and his instincts to perform that work are ingrained. Livestock guardians bond with flock animals, as well as their own families, with fierce possessiveness, making their own decisions about who is a friend and who is a foe, what is a threat and what is not. These strong-willed, highly intelligent, self-reliant dogs will take control of every situation unless you are an assertive leader who demands respect. He is serious and dignified, calm and quiet—unless provoked. Aloof with strangers, he will remain watchful every moment they are on his property. He is patient with his own children and other family pets, but requires careful introduction to those outside the family. Despite his bulk, he is remarkably agile, skilled at climbing and jumping, and requires a six-foot-high fence. He often prefers to be outdoors where he can view and patrol his territory; however, TMs have a deep, impressive bark, which they tend to use freely, especially at night when they are most attentive. They sometimes dig deep holes to lie in.

HISTORY

Thought by many to be the ancestor of most other mastiff and mountain dog breeds, the Tibetan Mastiff has been protecting flocks and guarding villages for thousands of years. Registered by the FCI.

PHYSICAL FEATURES

Males stand 26–30 inches and weigh 100–140 pounds. Females stand 24–26 inches and weigh 80–125 pounds.

Some lines are much larger and more imposing-looking than others. Brush his harsh coat once a week, daily during heavy seasonal shedding. The more profuse coats with cottony undercoats are prone to matting and need more maintenance. Colors include black, black-and-tan, brown, gold, cream, gray, and gray with gold markings. Some standards also allow cream and sable. His ears and tail are natural.

HEALTH ISSUES

Both parents should have OFA certificates (hips) and normal thyroid (full panel). Also ask about heart defects, allergies, and autoimmune problems in the lines. Eyelid disorders (entropion) can be a problem. With his low metabolism, he is sensitive to anesthetics, vaccines, and chemicals and should never be casually medicated or sedated. Females usually come into heat once a year, rather than twice. Lifespan: 8–14 years.

CAUTIONS WHEN BUYING

In a home where he is allowed to do his job yet is kept under control by experienced hands, he makes an impressive companion. However, without ongoing socialization and supervision, this somewhat primitive breed is simply too much dog.

Tibetan Spaniel

Fine for Novice Owners
Good with Older, Considerate Children
Small in Size
Feathered, Medium-Length Coat

EXERCISE REQUIRED — LOW
TRIMMING/CLIPPING REQUIRED — LOW
AMOUNT OF SHEDDING — MEDIUM
ACTIVITY INDOORS — MEDIUM
EASE OF TRAINING — MEDIUM LOW
SOCIABILITY WITH STRANGERS — MEDIUM

TEMPERAMENT

With his independent nature and quick agility, the Tibbie has been compared to a cat. Lively and playful, yet also calm and laid-back, this good-natured dog is easy to live with. He fits into an apartment or an estate with equal contentment—all he asks for in the way of exercise are daily walks and occasional romps in a safe enclosed area. Tibbies are family-oriented: They love to play games with their own people, are sensitive to moods and feelings, and do not like to be left alone for long periods of time. They are agile, surefooted climbers (they can often be found perched on the windowsill or the high back of a chair, looking out the window) and clever problem-solvers who often rely on their dexterity to get what they want. For example, they will use their paws to pry open a cabinet door. Most are conservative with strangers and don't like being swooped down on by people they don't know. Early socialization is important to develop a confident, outgoing temperament. Most are friendly with other animals. Though stubborn and self-reliant, he is also sensitive; obedience training should utilize food and praise. Jerking on the leash or other harsh handling only brings out his obstinate side.

HISTORY

The Tibetan Spaniel is misnamed, for although he hails from Tibet, he has no spaniel heritage. He served as a watchdog and companion in the Himalayan Mountains, lying on high monastery walls and barking to alert the true guard dog, the Tibetan Mastiff, whenever someone was approaching. AKC popularity: 105th of 146.

PHYSICAL FEATURES

He stands about 10 inches and weighs 9–15 pounds. Brush and comb his silky double coat twice a week, daily when he is shedding. Keep his ear canals clean and dry and his bottom trimmed for cleanliness. Colors include white, gold, cream, red, black, and others—in solid, sable, and particolor patterns. His ears and tail are natural.

HEALTH ISSUES

Both parents should have OFA certificates (hips and elbows), yearly CERF (eyes), and be screened for luxating patella. Also ask about liver shunt and allergies in the lines. Lifespan: 12–15 years.

CAUTIONS WHEN BUYING

Tibetan Spaniels have not caught the attention of mass commercial breeders, so their quality is high. If you need to be put on a waiting list, be patient and keep in mind that this small-scale, careful breeding is why quality is so high.

Tibetan Terrier

Fine for Novice Owners
Good with Older, Considerate Children
Small to Medium in Size
Long Coat

EXERCISE REQUIRED — MEDIUM
TRIMMING/CLIPPING REQUIRED — HIGH
    MEDIUM LOW
AMOUNT OF SHEDDING — LOW
ACTIVITY INDOORS — MEDIUM
EASE OF TRAINING — MEDIUM LOW
SOCIABILITY WITH STRANGERS — MEDIUM

TEMPERAMENT

The good-natured Tibetan Terrier is lively and playful, yet also calm and low-key. He is a moderate dog in all respects and can adapt to any home, city, or country, so long as he is given brisk daily walks and occasional romps in a safe enclosed area. He especially enjoys playing in the snow, his large, flat, snowshoe-like feet providing traction, and his long, heavy eyelashes protecting his eyes. He is athletic and agile, a surefooted climber, and a clever problem-solver who often uses his paws with great adeptness to open doors and hold toys. TTs are family-oriented: They love to play games and participate in activities with their own people, but most are conservative with strangers. In some individuals, caution can shade into timidity or shyness, so early socialization is important to develop a confident, outgoing temperament. Most are amiable with other animals, though perhaps a bit bossy. Though very stubborn, he should be trained with food rewards and praise, because he is proud and sensitive, and jerking on the leash only makes him more obstinate. Some individuals may enjoy digging in the garden.

HISTORY

Called "Little People" in their native Tibet, these sturdy dogs lived in the monasteries of the isolated Lost Valley and were considered good-luck charms. He is actually not a terrier at all—he was so named only because of his small size and shaggy coat. Nor is he a guardian or hunter, having always been bred solely for companionship. AKC popularity: 94th of 146.

PHYSICAL FEATURES

He stands 14–17 inches and weighs 20–30 pounds. His profuse double coat may be straight or wavy, with much hair overhanging his head, and should be brushed and combed every other day. Pet owners may choose to trim/clip the coat short every four to six weeks. Keep his ear canals clean and dry and his bottom trimmed for cleanliness. Colors include white, gold, silver, cream, black, and others—in solid, sable, brindle, and particolor patterns. His ears and tail are natural.

HEALTH ISSUES

Both parents should have OFA certificates (hips), yearly CERF (eyes), and be screened for luxating patella. Lifespan: 12–15 years.

CAUTIONS WHEN BUYING

Fortunately, Tibetan Terriers have not been singled out for mass production by unknowledgeable breeders, which means quantity is low and quality is high. You'll probably have to get on a waiting list, but the wait will be worth it if this is the breed for you. Keep in mind the grooming requirements.

Tosa (TOE-sa)

Best for Experienced Owners
Good with Children If Raised with Children
Giant in Size
Short Coat

EXERCISE REQUIRED — MEDIUM
TRIMMING/CLIPPING REQUIRED — LOW
AMOUNT OF SHEDDING — MEDIUM
ACTIVITY INDOORS — LOW
EASE OF TRAINING — MEDIUM
SOCIABILITY WITH STRANGERS — MEDIUM

TEMPERAMENT

The FCI Standard lists the key characteristics of the Tosa as "patience, composure, boldness, and courage." This stately, massive breed is quiet (seldom barks), calm, and relaxed—until aroused, which may mean a bad guy rushing at his family or a low-flying bird to be snatched out of the air. In other words, he is a laid-back sofa connoisseur until switched on. His athleticism and agility, combined with his immense power, mean that he must be respected, well socialized, well trained, and under control at all times. Weight pulling is an enjoyable activity, with some individuals pulling more than 3,400 pounds. Puppies should be friendly and trusting and become more discriminating as they mature, but this should always be a people-friendly breed. Protection training and Schutzhund are not recommended. Animal aggression (dogs, cats, livestock) is a real problem and requires committed socialization and training to keep under control. This stubborn breed is inclined to do things his own way, but he will defer to confident leadership that includes consistent rules and cheerful praise. This breed cannot be out-muscled. Unlike most mastiffs, the Tosa is not prone to drooling.

HISTORY

Often referred to as the "Sumo wrestler of the dog world" because of his great size and strength, he is also called Tosa-Ken or Tosa-Inu, especially in his native Japan. He was developed for dogfighting. Revered as a fearless warrior, he is often pictured in full ceremonial regalia. Registered by the FCI and UKC.

PHYSICAL FEATURES

Males stand 25–30 inches and weigh 120–160 pounds. Females stand 23–28 inches and weigh 100–140 pounds. His hard coat requires only an occasional quick brushing. Red is the preferred color, but he may also be fawn, apricot, black, black-and-tan, or brindle, often with limited white markings. His ears and tail are natural.

HEALTH ISSUES

Both parents should have OFA certificates (hips and elbows) and yearly CERF (eyes). Also ask about bloat and OCD in the lines. Eyelid disorders (entropion) can be a problem. Lifespan: 11 years.

CAUTIONS WHEN BUYING

This is not a breed for beginners. You must provide ongoing socialization and obedience training, supervision and control. Tosas are not vocally expressive and require a tuned-in owner who can read canine body language. Look for temperament titles (TT, CGC) in the pedigree.

Toy Fox Terrier

Fine for Novice Owners
Good with Older, Considerate Children
Little in Size
Smooth Coat

EXERCISE REQUIRED — LOW
TRIMMING/CLIPPING REQUIRED — LOW
AMOUNT OF SHEDDING — MEDIUM LOW
ACTIVITY INDOORS — MEDIUM
EASE OF TRAINING — HIGH MEDIUM
SOCIABILITY WITH STRANGERS — MEDIUM
    LOW

TEMPERAMENT

Bold and determined for his size, the spunky Toy Fox can be intensely focused and impulsive, but is more biddable and amenable than his larger cousin, the Smooth Fox Terrier. Both terrier and toy traits influence his personality and character. As a terrier, he is alert, proud, and spunky. As a toy, he is of quieter demeanor and loves to be held. Many dearly love to play ball and do a fine job of exercising themselves indoors; they are well balanced in rest time and playtime. The TFT is comical and entertaining and remains so throughout his long life. With his curiosity, quickness, and chasing instincts, he must always be leashed or fenced outdoors. *Securely* fenced, because he likes to explore—and that means the other side of the fence, whether he has to climb over, dig under, or squeeze through the cracks. With his keen eyesight and acute hearing, the Toy Fox is quick to announce strangers with his sharp, suspicious bark. He is described as "not easily intimidated by other pets," which means that not only will he not back down if challenged, but also that he may do much of the challenging himself. However, he does tend to get along well with other family pets. He has an independent mind and a mischievous sense of humor and prefers learning tricks to formal obedience exercises, but he is quite trainable when praise and treats are the primary motivators. Housebreaking can be difficult, especially in cold or rainy weather.

HISTORY

Bred down in size from the Smooth Fox Terrier, with the Chihuahua and Min Pin also playing roles in his development, the Toy Fox has long been a fixture on American farms as an excellent mouser and kitchen companion. Registered by the UKC.

PHYSICAL FEATURES

He stands up to 11 inches and weighs 3½–7 pounds. His satiny coat needs only an occasional quick brushing. The preferred color is mostly white, with a predominantly black head, with tan markings over the eyes and on the cheeks, and with or without black spots on the body. White-and-black is the same pattern with no tan trim. White-and-tan is the same pattern except that tan replaces the black on the head and body, and a different shade of tan constitutes the facial trim. Chocolate is also accepted by some registries. His ears are natural; his tail is docked.

HEALTH ISSUES

Both parents should have OFA certificates (hips) and yearly CERF (eyes). Also ask about heart problems and seizures in the lines. He should wear a sweater outdoors in cold or rainy weather. Lifespan: 15 years.

CAUTIONS WHEN BUYING

Be careful: Some breeders produce TFTs that cross the line between high energy and hyperactivity. Others pawn off patched mixed breeds as purebreds. Look for UKC registration papers and view both parents (and other relatives, if possible) for stable temperament.

Vizsla (VEESH-la)

Fine for Novice Owners
Good with Children
Large in Size
Smooth Coat

EXERCISE REQUIRED — HIGH
TRIMMING/CLIPPING REQUIRED — LOW
AMOUNT OF SHEDDING — MEDIUM
ACTIVITY INDOORS — MEDIUM
EASE OF TRAINING — MEDIUM
SOCIABILITY WITH STRANGERS — HIGH
    MEDIUM

TEMPERAMENT

The AKC Standard says, "Lively, gentle-mannered, demonstrably affectionate, and sensitive." The good-natured Vizsla has been called a "Velcro" dog because he is so tactile—he attaches himself to people, preferably in their laps. Athletic, agile, and light on his feet, he needs vigorous daily exercise and lots of personal attention. Too much confinement and too little companionship can lead to neurotic behaviors such as hyperactivity and destructiveness. Bored Vizslas are notorious chewers. He gets along well with everyone, including strangers and other animals, but does need a lot of early socialization to build confidence. Some Vizslas are excitable and/or easily startled in new situations. He has the independent spirit of all pointing breeds, but responds to training more willingly than most and is a capable performer in advanced obedience competition. Training should be motivational and persuasive rather than heavy-handed, as this breed is quite sensitive. You may need to control his tendency to mouth your hands—provide a box filled with toys so he can carry things around in his mouth.

HISTORY

This very old breed roamed the Hungarian plains with the nomadic Magyar tribes, hunting partridge and rabbits. *Vizsla* means "alert and responsive." AKC popularity: 48th of 146.

PHYSICAL FEATURES

He stands 20–25 inches. Males weigh 55–65 pounds; females weigh 45–55 pounds. His hard coat needs only an occasional quick brushing. There is also a wirehaired variety, more common in Europe but not yet recognized by the AKC. He comes in one color: golden rust. His ears are natural; his tail is docked.

HEALTH ISSUES

Both parents should have the following certificates: OFA (hips), yearly CERF (eyes), and a skin-punch biopsy for SA (sebaceous adenitis). Also ask about low thyroid, seizures, vWD, OCD, and cancer in the lines. Vizslas can be sensitive to anesthetics, vaccines, and chemicals and to cold weather. Lifespan: 11–14 years.

CAUTIONS WHEN BUYING

It is a tribute to Vizsla breeders that so many of these dogs are dual-purpose (both show and field) and even triple-purpose (show, field, and obedience). Look for a pedigree balanced with champion titles, field or hunting test titles, and obedience titles.

Weimaraner (WY-mah-rah-ner)

Best for Experienced Owners
Good with Children If Raised with Children
Large in Size
Smooth Coat

EXERCISE REQUIRED — HIGH

TRIMMING/CLIPPING REQUIRED — LOW

AMOUNT OF SHEDDING — MEDIUM

ACTIVITY INDOORS — HIGH

EASE OF TRAINING — LOW

SOCIABILITY WITH STRANGERS — MEDIUM

TEMPERAMENT

The high-energy Weimaraner, bred to hunt all day, needs an athletic owner who can meet his demanding exercise needs: running, biking, hiking, jogging, field work. Too much confinement leads to hyperactivity and destructiveness, as does being left alone too much. A bored Weim will bark up a storm, demolish your home and yard, even attempt to escape in search of adventure. Reserved and protective with strangers, dominant with other dogs, predatory toward small animals such as cats and rabbits, this breed needs an owner who can provide leadership, socialization, and training beyond the beginner level. He is headstrong, but in the right hands is capable of learning and doing virtually anything. Indeed, a well-matched owner will find him a loyal, aristocratic gentleman of great presence and character. A novice with little time and space will find him a rambunctious bully, difficult to control. He can be hard to housebreak.

HISTORY

"The Gray Ghost" was developed in the German republic of Weimar. Owned only by the aristocracy, he hunted both game birds and big game. AKC popularity: 37th of 146.

PHYSICAL FEATURES

Males stand 25–27 inches and weigh 70–90 pounds. Females stand 23–25 inches and weigh 55–75 pounds. His hard coat needs only an occasional quick brushing. Long-haired dogs are acceptable in Europe, but cannot be shown in conformation classes in the United States. His gray color ranges from light silver to dark mouse. His ears are natural; his tail is docked. His feet are webbed.

HEALTH ISSUES

Both parents should have OFA certificates (hips and elbows) and yearly CERF (eyes). Also ask about low thyroid, bloat, vWD, skin disease, and cancer in the lines. Weimaraners can be sensitive to anesthetics, vaccines, and chemicals. Lifespan: 10–12 years.

CAUTIONS WHEN BUYING

The Weimaraner is not as divided in type as some other sporting breeds, with many breeders aiming for show champions who can also hunt. For the most well-balanced, trainable Weimaraner, look for a pedigree balanced with champion titles, field or hunting test titles, and obedience titles.

Welsh Corgi (Cardigan)

Fine for Novice Owners
Good with Older, Considerate Children
Small to Medium in Size
Short Coat

EXERCISE REQUIRED — MEDIUM
TRIMMING/CLIPPING REQUIRED — LOW
AMOUNT OF SHEDDING — HIGH MEDIUM
ACTIVITY INDOORS — MEDIUM
EASE OF TRAINING — HIGH
SOCIABILITY WITH STRANGERS — MEDIUM

TEMPERAMENT

Spirited and athletic, yet steady and dependable, the Cardigan is a true "big dog on short legs." Herding, obedience, agility, or chasing balls (with surprising speed) are enjoyable outlets (both physical and mental) for his enthusiasm and desire to work. If his days include such moderate exercise, along with the loving companionship of his family, the Cardi is very adaptable and easy to live with. He is polite with guests, reserved with strangers, and makes a sensible, responsible watchdog. Most are fine with other family pets, though territorial with strange dogs and cats—one of his responsibilities was to chase strays away from his own farm. He is wonderful with livestock, including horses. This attentive breed learns quickly and responds well to obedience training. Yet he has the independent judgment and problem-solving abilities of a true herding breed, so you must have the confidence to establish and consistently enforce rules, or he may make up his own. Cardis prefer their flock (family members and other pets) to be gathered together and may try to accomplish this by circling and nipping. Barking can be a problem.

HISTORY

In Cardiganshire, Wales, he drove his master's cattle onto the common land to graze. He also drove off trespassing cattle and hunted vermin. He is related to the Dachshund, hence his low-slung build and slightly bowed front legs. In Welsh, *cor* means "dog" and *gi* means "dwarf." AKC popularity: 89th of 146.

PHYSICAL FEATURES

Most folks who first see a Corgi are surprised by the heavy bone packed onto his short legs. He stands 11–13 inches and weighs 25–40 pounds. From nose to tail tip, he is at least three feet long. Brush his harsh double coat once a week, daily when he is shedding. Along with heavy seasonal shedding, you'll see some loose hairs the rest of the year as well. He is brindle, black, blue merle, red (fawn to golden), or sable, usually with white markings. Blacks and blue merles may have tan or brindle points. His ears and tail are natural.

HEALTH ISSUES

Both parents should have OFA certificates (hips), yearly CERF (eyes), and a DNA certificate that shows whether they are affected, carriers, or clear of PRA (at least one parent must be clear). Long-backed breeds are susceptible to disk disease that can be exacerbated by excessive high-jumping, dashing down stairs, being picked up without proper support, and obesity. Lifespan: 12–15 years.

CAUTIONS WHEN BUYING

Compared to the Pembroke Welsh Corgi, the Cardi tends to be calmer and less outgoing with strangers and other dogs. Cardigans have a long tail (not docked), larger, rounder ears, a longer, heavier body, a deeper chest, and slightly bowed front legs.

Welsh Corgi (Pembroke)

Fine for Novice Owners
Good with Older, Considerate Children
Small to Medium in Size
Short Coat

EXERCISE REQUIRED — MEDIUM

TRIMMING/CLIPPING REQUIRED — LOW

AMOUNT OF SHEDDING — HIGH MEDIUM

ACTIVITY INDOORS — MEDIUM

EASE OF TRAINING — HIGH

SOCIABILITY WITH STRANGERS — HIGH
    MEDIUM

TEMPERAMENT

Spirited and athletic, yet steady and dependable, the Pembroke is a true "big dog on short legs." Herding, obedience, agility, or chasing balls (with surprising speed) are enjoyable outlets (both physical and mental) for his enthusiasm and desire to work. If his days include such moderate exercise, along with the loving companionship of his family, the Pembroke is adaptable and easy to live with. He is polite with guests, reserved with strangers, and makes a sensible, responsible watchdog. Most are fine with other family pets, though territorial with strange dogs and cats—one of his responsibilities was to chase strays away from his own farm. He is wonderful with livestock, including horses. This attentive breed learns quickly and responds well to obedience training. Yet he has the independent judgment and problem-solving abilities of a true herding breed, so you must have the confidence to establish and consistently enforce rules, or he may make up his own. Pems prefer their flock (family members and other pets) to be gathered together and may try to accomplish this by circling and nipping. Barking can be a problem.

HISTORY

In Pembrokeshire, Wales, he drove his master's cattle onto the common land to graze. He also drove off trespassing cattle and hunted vermin. He is descended from the spitz family, hence his foxy face. In Welsh, *cor* means "dog" and *gi* means "dwarf." AKC popularity: 34th of 146.

PHYSICAL FEATURES

Most folks who first see a Corgi are surprised by the solid bone packed onto his short legs. He stands 10–12 inches and weighs 25–30 pounds. Brush his double coat once a week, daily when he is shedding. Along with heavy seasonal shedding, you'll see some loose hairs the rest of the year as well. He is red, fawn, or sable, always with white markings, or tricolor (black with white markings and tan trim). A fluffy (feathered coat), whitelie (mostly white), or bluie (smoky blue) may not be shown in conformation classes. His ears are natural; his tail is docked.

HEALTH ISSUES

Both parents should have OFA certificates (hips) and yearly CERF (eyes). Each individual puppy must have his eyes examined by an AVCO-certified ophthalmologist (not just a regular vet) at six to ten weeks of age. Long-backed breeds are susceptible to disk disease that can be exacerbated by excessive high-jumping, dashing down stairs, being picked up without proper support, and obesity. Lifespan: 12–15 years.

CAUTIONS WHEN BUYING

Compared to the Cardigan Welsh Corgi, the Pembroke tends to be livelier, more excitable, and more outgoing with strangers and other dogs. Pembrokes have a docked tail, smaller more triangular ears, a shorter body, lighter bones, and straight front legs. Each of these breeds has its own heritage, but a similar delightful temperament. Training is important, for these dogs are not unquestioningly obedient.

Welsh Springer Spaniel

Fine for Novice Owners
Good with Children
Medium in Size
Feathered, Medium-Length Coat

EXERCISE REQUIRED — HIGH MEDIUM

TRIMMING/CLIPPING REQUIRED — MEDIUM

AMOUNT OF SHEDDING — MEDIUM

ACTIVITY INDOORS — MEDIUM

EASE OF TRAINING — HIGH MEDIUM

SOCIABILITY WITH STRANGERS — MEDIUM

TEMPERAMENT

The Welsh Springer is steadier, more sensible, and less exuberant than his cousin, the English Springer. A hardy, vigorous worker in the field, he loves the outdoors and needs as much running, hiking, or biking exercise as you can provide. Indoors he attaches himself with great devotion to his people. He is reserved with strangers, sometimes reticent, so he needs to be accustomed to people and noises at an early age. With other animals, he is peaceful and dependable. Because of his independence and tendency to be easily distracted, he requires early training so that good habits are instilled right from the start. However, he is physically and emotionally sensitive and "soft," so training should be done with a calm voice and a light hand on the leash. Corrections should be mostly verbal—these gentle dogs wilt under rough handling. Submissive urination (sudden wetting when excited or anxious) can be a problem in youngsters.

HISTORY

Developed in Wales, he is one of the oldest of the spaniels. AKC popularity: 118th of 146.

PHYSICAL FEATURES

Males stand 18–19 inches and weigh 40–45 pounds. Females stand 17–18 inches and weigh 35–40 pounds. Brush and comb his silky coat twice a week and occasionally trim straggly hairs. Keep his ear canals clean and dry and his bottom trimmed for cleanliness. He is red-and-white, usually with red ticking scattered throughout the white areas. Facial freckles are considered especially attractive. His ears are natural; his tail is docked.

HEALTH ISSUES

Both parents should have OFA certificates (hips) and yearly CERF (eyes). Also ask about seizures and low thyroid in the lines. Lifespan: 12–14 years.

CAUTIONS WHEN BUYING

If you like the general appearance and reputation of the spaniel as a mild-mannered, dependable family dog and want something sized between a Cocker and an English Springer, consider the Welshman. He has not been exploited as much by unknowledgeable breeders and is a safer bet in the health and temperament departments. The WSS is also more of a dual-purpose breed than the ESS, with most breeders seriously interested in preserving field instincts. Look for a pedigree balanced with obedience and field titles, as well as Ch. titles.

Welsh Terrier

Best for Experienced Owners
Good with Older, Considerate Children
Small in Size
Wiry Coat

EXERCISE REQUIRED — MEDIUM

TRIMMING/CLIPPING REQUIRED — HIGH
MEDIUM

AMOUNT OF SHEDDING — LOW

ACTIVITY INDOORS — HIGH

EASE OF TRAINING — LOW

SOCIABILITY WITH STRANGERS — MEDIUM
LOW

TEMPERAMENT

The compact Welsh Terrier, who looks like a small Airedale, is steadier, more sensible, and less excitable than some terriers, yet still full of energy and drive. The more exercise you can offer, the better. He is always alert and ready for a game, but his inquisitiveness and tenacity can get him into tight spots (literally) unless your fences are secure and/or he is well supervised. He does best with active owners who are confident and consistent, for he has a marked independent streak and will take advantage if indulged. Positive training methods are a must—terriers have a "What's in it for me?" attitude and do not react kindly to being jerked around. Welshies are more amiable with other dogs than some terriers, but they won't back down if challenged. They have a high prey drive, which means little creatures (often including cats) will be stalked. Most are friendly and outgoing with everyone, though proper socialization is important to develop this self-confidence. The alert Welsh Terrier can be counted on to sound the alert when anything is amiss; in fact, excessive barking may need to be controlled. True terriers, they love to tunnel and dig and can be possessive of their food and toys.

HISTORY

Not surprisingly, the Welsh Terrier hails from Wales, where he hunted otter, fox, and badger. AKC popularity: 99th of 146.

PHYSICAL FEATURES

He stands 14½–15½ inches and weighs 18–25 pounds. Brush and comb his hard wiry coat once a week. His beard should be combed daily for cleanliness. Likewise, keep his bottom trimmed for cleanliness. Show dogs are "stripped" (dead coat plucked out) every few months; pet owners may opt for more convenient clipping. He is born black, with the black receding from his head, chest, and legs by four months, leaving a tan or reddish brown dog with a black or grizzle (speckled) saddle. His ears are natural; his tail is docked.

HEALTH ISSUES

Both parents should have yearly CERF certificates (eyes). Ask about lens luxation, glaucoma, seizures, low thyroid, and allergies in the lines. Lifespan: 12–15 years.

CAUTIONS WHEN BUYING

Too many people choose one of these small square terriers (Lakeland, Welsh, Fox) without realizing that they are *more* energetic and excitable and *more* of a training challenge than larger Airedales, Kerry Blues, and Soft-Coated Wheatens. The larger terriers were developed to be more multipurpose and more responsive to humans, while the smaller were bred specifically for hunting and killing prey underground, requiring a tough, independent mind-set. Though their convenient size does mean that you can pick them up to keep them out of trouble, their intense character is not for the faint of heart.

West Highland White Terrier

Best for Experienced Owners
Good with Older, Considerate Children
Small in Size
Wiry Coat

EXERCISE REQUIRED — MEDIUM

TRIMMING/CLIPPING REQUIRED — HIGH
        MEDIUM

AMOUNT OF SHEDDING — LOW

ACTIVITY INDOORS — HIGH

EASE OF TRAINING — MEDIUM

SOCIABILITY WITH STRANGERS — HIGH
        MEDIUM

TEMPERAMENT

The AKC Standard says that he is "possessed with no small amount of self-esteem." Indeed. Along with the Cairn, the Westie is what many people picture when they hear "terrier," for he is everything a terrier was designed to be. Sturdy, spunky, and bold, he needs his daily walks and interactive play sessions, yet he is easier to handle and friendlier than some other terriers. He can adapt to any home in which he can be a full participant and busybody. Quick to announce anything amiss, including visitors, he usually proceeds to welcome them inside with a gaily wagging tail. Westies can be bossy with other dogs of the same sex, but otherwise coexist with other dogs and cats more readily than most terriers. Rabbits and rodents, however, are in for a stressful (and probably short) life, along with wild critters who venture into the Westie's yard. He will pursue with tenacity anything that moves and cannot be let off-leash except in a safe, enclosed area. Assertive but cheerful, with the typical stubbornness and cleverness of a true terrier, he must be shown that you are in charge, else he may become demanding and testy when he doesn't get his own way. He does respond well to consistent discipline and to obedience training that utilizes food rewards. Westies can be possessive of their food and toys, and they are determined diggers and barkers.

HISTORY

The Westie was developed in the Scottish Highlands as a vermin hunter. AKC popularity: 33rd of 146.

PHYSICAL FEATURES

He stands 10–11 inches and weighs 15–20 pounds. Brush and comb his straight, harsh coat twice a week. Keep his bottom trimmed for cleanliness. Show dogs are "stripped" (dead coat plucked out) every few months; pet owners may opt for more convenient clipping. As his name suggests, he is solid white. His ears and tail are natural.

HEALTH ISSUES

Both parents should be screened for luxating patella, and have GDC certificates showing they are clear of GCL (globoid cell leukodystrophy) and Legg-Perthes. Also ask about CMO, copper toxicosis, seizures, vWD, and allergies and skin conditions in the lines. Lifespan: 13–14 years.

CAUTIONS WHEN BUYING

The second most popular of the AKC-recognized terriers, the Westie has suffered from the irresponsibility of unknowledgeable breeders. There are a considerable number of health and temperament problems in the gene pool, and you must take care to choose a breeder who screens rigorously for these defects.

Whippet

Fine for Novice Owners
Good with Older, Considerate Children
Medium in Size
Smooth Coat

EXERCISE REQUIRED — MEDIUM

TRIMMING/CLIPPING REQUIRED — LOW

AMOUNT OF SHEDDING — MEDIUM LOW

ACTIVITY INDOORS — LOW

EASE OF TRAINING — MEDIUM

SOCIABILITY WITH STRANGERS — MEDIUM

TEMPERAMENT

The AKC Standard says, "Amiable, friendly, gentle, but capable of great intensity during sporting pursuits." The Whippet is sweet-natured and docile, yet playful and athletic. The same dog who will curl up under the blankets—a perfect couch potato, sleeping for hours—will tear enthusiastically around the yard, darting and zigzagging and turning on a dime without slowing down. He loves running games and requires short bursts of vigorous exercise each day. The area must be fenced, for this racy breed is the fastest dog of his weight: up to thirty-five miles per hour. Puppies can be mischievous and destructive, but adults are calm, undemanding, and unobtrusive indoors, trotting around with a light-footed, easy grace and seldom making a peep. They do insist on the luxury of being up on the furniture, so if this offends you, you shouldn't consider a sighthound. Polite with strangers, he should be accustomed to people and noises at an early age. He is peaceful with other dogs but has a high prey drive and cannot be trusted with smaller pets. Whippets are only mildly stubborn, but they are very sensitive and respond favorably only to calm, upbeat training methods that emphasize praise and food rewards. Sighthounds are touch-sensitive, tending to startle when touched unexpectedly or grabbed for a hug, so a verbal correction is less upsetting and distracting than a physical one.

HISTORY

Developed in England, the Whippet was bred down from the Greyhound and crossed with terriers. He ran down jackrabbits during the week and raced on weekends. AKC popularity: 64th of 146.

PHYSICAL FEATURES

He stands 18–22 inches and weighs 25–40 pounds. His hard coat needs only an occasional quick brushing. Some breeders offer "Longhaired Whippets," but according to the American Whippet Association, these are not purebred. Colors include brindle, white, white with colored markings, fawn, red, blue, and black, among others. His ears and tail are natural.

HEALTH ISSUES

Both parents should have yearly CERF certificates (eyes). Also ask about sebaceous adenitis, low thyroid, and heart problems in the lines. He is sensitive to anesthetics, vaccines, and chemicals and should never be casually medicated or sedated. He needs a sweater in cold weather, and to avoid pressure sores he requires soft blankets to sleep on. Lifespan: 12–15 years.

CAUTIONS WHEN BUYING

Whippet racing is very different from Greyhound racing—it is a hobby rather than a business. Unlike Greyhound racing, Whippet racing allows no gambling and no training on live prey. The racing Whippets double as pets and companions, returning home with their owner at the end of the afternoon's fun and curling up under the blankets on the bed.

White Shepherd

Best for Experienced Owners
Good with Children
Large in Size
Thick, Medium-Length Coat

EXERCISE REQUIRED — HIGH MEDIUM

TRIMMING/CLIPPING REQUIRED — LOW

AMOUNT OF SHEDDING — HIGH

ACTIVITY INDOORS — MEDIUM

EASE OF TRAINING — HIGH

SOCIABILITY WITH STRANGERS — MEDIUM

TEMPERAMENT

See the profile for German Shepherd Dog. White Shepherds need the same physical and mental exercise, but have been bred with an overall softer, more mellow, more sensitive personality. You seldom see the hard, businesslike, high-drive temperament present in many German Shepherds (especially those from German import lines). Because of this sweeter temperament, timidity is possible, and Whites need a great deal of early socialization to build a confident attitude. They seldom have dominant personalities, but they can be hardheaded, and all large working dogs need a confident, consistent owner who will establish and enforce rules. They can be quite vocal.

HISTORY

White has always occurred naturally in German Shepherds, but was disqualified by the GSD Club of America in the 1960s on the grounds that herding and guardian dogs should be dark to be easily distinguished from the sheep and less easily detected by criminals in the dark. White dogs *can* be registered with the AKC as German Shepherds and shown in AKC performance events (obedience, tracking, agility), but not in conformation classes. UKC allows White Shepherds to be registered as their own breed and to compete in conformation classes with other White Shepherds. The American White Shepherd Association also holds its own events.

PHYSICAL FEATURES

Males stand 24–26 inches and weigh 75–110 pounds. Females stand 22–24 inches and weigh 60–80 pounds. Brush his double coat every day or two to control shedding, which is constant all year and very heavy twice a year. The white color must be accompanied by black pigment: dark eyes and nose (though the nose pigment may fade in the winter, a phenomenon called "snow nose"). Blue-eyed or pink-eyed (albino) dogs are not acceptable. His ears and tail are natural.

HEALTH ISSUES

Parents should have OFA certificates (hips and elbows) and be screened for cardiac problems. Ask about bloat, vWD, seizures, low thyroid, sebaceous adenitis, OCD, panosteitis, and cancer. Skin conditions, autoimmune disorders, and digestive upsets are common. Lifespan: 12 years.

CAUTIONS WHEN BUYING

Be sure you see the hip and elbow clearances. Though some breeders will try to convince you otherwise, guarantees are not a substitute for having the hips and elbows X-rayed and certified before breeding. Avoid so-called "giant" lines—the bone structure of this athletic working dog was never intended to be massive.

Wirehaired Pointing Griffon
(griff-ON)

Fine for Novice Owners
Good with Children If Raised with Children
Medium to Large in Size
Wiry Coat

EXERCISE REQUIRED — HIGH

TRIMMING/CLIPPING REQUIRED — MEDIUM

AMOUNT OF SHEDDING — MEDIUM

ACTIVITY INDOORS — MEDIUM

EASE OF TRAINING — MEDIUM

SOCIABILITY WITH STRANGERS — MEDIUM

TEMPERAMENT

This rugged, athletic hunting dog has an alert expression and a pleasant, gentle disposition. Vigorous daily exercise (jogging, biking, hiking, fieldwork) is high on his list of Things to Do, as is companionship and personal attention. Too much solitary confinement makes him restless and prone to separation anxiety, which he may express by chewing destructively. He is politely aloof with strangers; to avoid his caution shading into timidity, he should be accustomed to people and noises at an early age. If thoroughly socialized with other animals, he is accepting, but some can be cat chasers. Though independent and easily distracted, he is not a dominant dog and is quite responsive to obedience training that includes a calm voice and light hand. He can be hard to housebreak and some bark excessively, especially without enough exercise or mental stimulation. Griffons are not for the fastidious household: They are sloppy drinkers, their beard soaking up water and depositing it as a trail of drips across your floor.

HISTORY

Developed in Holland and France by a Dutchman named Korthals, this dependable (but seldom seen) bird dog is known in Europe as Korthals Griffon. AKC popularity: 122nd of 146.

PHYSICAL FEATURES

Males stand 22–24 inches; females stand 20–22 inches. Weight is 45–60 pounds. Brush his harsh coat once or twice a week. Show dogs are "stripped" (dead coat plucked out) every few months; pet owners may opt for more convenient clipping. Keep his ear canals clean and dry and his bottom trimmed for cleanliness. His color is a patched/flecked combination of chestnut brown, steel gray, and off-white. His ears are natural; his tail is docked.

HEALTH ISSUES

Both parents should have OFA certificates (hips). A yearly CERF certificate (eyes) is also desirable. Lifespan: 12–15 years.

CAUTIONS WHEN BUYING

This breed has long been a well-kept secret among serious hunting dog enthusiasts. Compared to other sporting breeds, his quality has remained high; most individuals display keen field instincts and sound temperament and health.

Xoloitzcuintle (Miniature and Intermediate) (sho-lo-eets-QUEEN-tlee)

Best for Experienced Owners
Good with Older, Considerate Children
Small to Medium in Size
Hairless Coat

EXERCISE REQUIRED — MEDIUM

TRIMMING/CLIPPING REQUIRED — LOW

AMOUNT OF SHEDDING — LOW

ACTIVITY INDOORS — HIGH

EASE OF TRAINING — MEDIUM

SOCIABILITY WITH STRANGERS — MEDIUM
　　　LOW

TEMPERAMENT

This elegant, animated dog moves lightly and gracefully, runs swiftly, and jumps and climbs with agility. His webbed toes are somewhat prehensile, allowing him to grip toys (or your neck!) with dexterity. Tranquil in the home, he is exceptionally attentive to his owner and needs a lot of personal interaction, pining or acting out when left too long without the companionship of people or other pets. Wary of strangers, he makes an alert watchdog, exceedingly aware of his surroundings. Some are high-strung and/or timid of new people and new situations. Early and frequent socialization will help build a confident, stable temperament. Still somewhat primitive in behavior, he often reacts based on instinct, and his reflexes are lightning fast. The Xolo is most content with structure and consistency in his life. Though independent, he is smart and sensitive and responds best to gentle, reward-based obedience training. Harsh discipline only frightens him. Because of his athleticism and ingenuity, your fences should be high and secure. Don't allow too much barking.

HISTORY

In ancient Mexico and Central and South America, he was used as a medicinal bed-warmer and fattened for consumption by the native people. His skin and flesh were believed to have curative powers for physical ills. Considered "the dog of the god Xolotl," he was often sacrificed at Aztec burials so he could guide the human soul to heaven. The name is also spelled with an *i* at the end, rather than *e*. Registered by the FCI, FCM (Federación Canofila Mexicana), UKC, SKC, and AKC-FSS. Registered by CKC as the Mexican Hairless.

PHYSICAL FEATURES

Miniatures stand 10–14 inches and weigh 7–15 pounds. Intermediates stand 14–18 inches and weigh 15–40 pounds. He is hairless, though he often has sparse, bristly hair on the head, neck, tail, and/or feet. There is also a coated (short coat) variety, which cannot be shown in conformation classes in most of the world. Bathe weekly to keep the active sebaceous (oil) glands in his skin clean and open, especially those in the feet. Skin color may be charcoal, slate, red, liver, bronze, or spotted. His ears and tail are natural.

HEALTH ISSUES

Ask about luxating patella in the lines. He is sensitive to drugs (flea powders, anesthetics) and should never be casually medicated or sedated. He doesn't like cold or rainy weather and should wear a sweater in inclement conditions. The lighter colors sunburn easily, which leaves them susceptible to skin cancer. Hairless dogs have missing premolars and tend to lose some of their front teeth by age eight. Lifespan: 15 years.

CAUTIONS WHEN BUYING

The hairless Xolo is an interesting option for those who prefer a nonshedding, flealess animal with exotic beauty.

Xoloitzcuintle (Standard)

(sho-lo-eets-QUEEN-tlee)

Best for Experienced Owners
Good with Older, Considerate Children
Medium to Large in Size
Hairless Coat

EXERCISE REQUIRED — MEDIUM

TRIMMING/CLIPPING REQUIRED — LOW

AMOUNT OF SHEDDING — LOW

ACTIVITY INDOORS — HIGH

EASE OF TRAINING — MEDIUM

SOCIABILITY WITH STRANGERS — MEDIUM
       LOW

TEMPERAMENT

This elegant, animated dog moves lightly and gracefully, runs swiftly, and jumps and climbs with agility. His webbed toes are somewhat prehensile, allowing him to grip toys (or your neck!) with dexterity. Tranquil in the home, he is exceptionally attentive to his owner and needs a lot of personal interaction, pining or acting out when left too long without the companionship of people or other pets. Wary of strangers, he makes an alert watchdog, exceedingly aware of his surroundings. Some are high-strung and/or timid of new people and new situations. Early and frequent socialization will help build a confident, stable temperament. Still somewhat primitive in behavior, he often reacts based on instinct, and his reflexes are lightning fast. The Xolo is most content with structure and consistency in his life and needs to know exactly what is expected of him. Though independent, he is smart and sensitive and responds best to gentle, reward-based obedience training. Harsh discipline only frightens him. Because of his athleticism and ingenuity, your fences should be high and secure. Don't allow too much barking.

HISTORY

In ancient Mexico and Central and South America, he was used as a medicinal bed-warmer and fattened for consumption by the native people. His skin and flesh were believed to have curative powers for physical ills. Considered "the dog of the god Xolotl," he was often sacrificed at Aztec burials so he could guide the human soul to heaven. The name is also spelled with an *i* at the end, rather than *e*. Registered by the FCI, FCM (Federación Canofila Mexicana), UKC, SKC, and AKC-FSS.

PHYSICAL FEATURES

He stands 18–23 inches and weighs 40–80 pounds; some lines and individuals are more elegant and fine-boned, while others are stockier. He is hairless, though he often has sparse bristly hair on the head, neck, tail, and/or feet. There is also a coated (short coat) variety, which cannot be shown in conformation classes in most of the world. Bathe weekly to keep the active sebaceous (oil) glands in his skin clean and open, especially those in the feet. Skin color may be charcoal, slate, red, liver, bronze, or spotted. His ears and tail are natural.

HEALTH ISSUES

Ask about luxating patella in the lines. He is sensitive to drugs (flea powders, anesthetics) and should never be casually medicated or sedated. He doesn't like cold or rainy weather and should wear a sweater in inclement conditions. The lighter colors sunburn easily, which leaves them susceptible to skin cancer. Hairless dogs have missing premolars and tend to lose some of their front teeth by age eight. Lifespan: 15 years.

CAUTIONS WHEN BUYING

The hairless Xolo is an interesting option for those who prefer a nonshedding, flealess animal with exotic beauty.

Yorkshire Terrier

Fine for Novice Owners
Good with Older, Considerate Children
Little in Size
Long Coat

EXERCISE REQUIRED — LOW
TRIMMING/CLIPPING REQUIRED — MEDIUM
    LOW
AMOUNT OF SHEDDING — LOW
ACTIVITY INDOORS — HIGH
EASE OF TRAINING — MEDIUM
SOCIABILITY WITH STRANGERS — MEDIUM

TEMPERAMENT

There are two schools of thought on the Yorkie: (1) he is a vigorous terrier; (2) he is a delicate toy dog made for pampering. The owner's view of him has much to do with how an individual dog turns out. For certain, he is lively and inquisitive, physically and mentally quick, and spends much time trotting (or dashing) around checking things out. Larger dogs may view him as a delicacy, so he must always be leashed or fenced for his own protection; in addition, he can be an excitable chaser of birds and butterflies. A lover of comfort, he enjoys cuddling on laps and snuggling into soft pillows. Keen of eye and sharp of tongue, he won't fail to announce strangers, often in a high-pitched voice. Early socialization is required so that he doesn't become too shrill. Though he can be bossy and scrappy with other dogs, especially larger ones, Yorkies coexist well with other pets, but are overwhelmed by the roughhousing and mischief of small children. Some are bright and quick to learn, while others are willful and opinionated. Yorkies often dislike walking on a leash and may dart to and fro until taught how to behave. Housebreaking is notoriously difficult, especially in bad weather; consider an indoor litter box. Barking must be controlled from day one, and this spunky little fellow can be possessive of his food and toys.

HISTORY

Originally called the Scotch Terrier, he was brought to Yorkshire, England, by Scottish weavers. AKC popularity: 9th of 146 (the second most popular toy breed, behind the Chihuahua).

PHYSICAL FEATURES

He stands 7–8 inches and weighs 3–7 pounds. Larger individuals are common; while not suitable for showing, they make sturdy pets. Smaller individuals are often not sound or healthy. His single, exceptionally shiny, silky coat should be brushed and combed every other day. Pet owners may choose to trim the coat so that it doesn't drag on the ground. Keep his bottom trimmed for cleanliness. He is dark steel blue with rich tan trim. His ears are natural; his tail is docked.

HEALTH ISSUES

Both parents should be screened for luxating patella. Check parents' teeth for soundness—poor teeth run through some lines. Ask about liver shunt and allergies in the lines. He is sensitive to anesthetics, vaccines, and chemicals and should never be casually medicated or sedated. He doesn't like cold or rain and should wear a sweater in inclement conditions. Remember that falling objects and jumping from high places can crush delicate bones. Individuals under four pounds are more susceptible to hypoglycemia (low blood sugar). Lifespan: 12–14 years.

CAUTIONS WHEN BUYING

Yorkies are produced en masse by unknowledgeable breeders; an individual from such lines may be structurally unsound and neurotic. Look for outgoing lines with healthy teeth. Run from breeders who use the made-up term "teacup" or who sell puppies before twelve weeks of age.

STEP THREE

◆ ◆ ◆

Choosing the Right Breeder

◆ 5 ◆

Let's Talk about Responsible Breeders

Purebred puppies are not churned out of a plastic mold. The genetic makeup of the parents and the knowledge and skill of the breeder have a tremendous bearing on how your puppy will turn out. If you spend time and effort choosing the right breed, then buy your puppy from the wrong parents and/or the wrong breeder, you have wasted your time and effort, because one Golden Retriever puppy is most assuredly not the same as another.

Your goal is to find a breeder who knows what a good-quality Golden Retriever is supposed to look like and act like, and who has the knowledge and skill to match the right parents who have the right genes to produce such offspring. This is a responsible breeder.

RESPONSIBLE BREEDERS

• A responsible breeder breeds parents who are purebred and who have valid registration papers.

Wait—aren't purebred and registered the same thing? No, not at all. A dog can be purebred with-out having registration papers. Being purebred simply means that a dog and all of his relatives for a good number of generations have the same set of genes that reproduce with such consistency that the genes can be considered predictable and "fixed." Genes are what they are, and the presence or absence of registration papers has no effect on them.

Registration is a purely mechanical process. The AKC will register any puppy whose parents are already registered. And they registered your puppy's parents because *their* parents were already registered. And they registered *those* parents because . . . you get the idea. Registration is a chain of numbers. If the owners of your puppy's parents and grandparents were all good doobies who kept the chain intact by sending in their own money, the AKC will insert your puppy's name into their database, too. They will send you a piece of paper with a number on it. Voilà—he's registered. Dr. Herm David, Ph.D., says, "The AKC has an infinite supply of numbers. It's a good business to be in."

Registration operates entirely on the honor system. The AKC takes the owner's word for it that

243

King and Queen were really the parents of Solomon. Let's say someone has a nice male and also a horrible male, and the horrible male breeds a female. The breeder can say it was the nice male who bred her and no one will ever be the wiser. AKC papers can be falsified with one stroke of the pen. Fortunately, when the AKC's new DNA verification system is utilized by more breeders, accurate parental recording will be assured.

Even more important to understand is that registration papers are in no way a sign of "quality." The registry organization has not seen *any* of the dogs they register; thus they cannot and do not judge any dog's quality. A registration certificate (or the lack of one) has nothing whatsoever to do with a dog's quality (or lack of it). Quality can only be evaluated by examining the dog himself: his temperament, health, and structure.

But registration papers are a necessary first step in being a responsible breeder, because they provide registration numbers that allow the breeder to assemble a pedigree for the dogs he is considering breeding together.

• A responsible breeder evaluates the pedigree of both parents.

A pedigree is a family tree, a list of ancestors. Theoretically, every dog has a pedigree, because every dog, like every other living creature, came from parents who themselves came from parents, etc. If you were able to track down the names of your mixed breed's parents, grandparents, and so on, your mixed breed would have a pedigree, too.

Realistically, though, we do usually speak of a pedigree as the written family tree of a registered purebred, where all the names belong to other registered purebreds. However, just because the dogs are registered purebreds does not preclude them from being Black Barts. It's the actual dogs behind the names that are important, not the list

of names. The mere existence of a pedigree, like the mere existence of registration papers, says nothing at all about a dog's quality.

It is what a breeder *does* with the pedigree that counts. A responsible breeder uses it for research. He investigates each dog for positive and negative traits in the most important areas of temperament, health, and structure. These traits make up the genetic background of the sire and dam he is considering breeding, so pedigree evaluation before breeding is essential.

• A responsible breeder breeds parents who have undergone veterinary testing for the specific genetic health problems common to that breed.

It may be that the fulfillment of this criteria is what most clearly separates the responsible breeders from the irresponsible. In chapter 4, we discussed how prevalent health problems have become in purebred dogs today. We also discussed genetic health tests, such as having hips and elbows X-rayed, having eyes examined by a board-certified ophthalmologist, having EKGs performed for cardiac screening, having blood tested for thyroid function, and so on. Responsible breeders realize that not all of these tests are perfectly reliable, but they are willing to spend the time and money to have them performed because it is the best they can do with the current state of medical technology.

• A responsible breeder breeds parents with solid temperaments.

In many breeds, good temperament is easy to evaluate: A Labrador Retriever's tail should be waving much of the day. In other breeds, reserve toward strangers and even scrappiness toward other dogs is considered normal, but the breeder must be extra vigilant that this aloofness or feistiness doesn't shade into problematic aggression. So a sound temperament isn't always friendly and outgoing, but every dog of every breed should be able to interact reasonably well with the rest of the world, showing neither inappropriate aggression nor anxiety.

• A responsible breeder breeds parents whose structure and conformation are close to the official standard for that breed.

A breed standard is a written description of a breed, defining what that breed should look like and act like. Some refer to a breed standard as the "blueprint" of a breed. Standards are written by the national parent club of each breed and are used by judges in conformation classes as the written description against which each dog is mentally compared. Standards are also used by breeders and buyers as *the* reference for assessing breed attributes and negatives. A dog who fits the standard for his breed is said to be a good physical representative of his breed. He has most of the desirable characteristics, he does not have too many faults (undesirable characteristics), and he has no disqualifications (extremely undesirable characteristics).

Why are the standards important? The standards were written so breeders would have something concrete to aim at. With no organized guidelines, dogs would be bred willy-nilly, with countless personal prejudices determining how a breed looked and acted. Breeds look and act as they do for good reason. Those from desert climates have short coats; those from cold climates have thick coats. Those who chased prey across open terrain are long-legged and swift, with keen eyesight; those who chased vermin into underground dens are short-legged with a tenacious personality. Each breed was developed for a purpose, and certain characteristics were found to be best for accomplishing that purpose.

Those who love purebred dogs try to preserve them as they were intended to be. Thus, the standards are not about "show dogs"—they exist as quality control to keep one breed sharply distinct from another. A responsible breeder abides by this quality control, and a responsible buyer supports breeders who abide by this quality control.

To read the standard for the breed you're interested in, look for the American Kennel Club's *The Complete Dog Book*, Nineteenth Edition, Revised. Most libraries and bookstores carry it. You can also read the standards on the AKC Web site at www.akc.org. For non-AKC breeds, you can get a copy of the standard from the breed's national club (see the Appendix, National Clubs and Contacts), or on the Internet at www.rarebreed.com or www.ukcdogs.com/breedlist.html.

• A responsible breeder breeds parents whose working instincts are sound.

If the breed was intended to be a herding dog, hunting dog, or guardian, a responsible breeder makes sure such instincts are in evidence. Again, this goes back to the breed standard and the purpose behind breeding purebreds: to preserve each breed as it was intended to be.

• A responsible breeder is involved in canine activities such as obedience, agility, dog shows, fieldwork, kennel club membership, rescue organizations and animal shelters, and so forth.

Responsible breeders don't just churn out puppies. They are actively involved in the dog world, often showing their dogs in conformation and performance events to evaluate and prove structure, temperament, and working ability. Responsible breeders are proud of the titles their dogs have attained.

• A responsible breeder breeds selectively, only a few litters per year, and only one or two breeds.

• A responsible breeder interviews you.

Good breeders ask probing questions of prospective buyers to ascertain their ability to properly care for a puppy. Don't be put off by these questions. From the breeder's perspective, you're not buying a piece of merchandise but a little living creature whose future happiness rests on the breeder's ability to place him in the right home.

• A responsible breeder helps you select the puppy best suited to your family and lifestyle.

Responsible breeders take great pride in their knowledge of their breed, of their particular line, and of their puppies. They have been observing the litter since it was born and they may have formed their own opinion as to exactly what type of home and owner each puppy would be best suited to.

• A responsible breeder will provide the names and numbers of other responsible breeders (not just satisfied puppy buyers) as references.

• A responsible breeder sells all pets with limited (nonbreeding) registration papers, often accompanied by a neutering contract.

A "pet" puppy is one who has been produced by a responsible breeder, who has the temperament and health to be a great companion, but who deviates from the standard in some way that would prevent him from winning in the show ring or being used for breeding. Typically these deviations are in areas such as size, color, coat, head shape, curvature of the rear legs, positioning of the teeth, movement, and so on. The breeder doesn't want this puppy bred, so he issues limited registration papers. Limited registration means that any offspring of the puppy cannot be registered. Some breeders go a step further by including a neutering contract. Breeders who use limited registration and neutering contracts have the breed's best interests at heart.

You may be wondering about these "pet" puppies. It may seem as though I'm now encouraging you to accept puppies with faults and disqualifications when previously I stressed the importance of adhering to the standard. Actually what I've

stressed is that the *parents* must adhere to the standard. In other words, you're looking for a breeder who breeds only the best dogs possible so that the genetic background of your puppy has the most solid foundation possible. That doesn't mean every puppy will turn out perfect. Since invisible gene combinations can't be predicted with complete certainty, sometimes a breeder can conscientiously do everything right and the imprecise science of genetics simply does something unexpected.

So responsible breeders do produce pups with physical faults and disqualifications. And these matter not a whit, because they're not the result of breeder ignorance or irresponsibility. Thus, it is not really faults or disqualifications that are a threat to any puppy's potential as a good pet, but only the fact that they can be indicative of ignorance or carelessness that could well have slopped over into the more important areas of temperament and health. In other words, when a breeder deliberately breeds nonstandard dogs, or doesn't care that he's breeding nonstandard dogs, or doesn't even *know* that he's breeding nonstandard dogs, watch out. But if the breeder is aiming for the best and the parents are good and the lines are good, then an individual puppy who doesn't meet the standard is just fine. See the difference?

Always remember that your decision to buy from a particular person will affect other owners. Whoever you buy from will most likely breed again if he gets enough buyers this time around. It's wonderful to *adopt* a dog without any regard for where he came from or what his background is, but if you *buy* one, you may be rewarding and encouraging irresponsible people to keep right on doing what they're doing. Please try to buy only from someone who has done all the right things, someone who deserves to be rewarded and encouraged.

❖ 6 ❖

Let's Talk about Irresponsible Breeders

Now for the flip side. The majority of prospective pet owners buy their purebred puppy from an irresponsible breeder. Since they are the source of most of the health and temperament problems that have befallen the world of purebred dogs, you must learn how to recognize and avoid them. They don't wear signs around their necks identifying them as such, but there are plenty of clues that should enable you to spot them.

IRRESPONSIBLE BREEDERS

• An irresponsible breeder usually believes that *AKC registered* equals *breeding quality*.

This is their primary (and sometimes only) selling point: "Our dogs have AKC papers." Every year breeders produce thousands of AKC registered litters, the majority of them very poor quality. As you now know, registration papers mean only that the puppy's ancestors were also the same breed, even if they looked terrible, acted worse,

and/or were crippled by health problems. Registration papers don't suggest quality in dogs any more than they suggest quality in cars. (In fact, registration papers may suggest quality in cars *more* than they suggest quality in dogs, because in most states a car can be registered only if it has passed a smog check or mechanical safety check. The AKC registers dogs blindly, with no health or safety checks at all.)

• An irresponsible breeder may breed parents with no registration papers.

Though you know now that registration papers say nothing about a dog's breeding quality, the lack of them speaks volumes about the breeder. No registration papers means the breeder couldn't even be bothered with this simple step. Even with registration papers, parentage fraud can be committed, but it does carry repercussions from the registry if discovered. Without papers, lying is child's play.

• An irresponsible breeder may not know how to use a pedigree.

Without pedigree research, a breeder has no idea whether health or temperament problems are lurking in his puppies' genes. To an unknowledgeable breeder, the pedigree is just a list of names, rather than the embodiment of characteristics and genes that it represents to a knowledgeable breeder. How can a person possibly predict health, temperament, and sound structure in his puppies if he doesn't know anything about their background? Don't you agree that people buying pets have just as much right to a sound, healthy puppy as those buying show dogs?

• An irresponsible breeder breeds parents who have not undergone veterinary testing for the specific genetic health problems common to that breed.

This failure, in and of itself, should be enough to send you scooting out the door. In this day and age of rampant health problems, it is unconscionable for breeders not to test their dogs and, even worse, to dismiss the importance of testing and/or ridicule those breeders who do it.

• An irresponsible breeder may breed parents with unsound temperaments.

They may dismiss your concerns about a dog's seeming aggression or anxiety with excuses: "All mothers are like this when strangers come near their puppies" or "He was abused when he was young, so he doesn't trust men." In truth, you have no idea if a dubious temperament is environmental or genetic, and you should never take the chance.

• An irresponsible breeder breeds parents without regard for their structure or conformation according to the breed standard.

"We're not trying to produce show dogs, just pets" is the usual rationale. Because it sounds so reasonable, it's easy to fall into the trap of believing that two pet-quality dogs bred together make pet-quality puppies.

No. True pet-quality puppies are those whose parents were *breeding quality*, which means sound pedigree, sound health (proven by veterinary testing), sound temperament (often proven by success in performance events and temperament testing programs), and reasonable conformance to the breed standard (often proven by success in conformation shows). From these parents may come a couple of puppies who match the standard so closely they will be suitable for showing or breeding themselves. *The remaining puppies from this litter are your true pet-quality puppies.*

• An irresponsible breeder breeds parents without any consideration for working instincts.

When breeders choose a breed to become involved with, they have a responsibility to preserve *all* of that breed, including working instincts. A Cocker Spaniel with no field instincts is not a true Cocker. Oh, he may have the shape, coat, and color of a Cocker, but he is lacking the mind, heart, and instincts and should not have his genes perpetuated.

• An irresponsible breeder is seldom involved in other canine activities.

Irresponsible breeders tend not to socialize with the responsible breeders who make up the majority of participants at canine events.

• An irresponsible breeder may use incorrect terminology.

Unknowledgeable breeders often refer to purebred dogs as "full-blooded" or "thoroughbred." They may use "pedigree" as an adjective: "My dogs are pedigreed." They may refer to yellow Labs as "golden Labs." They may use made-up terms: "teacup" Poodle or "imperial" Shih Tzu. Rather than Shetland Sheepdog or Sheltie, they may say "toy collie" or "miniature collie." There is no excuse for such ignorance about one's own breed when one is being entrusted to manipulate the genes for that breed.

• An irresponsible breeder tends to ask few questions and offers little guidance in puppy selection.

He may not be able to offer much in the way of information about each puppy because he has paid them so little attention as they were growing up. "They're all cute and healthy" is his opinion. He is trying to make a sale, and he will encourage you to take your pick, even to take more than one. Such a breeder doesn't know or care whether you have toddlers or other pets, whether you work long hours, or how you're planning to raise and train the puppy. If you can pay for a puppy, that's good enough for him.

• An irresponsible breeder can't provide the names of responsible breeders as references.

Typically they'll offer the names of satisfied puppy buyers you can contact, but no breeders who belong to kennel clubs or who show and compete with their dogs. Satisfied puppy buyers aren't much help because most of them did far less research than you're doing. They bought their puppy because it was cute and because the breeder seemed nice. They know virtually nothing about the quality of the dog they bought or the skill or experience of the breeder.

• An irresponsible breeder may sell pets with full registration papers and no neutering contract.

Their cavalier attitude is "You can breed or not breed, whatever you want." But in a world where animal shelters are overflowing with unwanted pets, it is every breeder's responsibility to ensure that only his very best puppies are allowed full registration privileges so that they might pass on their excellent genes. All the rest should be neutered.

• An irresponsible breeder may breed extensively and advertise widely.

A red flag should go up whenever a breeder assures you that he always has puppies available. Generally, responsible breeders produce no more than three litters a year and maintain waiting lists for those. Advertising would only bring them a flock of inquiries that they can't satisfy. It's the larger-scale breeders churning out puppies who are bringing in enough money to run big ads, and one must question how they find enough time for socialization, testing temperaments, getting to know the puppies, and competing in shows and performance events. Smaller-scale breeders tend to devote more time and attention to each puppy.

The Truth about Pet Shops

• Finally, an irresponsible breeder may be willing to place his puppies in a pet shop or somewhere else for resale or consignment.

Every pet shop that sells puppies will assure you, solemnly, that their puppies are different. Their puppies don't come from puppy mills, but from fine local breeders. Pillars of the community, in fact.

The reality is that responsible breeders would never place one of their precious puppies in a pet shop or anywhere else for resale or consignment. Never, ever, ever. This cannot be emphasized enough. Most breed clubs include this pledge in their code of ethics: "I will never sell a puppy to wholesalers or pet stores." In so doing, a good breeder would no longer be able to use his knowledge and experience to screen homes and match suitable puppies with suitable owners. As commercial establishments, pet shops are required by law to sell a puppy to anyone who can pay. Responsible breeders wouldn't be able to sleep at night wondering which of their puppies might have gone to an unsuitable home and was not being properly cared for.

Pet shop puppies *always* come from irresponsible breeders who have not tested either parent for genetic disorders and who have not had either parent evaluated to make sure they fit the breed standard. Most pet shop puppies barely resemble their breed, and dedicated breeders cringe whenever they see a representative in a pet store window.

Pet shops won't admit any of this, of course. Their marketing ploys include:

• "We buy only from local breeders!"

As though being local makes the breeder any more responsible or knowledgeable. Why should irresponsible breeders live only in other states? Whether the breeder is local or lives in Timbuktu, whether he has produced only one litter or many, if he has placed his puppies in a pet shop, his breeding practices are irresponsible. I guarantee that if you get any of these breeders' phone numbers from the pet store and call them with the interview questions recommended in chapter 9, they will fail.

• "We buy only from USDA-licensed breeders."

USDA stands for the United States Department of Agriculture. They specialize in livestock, not pets. As long as breeding records are in order, the facilities are clean and disinfected, cages are a minimum size, and no infectious diseases such as distemper are immediately obvious, the kennel passes. The USDA has not the slightest interest in whether the breeder knows anything about his breed or in whether the adult dogs and puppies look like their breed, act like their breed, or are free of inherited health problems such as hip dysplasia or cardiac defects. "USDA Breeder" is a label to beware of. The only reason someone would apply for this license is to crank out lots of puppies. Such breeders always cut corners by not evaluating parents for correct structure and con-

formation and not testing parents for genetic health problems.

• "Health guaranteed!"

This is how pet shops and irresponsible breeders seek to get around the expenses of genetic testing. They offer to replace defective puppies rather than trying to avoid them in the first place. But guarantees offer little solace to the puppy who is born with or develops a genetic health problem that could have been avoided if his breeder had been seeking to produce healthy lives rather than seeking to keep his expenses down so as to make as much profit as possible. Pet shops know, in any case, that they won't have to honor many guarantees because most people won't return a puppy they've had for six months or a year or two years, which is when most genetic health problems show up. Guarantees *after* breeding are never a substitute for genetic testing *before* breeding.

As though poor conformation and poor health weren't enough, obedience instructors will attest to the disproportionate number of behavioral problems that develop in pet shop puppies as they grow. Whisked away from mother and littermates at six weeks of age, the pet shop puppy hasn't had enough time to absorb the concepts of authority and respect that are best taught by the sharp teeth of his mother and siblings. Pet shop puppies can be nippy, and raised in a small cage in which they're encouraged to eliminate freely, they are notoriously difficult to housebreak.

You may feel compelled to "rescue" a pet shop puppy. That's understandable: Everyone feels sorry for them. But your good intentions will backfire, because you are feeding the industry by rewarding it with money. You've emptied one cage, which creates demand for yet another litter to be produced to fill it. Even if your puppy turns out okay, a large percentage of the others will not, and your purchase contributes to

◆ The misery of the females who spend their lives in a cage, being bred again and again
◆ The misery of the future puppies born with health and temperament problems
◆ The misery of future families trying to cope with those health and temperament problems
◆ The misery of animal rescue groups as they have to deal with the myriad pet shop puppies dumped on their doorstep because the families gave up on the health and temperament problems

I hope it's clear that when you buy one of those cute puppies in the pet shop window, you buy more than the puppy. You buy the budding physical and behavioral problems created by poor early care and by the poor genes passed on by untested parents whom you never get to see and evaluate. A pet shop should not be anyone's choice as a source for a puppy.

The Myth of the Private Seller

Some people will tell you they got their dog from a "private seller," rather than a "professional breeder." They believe that if they buy from someone who simply had one litter and placed an ad in the paper, they're not buying from a breeder. Or if they buy from a neighbor or colleague who says, "Our Molly recently had pups. Would you like one?" they're not buying from a breeder. It is one of the biggest misconceptions of prospective

buyers that an individual is not a breeder because he owns only two dogs who produced a single litter, or because he doesn't take his dogs to dog shows, or because he doesn't have a sign in front of his house that says "Forestview Kennels."

Uh-uh.

A breeder is any person who owns a female who has a litter. One litter is all it takes. Any person with a single litter is the breeder of that litter. To be considered responsible, he must have taken exactly the same steps in evaluating and testing health, temperament, conformation and structure, and pedigree lines as "Forestview Kennels" does. Every dog was bred by someone. The question is, did that person do so responsibly, or irresponsibly?

Meeting any one of the criteria in this chapter makes a breeder unknowledgeable enough that he should not be breeding. He may be a nice person. He may love his dogs. Most people who breed animals are friendly and mean well—they're not out to cheat you or to make money. They simply don't know or don't care what they're doing. Their dogs may be purebred and registered, but their failure to spend the time, money, and effort to prove those dogs worthy of contributing to the gene pool, and to insure the genetic health and soundness of the resulting offspring, to save future puppy owners from heartache and excessive expenses, makes them irresponsible.

Whether done out of ignorance or with deliberate intent makes little difference in the result. Their puppies are not ones you want to take a chance on, and their efforts, however well-meaning, are not ones you want to reward.

◆ 7 ◆

Adopting from Animal Shelters and Rescue Organizations

I've raised puppies on many occasions—forget it! Give me the settled, laid-back, all-together, well-mannered, grateful, devoted, loving adult who knows what life is all about, who respects my authority, defends my property instead of chewing it to pieces, is grateful for everything I do, and gives so much in return. He may not be around as long as a young one. No matter. The quality of love he gives makes each day a special blessing. While the young dogs are running the fence, barking, digging, chewing, playing, ignoring my call for silence, the older dogs stand quietly at my side, content just to be with me. Oh yes, I'll miss them when God decides he needs them more than I do, but the memories and the lessons in love and devotion they are teaching me will live forever.

—AUTHOR UNKNOWN

Their signs plead, "Please save a life—adopt one of our dogs!"

Every evening, you drive by the Humane Society on your way home from work. Might there be any Miniature Schnauzers there? It's possible. Many purebreds end up at the animal shelter, and a popular breed may have a representative there, especially at a large city shelter. There are a hundred reasons why any dog, purebred or mixed, may have been dropped off at the animal shelter: "Our landlord says we can't keep him." "We're moving to Georgia and he doesn't like hot weather." "We have a new baby." "He's not housebroken . . . he chews . . . he barks . . . he digs . . ."

In other words, the owners couldn't or wouldn't keep their dogs any longer. Should you adopt one of them? An important consideration for some prospective buyers is money. Shelter dogs cost $25 to $75, a far cry from $300 to $600.

But what kind of dog will you be getting for fifty bucks? Maybe the worst dog in the world. Maybe the best dog in the world. The biggest disadvantage of Humane Societies is the unpredictability of what you'll find inside. If you do decide to go in, you'll have an advantage over the person who is impulsively "looking for a dog for the kids." That person will be faced with a bewildering number of decisions, and the barking bedlam of the animal shelter is not the best place to make wise decisions.

You're different. You've already made some decisions. You know you want a purebred and you know what breed(s) you're interested in. In Step Four of this book you'll learn how to evaluate a dog's temperament, health, and general structure, and then you'll be ready to apply your knowledge to the dogs at the Humane Society. You'll be able to choose the best one for you.

But you must go in with your eyes open, not just your heart. You don't know the background of these dogs, so you're taking a gamble, especially in the important area of health, and especially with those breeds who are most susceptible to devastating disorders such as hip and elbow dysplasia, eye diseases, heart abnormalities, and seizures/epilepsy. You should consider the potential heartbreak of dearly loving a dog who may soon become stricken with something serious.

On the other hand, much of life is risky, and the satisfaction and joy that come from giving such a dog a loving home for a few years may be worth it to you. I have adopted both purebred and mixed-breed dogs from our overcrowded humane societies. And I have bought from responsible breeders as well. Good dogs are everywhere, if you only know how to recognize them. So if the option still interests you, call the shelters of nearby large cities and ask them to notify you if a member of the breed you're looking for comes in.

And while you're on the phone, ask them if there is a breed rescue league in your area.

Suppose you're flipping through a magazine and you see a photograph of a pathetic-looking Irish Setter. The ad says, "The Irish Setter Rescue League is looking for good homes for abused and neglected Setters. Please call for an application." Should you call?

If you're looking for an adolescent or adult dog, and if you have a deep desire to make a difference in the life of a particularly needy dog, do call. Be prepared to answer as many questions as if you were trying to adopt a child. Rescue organizations don't want to save a dog from one bad home simply to place him in another, so they'll consider you very carefully before handing over a dog. Most rescue leagues scrupulously examine their dogs for temperament problems; they put aggressive dogs to sleep. Thus the dogs that these organizations offer for adoption are often among the gentlest, kindest representatives to be found anywhere. It is both astounding and shaming that many dogs will accept years of neglect or abuse without ever losing their kindly dispositions or their faith in mankind.

It's true that some rescue dogs are timid, distrustful, and in need of careful handling by people who know something about dogs. It's true that some of them have behavior problems that will need to be worked on. But many of them have absolutely no behavior problems and are sweet, trusting creatures.

Only you know if the idea of taking a hunted, haunted dog and turning his life around appeals to you. If it does, give the rescue organizations a call. In the Appendix, you'll find rescue contacts listed for most breeds.

◆ 8 ◆

Finding Breeders

Begin assembling a breeders' folder. If your breed is popular, you won't have to check every source listed here, but if it's uncommon, you may have to.

SOURCES FOR BREEDERS

National Clubs

Turn to the Appendix for the name and phone number of the national club for your breed. Call them and request phone numbers and/or E-mail addresses for breeders in your area. Some clubs will respond to your request by sending a list of breeders with mailing addresses only. This outdated practice requires that you write letters to each breeder, enclose a business-size SASE (self-addressed stamped envelope), then wait. And perhaps wait. And perhaps wait some more. Some breeders will respond within a few weeks, while others may take several mont\hs. Some may not respond at all.

If the club contact information in the Appendix includes a Web site, visit it and look for a directory of breeders. Print out the page and add it to your folder.

The biggest advantage of buying from a breeder who belongs to a national or regional club is that such clubs usually maintain codes of ethics that members must sign. Some of these codes are vague and ineffectual, while others have some teeth to them. Of course, it's possible for breeders to sign the code of ethics, then do as they please (at least until they're caught), but most breeders do comply. Club membership also means that a breeder has access to other responsible fanciers and their fine dogs.

Dog Magazines

If your breed is an AKC breed, call the American Kennel Club at 919-233-9767 and order a sample copy of their official publication, the *American Kennel Club Gazette*. Or call the largest library in your area and ask if they carry this magazine or if they can request a recent copy through the interlibrary loan program. If your breed is a UKC breed, call the United Kennel Club at 616-343-9020 and order a sample copy of *Bloodlines*. In either magazine, if you find any advertisements for your breed, photocopy or tear out the page and add it to your folder.

On many newsstands, you'll find *Dog World* and *Dog Fancy*. These monthly magazines include display and classified ads for most breeds, including many rare breeds. Unfortunately, a sizable number of ads (especially of guardian breeds and toy breeds) belong to irresponsible breeders. Add the pages to your folder, but be especially careful when contacting these breeders.

World Wide Web

If you have access to the Web, either at home or at your local library, you will find a plethora of breeders and breed clubs. You'll find the AKC clubs at www.akc.org. Some have their own home pages (go to a search engine such as www.yahoo.com and type in your breed's name: "Labrador Retriever"), while some are listed in all-breed directories (type in "dog breeders"). Do keep in mind that a sleek, impressive-looking Web site doesn't necessarily equal a responsible breeder, so exercise due caution when contacting them.

Local Veterinarians, Trainers, Groomers, and Pet Supply Stores

You would think that these sources would yield terrific results, but unfortunately, many vets seem to believe that a responsible breeder is one who faithfully utilizes the vet's services and has good-tempered dogs who don't put up a struggle in the office. I've heard too many people explain that they bred their pet store puppy with the blessings of their vet. So a vet may be able to steer you toward local breeders, but it will be up to you to interview them carefully and decide whether they are truly responsible or not. On the plus side, a vet may be able to assure you that a certain breeder is conscientious about genetic health testing, which

is valuable information. Vets may also know the contact numbers of local all-breed clubs, some of whose members may breed the type of dog you're interested in.

Likewise, local obedience trainers and pet supply stores may know breeders or breed clubs you can contact. Groomers are especially likely to know breeders of Poodles, Schnauzers, and other wiry-coated, curly-coated, or long-coated breeds. Whether these breeders are responsible or not is up to you to determine.

Newspaper Ads

The vast majority of these ads (at least nine of every ten) belong to irresponsible breeders. Virtually none of them can pass the interview questions in chapter 9. But you can certainly get lucky and find a good one, so if you wish, visit your library and photocopy the pet classifieds from local newspapers within driving distance.

Dog Shows

Want to find hundreds of breeders in one place? Go to a dog show! This is especially useful if you're still wavering between breeds.

First you have to find a show in your area. Look for a list of upcoming AKC/UKC shows in *Dog World* and *Dog Fancy*, or on the AKC Web site at www.akc.org. If yours is a rare breed, request a list of upcoming shows from your breed's national club.

For AKC shows, unless you can call a local exhibitor who knows the exact time your breed is being judged, try to arrive by 8:30 A.M. Locate the booth selling show catalogs. In the front of the catalog, you'll find an index of breeds and a judging schedule. Look up your breed and you'll see listed the number of representatives at the show, ring numbers, and judging times. Also head over to the obedience rings and see if your breed is competing in obedience.

Use your day at the dog show to observe the breeds up close, to chat with breeders and owners, and perhaps to get a few phone numbers. The names and addresses of all exhibitors are included in the catalog, so keep it for future reference, as you may be able to get phone numbers from Directory Assistance. Most breeders won't pressure you into buying a dog (just the opposite, in fact—most will be very cautious and noncommittal until they get to know and trust you), but just in case, don't get carried away by a breeder's glowing descriptions of his dogs or his breed. Don't let any breeder talk you into a breed that you know from your research is not right for you. Be affable, but a hard sell. You're not ready to buy your puppy just yet.

TERMS TO KNOW

As you're collecting your list of breeders from various sources, you'll be reading through display ads and classified ads. You'll start coming across terms you don't understand, so let's interpret some of that unfamiliar jargon.

You may notice *titles*:

Conformation Titles

By Ch. Ravenwood Lad x Ch. McKenna's Sassy Frassy. These are the parents of the litter. The sire's name comes first, after the word *by*, and the dam's name comes after the *x* or *ex* (which is pronounced "out of," as in "out of her body"). So the sire is Lad, from Ravenwood Kennels, and the dam is Sassy Frassy, from McKenna Kennels or owned or bred by the McKennas.

Ch. means that both dogs have won their AKC conformation championships: At several different dog shows, several judges felt that Lad and Sassy

Frassy fit the standard for their breed more closely than the other dogs present in the show ring on those days.

Dog shows were originally created to find the best dogs for breeding. Unfortunately, there are some "fleas" in the soup:

• Judging is subjective and can be political. Different judges feel that different body parts are more (or less) important than others. One may favor a perfect head, even though other traits may be lacking. Another may place a dog with an outstanding gait and poor head higher than those with good heads but faulty gait. You'll waste time and money entering under a judge who simply doesn't like your dog's "type" or color or astrological sign. Judges don't even agree on exactly what a perfect head and outstanding gait look like, because the wording of the standard is open to interpretation. So a win or loss on a particular day is just one judge's opinion. You can place first in your class on Saturday and last on Sunday—against the same competition, but under a different judge. And unfortunately, some judges award placings based on who is doing the handling, rather than on how good the dog actually is.

• The worth of a ribbon depends on the quality of the competition. Since show dogs are ranked according to the others in the class, if all the entrants that day were duds, the judge would simply be awarding first place to the best of a bum lot. An occasional dog accumulates most of his championship points in this fashion, winning what is termed "a cheap championship."

• Temperament isn't considered much. Though most show dogs do have excellent temperaments, it does happen that skittish dogs are sometimes handed ribbons and championship points by judges who are more interested in structure than behavior. Many judges look for showmanship ("He was up on his toes, asking for the win") rather than true breed temperament. And dogs with faulty temperaments can be conditioned to perform acceptably for the few minutes required in the ring.

• Genetic health isn't considered at all. Dogs do not need to be cleared of genetic health problems in order to win ribbons and championships.

So you must keep Ch. titles in perspective. Conformation classes are beauty contests that say little or nothing about a dog's intelligence, companionability, or health. But for the most part, Ch. titles are a pretty good indication that the dog fits the breed standard and an even better indication that the breeder is doing something with his dogs other than breeding them. Note that you may see multiple Ch. titles in front of a dog's name, because he may obtain championships in more than one country. *Am/Can/Ber Ch. Sterling's Cosmic Ray* has done so in America, Canada, and Bermuda.

Obedience/Tracking Titles

OTCh. Aleesha of Pinecrest UD TDX. A CD (Companion Dog) means the dog obeys basic commands, on- and off-leash. CDX (Companion Dog Excellent) means that he also retrieves and jumps hurdles. A UD (Utility Dog) means that he also obeys hand signals and locates objects by scent. These three titles are consecutive, and a dog must earn them in order. An OTCh. (Obedience Trial Champion) means that after attaining his UD title, he has gone on to capture first or second place in many more competitions. A TD (Tracking Dog), TDX (Tracking Dog Excellent), VST (Variable Surface Tracking), or CT (Champion Tracker) means that he has demonstrated his ability to follow human scent.

Some dogs have earned Canadian obedience titles, which look like this: *Aladdin's Jaded Waters Can CD.* Some have titles awarded by the United Kennel Club (UKC), which go in front of the dog's name: *U-CDX Aladdin's Jaded Waters.*

Temperament Titles

Brite Star's Maggie CGC, TT, TDI. These titles (Canine Good Citizen, Temperament Tested, and Therapy Dogs International) are awarded to dogs who have demonstrated basic obedience and normal reactions to strangers, odd sights, and sudden sounds. Every dog used for breeding should really obtain at least one of them, especially in the larger breeds.

Agility Titles

Sunnyhill's Ringleader NA. The sport of agility is played out over an obstacle course of hurdles, tunnels, hoops, and catwalks. Each dog must run around the course, off-leash, climbing on, over, and under the obstacles. Several organizations offer agility titles. The AKC awards NA (Novice Agility), OA (Open Agility), AX (Agility Excellent), and MX (Master Agility Excellent). The United States Dog Agility Association awards AD (Agility Dog), AAD (Advanced Agility Dog), MAD (Master Agility Dog), and many others.

Herding Titles

Stonehaven's Heather HIC. Herding events test a dog's ability to gather or drive sheep, cattle, or ducks. Several organizations grant herding titles, including HIC (Herding Instinct Certificate), HC (Herding Certificate), HT (Herding Tested), HS (Herding Started), HCT (Herding Capable Tested), HTD (Herding Trial Dog), STD (Started Trial Dog), and many others.

Field Titles

AFC Knollwood's Fleecy Jason MH. In field and hunting tests, a sporting dog (spaniel, setter, pointer, or retriever) must locate hiding birds and/ or retrieve birds that the hunter has shot. Jason is an Amateur Field Champion. NFC would be a National Field Champion. A Dual Ch. has won titles in both field and conformation. Titles that go *after* the dog's name include JH (Junior Hunter), SH (Senior Hunter), MH (Master Hunter), WC (Working Certificate), and WCX (Working Certificate Excellent), among others.

Schutzhund Titles

VA Canto vom Schonau SchH III AD FH. Canto has probably been imported from Germany. The Germans rate the quality of their dogs' conformation and structure by letters: VA is Excellent Select, while V is Excellent, a shade lower. AD is a physical endurance test and FH is a tracking test. The most common German title you'll see is SchH (Schutzhund) and then the Roman numeral I, II, or III, indicating the level of proficiency at this rigorous sport that combines protection work, obedience, and tracking, the highest proficiency being III. Schutzhund trials and titles are also given in the United States.

Earthdog Titles

Frydon's Here Comes Trouble CG. Terrier trials test a dog's instinct to "go to ground" in pursuit of vermin, which is safely confined in a cage at the end of an underground tunnel. Titles include JE (Junior Earthdog), ME (Master Earthdog), SE (Senior Earthdog), and CG (Certificate of Gameness).

Lure Coursing Titles

Colwyn's Turbo Diesel LCM. Sighthounds were bred to run down their prey across open terrain.

In the sport of lure coursing, sighthounds race against one another in pursuit of a lure dragged rapidly along the ground by a pulley system. Coursing titles are awarded by several organizations and include F.Ch. (Field Champion), LCM (Lure Courser of Merit), JC (Junior Courser), SC (Senior Courser), and others.

Breed Club Titles

Some national breed clubs award their own titles to members of their breed who have demonstrated working instincts such as carting, drafting, and water rescue. Finally, ROM (Register of Merit) is awarded to sires and dams who have produced several champion and award-winning offspring.

Grades of Puppies

Show quality: Show-quality puppies are those who, at a still-tender age, show promise of developing all of the characteristics called for in the AKC Standard, even ones that don't seem that important—for instance, feet shaped exactly so.

Predictions of show quality are risky because the puppy still has to grow up. The younger he is when the show-quality label is hung on him, the more time he has to develop faults that will hamper his chances in the ring. People who are looking seriously for a show winner should buy a puppy at least six months old. An older show prospect will cost more, of course, because the breeder has spent time and money raising him and now feels more certain about the dog's winning potential.

Breeders are reluctant to sell show prospects to novices because novices have a reputation for changing their minds about showing. Such a reversal is disappointing to the breeder. Some breeders will sell show prospects only on co-ownership, where both you and the breeder legally own the dog. This gives the breeder some control over the dog's show and breeding career and gives him the right to use the dog (if male) at stud. Co-ownerships are complicated contractual relationships and are not recommended.

Working quality: Some breeders prefer to sell their puppies to people who will work them in obedience competition, hunting, herding, Schutzhund, and other performance activities, as opposed to conformation shows. Most working breeders have their breeds' best interests at heart because they're trying to ensure that the breed retains its instincts. But just as some show breeders have disdain for working ability, some working-dog breeders have disdain for the breed standard. Neglecting to preserve a breed's unique appearance can affect and alter the breed in the same way as neglecting to preserve a breed's working instincts. It's that combination of appearance, temperament, and working instinct that makes each breed unique.

Pet/Companion quality: As we discussed in chapter 5, pet puppies fail to meet the standard in some way that would hamper their chances for success in the show ring: ears too small or too large, head too narrow or too wide, too many patches of color, and so on.

Here you may be tempted to say, "Aha! Finally, we've come to the grade of puppy for me. All this talk about show dogs and working dogs has been interesting, but I only want a pet."

No, you don't—you want a *quality* pet. I'm sure that by now you can recite what quality means: good temperament, sound genetic health, and a decent physical representative of the breed. Don't accept less just because a breeder is calling it "a pet puppy." Don't let a breeder show you a puppy whose parents are shy or nasty, who don't have all

of their health clearances, and/or who don't meet the standard for their breed. Such a puppy is simply a poorly bred puppy, not a pet/companion puppy.

Other Terms

Whelped 11/12: Born on November 12.

Imported stock: The breeder has imported his dogs, usually from the breed's country of origin. This claim is only as good or bad as the individual quality of each dog, but usually the breeder hasn't gone to all that trouble and expense to import dogs of dreadful quality.

Pointed stock: The breeder's dogs have attained some points toward their show championships. Points are accumulated by being judged better than other dogs present in the show ring that day. Fifteen points makes a champion.

Reservations being accepted for spring litter: Many breeders take reservations before they undertake a breeding. Some of the breeders you will soon be speaking to may have a current litter, but the puppies are already spoken for. For a future litter you'll have to put down a deposit, typically ranging from $100 to half the purchase price. The breeder will assign you first (or second or third) overall pick, or if you know what sex you want, first (or second or third) pick male (or female). Some breeders don't allow buyers to choose and will choose the puppy for you, based on their own knowledge and experience.

Home-raised and/or home-socialized: Puppies raised indoors grow accustomed to the sights and sounds of a normal home, which is a distinct advantage when the puppy goes to a new home. "Socialized" puppies have been carefully introduced to all sorts of people, sights, sounds, and situations, so that the puppy has learned to accept new things with calmness and confidence.

I once visited a home where four German Shepherd puppies sat behind a baby's tension gate off the living room. When a toy-laden toddler rushed into the room and tripped, toys crashed with a huge clatter. All four puppies simply perked their ears with interest and wagged their tails at the strewn toys, the bawling toddler, and the consoling mother. I chose Luke, my dear companion and enthusiastic obedience/Schutzhund competitor, from this home-raised and home-socialized litter.

Temperament-tested: This isn't the same as the TT (Temperament Tested) title I discussed earlier. When spelled out and referring to pups rather than adults, temperament testing means the breeder has performed a series of personality tests on each puppy to determine the type of family it would best fit into. Breeders who take the time to test temperaments care very much about their puppies' futures. You'll soon be learning how to do your own temperament testing.

Hips X-rayed, eyes cleared, OFA, CERF: If your breed is prone to genetic disorders like hip dysplasia or PRA/cataracts, look for these health assurances in the ad.

Guaranteed for hips, eyes, and/or temperament: We'll discuss later the specifics of good guarantees, but any offer of a guarantee is nice to see in an ad. However, a guarantee is not a substitute for pre-breeding tests.

Now, let's combine this terminology into three sample ads. What would a good ad say?

"Labrador pups for show, field, obedience, or pet, whelped 6/6. By Ch. Powderhorn Tamarack JH ex. Glenmoor's Emily CD (pointed). Both parents OFA and CERF. Home-raised, socialized, temperament-tested. Guaranteed."

This ad says all the right things. The breeder is interested in all aspects of the Labrador—the sire has a conformation championship and a Junior Hunter certificate for working ability, and the dam has an obedience title and some conformation points. Both have been checked for hip dysplasia (you'll need to inquire about elbow dysplasia, which is also a potential problem in Labs) and eye diseases. The puppies have been socialized so they'll be comfortable in a home environment and temperament tested to determine their personality. Most important, the tone and terminology sound as though the breeder knows what he's talking about. You'll still have lots of questions for this breeder when you call him, but he is definitely one to include on your list.

In contrast, let's look at an ad that has ignorance written all over it: "AKC purebred Dobies! Champion pedigreed! Giant size, some rare colors! Shots and wormed." I actually saw this ad in a newspaper. What's wrong with it?

1. If the puppies are AKC registered, they have to be purebred with a pedigree, don't they? No need to include either of these words. And knowledgeable dog people don't use "pedigreed" as an adjective.

2. A knowledgeable breeder wouldn't use the affectionate nickname "Dobies" in an advertisement.

3. Dobermans are not supposed to be "giant-sized." One of the breed's attributes is the athletic ability afforded by its moderate build.

4. Rare colors? Dobermans come in black, red, blue, or fawn. Although blue and fawn are not as common as black and red, they're not rare. But perhaps the dogs are white, which is indeed rare because it is a disqualification according to the breed

standard. White (albino) Dobermans often suffer from a plethora of health problems.

5. Since all puppies are vaccinated and checked for worms as a matter of course, good breeders seldom include this assurance in their ads. Unknowledgeable breeders have so little else they can say about the litter that they might push "shots and wormed" as the big selling point.

6. The worst thing about this ad is its overall tone. The incorrect terminology and exclamation point extravaganza reveal it as the ad of an unknowledgeable breeder.

Finally, let's look at perhaps the most common ad you'll find in your newspaper: "Irish Setter puppies. AKC-registered, champion lines, raised in our home, both parents on premises." This ad doesn't say much, but there's nothing overtly wrong with it, so you can put this breeder on your list to call. However, most newspaper ads belong to irresponsible breeders, so I'm willing to bet that the "champion lines" mean one grandparent was a champion (whoopie . . .) and that your first question ("Do both parents have OFA hips and have their eyes been CERF'd?") will be met with "Huh? What does that mean?" In the next chapter, we'll discuss each question you'll be asking breeders and the answers you should be looking for.

What if you work your way through all of the suggested sources and you don't find any local breeders? Call the breeder closest to you and ask if he knows of anyone in your area. Breeders maintain an informal network of who is producing what and who has what for sale and are usually willing to steer you in the right direction. Be polite when contacting breeders for this reason. Call at a reasonable time, say nine to nine, skipping the supper hour and remembering the time zone you're calling. If no one is home, don't leave a message on the answering machine asking the breeder to call you back at his expense.

What if the nearest breeder remains six states away? His ad says, "We will ship." He will secure a puppy in a shipping crate, put him on a plane, and you'll meet him at your end of the flight. Is this a good idea?

It can be if the breeder is extremely reputable, meaning you've spoken with a number of other responsible breeders and club members and they recommend him as a knowledgeable and ethical person to work with. But you must speak extensively with him on the telephone, because you need to feel confident that you can trust him to select the type of puppy you're looking for. Ask him all the questions in the next chapter ("Contacting Breeders") and be sure you see photos of the puppy and parents, the pedigree, copies of genetic health certificates, the sales contract, the health guarantee—all the paperwork described in chapter 12. Ask if he can make a videotape for you. From a distance, a breeder can give great lip service and can really fool you, so you must be careful. Ideally the breeder will be willing to ship on a trial basis and you can ship the pup back (at your expense, of course) if you and he don't hit it off.

Shipping requires a lot of coordination and expense and can be an unnerving experience for a dog. Still, it's an option, and with uncommon breeds, you may not have another choice. Sometimes you don't even have this choice—some breeders refuse to ship out of concern that something might go wrong. This concern is justified, because tragedies can and do occur when animals are shipped.

♦ 9 ♦

Contacting Breeders

You've assembled a folder of breeders. You've used your knowledge of correct and incorrect terminology to weed out the obvious duds. You're ready to start calling the most promising ones. But you're nervous because you don't know what to say.

It's true that some breeders will adopt a condescending attitude that implies that pet buyers are not worth their time. Some are gossip-happy and will repeat rumors that stir up dirt about other breeders. Some will stretch the truth to puff their puppies up over those of another breeder. Politics and clannishness do exist in the dog world. But most breeders are very nice people, enthusiastic about their breed, proud of their accomplishments, eager to educate, and willing to do whatever they can to help you find a nice puppy, even if it's not one of theirs.

Let's listen in on a telephone conversation between you, the prospective buyer, and a responsible German Shepherd breeder who offers all the right answers. There are no perfect breeders, but you'll learn from this conversation the important

topics of discussion and the answers you should be looking for. When you call, have pen and paper handy so you can take notes.

YOU: Mr. Kelly, I got your name from the German Shepherd Dog Club of America. I'm looking for a puppy and wondered if you might have any available.

If no, "I live in Westchester. Do you know of another breeder in my area who might have a litter?" and "Do you have any litters planned for the near future?" If the breeder does have a litter planned, chat him up, asking most of the questions that follow. Tell him you'll get back to him if you can't find any current litters. With the less common breeds, this is likely to be the case, and you'll have to put down a deposit and get onto a waiting list.

GENETIC HEALTH

If luck is with you and the breeder does have a litter *and* puppies are still available from it:

262

BREEDER: Yes, I do have two puppies right now.

YOU: Do both parents have OFA certificates?

BREEDER: Yes, they do.

YOU: For hips *and* elbows?

BREEDER: Yes.

YOU: What was the rating on the hips?

BREEDER: The sire is Excellent, the dam is Good.

The first question to ask is about the genetic health of both parents. That's *genetic* health— you're not looking for a general health certificate that says the dogs are healthy and happy and have all their shots and no fleas.

Depending on breed, genetic health tests mean X rays, opthalmological examination, blood tests, cardiac exams, hearing tests. If your breed's profile says both parents should be OFA-certified for hip dysplasia, CERF-certified for eye diseases, heart-tested for cardiomyopathy, BAER-tested for hearing, *be sure* they have been. Ask the breeder if he has the certificates or a veterinarian's report for each individual test, including the results or an official rating of their clearance status.

Sad to say, you'll hear a variety of excuses for why this has not been done:

"We've never had a problem with that."

"Those tests aren't reliable."

"That disease has never been proven to be genetic."

"I can't afford to have my whole kennel tested."

"A dog has to be two years old to be certified, and my dog is only a year old."

"We don't test, but if your puppy develops any problems, just truck him on back and we'll give you a new one." You'll hear this last "assurance" from one irresponsible breeder after another, as though a defective dog is as easy to replace as a defective toaster.

To all these excuses, you should reply, "I'm sorry, but I'm only buying from a breeder who has had these health checks done. Thank you for your time."

Stand firm. It's heartbreaking to discover, months down the road, that your puppy is showing the first signs of a disease that will cause him pain and suffering and perhaps cost him his mobility, his vision, or his life. It might have been prevented if the breeder had tested his dogs before breeding.

The cop-outs above require no further discussion, but there are some possible answers that do bear closer scrutiny.

"We screen for those problems, but we don't send the results to the OFA or CERF. We use our own judgment in evaluating the X rays and tests and deciding whether a dog is breedable." It's true that some breeders are perfectly capable of interpreting X rays and test results. But unless this particular breeder is your grandmother, you're taking a risk by simply accepting his word that he had the tests done and that he has the skills and the objectivity to evaluate them properly. Some breeders will offer you the X ray to look at yourself, which is fine and dandy if you know what you're looking at. But most people become understandably flustered when a breeder waves an X ray in their face and crows, "Look at these hips—best I've seen in twenty years of breeding!" Most people will frown at the X ray, pretending to study it, nodding sagely. Actually they could be looking at an X ray of a guppy and not know the difference.

Insist on official clearances: for hips, that means OFA (or PennHIP, GDC, or OVC). For eyes, that means CERF (or in a few breeds, a DNA test).

YOU: And have their hearts been examined?

BREEDER: Yes. Everything is OFA: hips, elbows, cardiac.

YOU: Great. I guess you can tell I'm really concerned about health. Will I be able to see the certificates?

BREEDER: Oh, yes.

YOU: What about the grandparents? What testing has been done on them?

BREEDER: All the hips are OFA for three generations.

Some certification programs are fairly new, but testing for hips and eyes has been going on for a while, so all four grandparents should be certified at least for hips and eyes (if recommended for your breed). If the breeder doesn't answer this first group of health questions satisfactorily, don't go any further with the interview.

AGE OF THE PUPPIES

YOU: How old are the puppies?

Less than seven weeks is out, as these puppies have not yet spent enough time with their mother and littermates, so have not learned how to use their teeth gently, how to respect authority, and how to interact appropriately with other dogs. It is appalling that irresponsible breeders are still trying to place puppies at six weeks, or as soon as they're weaned.

Advantages of a young puppy (seven to twelve weeks): He's fuzzy and adorable. He comes to you as a clean slate with no bad habits. It's easy to introduce him to other pets and to the routines of your family. You can mold most of the good habits you want him to develop. You can watch him grow up.

Disadvantages of a young puppy: He is a mouth on legs, eager to grab, swallow, and chew everything that fits into his mouth and some things that don't. Housebreaking will take months because he can't control his bodily functions for more than a few hours. You'll have to safeguard his health, especially around children and other pets. You can't be absolutely sure how his appearance and personality might turn out. Finally, any mistakes you make in raising him can greatly affect his behavior as an adult. This age group is not an option for the smallest toy breeds, such as Chihuahuas, Maltese, and Yorkies. These breeds are so fragile as puppies that the stress of being shifted to a new home can trigger hypoglycemia, parvovirus, coronavirus, or an outbreak of demodectic mange.

Advantages of an older puppy (three to eight months): He is stronger, more solid, more suited to active play and exercise. Assuming he doesn't have any bad habits to unlearn, housebreaking will go more quickly because he has more control. He may already have had some training, and you can better determine what his appearance and personality will be like as an adult.

Disadvantages of an older puppy: He's past the "cute stage." Indeed, this period is often called "the uglies." A teenage puppy can be boisterous and mischievous, flighty and uncertain, gawky and awkward as he plows through the physical and emotional stages of adolescence. Rebelliousness and dominance testing may rear their heads, and since the two of you haven't been together long enough to have established an "understanding," you might be in for some leadership struggles. Much depends on the breed and individual personality. You have to be patient, firm, and utterly consistent as you nip bad habits in the bud and establish control. Avoid older pups who have been raised in a kennel run—they may have "kennel syndrome," a deeply imprinted fear of new people, sights, sounds, and situations.

Advantages of an adult: Some breeders are willing to place retired show champions or retired breeding stock as pets. The appearance and personality of these dogs is settled—you know what you're getting. They're probably housebroken (or mostly so) and may have had some training. You've bypassed both the delicate baby stage and the frustrating adolescent stage.

Disadvantages of an adult: He may not be as pliable about new routines. Long-established bad habits may be more difficult to change. You missed his fun growing-up years, and you'll never know exactly what experiences he's had or what things he's seen. As with older pups, avoid adults who have been raised in a kennel run.

BREEDER: My puppies are ten weeks old.

SEX OF THE PUPPIES

YOU: Are they males or females?

BREEDER: One of each.

Males are often called boys or dogs, while females are often called girls or bitches—don't flinch! It's an accepted canine term. So which sex makes the better pet? The debate rages.

Generally, males are apt to be "lovable slobs" and "good ol' boys." They tend to be more openly affectionate, more "in your face." They enjoy being held and cuddled and will seek you out for attention. Males tend to be stable and reliable in mood, less prone to emotional swings. Though sometimes clumsy and silly and prone to acting like oversize puppies, they mean well and are easy to love. (Hmm. It's uncanny how similar they are to their human counterparts. . . .)

On the negative side, males are more apt to test their owners and engage in dominance struggles during the hormonal adolescent months. They have obvious genitals, which can make for embarrassing moments if they become aroused or decide to lick themselves when Mom is visiting. Most males lift their leg to urinate, a consideration if you have expensive shrubbery or lawn ornaments. Some males are compulsive markers who spray urine on vertical objects (ranging from telephone poles to blades of grass, depending on how obsessive they are) to mark it with their scent. Some males, especially toy breeds, are enthusiastic humpers who will mount stuffed toys, other dogs, and sometimes people's legs or ankles.

Generally, females are more subtle than males. They're affectionate, but on their own terms. They'll ask for petting, then assert their independence by moving away when they've had enough. They can be a bit more standoffish with strangers. Remarkably, female dogs also resemble their human counterparts: They're prone to mood swings and emotional theatrics. They can be sweet one day (or one hour) and grumpy the next, and they are masters (mistresses?) of "The Sulk."

Females are often quicker to learn and not as easily distracted during training sessions. They can be clever and manipulative about getting their own way, but are less likely to engage in open dominance challenges. Females are easier to take for walks because they pee more neatly and unobtrusively and don't tow you toward every bush and hydrant.

Here's a visual image of the differences: When you're sitting on the sofa, males are more likely to plop their big easygoing selves right on top of the book you're reading, while females are more likely to curl up beside you, then stalk off in a snit because you bumped them when you turned the page.

In some breeds and lines, certainly in many individuals, these generalizations may be reversed. Just be aware that since breeders keep more females, they often have males to place and do have a tendency to extol the virtues of males without mentioning the potential negatives.

Also consider the other dogs in your household. Some breeds, such as Beagles, are very accepting of newcomers, whatever their sex. Others, such as Akitas and Alaskan Malamutes, should never be kept with a dog of the same sex. Generally, it's easier on all concerned to bring home the opposite sex of the one you already have. Both should be neutered.

Finally, some neighborhoods have a resident canine bully who roams free and pesters other dogs being walked properly on-leash. If this happens to be an unneutered male, especially a large one, you'd be wise not to get a male yourself, else your daily walks may become stressful.

Let's touch on male and female reproduction. No, not "how to," but rather "how *not* to."

If you don't neuter (spay) your female, she will come into season every five to seven months. Each heat period is a three-week affair and includes swollen genitals, licking of same, and a bloody discharge (slight or copious). She may act restless, flirtatious, or perfectly normal. She must never be allowed off-leash or even left unsupervised in the yard, since this is the only time of the year when she can become pregnant. Unspayed females are at great risk for developing uterine infections, which are extremely serious and usually require an emergency spay. They may develop false pregnancies, which can disrupt their hormone levels in an unhealthy way. Mammary (breast) tumors are common in older unspayed females, and these may be cancerous.

If you don't neuter your male, he may embarrass you by sniffing and slobbering all over female dogs, rearing up on children or mounting your leg (sometimes growling if you try to pull away), or ignoring your commands when you go for a walk because his eyeballs are busy roving up and down the street looking for potential rivals. No, breeding him won't help—it will make things much worse. Males who have been bred may try to lift their legs in the house as a sign of dominance and masculinity. Just what you need, right?

I highly recommend neutering all pet females and any pet male who is highly sexed, energetic, or aggressive. Neutering encourages your dog to pay more attention to you, rather than to other dogs. It often calms excitable dogs. You may choose to neuter a well-behaved male simply for health reasons, since neutering prevents testicular cancer and reduces the risk of prostate disease. Neutering does not make a dog fat—overfeeding and lack of exercise make a dog fat. A neutered dog does have a lower metabolism, so offer less food and plenty of exercise and your neutered dog will stay slim and trim.

APPEARANCE OF THE PUPPIES

YOU: Are these pet-quality puppies?

BREEDER: Yes, they're not for show or breeding.

YOU: Are they being sold with limited registration and a neutering contract?

BREEDER: Yes, they are.

YOU: Could you tell me what faults they have that make them pet quality?

BREEDER: Well, the male is too heavily boned, and the female is just the opposite, too fine-boned and not enough angulation. These are nice puppies, just not "typey" enough for the show ring.

YOU: It sounds as though you evaluate them very honestly. What color are they?

BREEDER: The male is a black-and-tan saddle; the female is a dark gray sable.

It's best to be color-blind. Remember the old saying: "A good horse cannot be a bad color."

TEMPERAMENT AND SOCIALIZATION OF THE PUPPIES

YOU: Could you tell me about their temperaments?

BREEDER: The male is a big, easygoing guy, a real lover. The female is sharper and quicker, a real prima donna. She has an opinion about everything!

YOU: Do you do temperament testing, and how do you decide who gets which puppy?

BREEDER: Yes, we test temperaments at seven weeks. We use the Volhard testing program, to see if the puppy will follow us, if he'll retrieve a ball, if he's amenable to being handled and restrained. That gives us an idea as to the type of home we think each puppy would be best suited to. For example, this male puppy is probably too laid-back to be a competition dog, but he's so easy to handle, he'll be great as a family companion. The female would do better with someone who wants to compete in obedience or agility or herding, something that will keep her mind busy.

YOU: Have they been raised in your house or in a kennel?

BREEDER: We raise our kids right in the kitchen. They start out in a playpen, then they move to an ex-pen (exercise pen) with a swinging doggy door that leads outside. They practically housebreak themselves that way.

Needless to say, "raised in the garage" means the conversation is over.

YOU: Could you tell me what things you've done to socialize them?

BREEDER: We've been handling them since they were a few days old, carrying them around, talking to them, standing them up on a table and examining them, brushing them, clipping their nails. We have people in to play with them, including children. They're used to the TV, the stereo, the telephone. They've been up and down stairs. These are outgoing puppies. Temperament is very important to us.

Irresponsible breeders might not even know what socialization means. It is the process of introducing a puppy to friendly people and new experiences and other animals such as dogs, cats, and rabbits. By the age of seven weeks, a puppy's brain is fully functional and ready to learn. Despite the risk of being exposed to disease, it is vitally important that he become comfortable with the world, visiting with people of different ages, sexes, sizes, and races, playing with children, and seeing and hearing household sights and sounds, city traffic, people on bikes or skateboards. Anything that might be a part of a puppy's world should be introduced in a fun, nonthreatening manner at an early age. This will encourage an outgoing, confident attitude as an adult.

PARENTS AND PEDIGREE

YOU: What's the breeding on these puppies? What are their lines?

This question is a key one because you're using correct canine terminology to ask about the puppies' pedigree. This is an "insider's" question. Knowledgeable breeders will understand it and will discuss the sire, dam, perhaps a noteworthy relative, any titles the dogs have won. Unknowledgeable breeders won't understand what you mean and will say something unintentionally funny, like, "The breeding? Well, we bred their parents together. They're both Basset Hounds with AKC papers. I don't know what you mean by lines. . . ."

BREEDER: The sire is a champion, Ch. Forest-brook Penobscot. He's linebred on Ch. Jen-Jeans Aces High. I have pictures of him and I also have pictures of some of his sons and daughters so you can see what he produces. Also he has his CGC. The dam is champion-sired and has her CD and CGC. This is her second litter. Her lines are mixed German and American.

Translation: The sire is a conformation champion and has a Canine Good Citizen title for sound temperament. Aces High is a notable (i.e., top-winning) show dog in his pedigree. The dam also has the CGC title, plus a Companion Dog obedience title, and her father is a conformation champion.

What you don't want to hear is something like, "Belle is the mom; Taco is the dad. I'd have to look up their registered names, but they are AKC and they do have great pedigrees."

YOU: Will I be able to see both parents?

BREEDER: The dam is here, but the sire lives in New York. I do have photos of him and a video of him winning Best of Breed last year at the specialty show in Washington, D.C.

It's always better to be able to see both parents, yet *both parents on premises* is not always a positive sign. In newspaper ads, this phrase often means that someone bred two dogs together because they were the two he had on hand. A responsible breeder evaluates the strengths and weaknesses of his female, then looks around for a male who matches her strengths and compensates for the weaknesses. If the breeder happens to own the perfect male to do that, fine, but often he needs to use a stud dog from another breeder. If that other breeder lives close by, you could visit and see the dog in person, but as long as you can see photos and the pedigree, or even better, a video, that's considered sufficient.

YOU: Could you tell me about their temperaments?

BREEDER: The sire is one of the most easygoing German Shepherds you'll ever find. He takes life in stride and loves everyone. The dam is more aloof—she'll come over to get some attention, then she'll go lie down and keep her eye on you. She's terrific in obedience, very sharp. I suspect her daughter will be much the same way, whereas the male puppy takes after the father, more laid-back.

Now here's a real lulu of an answer: "The mom is so sweet but she's scared of strangers; she was abused when she was young. The dad is a great watchdog, very protective, so you won't be able to pet him. But you can see him through the window."

YOU: What size are the parents, and what size do you expect the puppies to be?

BREEDER: The sire is a big guy, just over twenty-six inches, just over one hundred pounds. The dam is twenty-four inches and eighty pounds. The male puppy is large-boned; I expect him to be about the same size as his father. The female puppy is more elegant, so I would expect her to be on the small side of the standard, not as large as her mother.

If the breeder were to tell you that his German Shepherds or Dobermans or Rottweilers were "giant," or that his Chihuahuas or Maltese or Yorkies were "teacups," you would roll your eyes, thank him politely, and hang up.

YOU: Why did you choose these two dogs to breed together?

BREEDER: The dam comes from a line of long-lived Shepherds (all of her grandparents are over thirteen) and she has an excellent working background. Her head could be better—it's a little narrow—so I chose Penobscot to improve that. His head is very strong and masculine, and his topline . . .

There are many ways a breeder might answer this question. What's most important is that he had a goal, that he studied individuals and pedigrees and chose these breeding partners for a reason. A reason other than: "Well, these are the two we have. Everyone told us they've never seen German Shepherds as nice as ours and that we should breed them together." Or: "It was an accident. We had no idea a brother and sister would breed together."

THE BREEDER'S EXPERIENCE

YOU: How many years have you been involved with German Shepherds?

BREEDER: I've had shepherds for eighteen years now. I started out showing my first Shepherd in obedience, let's see, that was back in . . .

Most breeders enjoy talking about how they got involved with dogs and their breed in general. Such a conversation puts the breeder in a relaxed mood and helps the two of you feel comfortable with each other.

YOU: How many litters do you breed each year?

BREEDER: No more than two litters a year.

Generally, responsible breeders produce no more than three litters a year. It's possible to have more, but without assistance, one must question whether the breeder would have enough time for socialization, testing temperaments and getting to know the puppies, and competing in shows and performance events. Smaller-scale breeders tend to devote more time and attention to each puppy.

YOU: Do you breed just German Shepherds, or do you have other breeds?

You want a kennel specializing in only one or two breeds. A kennel claiming three or more has spread itself too thin and cannot really know enough about each breed.

BREEDER: Just German Shepherds. Well, I take that back; we also breed quarter horses.

YOU: Ah, then I'll know who to call when I'm looking for a horse! Could you tell me, what are the characteristics of your lines? What qualities do you focus on in your breeding program as most important?

BREEDER: Temperament, first and foremost. It has to be confident and stable, not this nervous hyperactivity that you'll see in some lines. Health is next on the list, especially longevity and sound hips, elbows, and hearts. I'm determined not to let heart problems into my line. Intelligence is essential, and trainability, which is why I work in obedience and all my dogs have CGCs. Oh, and I'm concerned about washed-out colors, so I aim for rich pigment: black-and-red, dark sable. . . .

Let the breeder have a long leash and listen for goals based on temperament, health, intelligence, trainability, longevity. Breeders who launch right into conformation and appearance (topline, angulation, gait, head, coat) as their main goals are geared toward the show ring rather than the features that make a fine companion. Similarly, breeders who stress high Schutzhund scores and "courageous, hard-driving temperaments" are producing competitive working dogs who won't fit the average household.

YOU: What activities do you show your dogs in? What do you like to participate in?

BREEDER: I've been showing for about fifteen years and I've finished eight champions. But my real interest is obedience, and I'm just getting involved in agility, and as I said, all my dogs have CGCs. . . .

YOU: Do you belong to any clubs?

BREEDER: Yes, to the German Shepherd Dog Club of America, where you got my name, and also to the (such and such) regional club, and the (such and such) obedience club.

MORE ABOUT HEALTH

YOU: Besides hips, elbows, and hearts, do you do any other screening for health problems?

BREEDER: We do skin-punch biopsies for sebaceous adenitis. That's a serious skin disease. There's no cure for it and I don't want it in my lines.

You've already inquired about the major tests at the very beginning of the conversation, so any additional testing the breeder does is a bonus. For example, some may run full blood panels for low thyroid, some may run blood tests for vWD, and this breeder does skin-punch biopsies.

YOU: Have you had any incidences of hip dysplasia in your lines? Elbow problems? Heart problems? Bloat, vWD, seizures, low thyroid, sebaceous adenitis, OCD, panosteitis, cancer, allergies, skin conditions, autoimmune disorders, digestive problems?

Run through the health problems listed in the profile. If the breeder doesn't admit to anything ever having occurred in his lines, it's too good to be true and probably isn't. You're not looking for perfection, just honesty.

YOU: What health guarantees do you offer?

BREEDER: We guarantee our puppies to be free of general illness such as distemper or parvo for forty-eight hours, during which time we encourage you to take the puppy to your own vet for a checkup. If he finds anything wrong, return the puppy and we'll refund your money or replace the puppy with another one.

YOU: And that option would be mine? Whether I wanted a refund or a replacement?

BREEDER: Yes, your option.

This forty-eight-hour guarantee is standard among breeders, though some allow seventy-two hours. The problem is that many diseases have a ten- to fourteen-day incubation period from the time the puppy contracts the disease to the time he begins showing symptoms. Two or three days is not nearly enough time to detect whether a puppy was indeed carrying something when he left the breeder's home. Unfortunately, this guarantee is so standard that the breeder is unlikely to extend it. However, you can at least make sure that the option of refund/replacement is *yours*, not his. You must reserve the right to reevaluate a breeder who has already sold you one sick puppy.

YOU: Do you offer a guarantee against hereditary problems as well?

BREEDER: Yes, we offer a written guarantee for two years against hip dysplasia, elbows, heart, bad temperament, and other hereditary problems. These would have to be put in writing by your vet, and we require that our own vet concur with those findings.

Hereditary guarantees vary widely, from a useless six or twelve months to a more reasonable two years to a generous lifetime guarantee. Will you get a refund if your puppy develops a hereditary problem? No. This guarantee almost always promises to replace your puppy. The problem here, of course, is that once you've owned a puppy for several months or years, you're attached to him, and except in the case of poor temperament are unwilling to "exchange" him. Better that the breeder promises an *additional* puppy—although you may not want two dogs, especially if you need to pay vet bills to treat the hereditary problems of the first one.

From an owner's point of view, an ideal guarantee would be one whereby the breeder promises to pay some of the vet bills. However, since most responsible breeders are small in size, and since many hereditary problems come from "carrier" parents who tested clear of the disorder, such a guarantee could bankrupt a breeder who did everything right and honestly wasn't aware that a hereditary problem was hidden in his line.

Breeding animals is not an exact science. As a prospective buyer, all you can do is to carefully screen your breeder with thoughtful questions, ensure that he tests and certifies his dogs, check his references, and request reasonable guarantees. Beyond that, you do accept some risk for the occasional act of Mother Nature.

TURNABOUT IS FAIR PLAY . . . BREEDER QUESTIONS

This interview shouldn't be a one-way street. Don't expect to simply call a good breeder and be greeted with an immediate invitation to come pick out any puppy you want. A good breeder wants to make sure you've done some research, that you didn't decide this is the breed for you based on an old episode of *Rin Tin Tin*. He wants to feel reassured that his puppy will receive proper care in a permanent home. Don't be offended by his concern. Look at it as your opportunity to reassure him about your knowledge and what you have to offer as an owner.

BREEDER: How did you become interested in German Shepherds? Have you owned one before? Have you had other breeds? What happened to them? Do you have pets now? Do you have children? How old? How would you describe them? What do you do for a living? Who else lives in your household or is there on a regular basis? Who is home during the day, and for how long? Where do you live? Do you have a yard? What

type of fencing? Where will the dog spend his days? His nights? Do you have a crate, or will you purchase or borrow one? Is anyone in your family allergic to dogs? What recent books have you read on raising and training a dog? What types of socialization are you planning to do? How will you handle housebreaking? Do you rent? Will your landlord okay a dog in writing? Could I have the phone number of your vet as a reference? Would I be able to come visit your home or have a friend do so?

PRICE

YOU: What price are you asking for the puppies?

Price should be one of the last questions you ask. The quickest way to turn off a breeder is to ask, right off the bat, how much his puppies cost. It makes him think you're a discount shopper.

BREEDER: Four hundred and fifty dollars.

As we've discussed, reasonable price range for a pet-quality puppy in most breeds is $300 to $600. Lower than that, and the breeder has virtually always cut corners. Especially in breeds that require a great deal of medical testing, no one can put in all that time and expense and charge only $200 for a puppy. On the other hand, some big-name show breeders inflate their prices simply because their dogs win lots of ribbons in the show ring.

Watch out for price differences based solely on sex ("females $295, males $250") rather than on individual quality. Finally, anyone who offers a puppy at one price "with papers included" and at a lower price "without papers" is breaking AKC rules, which say that money can never be connected to the registration papers. If papers are present, they stay with the dog. The exception is a neutering contract, where the breeder may withhold the papers until the dog has been neutered, but he cannot make you pay extra for them and he cannot give you a discount if you don't take them.

In case you're wondering, trying to negotiate a lower price is not looked kindly upon by a responsible breeder. You're not buying a car.

YOU: How would payment need to be made?

BREEDER: Cash or a cashier's check.

Most breeders don't accept personal checks or credit cards, but it never hurts to ask.

THE APPOINTMENT

YOU: I'd like to see your puppies. When would be a good time?

BREEDER: Well, I'll be away at shows this weekend, but next Tuesday night would work for me. Around seven?

YOU: Sounds good. Before I get directions, would you mind giving me some references, perhaps a couple of other club members I could call?

BREEDER: Sure, let me get some numbers for you.

Don't even consider visiting someone who can't answer this question with a resounding YES. If the breeder says he doesn't know anyone who belongs to a club, or that he doesn't associate with any club members because they're all snobs, forget it.

Are you thinking, "I'd be embarrassed to ask so many questions"? Please try not to be. A good breeder welcomes questions. The long conversation gives them a chance to get to know you better. Responsible breeders rely heavily on what you sound like on the phone. They will listen to the questions you ask and the terminology you use and they will be impressed by your sincerity and thoroughness. Only irresponsible breeders will become irritated, because it will eventually become

clear to them, based on your reaction, that they're not giving appropriate answers.

Perhaps you're tempted to write a letter, but most breeders prefer phone calls because they're interactive and the breeder can get a better feel for you. You could try writing letters initially, then calling those whose responses you like best, but in this day and age of instant communication and busy lifestyles, many breeders just don't get around to answering letters. Stick with the telephone, if possible. E-mail is also very effective; more and more breeders have E-mail addresses and even Web sites.

Here's an appropriate E-mail message:

Dear Mr. Kelly,

I've just finished visiting your Web site—thank you for providing such comprehensive information. I'm looking for a German Shepherd puppy for our family. My husband and I live in Westchester and have two children, ages ten and twelve, and no other pets. We both grew up with mixed-breed dogs, so do have some experience raising a puppy to be happy and well-mannered.

We've done a lot of reading and research and have settled on a German Shepherd as the right breed for us. We admire their intelligence and trainability and will be happy to provide the exercise and training they need and enjoy. Someone is home all day at our house, so we can provide continued socialization and companionship. The Westchester Kennel Club offers obedience classes, which we plan to attend, starting with puppy kindergarten. Though our dog will live indoors with us, we have a large fenced (six-foot-high) yard for safety and play.

We would prefer a male puppy. Sire and dam must have OFA certificates for hips and elbows and be screened for cardiac problems. I was so pleased to read on your Web site that you do this type of testing, and also that you show your dogs in obedience and agility, so I feel confident that your breeding program produces intelligent, healthy dogs, and that's just what we're looking for.

Might you have a puppy available who would fit well into our family, either now or in the near future? We look forward to hearing from you.

THE NEXT STEP

Assuming that you've gotten over your stage fright and spoken at length with the breeder on the telephone, and that the answers to all your questions are satisfactory, and that you've called the breeder's references, let's head out to his home!

◆ 10 ◆

At the Breeder's Home

Don't be surprised if the kennel is one in name only. Most breeders own only a few dogs, all of which may live in the house, and have only a couple of outside runs or a large yard for exercise. Rare today (fortunately) are large kennels with runs for thirty or forty dogs, few of whom ever see the inside of the breeder's home.

Some responsible breeders pay so much attention to their dogs that their own house goes to pot. Don't be too quick to fault a cluttered living room or dishes heaped in the sink. What's important is the area where the dogs are kept. It should be warm, well lit, and roomy enough for playing. It should include toys and beds. It should be clean, with no piles of dried waste or stale canned food. Water bowls should be fresh and full. Food bowls should not be overrun by ants. Doghouses and fences should be sturdy, with no sharp edges or protruding nails. There should be no broken glass or tin cans littering the ground, no thumbtacks or elastic bands lying on the floor waiting to be swallowed by puppies.

Clean and *safe* are the operative words. If the place looks dirty or unsafe, trust your instincts. Tell the breeder you're not feeling well or you've just remembered another appointment, thank him, and drive away. A breeder who doesn't care about his dogs' safety is not the breeder for you, no matter how many show ribbons are plastered on the walls.

What can the adult dogs at the breeder's home tell you? A great deal.

Health: Adults should be clean and brushed, with no mats, tangles, or patches of missing hair. Their eyes should not be weepy or tearing. They shouldn't be limping or scratching, unless a dog is simply nursing a sprained leg or battling a skin condition for which he is being treated. Ask.

Temperament: Adult dogs may rush up to greet you, they may stand back and look you over, or they may bark furiously at you. Most dogs are bolder behind a fence, where even sweet dogs may gleefully pretend to be maniacal killers. The response you'll see will depend to some extent on the breed you're looking at. Salukis aren't likely to jump all over you with madly waving tails, but Flat-Coated Retrievers might. However, no matter what the breed, the adults should soon become accepting of your presence. If more than one individual (1) has to be locked up because he won't relax and shut up; (2) spooks if you happen to shift your feet; or (3) cringes away from your hand with his tail tucked between his legs, this line is not one you want to be involved with.

Pay special attention to the parents, grandparents, and any previous offspring of either parent. The mother's temperament is especially important because the puppies will be with their mother for several months. They will tend to copy her attitude toward strangers, her reactions to loud sounds, and so on. Make sure she is the confident, well-adjusted dog you want your own puppy to become. If she is still with her puppies, she may display a somewhat suspicious maternal instinct, so ask to see her away from the puppies so you can more fairly judge her temperament.

You may be asking, "Why do I have to spend all this time evaluating the adults when I want to buy a puppy?" Canine authority Roger Caras wisely advises, "Never buy the puppy. Buy the dog the puppy one day will be." The puppies you'll see today, no matter how friendly they seem right now, will likely grow into something very similar to the adult dogs you see. The way you raise your puppy will also influence his temperament and behavior, but you can't change the genes he was born with. Those fixed genes of a purebred can act against you if you look at a cute puppy and rationalize that surely, with all the love you're going to give him, he'll not turn out like the spooky adults in the breeder's yard. Use those fixed genes to act *for* you by assuring yourself that the adults you see are the kind of dog you want your puppy to become.

As the breeder is showing you around, form an impression of him. Is he proud of his dogs? Does he pet them and speak fondly to them? Can he control them? Are they happy to see him? Chat with him about his breed and his dogs. Is he the type of person you'll feel comfortable calling on the phone if you have any questions or problems? When you mention other breeders you may have contacted, is he diplomatic or does he talk them down? Does he express an interest in keeping up with the puppy's progress? Does he invite you to call and send photos?

Since you wouldn't have come unless his telephone answers were satisfactory, the impression you'll form in person will probably also be satisfactory. The chances are good that you're talking to a friendly and dedicated person who knows dogs, loves dogs, and is doing his best to improve his breed. But you're making a major addition to your life here, so don't be embarrassed about double-checking his expertise as a breeder. He isn't embarrassed about checking you out as an owner. Both of you are doing the right thing.

One caution: Don't use the criteria in this chapter to *choose* your breeder. It is not enough that a breeder keeps his puppies clean and safe in the living room, loves them, and is personable. Love and friendliness do not translate into a knowledge of genetics, health problems, or the breed standard. If you simply called any breeder from the newspaper and rushed right over to see his puppies, you'd likely find that he was a nice person who loved his dogs. That will be no solace whatsoever when your puppy develops hip dysplasia, temperament problems, horrible teeth, or grows up with a strange-looking head and body because the breeder had no idea what he was doing.

Make sure a breeder measures up in knowledge, not just personality. You can do that only with the qualifying questions from chapter 9—*before* you visit his home.

You've done all that. You're satisfied with the breeder. Now let's go look at the puppies!

STEP FOUR

◆ ◆ ◆

Choosing the Right Puppy

◆ 11 ◆

Evaluating Puppies and Older Dogs

I'm assuming the breeder is allowing you to evaluate the litter yourself and choose your own puppy. However, if you are a novice and the breeder is very experienced, he may have a firm policy of making the choice for you. Many breeders take great (and usually justified) pride in their knowledge of their breed, of their particular line, and of their puppies. They have been observing the litter since it was born, they may have already temperament tested the puppies, and they may have formed their own opinion as to exactly what type of home and owner each puppy would be best suited to. An experienced breeder is usually far more qualified than you are to make this decision, and you may choose to either accept their decision or go elsewhere.

But if the breeder is allowing you to make a choice, there they are! One or two or six or eight cute, fuzzy, wriggling puppies. Your puppy may be among them!

You may have been advised by well-meaning friends to let a puppy choose *you*. But that usually results in all the bold and pushy puppies being taken first, while the gentle puppies who usually make calmer pets wait politely in the background or are pushed out of the way. Most families are making a mistake when they let the most brash, forceful puppies choose them. These little dynamos are a blast to play with for an hour at the breeder's, but depending on your personality, they could drive you crazy in the same amount of time in your own home. A puppy can love you without being suited to you, and a puppy can be perfectly suited to you without launching himself immediately into your lap. So resolve to give each puppy a fair evaluation and to do the choosing yourself.

Your first look should be at the entire litter as a group. If there are seven puppies and six of them are running away or barking suspiciously at you and staying at arm's length, I'm sorry to say that your visit is over. No, you shouldn't buy the seventh puppy; the chances are too great that shyness or distrustfulness is in the genes and simply hasn't caught up to him yet. Don't let a breeder try to laugh off his puppies' timidity with assurances of, "Oh, they're just a little hesitant because they haven't been handled much." There is no excuse for lack of socialization other than laziness or ignorance on the part of the breeder. You do not want a puppy from a lazy or ignorant breeder.

Let the puppies show you their true temperament, whatever it happens to be. Don't coax a frightened puppy to be brave, trying to convince yourself that you'll be able to "bring him out of his shell." You don't know what's going on in this puppy's mind or genes. Shy puppies usually become shy dogs who won't take part in anything around them, who may even snap defensively at anything that startles them.

If the litter isn't running away, what should they be doing? Normal puppies of most breeds are friendly, curious, and trusting. They'll mill around your feet, tug at your shoelaces, swarm into your lap, nibble on your fingers. After a while, they may stop playing with you and begin wrestling with one another, which is good because you can tell a lot about the individual puppies by the way they interact with their littermates. Which ones are strong, outgoing, bossy, noisy? Which ones are quiet, submissive, gentle? Which ones grab all the toys and start and win the tugs-of-war and tussles? Which ones seem weak and picked on? Most families do best with a puppy who is neither the boss of the litter nor the lowest on the totem pole, so look for good-natured puppies who do not initiate the games and play fights, but who do join in and hold their own.

Clap your hands gently, snap your fingers, jingle your car keys, shuffle your feet, whistle softly, cluck your tongue. Which pups are interested? Which ones come over to investigate? Which ones are apprehensive? You want an attentive, confident puppy. A nervous puppy who is afraid of sudden sounds or quick movements will not do well in a busy household. A puppy who is completely oblivious may be too dull, too independent, or sick.

In fact, if most of the puppies seem apathetic or drowsy, ask the breeder if they've just been eating or playing, as these activities can slow puppies down. If so, perhaps you could head over to a nearby mall or restaurant while the puppies nap for a while. A considerate breeder tries to arrange appointments so that the puppies are alert when a prospective buyer arrives, but this is not always easy to coordinate.

Next, ask the breeder if you can see each puppy who is available for sale individually, while the others are removed. You want to see how each puppy reacts when he is alone with the breeder and your family and away from his littermates. Sometimes a puppy who seems bold when other dogs are "backing him up" will become uncertain or anxious on his own. At the other extreme, sometimes a feisty, active individual will calm down when not being egged on by the others; given your undivided attention, he may become quite the lap-sitter.

What is his general expression and body language? Does he keep his tail up or mostly down? Is it wagging, even hesitantly? When you talk to him, does he look at your face? Does he cock his head and listen? Guide him into a sitting position, and if possible, into a lying-down position. Does he melt easily under your hands or does he resist? When you pick him up, is his body pliable and relaxed, or does he throw out all four limbs like a suction-cup Garfield? Open his mouth and touch his teeth—is he okay with that? Ask the breeder to put the puppy on a table and show you how he responds to grooming. Ask him to clip one of the puppy's nails—is he accepting or does he pitch a fit (I mean the puppy, not the breeder!)?

Now try these five temperament tests:

At some point when he is across the room, kneel down and clap your hands gently a few times, close to the floor in a quick, encouraging manner. A normal puppy should come readily to you. A dominant puppy may rush wildly at you, leaping or nipping when he arrives. A submissive puppy will come hesitantly, often with belly low to the ground or tail down. An independent puppy won't pay any attention to your clapping or will glance at you, then keep on doing his own thing.

Stand up and walk away from the puppy, bending down as you walk and gently clapping your hands to encourage him to follow. A normal puppy will follow you. A dominant puppy will, too, but he'll entangle your feet or pounce on your shoes or try to grab your pant leg. A submissive puppy will follow hesitantly, perhaps with his tail down. An independent puppy will just stand there watching you leave, or wander off to explore.

Gently roll the puppy onto his back and hold him there, with one hand on his chest, for fifteen seconds. A normal puppy will struggle a little, then settle down. A submissive puppy will lie passively, perhaps licking your fingers. A dominant or independent puppy will struggle fiercely the whole time, perhaps crying or trying to nip.

Lace your fingers together and cradle them, palms up, under the puppy's tummy. Raise him up so that his four feet are just off the floor. Hold him there for fifteen seconds. A normal puppy will struggle a little, then settle down. A submissive puppy will hang passively, perhaps licking your fingers. A dominant or independent puppy will

struggle fiercely the whole time, perhaps crying or trying to nip.

Get the puppy's attention with a ball or toy. Roll it across the floor and encourage the puppy to run after it and bring it back. An ideal puppy will bring it back and drop it for you, or allow you to take it from him. The average puppy will chase it and pick it up, but is more likely to carry it off to chew on it than to bring it back to you; however, when you go over to take it from him, he's willing to give it up. A dominant puppy will carry it off and will hold on stubbornly when you go over to get it from him. A submissive puppy may be nervous when the toy rolls by or hesitant to approach the toy when it stops moving. An independent puppy or one who simply has no prey instincts will show little or no interest in chasing or picking up the toy.

Most families, especially those with children, will do best with a puppy who behaves normally in at least three of the tests. A puppy who displays dominant or independent behavior in several tests will careful training and socialization, else he could become overly bold or aggressive. A puppy who displays submissive behavior in several tests will also need careful training and socialization, as an overly meek, docile puppy could mature into a skittish adult. A puppy who is a real mixed bag of labels (one normal, one dominant, one submissive, one independent) will probably be unpredictable in his response to training and to unusual situations; such a puppy will be hard to read and is not a good choice for most owners.

Caution: Keep in mind the breed you're testing. In a dominant or independent breed, the responses of most of the puppies may be dominant or independent. In a submissive breed, the responses of most of the puppies may be submissive. Indeed, such a uniform response that follows typical breed character is an indication that most of the litter will turn out to have the dominance, independence, or submissiveness typical for their breed. This type of uniform litter is a tribute to the breeder and makes the buyer's choice much easier. However, even in dominant breeds, submissive breeds, and independent breeds, most families will still do best with the puppy whose responses lean toward the normal.

After you've evaluated each puppy's temperament, give him a brief physical exam.

His *build* should be uniformly rounded: He should not have thin ribs combined with a fat potbelly, which could mean worms.

His *skin* should be free of fleas. Part the hair and look for the little creatures themselves or the dark specks of their waste, which they leave attached to the hair. He should not be scratching furiously at his coat or ears or turning around to bite at the base of his tail or rear end. Especially watch out for thin or bare areas around the eyes and mouth and on the front legs, which may be demodectic mange.

His *coat* will be a "puppy coat." Long-coated breeds will be fuzzier than short-coated breeds, but don't expect Old English Sheepdog or Afghan Hound puppies to look anything like the adults they will become. For some months, their hair will appear to grow outward rather than downward, and they'll look like fluffballs.

His *color* may be different from an adult's. As with coat length, correct color can take months or even years to develop.

His *eyes* should be bright and clear, not watery. The whites of the eyes should be white, not yellow or streaked with red. There should be no tearstains down the face. Puppy eyes may still be blue, or they may be changing toward their adult color, which is brown in the vast majority of breeds.

His *ears* should not be dirty or smelly, and the puppy should not be shaking his head, which could mean ear mites. Ears that stand up by themselves—prick ears—may not be up yet. Some breeds have them up at six weeks, while others do not have them up until twelve or fourteen weeks (especially in the larger breeds). When they do come up, they may come up quarter-mast or half-mast for a while until they finally straighten all the way up. Also, ears often go up and down during teething. But beware of a puppy of four months or older with heavy ears that are fully hanging—these may not come up at all, or they may need extensive taping and bandaging to bring them erect.

His *nose* should not be running. You should not hear him breathing through it, nor should he be wheezing or coughing.

His teeth should be straight and white. As for their arrangement—a dog's *bite* is the way in which his upper and lower teeth meet. Most common is a scissors bite, where the back of the upper front teeth slightly overlap but still touch the front of the lower front teeth. Also common is a level (or even) bite, where the bottom of the upper front teeth meet the top of the lower front teeth edge to edge. Undesirable in all breeds is an overshot bite, where the upper front teeth jut out beyond the lower front teeth. Undesirable in *almost* all breeds (a few, such as the Bulldog, require it) is an undershot bite, where the lower front teeth jut out beyond the upper front teeth.

Why is a proper bite important? From a historical perspective, most breeds were developed for working purposes, and they needed the most efficient arrangement of teeth for nipping livestock to drive them in the desired direction, seizing prey such as rabbits and rats, retrieving and holding fallen birds, defending their flock and family against intruders, and so on. From a practical perspective, a proper bite allows a dog to grip and chew his food easily. It is a breeder's responsibility to maintain a healthy bite in his breeding stock.

Most breeds require a scissors bite, but some breeds allow or even prefer a level bite. In a seven- to twelve-week-old puppy, the bite may already be scissors or level. However, upper and lower jaws grow at different rates, so the bite you see in a young puppy may not be the bite you end up with. A perfect bite may stay perfect or go slightly off in the next few months, while a slightly overshot bite (just a wee bit) may correct itself. A severely overshot or undershot bite will not correct itself.

A *dewclaw* is a useless fifth claw on the ankle. Some dogs are born with these and some aren't. Dewclaws are acceptable on the front legs, but on the rear legs they're susceptible to snagging and tearing when a dog scratches himself. Unless you're looking at a Great Pyrenees, Briard, or Beauceron (who, for no practical reason, *require* dewclaws on their hind legs), the breeder should have had any rear dewclaws snipped off by the vet. If you see a puppy or adult with rear dewclaws, it tells you something (bad) about his breeder.

Nails should be short. Long nails are a sign of poor care.

The *anal area* should be clean, with no irritation or wet stains, which could be a sign of diarrhea. Perhaps you'll also have a chance to observe stools for firmness and lack of worm segments.

Testicles should be down by twelve weeks, though they may go back up when the puppy gets excited or cold. If both have come down at least once, they'll eventually come down to stay. Some dogs will keep one up as late as ten or twelve months, then suddenly drop it. But males who retain a testicle past twelve months should always be neutered, else the retained testicle is likely to develop cancer. These dogs cannot be shown anyway, and monorchidism (one testicle retained) and cryptorchidism (both testicles retained) are genetic traits, so these dogs must never be bred.

Conformation faults (physical deviations from the breed's standard) will be difficult or impossible for a novice to notice, so ask the breeder to point them out. In any case, they are probably the reason the puppy is being offered as a pet rather than as breeding or show quality. As long as you're purchasing from a responsible breeder, conformation faults do not affect the puppy's ability to make a wonderful companion.

After you've evaluated and examined each puppy, tell the breeder that you and your family would like a few minutes alone to talk things over and make a decision.

EVALUATING AN OLDER DOG

If you're looking at a dog over four months old, you'll test him and examine him a little differently.

With the dog on-leash, go for a stroll along the sidewalk or to the park. Notice how he reacts to traffic, bicycles, skateboards, rustling leaves. Ideally, he will be calm and controlled, but if he strains eagerly on the leash, trying to visit passersby and check out all the sights, that's a good sign that he's interested in and unafraid of the world around him. The pulling can be controlled with obedience training. Use your common sense, though. If his strength or excitability make you uncomfortable, if you're uncertain of your ability to hold on to him, he may be too much dog for you. You'll be living with this dog, walking him, training him, for a long time. Don't get a dog who makes you feel uncomfortable or uncertain.

Walk up to passersby under the pretense of asking for directions or for the correct time. Observe the dog's reaction. He should act friendly or indifferent. He should never be fearful or apprehensive.

Try to find children who will interact with the dog. He should never nip at them, even in play, and he should never be skittish of them.

Try to find other dogs to walk past, and gauge his reactions.

Hand the leash to the breeder and ask him to walk the dog past a bush or tree where you will be hiding. As the breeder and dog go by, shake a coffee can full of pebbles or make some other sudden sound. The dog may alert sharply to the sound, he may startle a little, or he may seem not to notice or care. He should not bolt to the end of the leash or stand trembling with his tail tucked and eyes wide.

Emerge from your hiding place, pulling a rattling pull toy or some other unusual object across the path of the dog and breeder. As with the sound test, he should be either interested or indifferent, but not afraid. He'll see many new things in the world, and he must be willing to accept them with equanimity.

Ask the breeder about any training the dog has had: housebreaking, riding in the car, crate training, any commands he knows. How easy was he to train? How is he with other dogs? Cats? Is he a barker? A digger? A chewer? If there is some character trait or behavioral trait that you and your family cannot tolerate, make it clear to the breeder. Many breeders will sell an older dog on a trial basis. They will take the dog back and refund your money if he doesn't fit into your household, including getting along with your other pets, within a week or two.

Sit with the dog in the yard or house. Pet him, talk to him, play with him. Try to get a feel for him. Depending on his breed, personality, and age, he may not be very outgoing with you yet, but that will change with time, so don't let his reserve bother you. After all, you're a complete stranger to him. The important question is, Do you like him?

Also take this quiet time to examine him physically, much as you would a puppy. Then tell the breeder that you and your family would like a few minutes alone to talk things over and make a decision.

Saying Yes; Saying No

If you decide that a puppy is perfect for your wants, needs, personality, and lifestyle, congratulations! You've made the most informed decision a prospective dog buyer could ever hope to make. You're to be commended for the time and effort you've spent.

Now it's time to go over the paperwork.

You first need to see any genetic health clearances required for your breed: OFA certificate, CERF certificate, BAER printout, veterinary reports disclosing cardiac status, thyroid status, vWD status, and so on.

HOW TO READ OFA AND CERF CERTIFICATES

First make sure the names on the certificates are the same as the sire and dam of the litter and that the AKC registration numbers match. (Yes, some breeders really do try to pass off the certificates of other dogs . . .)

The OFA hip number looks like this: PO-4567G34F-T

PO = the initials of the breed (i.e. PO = Poodle, AS = Australian Shepherd)
4567 = the certificate number
G = the result (E=excellent, G=good, F=fair)
34 = age in months at exam time (should be at least 24)
F = gender of dog
T = dog also has permanent ID (tattoo or microchip) for a more positive identification

The OFA elbows number looks like this: PO-EL455-T

PO = the initials of the breed
EL = elbows
455 = the certificate number
T = dog also has permanent ID (tattoo or microchip) for a more positive identification

The OFA cardiac number looks like this: PO-CA51/28F/C-T

PO = the initials of the breed
CA = cardiac
51 = the certificate number
28 = age in months at exam time (should be at least 12 months)
F = gender of dog
C = exam was done by a cardiologist;
  S = specialist (an internist with cardiology training); P = practitioner (general vet)
T = dog also has permanent ID (tattoo or microchip) for a more positive identification

The OFA thyroid number looks like this: PO-TH12/31F-T

PO = the initials of the breed
TH = thyroid
12 = the certificate number
31 = age in months at exam time
F = gender of dog
T = dog also has permanent ID (tattoo or microchip) for a more positive identification

The CERF number looks like this: PO-256/99-28

PO = the initials of the breed
256 = the certificate number
99 = year of exam (must be within the past year, as this test must be repeated annually)
28 = age in months at exam time

If you have Internet access, all of this information can be verified through the free database on the OFA Web site at www.offa.org (yes, that's two *f*'s rather than one!) or on the CERF Web site at www.vet.purdue.edu/~yshen/cerf.html.

REGISTRATION APPLICATION OR CERTIFICATE

When you buy a purebred puppy who is represented as being eligible for AKC registration, you are entitled to his registration papers. These belong to the puppy and may not be withheld unless there is an agreement regarding their withholding, signed by both the buyer and the seller. Be sure the breeder fills out and signs his part of the registration application or certificate that acknowledges himself as the breeder and you as the new owner.

PEDIGREE

Here is an example of a nice three-generation pedigree:

Ch Fanfair Mystic Wizard
Ch Foxnoir Fashion Bug CD (grandfather)
Ch Foxnoir Super Star
Ch Boxwood's Don Miguel CGC (sire)
Ch Shadowmist Porky Pig
Ch Rosewood's Miss Jasmine CD (grandmother)
Ch Paxson's Faith
Puppy
Ch Candlebelle's Rebellion
Madric's Black Gold CDX TD (grandfather)
Starfire's Ebony Rose
Rosewood's Elvira TDI TT (dam)
Kountrydale's Hiawatha
Eden's Bluebell (grandmother)
Eden's Bay Wind

Notice how each registered name is made up of a kennel name (Foxnoir, Rosewood) plus an individual name or "cool" phrase. This is the way knowledgeable breeders name their dogs. Imagine a Dachshund named Mikey, whose registered name is Willowrun's Hocus Pocus. Willowrun is the kennel name attached to all the pups produced by Mikey's breeder. Hocus Pocus is the cool phrase that sets Mikey apart from his siblings and cousins from that same breeder.

Notice the titles: You may remember from chapter 8 that Ch. means conformation champion (structure and gait), while CD is an obedience title, and CGC, TT, and TDI are temperament titles. Titles don't prove quality, but they do show that the breeder is making an attempt to accomplish something with his dogs besides breeding them. See chapter 8 for the titles you should be looking for on a pedigree.

Now look at this pedigree:

> Tinker Red Fox
> Smith's King Gus
> Chico's Shy Boots
> Popcorn Peanut Pete
> Casey XXIX
> Smith's Little Nina
> Fee Fee XIV

Puppy

> Copper John
> Mister Saucy Chico
> Cookie Girl III
> Miss Chiquita Jane
> My Little Buddy IV
> Bitsy Johnson
> Honey Bee Buzz

See the difference? There are no titles here and virtually no kennel names. The people who owned these individuals didn't know enough about purebred dogs to name them in the accepted manner, so they gave them the same kind of "call name" we use every day with our pets. All those Roman numerals had to be added by the AKC because there were so many other people who didn't know how to give their dog a more distinctive name.

Mind you, these kinds of names are not a crime. Many people enjoy naming their dogs as though they were children; for example, Tiffany Marie Johnson. But people who have done research into responsible breeding practices would have learned about accepted naming patterns. Even if they had already named their dog Tiffany Marie Johnson, they would have sought out a stud dog from a responsible breeder who did know how to name his dog and whose whole line was properly named.

That didn't happen here. Each of the dogs in this second pedigree was bred to another dog with the same kind of name. This clueless breeding has gone on for several generations, with each person who didn't know any better linking up with other people who didn't know any better. When people don't educate themselves about such simple breeding practices as registered names, how likely is it that they learned about anything else?

Some pedigrees will include kennel names, but it will be virtually the same one throughout: Smith's, Betty's, Joe-Bob's. Such a breeder has established a long line of dogs, and if they have no titles, you are probably looking at a puppy from a puppy mill or pet shop. Oh, there might be one title: perhaps a great-grandfather named Ch. Eaglecraft's Lightning Bolt. The breeder or pet shop owner will point proudly to ol' Lightning Bolt, but one or two good dogs in the pedigree won't affect your puppy enough to balance the dozen poor-quality dogs. Always focus on the parents and grandparents when looking for titles in a pedigree.

To give the pedigree more meaning, ask the breeder if he has photos of any of the dogs. Ask him to tell you about their temperaments, strengths, and weaknesses. Knowledgeable breeders enjoy talking about their puppies' ancestry, and you can learn about the kind of dog your puppy might turn out to be by letting the breeder add descriptions and personalities to otherwise meaningless names. You'll also learn how much the breeder actually knows about his line. Most breeders have an album or shoebox full of pictures and will whip it out on a moment's notice.

SALES CONTRACT

Not all breeders use sales contracts, and I am wary of those that are excessively lengthy and complex. I dislike legalese. Contracts that specify that you're buying a pet-quality puppy, that you'll take good care of him, that you won't keep him chained outdoors or let him run loose, that you won't sell him or give him away without contacting the breeder first, and other commonsense requirements, are fine.

Do not agree to any contract that stipulates co-ownership, where both you and the breeder own the dog, or that makes demands that you breed or show your dog. These clauses, which you won't see when you're buying a pet-quality dog, but might see when you're buying show quality, interfere with your ability to raise your dog the way you want to. What if you want to neuter because a female's heat periods become a nuisance or because a male is lifting his leg all over the house? What if he/she develops a health or temperament problem that makes him unsuitable for breeding, yet the breeder wants to breed him anyway? Who is responsible for the medical bills for C-sections?

It is impossible to come up with every possible scenario in co-ownership contracts and breeding contracts. They have ruined friendships and caused so much emotional stress that they are simply not worth it. Even the AKC recommends against them. I urge you not to get involved in them. If you buy a dog, he should be yours, free and clear.

Here is a simple contract:

Names, address, phone numbers of buyer and
  breeder
Puppy's name or description
AKC litter registration number
Birth date, sex, color

1. The Buyer shall provide the dog with good food, fresh water at all times, daily companionship and affection, and veterinary care upon sickness, disease, or injury.
2. The Buyer shall keep the dog as an indoor pet, providing a fenced yard or other means of safe outdoor exercise (walking on-leash).
3. The Buyer shall provide a collar and identification tag for the dog to wear at all times when allowed outdoors.
4. The dog is being sold as pet quality, with limited registration. The Buyer agrees not to breed the dog and to have the dog neutered by the age of twelve months. The Buyer agrees to furnish proof (a copy of the veterinary neutering certificate) to the Breeder that this has been done.
5. The dog shall reside at the Buyer's address. The Buyer and Breeder agree to keep each other informed of their current addresses.
6. The Buyer agrees to keep in touch with the Breeder at least once a year to

report on the dog's condition, health, temperament, etc.

7. If the dog cannot be kept by the Buyer, the Buyer shall notify the Breeder immediately. The dog shall not be sold, transferred, or given to any individual without the Breeder's consent.

8. For the life of the dog, the Buyer may return the dog to the Breeder at any time and for any reason. At the time of return, the Buyer agrees to sign the necessary AKC papers to list the Breeder as sole owner of the dog.

9. The Buyer agrees that the Breeder is in no way liable or responsible for any damage, accident, or injury resulting from the dog.

10. The Buyer shall pay a purchase price of _____, as well as any shipping charges and related expenses with regard to the delivery of the dog to the Buyer.

11. Should the Buyer be unable or unwilling to fulfill any of the above provisions, the Buyer agrees to return the dog to the Breeder at the Breeder's request. Should the Buyer refuse to return the dog, the Buyer hereby authorizes the Breeder to pick up and remove the dog from the Buyer's control.

12. The Buyer agrees to pay the Breeder any and all expenses, including court costs and reasonable attorney fees, in enforcing the terms and provisions of the contract.

WRITTEN HEALTH GUARANTEE

If the breeder doesn't use a sales contract or if the health guarantee is not specified in the sales contract, it should be on a separate sheet of paper.

We discussed health guarantees in chapter 9: Expect a forty-eight-hour guarantee where you can return the puppy for a full refund if he doesn't pass your vet's examination. Also expect a two-year guarantee against hereditary diseases, including bad temperament.

MEDICAL RECORD

Ask the breeder if the puppy has had any illnesses or incidences of fever, coughing, limping, skin conditions, or anything else. Be sure the medical record includes:

1. Vaccinations: A schedule of dates and types of vaccines used and the name of the person who administered them. Sometimes the breeder administers his own shots. Ask about any adverse reactions the puppy may have had.

2. Worming: A schedule of dates when the puppy's stool was checked for worms and any worming that had to be done.

3. General health certificate: Signed by a veterinarian.

FEEDING SCHEDULE

This should include the type of food the puppy is accustomed to eating, how it is prepared, how much, and when. You don't want to stress his digestive system with a sudden change of diet. You will, however, almost certainly want to change his diet very soon.

New puppy buyers are always warned, "Regarding food, listen to your breeder." How absurd. Feeding is one of the most controversial subjects in dogdom. Why should one breeder's opinion matter any more than another's, especially when most breeders have done little research? Do your own research, especially checking out natural feeding methods.

READING MATERIALS

Some breeders include pamphlets or written instructions on puppy care and training, a recommended reading list, or contact information for joining the breed's national club.

FAVORITE TOY OR BLANKET

If the breeder doesn't include this, ask. A familiar toy eases the puppy's transition to a new home.

PHOTOS

Ask the breeder if he has any photos of your puppy's parents that you can keep. Some thoughtful breeders will even give you a photo of your puppy taken soon after birth.

You've just bought yourself a fine purebred dog!

If you decide that none of the puppies is right for your wants, needs, personality, and lifestyle, say politely: "These are really nice puppies, but we just don't see exactly what we're looking for right now. Thank you so much for your time, and thank you for showing them to us."

I know you're disappointed, but you'd be *more* disappointed if you chose the wrong puppy. Reflect on everything that this valuable first experience has taught you about the breed and about the evaluation process. Call the next breeder on your list. Take your time. The search will be worth it.

APPENDIX:
NATIONAL CLUBS AND CONTACTS

Web sites are included when the domain name is unique, breed-related, and/or owned by the club, i.e., www.afghanhound.net. Clubs that are being hosted on personal pages, such as on AOL or Geocities, are likely to change, so to avoid getting outdated information, visit www.akc.org to find the current site of your breed's national club. Or use a search engine such as www.yahoo.com and type in the breed name: "Afghan Hound."

Affenpinscher Club of America: 410-378-4075; Rescue: 608-455-1828

Afghan Hound Club of America: 602-994-0150; Rescue: 413-268-0208, www.afghanhound.net

Airedale Terrier Club of America: 650-225-9140, www.airedale.org; Rescue: 602-996-9648 or 610-873-9054

Akita Club of America: 909-943-1811, www.akitaclub.org; Rescue: 973-427-5985

Alaskan Malamute Club of America: 973-584-7125; Rescue: 505-281-3961

Working American Bulldog Association: 714-903-9688; National American Bulldog Association: 413-566-8637; American Bulldog Association: www.american-bulldog.com

American Cocker Spaniel Club: 931-484-5030; Rescue: 770-974-7931

American Eskimo Dog Club of America: 828-625-0125; Rescue: 770-963-6120, www.heartbandits.com

American Foxhound Club: 254-778-4887

American Hairless Terrier Club: 704-892-5104; American Hairless Terrier Federation: 954-946-7297, www.ahtfederation.com

National American Pit Bull Terrier Association: 203-669-0258

(American) Staffordshire Terrier Club of America: 716-234-3647; Rescue: 810-349-0088

American Water Spaniel Club: 800-555-2972; American Water Spaniel Field Association: 248-363-0858; Rescue: 512-357-2591

Anatolian Shepherd Dog Club of America: 619-445-3334; Anatolian Shepherd Dogs International: 931-647-0586; United Anatolian Guardians: 707-668-4268

Appenzell Mountain Dog Club of America: 302-999-1542

Australian Cattle Dog Club of America: 913-856-2162, www.cattledog.com; Rescue: 760-366-3593; Other: www.australiancattledog.com

North American Australian Kelpie Registry: 309-523-2188

Australian Shepherd Club of America: 409-778-1082, www.asca.org; United States Australian Shepherd Association: 408-663-3900, www.australianshepherds.org; Rescue: 877-277-4779 or 877-372-8387, www.aussierescue.org

Miniature Australian Shepherd Club of America: 619-284-0840 or 619-486-4339; North American Miniature Australian Shepherd Club of the USA: 805-929-2195

Australian Terrier Club of America: 850-444-3426, www.aussies.inna.net/atca.htm; Rescue: 970-482-9163

Basenji Club of America: 206-362-4202, www.basenji.org; Rescue: 303-795-5382; Other: www.barkless.com

Basset Hound Club of America: 330-725-7353, www.basset-bhca.org; Rescue: 908-874-0508; Other: www.basset.net, www.dailydrool.com

National Beagle Club: 423-986-9406; Other: www.beagles-on-the-web.com

Bearded Collie Club of America: 870-837-2930, www.beardie.net/bcca/; Rescue: 516-724-0871

North American Beauceron Club: 540-659-7480, www.beauce.org; Beauceron Club of America: 909-767-9163; United States Beauceron Alliance: 770-772-6555, www.beauceronus.org

Bedlington Terrier Club of America: 573-468-5282; Rescue: 804-232-3748

Belgian Sheepdog (Groenendael) Club of America: 360-577-6636; Rescue: 517-627-2549 or 508-947-6640

American Belgian Laekenois Association: 607-533-4767 or 719-444-8526

American Belgian Malinois Club: 520-825-0278, www.breedclub.org/ABMC.htm

American Belgian Tervuren Club: 828-837-8870 or 904-778-1093, www.abtc.org; Rescue: 414-642-2286

Bernese Mountain Dog Club of America: 850-594-4636, www.bmd.org; Rescue: 309-596-2633

Bichon Frise Club of America: 336-945-9788, www.bichon.org; Rescue: 314-892-1748

American Black and Tan Coonhound Club: 813-963-2033, www.abtcc.com; Rescue: 919-776-7375

American Bloodhound Club: 904-756-0373, www.bloodhounds.org; Other: www.bloodhounds.com

Bolognese Club of America: 812-923-8066

Border Collie Society of America: 414-656-1554; United States Border Collie Club: www.bordercollie.org; American Border Collie Association: 316-635-2356

Border Terrier Club of America: 860-546-6674; Rescue: 706-863-0951

Borzoi Club of America: 908-647-3027, www.borzoiclubofamerica.com; Rescue: 908-859-4554 or 888-264-8898; Other: www.borzois.com

Boston Terrier Club of America: 303-857-6016; Rescue: 724-883-4732 or www.bostonrescue.net; Other: www.bostonterrier.org, www.bostons.com

American Bouvier des Flandres Club: 919-851-9325, www.bouvier.org; Rescue: 978-948-7039

American Boxer Club: 703-385-9385; Rescue: 504-738-5820

Briard Club of America: 908-647-7329; Rescue: 910-869-5490

American Brittany Club: 402-553-5538 or 618-985-2336; Rescue: 510-582-2714, www.brittanyrescue.com

American Brussels Griffon Association: 612-427-7687, www.brusselsgriffon.org; Rescue: 713-783-8887

Bulldog Club of America: 540-775-3015, www.thebca.org; Rescue: 248-945-8009 or 800-594-4289; Other: www.bulldog.org, www.bulldogbytes.com

American Bullmastiff Rescue: 978-939-5300

Bull Terrier Club of America: 423-842-2611; Rescue: 800-282-8911, 401-231-0927, www.btwf.org; Other: www.bullterrier.org

Cairn Terrier Club of America: 517-545-4816, www.cairnterrier.org; Rescue: 817-783-5979

Canaan Dog Club of America: 707-226-3353, www.cdca.org; Israel Canaan Dog Club of America: 319-984-5139, www.itb.it/canaan/

International Cane Corso Federation: 973-691-3244, www.canecorso.org; Rescue: 718-279-2686

Cavalier King Charles Spaniel Club: 513-831-6755, www.ckcsc.org; American Cavalier King Charles Spaniel Club: 805-477-2667, www.ackcsc.org; Rescue: 541-726-3850 or 717-235-2120

National Cesky Terrier Club: 919-778-2318, www.cesky.org; Rescue: 973-627-9050

American Chesapeake Club: www.amchessieclub.org; Rescue: 207-529-451, www.cbrrescue.org

Chihuahua Club of America: 203-762-2314; Rescue: 203-762-2314

American Chinese Crested Club: 603-547-2804; Rescue: 602-870-4928, www.crest-care.com

Chinese Shar-Pei Club of America: 907-345-6504, www.cspca.com; Rescue: 610-341-0346 or 708-848-2226

Chinook Owners Association: 406-454-3598, www.chinook.org; Chinooks Worldwide: 207-832-6182, www.chinook-dogs.org

Chow Chow Club: 513-398-0206, www.chowclub.org; Rescue: 608-756-2008, www.chowwelfare.com; Other: www.chowchowbaby.com

Clumber Spaniel Club of America: 914-738-3976, www.clumbers.org; Rescue: 908-580-1055

Collie Club of America: 815-337-0323; Collie Club of America Foundation: www.cca-foundation.org; American Smooth Collie Association: 603-352-8597; Rescue: 412-364-5742

Coton de Tulear Club of America: 609-268-9737; United States of America Coton de Tulear Club: 817-572-7387; American Coton de Tulear Association: 516-549-3963

Curly-Coated Retriever Club of America: 978-281-3860; Other: www.curlycoats.com

Dachshund Club of America: 504-835-1025, www.dachshund-dca.org; Rescue: 724-846-6745

Dalmatian Club of America: 708-687-5447, www.thedca.org; Rescue: 540-349-9022

Dandie Dinmont Terrier Club of America: 719-473-9560; Rescue: 770-975-3773

Doberman Pinscher Club of America: 828-884-3487, www.dpca.org; Rescue: 757-482-3762

Dogo Argentino: Karolyn Harris 580-246-3550

Dogue de Bordeaux Society: 732-723-1876; Rescue: 916-687-7461, www.ddbsrescue.homepage.com

English Cocker Spaniel Club of America: 414-529-9714, www.ecsca.org; Rescue: 703-548-7641

English Foxhound Club of America: 301-372-1073

English Setter Association of America: 440-285-4531, www.esaa.com; Llewellin (Field) Setter Association: 501-849-3383, www.llewellin.com; Rescue: 336-854-7142

English Shepherd Club: Karen Zumwalt 813-655-8936, www.englishshepherd.org

English Springer Field Trial Association: 702-656-7116 or 212-481-7792, www.essfta.org; Rescue: 800-377-3824

English Toy Spaniel Club of America: 847-662-1000 or 860-399-0090; Rescue: 609-397-3148 or 219-848-7429

National Entlebucher Mountain Dog Association: 604-541-2822; www.entlebucher.org

Field Spaniel Society of America: 815-625-0467; Rescue: 714-761-7144

Fila Brasileiro Club of America: 972-783-0341

Finnish Spitz Club of America: 801-774-9045; Rescue: 919-359-1150

Flat-Coated Retriever Society of America: 904-268-0325; Rescue: 616-846-0773 or 603-547-8607

American Fox Terrier Club (Smooth and Wire): 425-483-6177; Rescue: 800-369-8377

French Bulldog Club of America: 205-553-3817, www.frenchbulldog.org; Rescue: 818-557-6565; Other: www.frenchbulldogs.org

German Pinscher Club of America: 401-397-4301, www.iag.net/~lakai/; American German Pinscher Breeders Association: 814-736-9699

German Shepherd Dog Club of America: 201-568-5806, www.gsdca.org; German Shepherd Dog Working Dog Association: www.gsdca-wda.org; Rescue: 630-529-7396

German Shorthaired Pointer Club of America: 803-499-4140 or 315-626-2990; Rescue: 309-787-4266, www.gsprescue.org

German Wirehaired Pointer Club of America: 360-985-2776, www.gwpca.com; Verein Deutsch-Drahthaar: 515-993-5982, www.drahthaar.com; Rescue: 978-861-0820

Giant Schnauzer Club of America: 603-894-4938, www.schnauzerware.com; Rescue: 303-988-6564

Glen of Imaal Terrier Club of America: 540-885-7846

Golden Retriever Club of America: 281-861-0820 or 540-341-7356, www.grca.org; Rescue: 218-861-0820, www.golden-retriever.com

Gordon Setter Club of America: 303-841-2015, www.gsca.org; Rescue: 612-413-0612

Great Dane Club of America: www.gdca.org

Greater Swiss Mountain Dog Club of America: 440-237-9572, www.gsmdca.org; Rescue: 609-384-8595

Great Pyrenees Club of America: 540-731-0229

Greyhound Club of America: 804-883-7800; Rescue: 805-684-4914; Greyhound Pets of America: 800-366-1472, www.greyhoundpets.org; National Greyhound Adoption Program: 800-348-2517, www.ngap.org; Greyhound Protection League: 800-446-8637; The Greyhound Project: www.adopt-a-greyhound.org

Harrier Club of America: 707-463-0501; Rescue: 619-377-4758

Havanese Club of America: 352-568-8172 or 203-756-1753

Ibizan Hound Club of the United States: 360-856-2139; Rescue: 806-746-5521

Irish Setter Club of America: 209-295-1666

Irish Terrier Club of America: 508-285-9655; Rescue: 423-538-8648

Irish Water Spaniel Club of America: 773-725-5434; Rescue: 301-724-9162

Irish Wolfhound Club of America: 937-845-9135, www.iwclubofamerica.org; Rescue: 609-268-9373

Italian Greyhound Club of America: 909-679-5084, www.italiangreyhound.org

Italian Spinone Club of America: 804-333-0309, www.spinone.com

Jack Russell Terrier Association of America: 860-738-0492, www.jrtaa.org; Jack Russell Terrier Club of America: www.terrier.com; Rescue: 804-469-4744; Other: www.jack-russell.com

Japanese Chin Club of America: 931-836-8150, www.japchin.com/jcca/; Rescue: 425-255-7119 or 410-392-5645

Keeshond Club of America: 215-637-7731; American Keeshond Society: 301-293-9556; Rescue: 310-457-3569, www.keeshond.com

United States Kerry Blue Terrier Club: 757-766-8097; Rescue: 513-742-3745; Other: www.kerryblues.org

Komondor Club of America: 734-433-0417; Rescue: 414-594-3374

Kuvasz Club of America: 219-921-1529, www.kuvasz.com; Rescue: 313-271-5438

Kyi-Leo Club of America: Harriet Linn 510-685-4019

Labrador Retriever Club: 440-473-5255 or 440-729-2064, www.thelabradorclub.com; Rescue: 512-259-3645

United States Lakeland Terrier Club: 602-998-8409; Rescue: 303-733-4220

Leonberger Club of America: 505-867-3599, www.leonberger.com

American Lhasa Apso Club: 219-462-9520, www.lhasaapso.org; Rescue: 800-699-3115; Other: www.lhasa-apso.org

National Association of Louisiana Catahoulas: 504–665-6082 or 225-665-6082; American Catahoula Association: 504-892-6773, www.catahoulas.org; Other: www.catahoulaleopard.com

Löwchen Club of America: 330-666-8279 or 941-575-4515

American Maltese Association: 941-549-4446, www.americanmaltese.org; Other: www.maltesedog.com

American Manchester Terrier Club: 908-996-7309; Rescue: 215-957-0109

Mastiff Club of America: Sandra Shults 602-843-6995, www.mastiff.org; Rescue: 440-639-1160

Miniature Bull Terrier Club of America: 352-351-3333, www.bullterrier.org/~mbtca; Rescue: 603-679-9507

Miniature Pinscher Club of America: 407-632-6547; Rescue: 757-853-5811

American Miniature Schnauzer Club: 561-366-1038; Rescue: 214-363-5630; Other: www.schnauzerware.com

United States Neapolitan Mastiff Club: 630-858-5298, www.neapolitan.org; Rescue: 301-473-5721

Newfoundland Club of America: 256-852-7015, www.newfdogclub.org; Rescue: 608-437-4553

Norwegian Buhund Club of America: 618-377-3714, www.buhund.org

Norwegian Elkhound Association of America: 864-243-5816, www.neaa.com; Rescue: 909-351-2554

Norwegian Lundehund Club of America: 360-598-6118

Norwich and Norfolk Terrier Club: 908-766-3468; American Norfolk Terrier Association:

www.norfolkterrier.org; Rescue: 908-766-5429

Nova Scotia Duck Tolling Retriever Club: 508-636-5386

Old English Sheepdog Club of America: 406-563-6712; Rescue: 805-821-0416

Otterhound Club of America: 402-441-7900; Rescue: 601-634-0199 or 847-838-3889

Papillon Club of America: 409-357-2701, www.papillonclub.org; Rescue: 703-644-7949

Pekingese Club of America: 518-885-6864, www.pekingeseclub.org; Rescue: 253-847-3537

Petit Basset Griffon Vendeen Club of America: 805-527-6327, www.pbgv.org; Rescue: 505-820-6624

Pharaoh Hound Club of America: 352-357-8723; Rescue: 305-246-9598 or 702-782-6542

American Pointer Club: 301-926-1599, www.pointers.org; Rescue: 608-241-1613, www.pointerrescue.org

American Polish Lowland Sheepdog Club: 410-551-6750, www.aponc.com; Other: www.pon.com

American Pomeranian Club: 218-741-2117

Poodle Club of America: 956-447-1939; Rescue: 713-526-9619; Versatility in Poodles: www.pageweb.com/vipoodle/

Portuguese Water Dog Club of America: 360-675-9539, www.pwdca.org; Rescue: 610-346-9370

Pug Dog Club of America: 314-207-1508, www.pugs.org; Rescue: 320-485-2876

Puli Club of America: 405-359-0322, Rescue: 207-283-3528; Other: www.puliworld.com/puliworld

National Rat Terrier Association: 860-563-2293, www.nrta.com; American Rat Terrier Association: 860-569-6844, www.arta.net; Rat Terrier Club of America: 805-945-4051, www.ratterrierclub.com; Rescue: 818-951-8888

Rhodesian Ridgeback Club of the United States: 919-496-3389, www.rrcus.org; Rescue: 773-281-5569

American Rottweiler Club: 208-424-1304, www.amrottclub.org; Rescue: 330-722-3682

Saint Bernard Club of America: 414-392-2852; Rescue: 541-878-8281

Saluki Club of America: 817-379-1355, www.saluki.com; Rescue: 908-257-9134

Samoyed Club of America: 504-898-0864, www.samoyed.org

Schipperke Club of America: 541-259-3826; Rescue: 716-985-4137

Scottish Deerhound Club of America: 810-329-3841, www.deerhound.org; Rescue: 608-877-4140

Scottish Terrier Club of America: 916-483-9069; Rescue: 210-653-3723

American Sealyham Terrier Club: 301-699-9507; Rescue: 330-239-1498

American Shetland Sheepdog Association: 831-726-1660, www.assa.org; Rescue: 815-485-3726; Other: www.dogpatch.org/sheltie/

National Shiba Club of America: 541-265-8301

American Shih Tzu Club: 717-432-4351; Rescue: 760-942-0874

Shiloh Shepherd Dog Club of America: 716-493-5747, www.shilohshepherds.org; International Shiloh Shepherd Dog Club: 818-993-7111, www.shilohshepherd.org

Siberian Husky Club of America: 360-260-2162, www.shca.org; Rescue: 908-782-2089

Silky Terrier Club of America: 303-988-4361; Rescue: 219-322-7719

Skye Terrier Club of America: 610-965-8619; Rescue: 843-726-3237 or 301-699-9507

Sloughi Fanciers Association of America: 712-545-9098, www.sloughi.org; American Sloughi Association: 319-626-6446, www.sloughi-international.com

Soft-Coated Wheaten Terrier Club of America: 650-299-8778, www.scwtca.org

Staffordshire Bull Terrier Club: 352-357-4215 or 360-331-3412; Rescue: 718-898-0298

Standard Schnauzer Club of America: 914-565-4604; Rescue: 651-739-0062; Other: www.schnauzerware.com

Sussex Spaniel Club of America: 217-364-9603

Swedish Vallhund Club of America: 810-791-3299, www.swedishvallhund.com

Teddy Roosevelt Terrier Association: 210-623-1778, www.trta.freeservers.com

American Tibetan Mastiff Association: 757-421-2161, www.tibetanmastiff.org; Tibetan Mastiff Club of America: 909-685-5162, www.tibetanmastiffs.com/tmca; United States Tibetan Mastiff Club: 770-258-9334

Tibetan Spaniel Club of America: 541-533-2777, www.tibbies.net

Tibetan Terrier Club of America: 954-340-9356; Rescue: 973-839-5320 or 877-790-0006

Tosa Owners Service Association: 815-626-6382

American Toy Fox Terrier Club: 541-523-3368; National Toy Fox Terrier Association: 334-267-2833

Vizsla Club of America: 908-789-9774; Rescue: 610-294-8020, www.vizsladogs.com

Weimaraner Club of America: 618-236-1466, www.weimclubamerica.org

Cardigan Welsh Corgi Club of America: 303-530-7107, www.cardigancorgis.com; Rescue: 703-836-1963

Pembroke Welsh Corgi Club of America: 616-625-2560, www.pembrokecorgi.org

Welsh Springer Spaniel Club of America: 914-856-4533; Rescue: 316-244-3782; www.welshspringer.com

Welsh Terrier Club of America: 949-488-0178; Rescue: 404-351-1330 or 408-725-0424

West Highland White Terrier Club of America: 843-795-9966; Rescue: 314-991-8819

American Whippet Club: 804-295-4525; Rescue: 214-337-1758

American White Shepherd Association: 517-832-7097, www.awsaclub.com

American Wirehaired Pointing Griffon Association: 407-846-0484, www.awpga.com; Rescue: 609-265-9195; Wirehaired Pointing Griffon Club of America: 503-296-6725, www.wpgca.org

Xoloitzcuintle: Gary and Roxie Lindsey 770-477-1459

Yorkshire Terrier Club of America: 360-651-7543, www.ytca.org; Rescue: www.yorkshireterrierrescue.com

GLOSSARY

Colors

Black-and-tan is mostly black with tan "points" or "trim" above the eyes, on the cheeks, muzzle, throat, chest, legs, feet, and under the tail. Example: Rottweiler.

Blue ranges from silver to gray to steel blue. Nose, paw pads, and toenails are blue/gray. Example: Italian Greyhound.

Brindle is a light background color (often fawn) speckled with darker hairs. This "brindling" pattern may occur only in the tan areas of a particolored dog, or it may run through the entire coat, producing tiger-like stripes. Example: Greyhound.

Chocolate is dark brown, with a brown nose, paw pads, and toenails and usually light or yellowish eyes. Example: Labrador Retriever.

Dapple is a swirling, mottled mixture of several colors and is called *merle* in most other breeds. Example: Dachshund.

Double dapple is *dapple* with white markings. Example: Dachshund.

Fawn ranges from beige to tan. Example: Chihuahua.

Harlequin is an unusual color term, used in Great Danes to mean white with ragged black patches and in Beaucerons to mean blue *merle*.

Isabella is a shade of fawn. Example: Doberman.

Liver is brown, with a brown nose, paw pads, and toenails and often light or yellowish eyes. Example: German Shorthaired Pointer.

Merle is a swirling, mottled mixture of several colors, most commonly gray/white/black (blue merle). Example: Australian Shepherd.

Piebald is white with colored patches. Example: Bulldog.

Pinto is white with colored patches. Example: Akita.

Roan is a white background speckled with colored hairs. Example: English Cocker Spaniel.

Sable consists of light-colored hairs (usually fawn), tipped with a darker color (usually black or chocolate). "Sabling" may occur only in the fawn areas of particolored dogs, or it may run through most of the coat. Example: Collie.

Salt and pepper (or pepper and salt) consists of hairs that are banded with both black and white. Example: Schnauzer.

Health Problems/Tests

Addison's disease (hypoadrenocorticism) is an insufficient production of essential adrenal hormones. The disease is fatal unless diagnosed by blood tests and managed throughout a dog's life. Unfortunately, drug therapy tends to be accompanied by unpleasant side effects.

Allergies are the result of the immune system overreacting to some stimulus, such as a flea bite, grass or pollen, food, detergent, chemicals, etc. Allergies are virtually an epidemic in pets today, possibly because unnatural commercial diets, excessive vaccinations, and chemical-laden homes and yards put enormous stress on the immune system, which has to constantly battle against these toxic substances. Holistic vets will recommend a natural health care program to build the immune system and calm its hypersensitivity.

Amyloidosis is a serious disease in which a waxy protein substance called amyloid is deposited into bodily tissues, primarily in the kidney, where it surrounds the cells and crushes them. The disease exists in several forms and degrees from chronic to fatal and may actually be the end point of another (underlying) inflammatory disease, such as *familial Shar-Pei fever* (FSF).

The **BAER test** (Brainstem Auditory Evoked Response) records brain responses to clicking sounds delivered to a dog's ear. The test gives a definitive record of each ear's response to sound as early as three weeks of age. An individual may have bilateral hearing (hearing in both ears), unilateral hearing (hearing in one ear; such dogs make fine pets but must not be bred), or be completely deaf.

Bloat is a life-threatening emergency primarily seen in large or deep-chested dogs. The stomach swells with air and gas (gastric dilation) and may suddenly rotate (gastric torsion), trapping the air and gas and cutting off blood flow to the spleen and liver. Without immediate veterinary intervention, this condition is fatal. Dogs can have a hereditary disposition to suffer from this disease; contributing factors may include dry kibble diets (as opposed to natural fresh foods), eating one large meal rather than several small ones, and excessive drinking or exercising after eating.

Cardiomyopathy is a serious abnormality of the heart muscle that can cause weakness during exercise, edema of the lung, and sudden death.

A **cataract** is an opaque (whitish or bluish) spot on the lens of the eye that obscures vision and may cause blindness. Some forms (such as juvenile cataracts) have a hereditary basis, while others are the result of injury, diabetes, or old age.

Cerebellar ataxia (cerebellar hypoplasia) is an underdeveloped brain at birth, or a degeneration of the brain a few months after birth, that results in tremors, lack of coordination, and a staggering gait.

CERF (Canine Eye Registration Foundation) is an organization that issues numbers and certificates to dogs whose eyes have been examined by a board-certified (AVCO) ophthalmologist and found to be clear of eye defects that CERF recognizes as genetic.

CMO (craniomandibular osteopathy) is a noncancerous growth of bone, usually on the lower jaw. It is usually recognized when a puppy shows discomfort while chewing, between three and seven months of age. The rough surface can be detected by palpation, with confirmation by X ray. Most dogs recover with treatment.

Collapsing trachea is a serious disorder that worsens over time. The trachea (windpipe) is a flexible breathing tube made of cartilage rings and connective tissue. If these are genetically soft or damaged from injury (such as excessive jerking on a choke collar), they can fold inward, collapsing the airway like a paper straw being drawn on too vigorously. A honking cough during exercise is symptomatic. Eventually the chronic coughing may cause enlargement of the heart and fluid buildup in the lungs. Fortunately, this usually takes many years, and the condition can be managed so the dog is comfortable. Surgery is usually ineffective.

Collie eye anomaly (CEA) is the most common eye disease found in Collies. It is also common in the Border Collie, Bearded Collie, and Shetland Sheepdog (Sheltie). Severity ranges from mild obstruction of vision to blindness.

Copper toxicosis (CT) is an inborn error in metabolism that allows copper to accumulate in the liver, resulting in cirrhosis of the liver. It is fatal if not treated.

Cushing's disease (hyperadrenocorticism) is a serious disease caused by excessive production of adrenal hormones. The underlying cause is usually a tumor, and surgical removal or drug therapy is tricky. Improper management of Cushing's can produce its counterpart, *Addison's disease*.

Deafness: see *BAER test*

Demodectic mange is a skin disease caused by the demodex mite, which exists on all dogs and usually causes no harm. But some young dogs are genetically predisposed to react adversely to the mites, especially during times of stress or illness. Then the little buggers multiply into localized demodectic mange, which is manifested by hair loss around the eyes and mouth and on the front legs, with little or no itching. Almost always, no treatment is required, as the dog's immune system wipes out the mites by the time he's twelve to fourteen months of age. In a few individuals, the mite spreads over the body and becomes general demodectic mange, with extreme hair loss, skin thickening, and pimples and discharge created by staph bacteria. General demodectic mange is serious and requires veterinary treatment.

Distichiasis is an abnormal growth of an eyelash on the inner surface of the eyelid, causing discomfort, tearing of the eye, and possibly corneal ulcers. Surgery is the treatment.

Ectropion is a condition where the eyelids turn outward and are unable to properly spread tears across the eye. Surgery is the treatment.

Elbow dysplasia is an umbrella term encompassing several serious orthopedic disorders: Osteochondritis dissecans (OCD), fragmented coronoid process (FCP), and ununited anconeal process (UAP) are the most common forms. Elbow dysplasia is detected by X ray, ranges from mild to crippling, and may require surgery.

Entropion is a condition where the eyelids turn inward, irritating the cornea. Surgery is the treatment.

Epilepsy is a broad term used to describe seizure activity (trembling, salivating, falling over, loss of control of bodily functions, and/or sudden strange behaviors such as biting at the air or staring rigidly into space as though in a trance) that cannot otherwise be explained by identifying a specific disease, tumor, or head trauma. If blood work, X rays, and EEGs come back negative, most vets diagnose epilepsy. Thus, epilepsy is not proven by any test, but is a fallback diagnosis when no other cause can be found. Holistic vets have discovered that chemicals, pesticides, and vaccinations can trigger seizures and that a switch to natural health care minimizes seizures in many dogs. In any case, epilepsy is seldom fatal, though managing it is a lifelong commitment.

Eyelid/eyelash defects include *entropion* and *distichiasis*.

Familial Shar-Pei fever (FSF) is a painful inflammatory disorder producing episodic fever, abdominal sickness, and swelling of the muzzle and/or joints. The hock is most commonly affected, hence the alternate name of swollen hock syndrome. FSF is thought to be caused by an individual's inability to regulate his immune system. FSF episodes occur chronically and can often be managed, but they may also lead to *amyloidosis* or other diseases that can cause death at three to five years of age.

GCL (globoid cell leukodystrophy, Krabbe's disease) is an enzyme deficiency that produces degeneration of the brain and spinal cord. Symptoms include lack of coordination, loss of control of the hindquarters, and paralysis, beginning before six months of age and progressing rapidly to death.

Glaucoma is an increase of fluid pressure within the eyeball, usually leading to partial or total blindness. Primary (congenital) glaucoma has a hereditary basis. Secondary glaucoma results from an underlying condition such as eye injury or infection.

Hemolytic anemia is a serious condition in which red blood cells are destroyed, usually by the dog's own immune system for no apparent reason. The prognosis is poor, with most dogs living only a year or two. However, if the red blood cells are being destroyed for a legitimate reason, i.e., because they have been altered by a parasite, virus, or toxin, then treating the underlying cause can bring the condition under control. Another cause is a genetic deficiency of the PK enzyme: See *PKD*.

Hip dysplasia is a major orthopedic disorder in which the ball of the hip doesn't fit properly into its socket. The result is lameness of varying degrees, eventually leading to degenerative joint disorder (arthritis). The origin of hip dysplasia is a hot subject for debate, though heredity is clearly involved. Some researchers also implicate nutrition and believe it can be avoided or minimized by natural feeding and supplementation with vitamin C. Environment may also be a factor: too much exercise forced on growing pups, along with high-protein puppy kibble that encourages rapid growth. All breeds are susceptible, but it is most common in large and giant breeds. Hip dysplasia is a developmental disease, meaning it is not present at birth. Severe cases manifest themselves between five and twelve months of age, while moderate to mild cases may not show up until eighteen months or later. Depending on severity, treatment includes diet and pain management and/or surgery.

HOD (hypertrophic osteodystrophy) causes acute lameness in young, growing dogs, especially large breeds. It often affects all four legs simultaneously and may be accompanied by extremely painful swellings around the joints. HOD may resolve spontaneously in a week or two, it may recur as a chronic condition, and/or it may cause permanent disability. Pain management is the major goal. Some research indicates that HOD can be triggered by vaccinations or by viral or bacterial infections.

Hypoglycemia (low blood sugar) results when glucose (sugar) levels in the blood drop, whereupon the body weakens and the brain can go into seizures. Toy breeds are most susceptible, especially young or tiny individuals, and especially when physically or emotionally stressed. Hypoglycemia comes on very fast, often within a few minutes. Without immediate sugar supplementation (a fingerful of honey or Nutrical supplement usually does the trick, though some pups will require intravenous glucose), the puppy can die. Never buy a toy breed puppy less than ten weeks old, and never less than 1½ pounds. The shock of a new home at such a fragile age/weight is a perfect opportunity for hypoglycemia (and other stress-related problems such as parvovirus and demodectic mange) to strike.

Hypothyroidism: See *low thyroid*

Inflammatory bowel disease is not so much a disease as a group of clinical signs involving the gastrointestinal tract: vomiting, loose or bloody stools, weight loss. The underlying pathology is infiltration of the gut wall by inflammatory cells, causing thickening of the wall, which interferes with digestion of food and absorption of nutrients (malabsorption syndrome). Diagnosis is by blood and fecal testing and/or intestinal biopsy. Causes are varied, but include food allergies, so holistic veterinarians will usually recommend a natural, fresh-foods diet.

Legg-Perthes disease (also called Legg-Calve-Perthes) is a disintegration of the femoral head, the ball part of the ball and socket that make up the hip joint. The result is painful lameness starting at four to twelve months of age. The condition is confirmed by X ray. Mild cases may resolve with only pain management, while severe cases may eventually require removal of the femoral head.

Lens luxation occurs when the ligament fiber holding the eye lens in place deteriorates, causing the lens to dislocate (either partially or completely) from its normal position. If the lens luxates forward, it will rub against the cornea, causing discomfort, tearing, and a bluish cast over the eye, and often leading to glaucoma. Treatment ranges from drops and medication, to surgical removal of the lens, to surgical removal of the eye. Primary lens luxation has a hereditary basis, while secondary lens luxation is associated with trauma to the eye.

Liver shunt (portosystemic shunt) is a serious malady in which the blood that normally goes to the liver to be detoxified (rid of excess bile acids and other toxic by-products of normal digestion) bypasses the liver. The toxins then build up in the blood. Liver shunt may be suspected when a puppy or young dog fails to thrive and grow. Diagnosis is by blood test, ultrasound, and dye-contrast X ray. Treatment includes diet modification and possibly surgery to repair the shunt.

Low thyroid (hypothyroidism) is a chronic condition where the thyroid gland does not produce enough hormone to adequately maintain the dog's metabolism. Often this is the result of the dog's own immune system attacking the thyroid gland. Among a host of possible symptoms, hair loss, weight gain, and lethargy are the most common. Diagnosis can be tricky and must include blood testing for T3, T4, and

TSH, not just a simple T4 test. Low thyroid is easily treated with daily pills, but it is a lifelong commitment.

Luxating patella (slipped stifle) is a dislocating knee—the kneecap keeps slipping out of its socket. The ligaments or muscles around the kneecap may be genetically weak, or the socket may be too narrow or shallow. Suspect luxating patella when a dog (especially a small dog) sometimes lifts one rear leg while running or moves both rear legs at the same time, like a hopping bunny. Sometimes the knee slips only for a moment, then slides back. Sometimes it stays out until you or the vet manipulate it back. Most cases (first or second degree) are not severe and can be easily managed, but chronic (third degree) and severe (fourth degree) cases require surgery, which may or may not be successful.

Mitral valve disease (MVD) is a serious heart defect responsible for premature death or compromised quality of life. MVD is best diagnosed by Doppler ultrasound.

OCD (osteochondritis or osteochondrosis) is a serious disorder of the joints. See *elbow dysplasia*.

OFA (Orthopedic Foundation for Animals) is an organization that evaluates X rays and veterinary reports for the presence and/or degree of hip dysplasia, elbow dysplasia, luxating patella, heart defects, and hypothyroidism.

Pancreatitis is a leakage of digestive enzymes, which damages the pancreas and causes abdominal pain and sickness. Causes include high-fat foods, obesity, lack of exercise, Cushing's disease, and genetic factors that make some breeds more prone to the disorder than others. Mild, recurrent attacks are most common, though a single acute attack can occur and can be fatal.

Panosteitis, commonly called *pano*, is an inflammation of the membrane covering the leg bones, producing sudden lameness in large breeds, usually males, between five and eighteen months of age. Typically a front leg is affected first, with the syndrome then shifting to different legs. Pressure applied over the long bones usually produces pain, and X rays reveal that the bones have greater density than is normally found. Pain management and rest are the goals, as the condition is self-limiting and will eventually go away.

PDA (patent ductus arteriosus) is a heart defect in which the vessel between the aorta and the pulmonary artery, which is open in the fetus so that blood can travel between mother and puppy, doesn't close at the time of birth. The open vessel causes heart murmurs and weakness during exercise and may cause death.

Persistent pupillary membranes (PPM) are blood vessel remnants/strands in the eye. Depending on type and severity, visual impairment or blindness may occur. There is no effective treatment.

PKD (pyruvate kinase deficiency) is an enzyme deficiency in which the lack of PK enzymes in the red blood cells results in the destruction of those cells, leading to *hemolytic anemia*. Diagnosis is by DNA analysis of the blood. Treatments have not been effective to date, and affected dogs usually die at one to four years of age.

PRA (progressive retinal atrophy) is a painless but serious degeneration of the retina, a tissue within the eye. Breeds differ in the age of onset (from puppyhood to middle age) and the rate of progression, but PRA always leads to blindness. Diagnosis is by ophthalmoscopic examination and/or electroretinography (ERG). There is no treatment.

Renal dysplasia is an abnormal or arrested development of the kidney. Severe to moderate cases seldom live past a year, but mild cases can usually live a normal life.

Retinal dysplasia is an abnormal development of the retina that may lead to blindness. See *PRA* for more information about the importance of the retina.

SAS (subaortic stenosis) is a progressive type of heart disease that is usually fatal. Diagnosis is by Doppler EKG.

Scotty cramp is a chronic syndrome in which excitement or exercise triggers sudden muscle cramps, a hopping gait, or a complete inability to walk.

vWD (von Willebrand's disease) is a deficiency in the amount or function of the von Willebrand factor blood protein. The vWD factor binds platelets to blood vessels when they are injured; thus, absence or deficiency can lead to spontaneous bleeding, typically from the mouth, nose, or gastrointestinal tract, and hemorrhaging from a cut or minor surgery. For most breeds, diagnosis is done by the ELISA assay blood test; however, the results are so commonly affected by illness, stress, recent medication or vaccination, and hormonal changes such as heat period or pregnancy that they are unreliable. A reliable DNA test is now available for some breeds.

White shaker dog syndrome is not a very scientific name, but it does paint an accurate picture of this unusual condition in which small white dogs such as the Maltese, Bichon Frise, and West Highland White Terrier develop tremors during times of stress or excitement. The cause is unknown.

Wobbler's syndrome is a complex disease in which the neck vertebrae are unstable. Some dogs experience no pain but are paralyzed, while others are in extreme pain but are mobile. Diagnosis by myelogram is difficult and risky, and there is no cure. The value of surgery as treatment is hotly debated.

PHOTOGRAPHIC CREDITS

Affenpinscher: Multi Ch. Balu's Schwarz Wipfel Schatzen and Multi Ch. Balu's Schwarz Mingeri, owned by Lucille Meystedt

Afghan Hound: Ch. Chaparral Soylent Blue Ro-Jan CDX, FCH, TT, owned by Shelley Hennessy

Airedale Terrier: International Ch. Stone Ridge Bengal Bravo, owned by Janet Johnson Framke

Akita: Ch. Masumi's Lady Sunshine ROM, owned by Judythe Dunn

Alaskan Malamute: Ch. Poker Flat's Paper Chase WTD, WWPD, Ch. Poker Flat's Rainman CD, and Kesha, owned by Robin Haggard and Jim Kuehl, photo by Jim Kuehl

American Bulldog: Razors Edge Sultan, owned by Calvin Middlebrook

American Cocker Spaniel: Ch. Barbandale's TC Cherub, owned by Barbara Prentiss, photo by Vaora

American Eskimo Dog (Miniature): U-CD, U-CH White Star Panda's First Noel, owned by Cynthia Boccia, photo by Dianna James

American Eskimo Dog (Standard): Grand Ch. Sierra's Snow Shadow, owned by Charline Dunnigan, photo by Carl Lindemaier

American Eskimo Dog (Toy): Ch. Withingtons Sashi at Carara TT, owned by Jeannie Halmo-Cone

American Foxhound: Am/Mex Ch. Brown's Mr. Mighty, owned by Christian and Rebecca Blatter

American Hairless Terrier: Trout Creek's Boss and Trout Creek's Jay Are, owned by Edwin Scott

American Pit Bull Terrier: Redwoods Brytessa Ca. Cud, owned by Teresa Givens and Sterling Bright, photo by Teresa Givens

American Staffordshire Terrier: Ch. Intrepid Nefertiti, owned by Denise Wedel

American Water Spaniel: Barth's Super Star of Swan Lake, owned by John Barth

Anatolian Shepherd Dog: Masgallah Pasit, owned by Carol Oleksak, photo by Jennifer Floyd

Appenzell Mountain Dog: Glenn vom Schwarzwaldblick, owned by Audrey and Stephen Lyke, photo by Stephen Lyke

Australian Cattle Dog: Am/Can Ch. Maitlands SilverDust Sydni, owned by Deb Casey and Gina McDonnell

Australian Kelpie: Noonbarra Tracey, owned by Mary and Stephen Bilson

Australian Shepherd: Lyveden Fairapache Nitido At Remuda, owned by Linda Whyman

Australian Shepherd (Miniature): Ch. Taycins First Edition, owned by Karen Keller, photo by Juli Carralejo

Australian Terrier: Ch. Southern Cross' Eagle Dancer, owned by Michael and Mary Palazzo, photo by Marsha Gray

Basenji: Ch. Sukari Raider of the Lost Bark and Ch. Sukari's Mindiana Jones CD, FCH, owned by Kathleen Jones and Laura Richarz

Basset Hound: Holly Hill's Carrot Top and Barbory's Amaris, owned by Amandy Hettich, photo by Don Menard (Graphic Expressions)

Beagle: Gracebee's Ol'Fash'n Root Beer and Ch. Just-Wright Wayward Windy, owned by Grace Rychliski

Bearded Collie: Ch. Ha'Penny Moon Shadow, owned by Robert W. Greitzer and J. Richard Schneider

Beauceron: Multi Ch. Hammer de Keramezec CGC, owned by Karla Davis

Bedlington Terrier: Carillon Tyler Blue CD, CG, owned by Donna Hurley and Lucy Heyman

Belgian Groenendael: Ch. OTCh. U-UD Qazar Charfire V Siegestor BH, WH, HIC, TT, SchH I, HOF, owned by Elaine Havens, photo by Jan Haderlie

Belgian Laekenois: Lalique du Mas de Turco, owned by Cindy Fitzgerald, photo by Carol Corbin

Belgian Malinois: Ch. Trew Bleue Anticipation HCT, CGC and Belgian Ch. O'Neill van Balderlo HS, CQN, JHD, CGC, owned by Catherine Shields, photo by Catherine Shields

Belgian Tervuren: Ch. Patana's Quest For Liberty UD, owned by Lillian White

Bernese Mountain Dog: U-CDX Sandusky's Brighteye Abigail TD, TT, Am/Can CDX, owned by Deborah Hotze

Bichon Frise: Multi Ch. C&D's Count Kristopher, owned by Dolores Wolske

Black and Tan Coonhound: Ch. Sandstone's Full Volume, owned by Shelley and James Cafferty Jr.

Bloodhound: Ch. Churchil's Col. Sherman Potter and Ch. Churchil's Notorious Natalie, owned by Van Buck and Michele McKinney, photo by Olan Mills Studios

Bolognese: Jabir's Bo-Blanc Petienne, owned by Nancy and Norman Holmes

Border Collie: Standsure's Flying Scotsman ADC, owned by Kay Whitehead, photo by Kimberley Collins

Border Terrier: Ch. Luvemur's First Edition UD, CG, TT, owned by John and Laurale Stern

Borzoi: Ch. Songmaker's Syren CD, FCH, owned by Jan McKenney

Boston Terrier: Ch. Bonnie's Jet Pilot and Ch. Bonnie's Touch of Magic, owned by Rita Otteson and Mae Wiger

Bouvier des Flandres: Ch. Briarlea Norstar Rose O'Luke CD, TD, owned by Sunny and Jack Rozycki

Boxer: Ch. Bentbrook's Competitive Edge, owned by Barb Carroll, and Bentbrook's High Impact, owned by Samantha Wooldridge, photo by Marcia

Briard: Ch. Mon Jovis Digby de L'Etat D'Or, owned by Donavon Thompson and Mary Lopez, photo by Fox and Cook

Brittany: Roja's Malibu Jazz Matazz CD, owned by Gail Wilder, photo by Michael Wilder

Brussels Griffon (Rough): Jeni, owned by Darryl Vice

Brussels Griffon (Smooth): Ben, owned by Sharon Sakson, photo by Robin Schwartz

Bulldog: Brynne's Sir Winston, owned by Vicki and Tony Ruiz

Bullmastiff: Ch. Tauralan Turkish Delight, owned by Carol Beans

Bull Terrier: Shavin-Kingsmere Sheez It, owned by Roland and Patricia Edwards, Linda Lethin, and R. Bollong

Cairn Terrier: Ch. Cairmar Cowardly Lion, owned by Betty Marcum, Anna Lee Rucker, and Brenda Carroll, photo by Pegini

Canaan Dog: U-UD Ch. Lahatut me Shaar Hagai UD, CKC-CDX, TT, owned by Victor Kaftal, photo by Hillside Studio (Donna Coss)

Cane Corso: Ch. Ravencreek's Al Capone, owned by Garry Gerardot and Kim Yeager, photo by Wolf Studios

Cavalier King Charles Spaniel: White Sawn Winston, owned by Bart and Kim Crider, photo by PetsMart

Cesky Terrier: Wee Toons Ariel, owned by June and George Perry

Chesapeake Bay Retriever: Ch. Mitsu Kuma's Pond Mist CD, JH, WD, Pond Hollow Dowitcher, and Ch. Pond Hollow's Spindrift CD, SH, WD, owned by Bill and Dyane Baldwin

Chihuahua (Long Coat): Laguna Mucho Man of Jobarbs, owned by Susan Sine

Chihuahua (Smooth): Royal Acres Tina Marie and Royal Acres Cisco Kid, owned by Joyce Flint

Chinese Crested (Hairless): Am/Can Ch. Xcel's Rated-R, owned by Lyn Brownell, photo by Kurt Brown

Chinese Crested (Powderpuff): Gaea's Gala Affair, bred by Lyn Brownell, photo by Kurtis Photography

Chinese Shar-Pei: Ch. Singh Dynasty's Rolovr Honey, owned by Darla and Michael Singh, photo by Donna Coss

Chinook: Multi Ch. Winterset's Heyokakaga Suka CGC, HIC, owned by Cheryl Kubart, photo by Steinley's

Chow Chow (Rough): Ch. Don-Lee Chowtime, owned by Desmond Murphy and Susie Donnelly

Chow Chow (Smooth): Am/Can Ch. Chinarose A Ladies' Man, owned by Sandra and Steve Miller

Clumber Spaniel: Villa De's Thelma Lou, owned by Lisa and Claude Olsen-Rankin and Kathleen Tumey

Collie (Rough): Holmhaven Magic Flash UD, owned by Lily Sayre

Collie (Smooth): Am/Can Ch. Valiant Quick Silver, owned by Athena Lethcoe-Harman, photo by Steven Ross

Coton de Tulear: Ch. Cotonbrie Moonraker of Bar-Ken, owned by Barbara Adcock, photo by Barbara Adcock

Curly-Coated Retriever: Mayhem Mum's The Word CD, TD, TDI and Ch. Charwin Paisley CR. Porsche CDX, WC, TDI, owned by Kathleen Kardash

Dachshund (Longhaired): I Spy Star Jester L, UD, Can CDX, U-CDX, CG, HC, CGC, TDI, owned by Dee Dee Murry

Dachshund (Smooth): Ch. Fleming's Turbo Diesel, owned by Stephen and Cheryl Shultz

Dachshund (Wirehaired): Welwyn Bonny Bryann MW, owned by Bruce and Nancy Silk

Dalmatian: Am/Bah Ch. Ravenwood Yankee Clipper CDX, Bah CD, owned by Kathy and Lee McCoubrey

Dandie Dinmont Terrier: Ch. Ephan Clydes Kid Colonel, owned by Patti Perkins

Doberman Pinscher: Easy Does It Wind Walker

UDT, Can CDX and Easy Does It Lite 'N Lacey UDT, Can CD, owned by Bobbie Crissey

Dogo Argentino: JLAS/Mex/JCM Ch. Leguero De Los Medanos and Mex/JCM Ch. Malena De Los Medanos, owned by Michelle Smith Barbour, photo by Alex Smith Photography of Canada

Dogue de Bordeaux: Australian Ch. Barbarian Thorny Dragon, owned by Kerri and Nick Trikilis, photo by Davies Brothers

English Cocker Spaniel: Ch. Cabin Hill I'm Gordon, owned by Rebec and Harvey Riggs

English Foxhound: Am/Can Ch. Crackerland Trailblazer, owned by Sandra Zornes, M.D., and Terrell Templin

English Setter (Bench): Am/Can Ch. Kameric Solitaire of Clariho and Multi Ch. Clariho London, owned by Jim Jannard and Paula Dempsey, photo by Jim Jannard

English Setter (Field): Advie Savage, owned by Edward and Annie Cyr

English Shepherd: Bracken's Sudden Spring CGC, owned by Kathy Lofthouse

English Springer Spaniel: Ch. Nokola Ziggy Stardust UD, owned by Ron and Gayle Hutchison, photo by Art Stewart

English Toy Spaniel: Ch. Kis'n Knoble Sir Walter, owned by John and Sue Kisielewski

Entlebucher Mountain Dog: Alpine Box Elder, owned by Barry and Jan Vincent, photo by Mark Walker Smith

Field Spaniel: Ch. OTCh. Calico's So Fine Four-O-Nine UDX, HOF, ROM, owned by Becki Jo Wolkenheim

Fila Brasileiro: Ch. Deer Graze's The Un-Forgiven (brindle), owned by Susan Williams

Finnish Spitz: Multi Ch. Arkle's Firefox of Subira CD, owned by Richard and Dawn Woods, and Mex/Can Ch. Audacious Arkle CD, owned by

Michele Sevryn and Judi Burll, photo by Judith Lee Smith

Flat-Coated Retriever: Ch. Petersfield Karmel Lalique, owned by Pat Debree, photo by Kurt Anderson

Fox Terrier (Smooth): Ch. Morgansonne Gallant Legacy, owned by Eileen Olmstead, photo by Eileen Olmstead

Fox Terrier (Wire): Ch. Libwyre Painted Lady, owned by Ruth Libner

French Bulldog: Ch. Smokey Valley's Bullwinkle CD, owned by Richard and Michelle Shannon

German Pinscher: Ch. Tanner's Fire Coral of Sea Br'ze and Grand Ch. Sea Breeze Barracuda, owned by Donna Tanner, photo by Pets by Paulette (Paulette Braun)

German Shepherd Dog: Valiantdale's Michelle CDX, Valiantdale's Katie UD, SchH III, Valiantdale's Icon UDT, SchH III, and Valiantdale's Shadow CDX, SchH I, owned by Kathy Watson

German Shorthaired Pointer: Ch. Fieldfine Cinnamon Schnapps SH, owned by Fred Cohen and Fieldfine Kennels

German Wirehaired Pointer: Ch. Von Duffin's Rockland Wags, owned by Terry and Ann Duffin, photo by Ann Duffin

Giant Schnauzer: Ch. Skansen's Handsome Stranger, owned by Sylvia Hammarstrom

Glen of Imaal Terrier: Ch. Glen Tyr's Kelly Callahan, owned by Mary Brytowski

Golden Retriever: OTCh. "Gaines Top Dog" Shoreland's Big Harry Deal, owned by Sue Mayborne

Gordon Setter: Timbaray's King Arthur, owned by Barb Meining, DVM

Great Dane: Ch. Waterwood's Just As I Am CD, owned by Margaret Shappard, photo by Diana Alverson

Greater Swiss Mountain Dog: Ch. Rigi v Both-swain CD, TT, owned by Doug and Sandy Nyeholt

Great Pyrenees: Ch. Summerhill's Royal Knight, owned by Lynne Gomm

Greyhound: Huzzah Reddy Willing And Able UD and Ch. Huzzah Ishidot Get Up and Glow UD, owned by Charlene Vincent

Harrier: Ch. Landlubber's Liberty, owned by Betty Burnell, photo by Steve Eltinge

Havanese: Smallhaven Harlequin and Smallhaven Montezuma, owned by Kachina Havanese, photo by PetsMart

Ibizan Hound: Ch. Smotare's Scarlet PJ's, FLD CH, owned by Nancy Hiles, and Seti, FLD CH, owned by Will and Sarah Martens

Irish Setter: Lunn's Say Goodnight Gracie and Lunn's I Love Lucy, owned by Gaye Cocoman, photo by Thomas & Thomas Studio

Irish Terrier: Rhiannon Baystone Firebug, owned by John Childers, photo by Dog Ads

Irish Water Spaniel: Ch. Co-R's Maeve O'Blu Max CD and Ch. Co-R's Sullivan O'Blu Max CD, owned by Ruth Roes

Irish Wolfhound: Glenamadda Calypso Kellyscot, Demage Marchand de Reves, and Emrys Carageen, owned by Helga Lavigne and Katri Helava, photo by Indra Ancans

Italian Greyhound: Ch. Littleluv's Superman CD, owned by Kathryn Holmes, photo by Joan Ludwig

Italian Spinone: Orion Bogwalker, owned by Joe Zawadowski

Jack Russell Terrier (Broken Coat): Hawksfield Tags of the Bowery, owned by Cheryl Edwards

Jack Russell Terrier (Smooth): Eastlake Ava, owned by Will Hahn

Japanese Chin: Ch. Inuhaus Fujiyama Fireball, owned by Jari Bobillot

Keeshond: Winsome's Here Comes Trouble CD and Rakker's Most Excellent Promise CD, owned by Connie Jankowski, photo by Missy Yuhl

Kerry Blue Terrier: Am/Can Ch. Lisiji Christmas Hope, owned by Lisa and C. J. Favre and Juanita Traylor

Komondor: Ch. Szentivani Ingo, owned by Marion Levy Jr.

Kuvasz: Ch. Bjel-Saros Autumn Prince TDI, B, WH and Ch. Bjel-Saros Autumn Starlight TDI, owned by Fred and Gudrun Stein

Kyi-Leo: Mig-Gi Mui of Lin-Kai and Nan-Di of Lin-Kai, owned by Al and Harriet Linn

Labrador Retriever: Cirques Emmy, owned by Abby Kagan, photo by Greg Goebel

Lakeland Terrier: Ch. Kilfel Pointe of Vu, owned by Patricia Peters

Leonberger: Bill du Barrsaint and Apollo du Barrsaint, owned by Lucie Barriault and Richard Saint-Jean

Lhasa Apso: Benbridge Hazel's Little Sophie CD, CGC, owned by Hazel Waring and Gail Zurawski, photo by Gail Zurawski

Louisiana Catahoula Leopard Dog: Blue Diamond's Cimmaron, owned by Jeff and Jeanne Treder, photo by Jeff Treder

Löwchen: Ch. Pepperland Miss Piggy CD, owned by Earlemarie Dingel

Maltese: Ch. Cedarwood Sunshine Zina, owned by Marti Klabunde, photo by Don Petrulis

Manchester Terrier (Standard): Ch. Invermood's Call Me Madeline Am/Can CD HOF and Ch. Invermood's Charms My Game Am/Can CD, owned by Marla Brick, photo by Wandel Studio

Manchester Terrier (Toy): Firefly's Facination, owned by Juli Laskujari

Mastiff: Ch. Brite Star's Phoebe, Ch. Brite Star, and Ch. Brite Star's Titas, owned by Lance and Barbara House, photo by Vaora

Miniature Bull Terrier: Graymoor Genghis, owned by Donly Chorn

Miniature Pinscher: Can Ch. Meyerling's I Luv Lucy, owned by Faith Gordon

Miniature Schnauzer: Ch. Aljamar Hot Ice CD, owned by Janice Rue and Marilyn Laschinski, photo by Graham

Neapolitan Mastiff: La Tutela Nunziello di Tuono, owned by Helen Splan

Newfoundland: Ch. Picabos Hausblomma Nereid, owned by Rory Hedin Leonard

Norfolk Terrier: Ch. Tylwyth Just Chelsea, Am/Can UD, CG, owned by Mary Fine, photo by Ashbey

Norwegian Buhund: Ch. Leifegard's Ruby, owned by Malfrid Byshja

Norwegian Elkhound: Ch. Statton's Jaded Watters UD, Can CD, owned by Stan and Cotton Silverman, photo by Stan Silverman

Norwegian Lundehund: Lundecock's Free & Footloos, owned by Kim and Kimberly Richey

Norwich Terrier: Mexican Ch. Psalm's Contessa, bred by Linda Kenyon, photo by Jose Arturo

Nova Scotia Duck Tolling Retriever: Ch. Driftwood's Clipper WC, owned by Paul and Carol Milbury

Old English Sheepdog: Can Ch. Klaumar Crystal Keepsake CD and Can Ch. Klaumar Glencroft Toy Maker, owned by Glenna Royston, photo by Glenna Royston

Otterhound: Am/Can Ch. Follyhoun First in Line, owned by Louise and Rex DeShon Jr.

Papillon: Majestic Joy Lady Tinkerbell, owned by Rita Koy, photo by Reflections in Oil

Pekingese: Shadow Hills Kiss of Kismet, owned by Bonnie Eriksson

Petit Basset Griffon Vendeen: Kasani Honette, owned by Valerie Link

Pharaoh Hound: Ch. Auten's Aladdin, owned by Ron and Carol Auten

Pointer: Ch. Scanpoint's Barefoot Contessa CD and Am/Can Ch. OTCH Scanpoint's Sunrise Serenade UD, owned by Lynn Deering

Polish Lowland Sheepdog: Multi Ch. Lechsinska's Chocolate Truffle, owned by Phyllis Vlasaty

Pomeranian: Hupkas Mr. Giggilo, owned by Marian Coy

Poodle (Miniature): Genals Gena La Beaute Noire, Am/Mex UD, owned by Connie Sullivan

Poodle (Standard): Lido's Miss Strawberry Pic CDX, owned by Susie Osburn

Poodle (Toy): Bobbil's Red Clay O'Sweeney, owned by Bobbie Wright

Portuguese Water Dog: Ch. Matia, owned by Joyce Vanek-Nielsen

Pug: Lazy J Kola, owned by Richard and Frances Weaver

Puli: Ch. Bowmaker's Ted E. Bear CD, owned by Sherry Gibson, photo by Rayleen Hendrix

Rat Terrier: Daphnie Pooch (tricolor), owned by Julia Kleutsch

Rhodesian Ridgeback: Filmmaker's Starlet, owned by Gerry Gilmore and Kate Graham

Rottweiler: Am/Can Ch. Von Worley's Alexander, Am/Can CD, owned by Dawn and Jim Worley

Saint Bernard (Longhaired): Ch. Legend, owned by Twin Branch Saints, photo by Brenda McWhorter

Saint Bernard (Shorthaired): Twin Branch's Quest for Fame, owned by Dwayne and Nola Fairchild, photo by Brenda McWhorter

Saluki: Ch. Ranesaw Imperial Beach, JC, owned by Ron and Jackie Wassenaar, photo by Ross

Samoyed: Multi Ch. Aladdin's Solitary Man TT, owned by Sandra and Bruce Krupski

Schipperke: Ch. Jetstar's Jumpin Jehosphat, owned by Mary Ann and Terrie Johnson

Scottish Deerhound: Fairyfort's Black Narcissus, owned by Madelyn Larsen, photo by Caroline Brown

Scottish Terrier: Ch. Claudon's Is It Really Love, owned by Nancy Clements and Claudia Leffler, photo by Wayne Cott

Sealyham Terrier: Ch. Trailview Mozambique, owned by Christine Hawley, photo by Brad Hawley

Shetland Sheepdog: Ch. Minos Remember My Name and Ch. Minos The Escape Artist, owned by Chris Gabrielides

Shiba Inu: Multi Ch. Ranchlake's Tamarisk Samsara ROM, owned by Dorothy Warren, photo by James Meager Paw Prints

Shih Tzu: Conleys' Sweet September, owned by Sharon Conley, photo by Mark Conley

Shiloh Shepherd: Ch. CJ's Lobo Amado De Windsong ROM, TDI, CGC, owned by Carl and Judy Vaneman, photo by Ms. Randi Handwerger

Siberian Husky: Ch. Silistra's Thief of Hearts, Am/Can CD, Mex PC, SD, owned by Gene and Karen Stinson

Silky Terrier: Ch. Lyneloor's Salty Sailor UD, owned by Mimi Elaine Lorie, photo by Joni

Skye Terrier: Ch. Druidmoor Sweeney Todd CD, owned by Charles Brown Jr., photo by Ludwig

Sloughi: Jalandad Schuru esch Schams, Iricho de Moreau, and Noub de la Cite du Guerrier, owned by Ermine Moreau-Sipiere, photo by Ermine Moreau-Sipiere

Soft-Coated Wheaten Terrier: Am/Mex Ch. Gleangay Hi-Jinks CDX, TT, Mex PCE and Multi Ch. Dounam's Blarney-Stone CD, Mex PC, owned by Douglas and Naomi Stewart

Staffordshire Bull Terrier: Ch. Yankeestaff Fireflash, owned by Mr. and Mrs. D. C. Judd, photo by Anthony Lopez

Standard Schnauzer: Ch. Sterling Rikki Lynn Hansen CDX and Yamadas Robyn Lynn Hansen CDX, owned by Richard and Judy Hansen

Sussex Spaniel: Ch. Topjoys Sussex Mooncloud, owned by Kathy Perry and Ruth Gardner

Swedish Vallhund: Svedala Lilla Holger, owned by C. Gardner, photo by A. Whitmarsh

Teddy Roosevelt Terrier: Broken Wing's Midget, owned by Patricia Blankenship

Tibetan Mastiff: Ch. Shay Ri Gentle-Ben v.d. Zegse Heide, Ch. Himalaya's Dred Mo, Himalaya's Lokeshvara, and Ch. Loyal Rak-pa Ni A Soechavati, owned by Susan Ochsenbein and Mary and Bill Akis, photo by Jeff Kaiser

Tibetan Spaniel: Ch. Deetree Por-Sha, owned by Deb Henson, photo by Deb Henson

Tibetan Terrier: Ch. Kyirong's Cedarbar Shogun, owned by Linda Immel and James Joseph, photo by David Gossett

Tosa: Multi Ch. Straw Dog's B.A. Aki, owned by Laura Carril

Toy Fox Terrier: National Grand Ch. Gorden's Shamrock Lad, owned by Doug and Betty Gorden

Vizsla: Ch. Red Rock's Copper Quest, owned by Norita and Ricky Prindle, photo by Nica Lyons

Weimaraner: Ch. Liberty's Angel O'er GraytSky JH, NSD, and Ghostmar's Silk Stockings JH, SD, NRD, CGC, TDI, owned by Amy and Michael Anderson, photo by Bill Gray

Welsh Corgi (Cardigan): Ch. Coedwig's Buckeye, owned by Kim Shira, photo by Chelsea Thompson

Welsh Corgi (Pembroke): Ch. OTCh. Aberdare Eliza of Taliesin, owned by Peggy McConnell, photo by Bryce Beasley

Welsh Springer Spaniel: Ch. Colwyn's Winchester Special, owned by Lisa and David Hubler

Welsh Terrier: Brynhir Shelby and Am/Can Ch. Lichen Run's Laddie, owned by Bonnie Ross

West Highland White Terrier: Am/Can Ch. Barley O'The Ridge, owned by Marjadele Schiele

Whippet: Multi Ch. Topnotch McFadden and Multi Ch. Topnotch Buttons & Bows TT, owned by Ellen Frenkel and Pamela Miller, photo by John Ashbey

White Shepherd: Ch. U-CD Ve-Lin's Sabre of Braehead CDX, TT, CGC, owned by Susan Ewart, photo by Susan Ewart

Wirehaired Pointing Griffon: Acer V. 'T Holt-laand, bred by Eric V/D Schouw, photo by Shannon Ford

Xoloitzcuintle (Intermediate): Multi Ch. Zoyatl, owned by Patricia Hoover, photo by Ken Mills

Xoloitzcuintle (Standard): Multi Ch. Yopico-Balam, owned by Patricia Hoover, photo by Ken Mills

Yorkshire Terrier: Lovely Samantha, owned by Carol Panza, Portrait by Shutter Pup, Inc.

INDEX

Bernese Mountain Dog, 73
Bichon Frise, 74
bitches (females), advantages and
    disadvantages of, 265–66
bite, examining puppy's, 282–83
Black and Tan Coonhound, 75
blanket, puppy's, 290
Bloodhound, 76
Bloodlines, 254
boarding costs, 7
Bolognese, 77
books
    on diet and health, 7
    on individual breeds, 38
Border Collie, 78
Border Terrier, 79
Borzoi, 80
Boston Terrier, 81
Bouvier des Flandres, 82
Boxer, 83
Brainstorm Auditory Evoked Response
    (BAER) testing, 36
breed clubs, listing of, 291–97
breeders
    appointment to view puppies, making an,
        272
    cleanliness of home, 274, 275
    defined, 251
    finding, 254–56
    forming an impression of, 275–76
    home visits, 38, 274–76
    interviewing, *see* interviewing breeders
    interviewing potential owners, 245–46,
        271
    irresponsible, *see* irresponsible breeders
    of "poo breeds," 18
    private seller, myth of the, 251
    responsible, *see* responsible breeders
    visiting, 38, 274–76
breeding, selective, *see* selective breeding
breed profiles, 41–240
    using the, *see* using the breed profiles
breed selection, 6, 19–240
    for hunting, herding, or Schutzhund,
        28
    narrowing your list of suitable breeds,
        37–38
    for your personality and lifestyle,
        21–29
    questionnaire, 22–28
    special circumstances, 28–29
    using the breed profiles, *see* using the
        breed profiles
    for watchdogs, 28–29
    Web sites to aid in, 38
breed standards
    conformation titles and, 256, 257
    finding, 245

irresponsible breeders and, 248
    purpose of, 245
    responsible breeder's attention to, 245
    writing of, 245
Briard, 84, 283
Brittany, 85
brush and comb, 7
Brussels Griffon
    Rough, 86
    Smooth, 87
Bulldog, 5, 88, 282
    American, 46
    French, 132
Bullmastiff, 89
Bull Terrier, 90
    Miniature, 172

Caesarean section, 5
Cairn Terrier, 91
Canaan Dog, 92
Canadian Kennel Club (CKC), 17–18, 32
Canadian Ontario Veterinary College
    (OVC), 35, 263
Cane Corso, 93
Canine Eye Registration Foundation
    (CERF) certificates, 35, 263, 264
    how to read, 286
Caras, Roger, 275
cardiac certification programs, 35, 263,
    285
Cardigan Welsh Corgi, 230
cardiomyopathy, 35
cataracts, juvenile, 35
cats, 10
cautions when buying, breed profile section
    providing, 36–37
Cavalier King Charles Spaniel, 94
CERF, *see* Canine Eye Registration
    Foundation (CERF) certificates
Cesky Terrier, 95
championship, conformation, 256–57
"cheap championship," 256
Chesapeake Bay Retriever, 96
Chihuahua, 264
    Long Coat, 97
    Smooth, 98
children
    breed selection questionnaire, 23
    decision to get a dog and, 13
    older puppy's behavior around,
        284
    pack instinct and, 10–11
    proper behavior around dogs, 23
Chinese Crested
    Hairless, 99
    Powderpuff, 100
Chinese Shar-Pei, 101
Chinook, 102

choosing the right breed, *see* breed selection
choosing the right puppy, 279–84
    entire litter, viewing, 279–80
    general expression and body language,
        280–81
    individuals, viewing, 280–83
    letting puppy choose you, problem with,
        279
    looking further, 290
    making the final decision, 285, 290
    older dogs, 283–84
    paperwork, *see* paperwork
    physical examination, 282–83
    responsible breeder's assistance in, 246,
        279
    temperament tests, 281–82
Chow Chow
    Rough, 103
    Smooth, 104
cleanliness of breeder's home, 274, 275
clipping required, *see* grooming
clubs, national, 291–97
    breed standards written by, 245
    codes of ethics, 254
    finding breeders through, 254
    titles awarded by, 258
Clumber Spaniel, 105
coat, 32
    breed selection and, 24–25
    examining puppy's, 282
    see also grooming
Cocker Spaniel
    American, 47
    English, 118
collar, 7
Collie
    Rough, 106
    Smooth, 107
color, 266, 282
    ability to see, 9
    in breed profile, 32
comb and brush, 7
commitment and responsibility,
    13–14
communication, 8–10, 11, 12
companion quality puppies, *see* "pet-
    quality" puppies
companionship as reward of dog ownership,
    13
Complete Dog Book, The (American Kennel
    Club), 245
conformation
    standards, *see* breed standards
    titles, 256–57
Continental Kennel Club, 18
contracts
    neutering, 246, 249, 266, 271–72
    sales, 261, 288–89

groomers, finding breeders through, 255
grooming
    in breed profile, requirements in, 32
    breed selection questionnaire, 25
    costs of professional, 7
    equipment, 7
guarantees about health problems, 34, 260,
    261
    interviewing breeders about, 270–71
    from irresponsible breeders, 250, 263
    standard, 270
    written, 289
guard and watchdogs, 28–29
    breed selection, 28–29
    defined, 28
    obedience training, 28

handlers, dog show, 256
Harrier, 145
Havanese, 146
health issues
    breeder's home, observations at, 274
    in breed profiles, 34–36
    conformation titles and, 257
    genetic health certificates, *see specific
        certificates,* e.g., Canine Eye Registra-
        tion Foundation (CERF) certificates;
        Orthopedic Foundation of America
        (OFA) certificates
    guarantees about health problems, *see*
        guarantees about health problems
    interviewing breeders about, 262–64,
        270–71
    medical record, 289
    veterinarians, *see* veterinarians
    veterinary testing, *see* veterinary testing
        for genetic health problems
    see also specific issues
hearing, sense of, 9
    BAER testing, 36
    communication with your dog, 9–10,
        11, 12
    deafness, 36
    reaction of puppies to noises, 280, 284
heart disease, 35, 263, 286
heat period, female, 266
herding dogs, breed selection for, 28
herding titles, 257
heredity and selective breeding, *see* selective
        breeding
hip dysplasia, 34–35
    OFA certificates, 34–35, 263, 264, 285
    X rays to detect, 35, 260
history in breed profile, 32
holistic or natural medical philosophy, 6–7
home of breeder, visiting, 38, 274–76
home-raised and/or home-socialized
    puppies, 259–60

hound
    lure coursing titles, 258
    see also specific breeds
housebreaking, 267, 284
    adult dogs, 265
    age of puppy and, 264
    crate or pen for, 7
    of pet shop puppies, 250
Humane Societies, adopting a puppy from,
    6, 252–53
hunting, selecting a breed for, 28
hypoglycemia, 264
hypothyroidism, 35

Ibizan Hound, 147
identification tag, 7
independent behavior, 281–82
Innova, 7
Institute for Genetic Disease Control in
    Animals (GDC), 35, 263
Internet sites, *see* Web sites
interviewing breeders, 262–73
    about age of puppies, 264–65
    about appearance of puppies, 266
    appointment to view puppies, 272
    about experience as breeder, 269–70
    about genetic health, 262–64,
        270–71
    about health screenings and guarantees,
        262–64, 270–71
    about parents and pedigree, 267–69
    about price, 271–72
    about sex of puppies, 265–66
    about socialization of puppies, 267
    about temperament, 267, 268
interviewing of potential owner by breeder,
    245–46, 271
Irish Setter, 148
Irish Terrier, 149
Irish Water Spaniel, 150
Irish Wolfhound, 151
irresponsible breeders, 247–51, 272
    advertising by, 249, 255, 260–61
    breeding parents with registration papers,
        247
    breed standards and, 248
    equating breeding quality with AKC
        registration, 247
    full registration papers given by, for "pet-
        quality" puppies, 249
    health guarantees from, 250, 263
    lack of involvement in dog world, 248
    number of litters per year, 249
    pedigree research and, 247–48
    pet shops, puppies from, 249–51
    private seller, myth of the, 251
    references, 249
    socialization of puppies and, 267

temperament, breeding parents of
    unsound, 248
terminology, incorrect use of, 248–49,
    267, 268
veterinary testing, breeding parents
    without prior, 248
Italian Greyhound, 152
Italian Spinone, 153

Jack Russell Terrier
    Broken Coat, 154
    Smooth, 155
Japanese Chin, 156
judging at dog shows, 256

Keeshond, 157
kennel runs, puppies raised in, 264, 265
"kennel syndrome," 264
Kerry Blue Terrier, 158
"knees, bad," 35
Komondor, 159
Kuvasz, 160
Kyi-Leo, 161

Labrador Retriever, 162
Lakeland Terrier, 163
large dogs
    hip dysplasia in, 34
    selection of, 24
leader, establishing yourself as the, 10–12,
    264
leash, 7
Leonberger, 164
Lhasa Apso, 165
lifestyle and personality, choosing a breed
    based on your, 21–29
    questionnaire to help in, 22–28
limited registration papers, 246, 266
litters per year, 269
    responsible breeders, 245
little dogs, selection of, 23–24
long coats, 24–25, 32
Louisiana Catahoula Leopard Dog, 166
love, 8, 12
    unconditional, 13
Löwchen (Little Lion Dog), 167
lure coursing titles, 258
luxating patella, 35

magazines, finding breeders through dog,
    254–55
males, advantages and disadvantages of,
    265–66
Maltese, 168, 264
mammary tumors, 266
Manchester Terrier
    Standard, 169
    Toy, 170